A Very Merry Garfield Christmas

Season's Eatings

A Very Merry Garfield Christmas

By Jim "Jingle Bell" Davis

With his little humor helpers
Scott "Sugarplum" Nickel & Mark "Mistletoe" Acey

Ballantine Books   •   New York

A Ballantine Book
Published by The Random House Publishing Group
Copyright © 2003 by PAWS, Inc. All Rights Reserved.

All rights reserved under International
and Pan-American Copyright Conventions.
Published in the United States by
The Random House Publishing Group,
a division of Random House, Inc.,
New York, and simultaneously in Canada by
Random House of Canada Limited, Toronto.

Ballantine and colophon are registered
trademarks of Random House, Inc.

"GARFIELD" and the GARFIELD characters
are registered and unregistered trademarks of PAWS, Inc.

www.ballantinebooks.com

www.garfield.com

Library of Congress Control Number: 2003092740

ISBN 0-345-46338-2

Manufactured in the United States of America

First Edition: November 2003

10 9 8 7 6 5 4 3 2 1

EDITORS AND WRITERS
Mark Acey, Scott Nickel
·
ART DIRECTOR
Betsy Knotts
·
DESIGNER
Kenny Goetzinger
·
ILLUSTRATORS
Gary Barker, Lori Barker, Larry Fentz,
Mike Fentz, Lynette Nuding
·
COVER DESIGNER
Tom Howard
·
COVER ILLUSTRATORS
Gary Barker, Larry Fentz, Mike Fentz
·
PRODUCTION ARTIST
Linda Duell

HO! HO! HO!

Christmas comes but once a year (unfortunately).

Like Garfield, I like everything about this special season . . . the food, the friends, the gifts. But, most of all, I like the spirit. Because, when it comes to Christmas, it's not the giving, or the getting . . . it's the loving!

Have a Wonderful Holiday!

JIM DAVIS

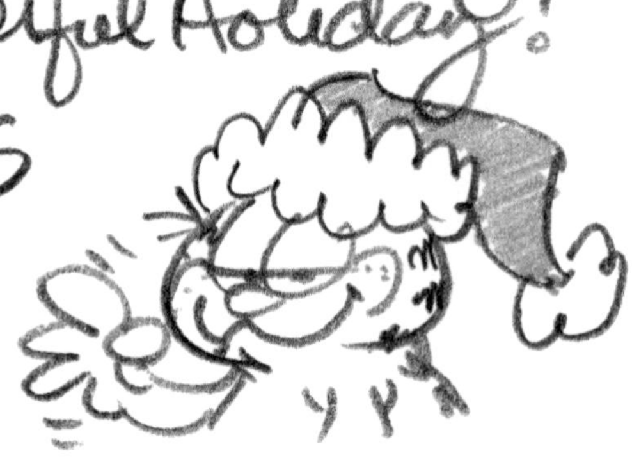

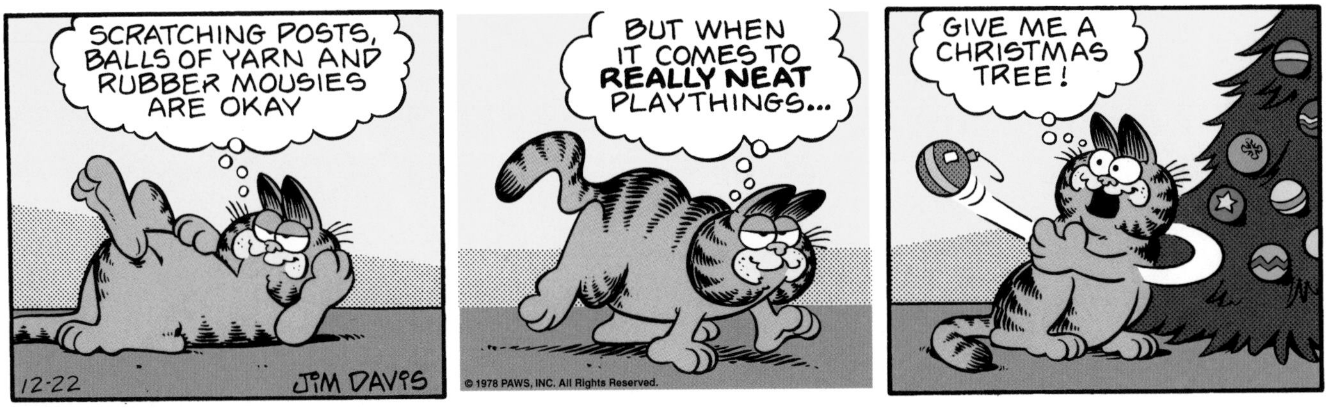
SCRATCHING POSTS, BALLS OF YARN AND RUBBER MOUSIES ARE OKAY
12-22
JIM DAVIS
BUT WHEN IT COMES TO **REALLY NEAT** PLAYTHINGS...
© 1978 PAWS, INC. All Rights Reserved.
GIVE ME A CHRISTMAS TREE!

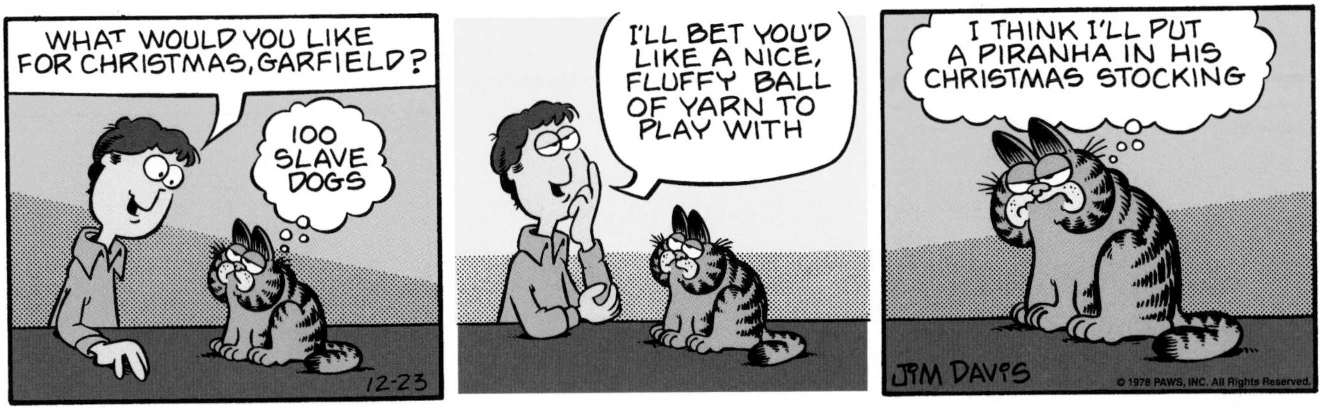
WHAT WOULD YOU LIKE FOR CHRISTMAS, GARFIELD?
100 SLAVE DOGS
12-23
I'LL BET YOU'D LIKE A NICE, FLUFFY BALL OF YARN TO PLAY WITH
I THINK I'LL PUT A PIRANHA IN HIS CHRISTMAS STOCKING
JIM DAVIS
© 1978 PAWS, INC. All Rights Reserved.

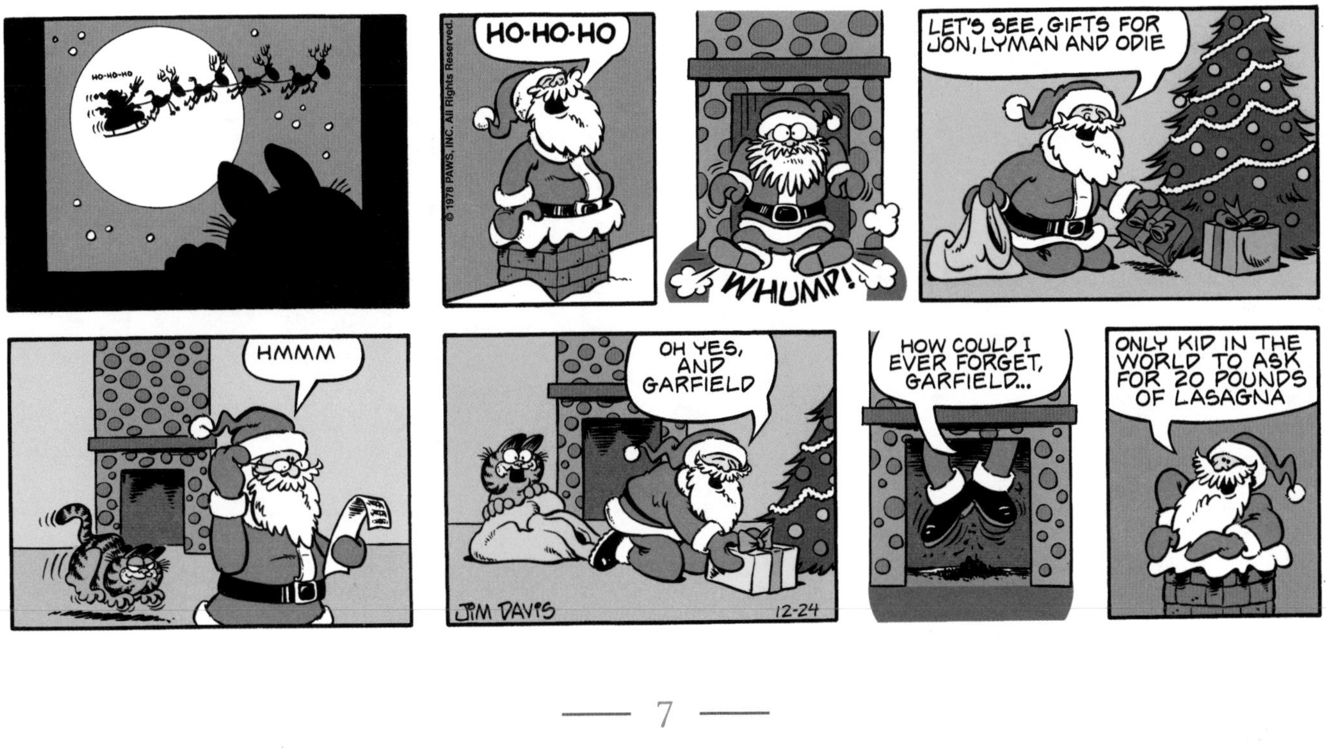
HO-HO-HO
© 1978 PAWS, INC. All Rights Reserved.
HO-HO-HO
WHUMP!
LET'S SEE, GIFTS FOR JON, LYMAN AND ODIE
HMMM
OH YES, AND GARFIELD
JIM DAVIS
12-24
HOW COULD I EVER FORGET, GARFIELD...
ONLY KID IN THE WORLD TO ASK FOR 20 POUNDS OF LASAGNA

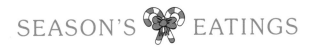

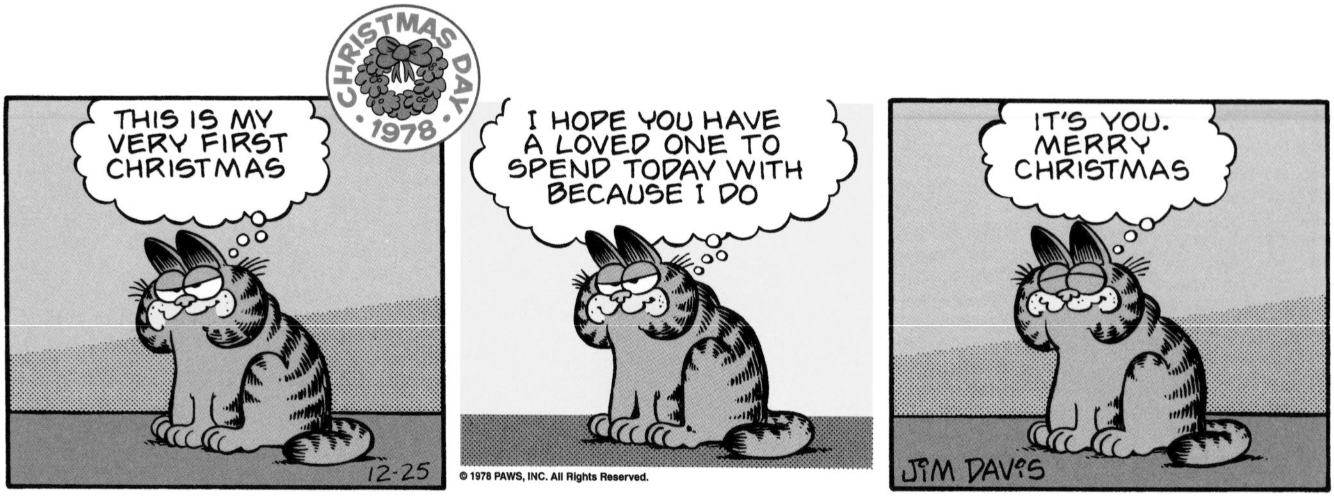
CHRISTMAS DAY 1978
THIS IS MY VERY FIRST CHRISTMAS
12-25
I HOPE YOU HAVE A LOVED ONE TO SPEND TODAY WITH BECAUSE I DO
© 1978 PAWS, INC. All Rights Reserved.
IT'S YOU. MERRY CHRISTMAS
JIM DAVIS

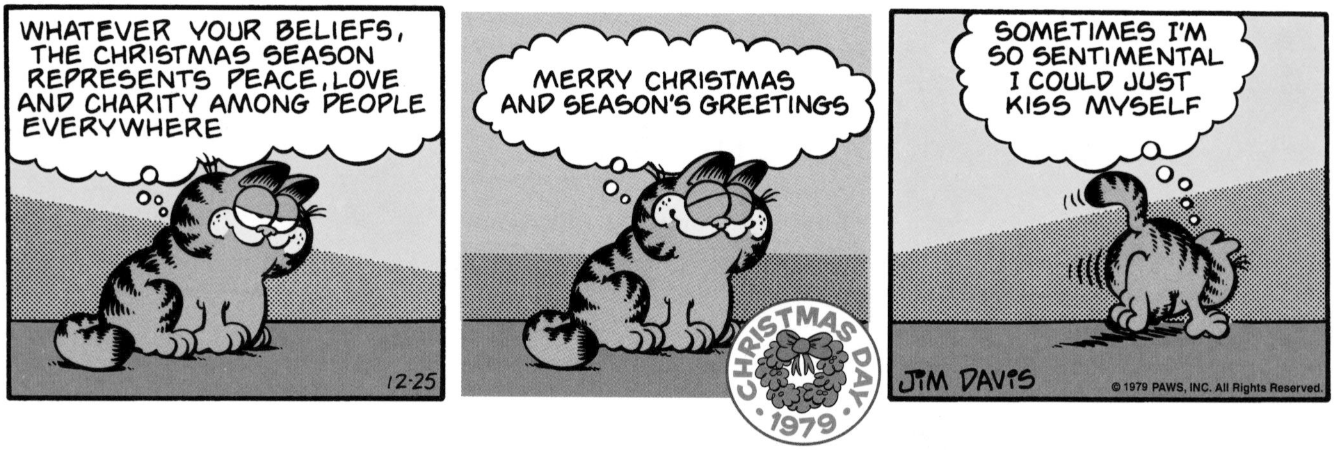
WHATEVER YOUR BELIEFS, THE CHRISTMAS SEASON REPRESENTS PEACE, LOVE AND CHARITY AMONG PEOPLE EVERYWHERE
12-25
MERRY CHRISTMAS AND SEASON'S GREETINGS
CHRISTMAS DAY 1979
SOMETIMES I'M SO SENTIMENTAL I COULD JUST KISS MYSELF
JIM DAVIS
© 1979 PAWS, INC. All Rights Reserved.

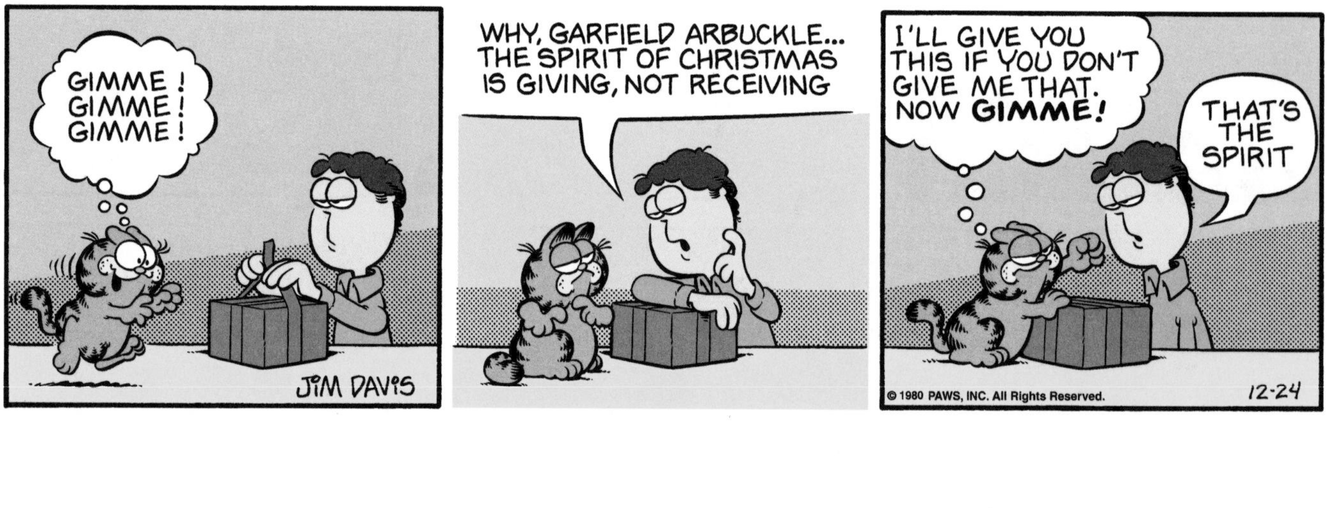
GIMME! GIMME! GIMME!
JIM DAVIS
WHY, GARFIELD ARBUCKLE... THE SPIRIT OF CHRISTMAS IS GIVING, NOT RECEIVING
I'LL GIVE YOU THIS IF YOU DON'T GIVE ME THAT. NOW GIMME!
THAT'S THE SPIRIT
© 1980 PAWS, INC. All Rights Reserved.
12-24

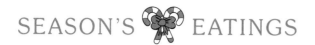

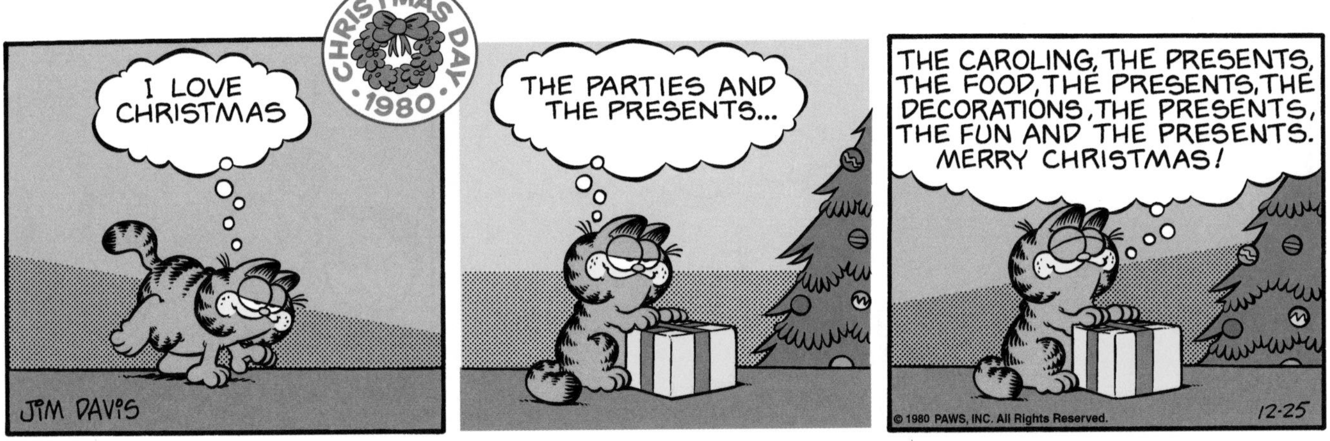
CHRISTMAS DAY 1980
I LOVE CHRISTMAS
THE PARTIES AND THE PRESENTS...
THE CAROLING, THE PRESENTS, THE FOOD, THE PRESENTS, THE DECORATIONS, THE PRESENTS, THE FUN AND THE PRESENTS. MERRY CHRISTMAS!
JIM DAVIS
© 1980 PAWS, INC. All Rights Reserved.
12-25

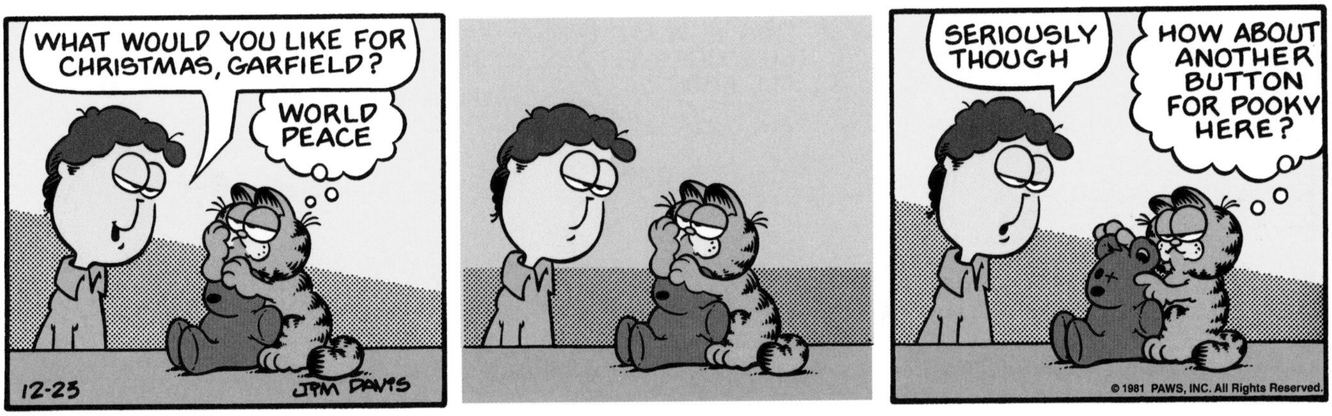
WHAT WOULD YOU LIKE FOR CHRISTMAS, GARFIELD?
WORLD PEACE
SERIOUSLY THOUGH
HOW ABOUT ANOTHER BUTTON FOR POOKY HERE?
12-23
JIM DAVIS
© 1981 PAWS, INC. All Rights Reserved.

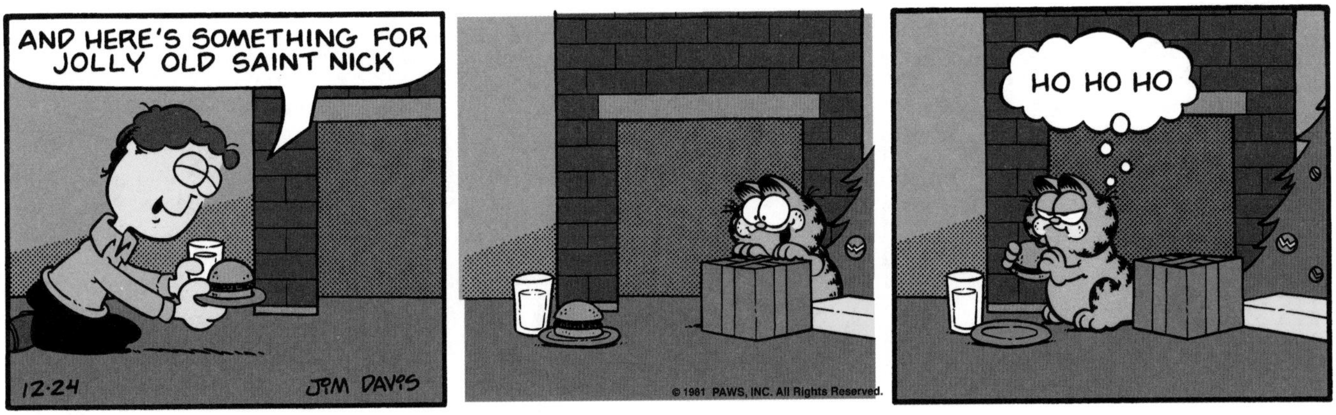
AND HERE'S SOMETHING FOR JOLLY OLD SAINT NICK
12-24
JIM DAVIS
© 1981 PAWS, INC. All Rights Reserved.
HO HO HO

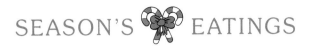

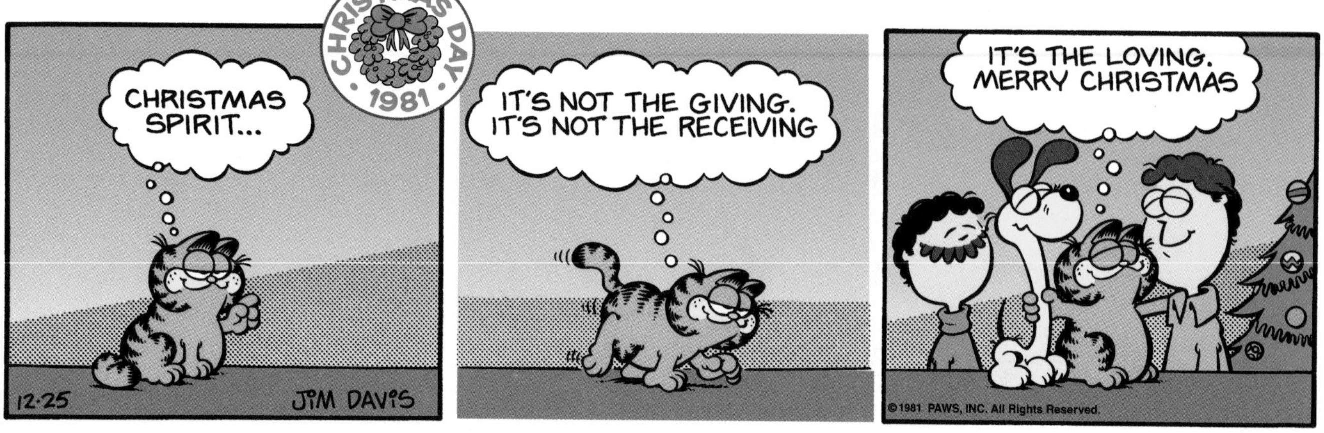
CHRISTMAS DAY 1981
CHRISTMAS SPIRIT...
IT'S NOT THE GIVING. IT'S NOT THE RECEIVING
IT'S THE LOVING. MERRY CHRISTMAS
12-25
JIM DAVIS
©1981 PAWS, INC. All Rights Reserved.

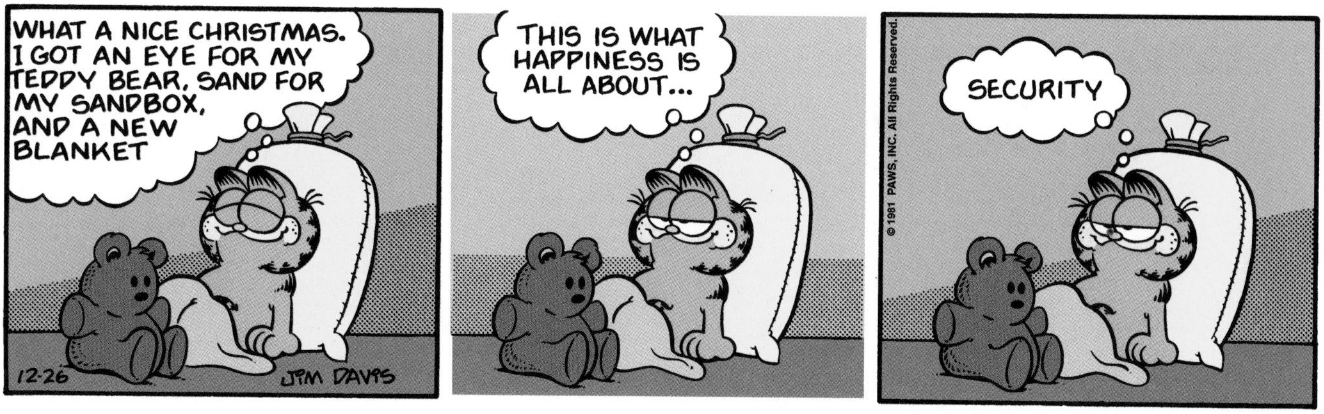
WHAT A NICE CHRISTMAS. I GOT AN EYE FOR MY TEDDY BEAR, SAND FOR MY SANDBOX, AND A NEW BLANKET
THIS IS WHAT HAPPINESS IS ALL ABOUT...
SECURITY
12-26
JIM DAVIS
© 1981 PAWS, INC. All Rights Reserved.

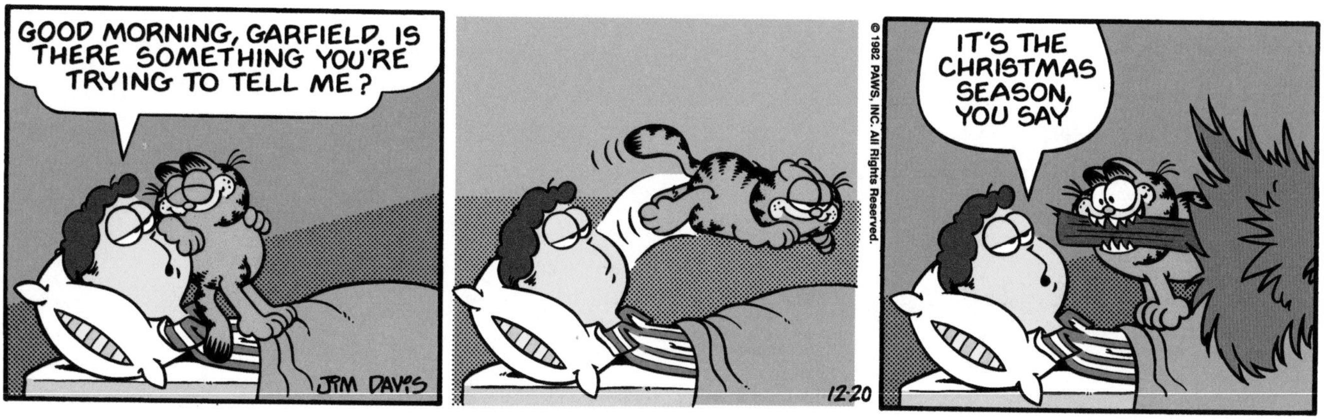
GOOD MORNING, GARFIELD. IS THERE SOMETHING YOU'RE TRYING TO TELL ME?
IT'S THE CHRISTMAS SEASON, YOU SAY
JIM DAVIS
12-20
© 1982 PAWS, INC. All Rights Reserved.

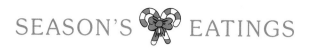

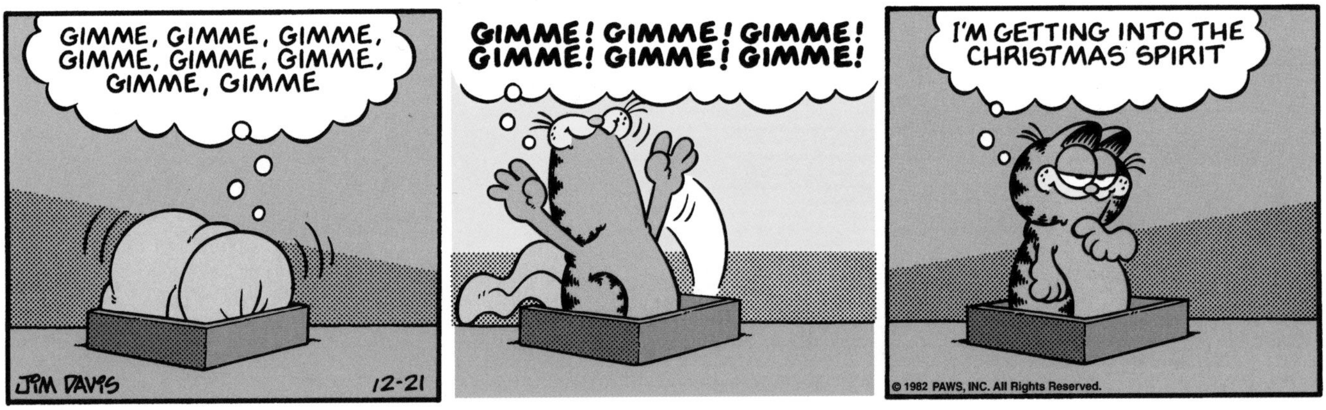
GIMME, GIMME, GIMME, GIMME, GIMME, GIMME, GIMME, GIMME
JIM DAVIS
12-21
GIMME! GIMME! GIMME! GIMME! GIMME! GIMME!
I'M GETTING INTO THE CHRISTMAS SPIRIT
© 1982 PAWS, INC. All Rights Reserved.

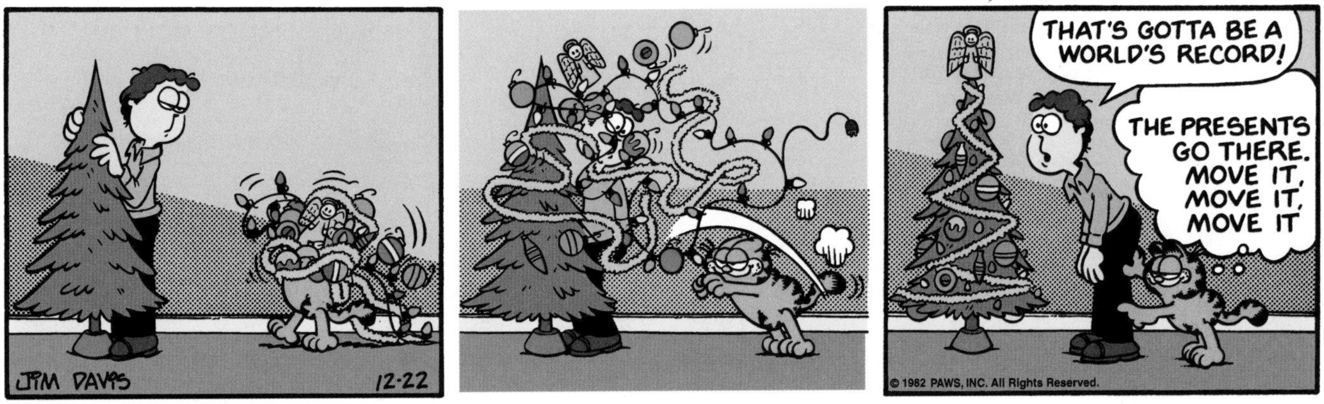
JIM DAVIS
12-22
THAT'S GOTTA BE A WORLD'S RECORD!
THE PRESENTS GO THERE. MOVE IT, MOVE IT, MOVE IT
© 1982 PAWS, INC. All Rights Reserved.

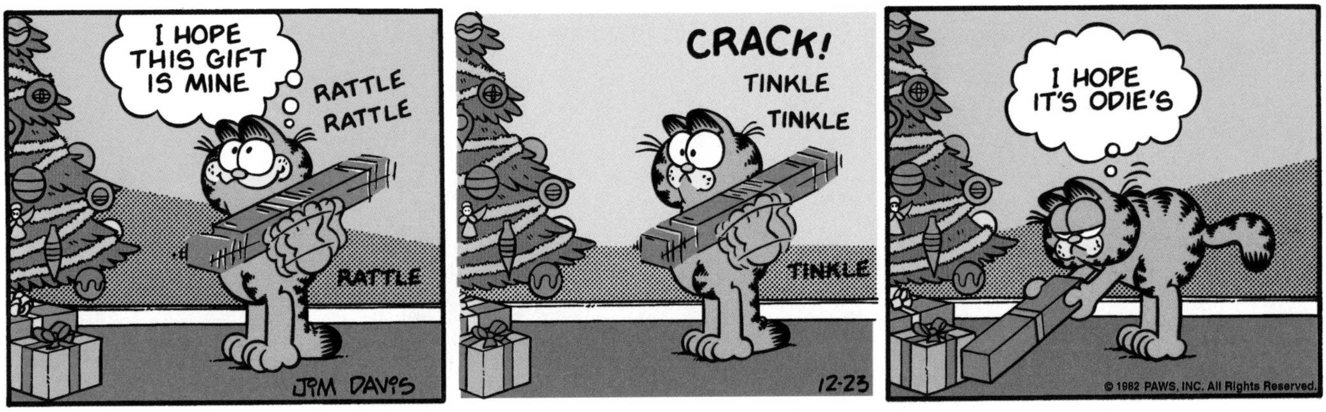
I HOPE THIS GIFT IS MINE
RATTLE
RATTLE
RATTLE
JIM DAVIS
CRACK!
TINKLE
TINKLE
TINKLE
12-23
I HOPE IT'S ODIE'S
© 1982 PAWS, INC. All Rights Reserved.

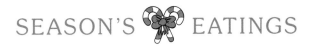

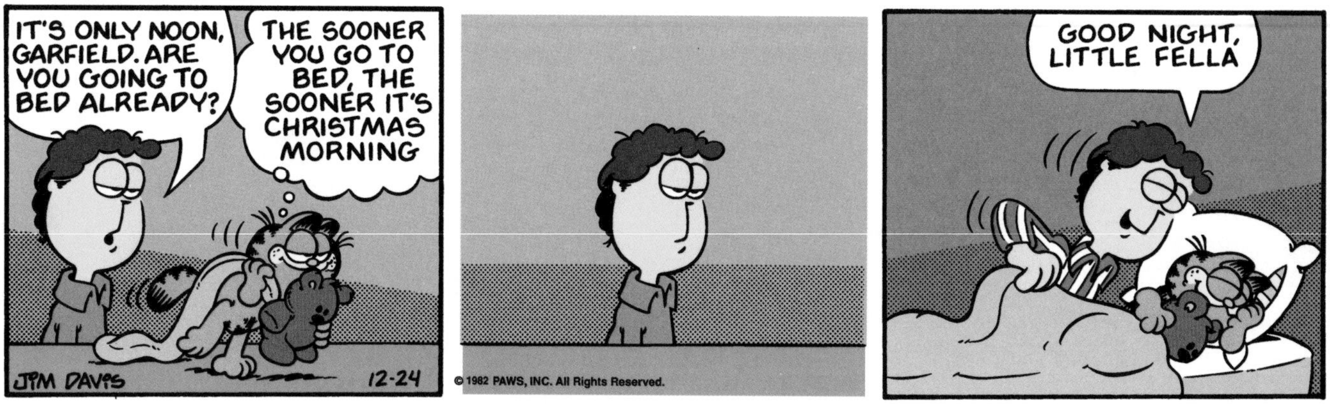
IT'S ONLY NOON, GARFIELD. ARE YOU GOING TO BED ALREADY?
THE SOONER YOU GO TO BED, THE SOONER IT'S CHRISTMAS MORNING
JIM DAVIS
12-24
© 1982 PAWS, INC. All Rights Reserved.
GOOD NIGHT, LITTLE FELLA

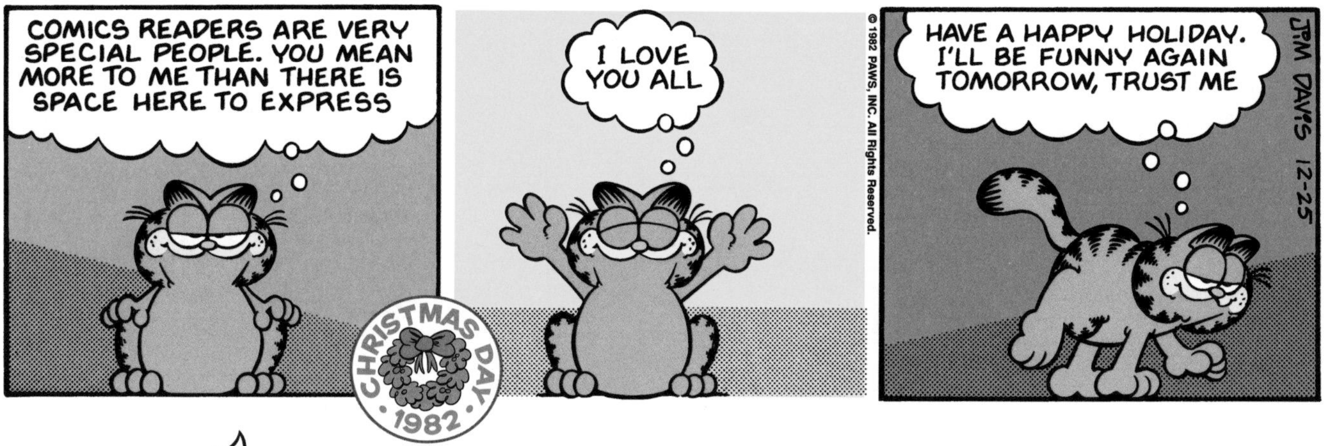
COMICS READERS ARE VERY SPECIAL PEOPLE. YOU MEAN MORE TO ME THAN THERE IS SPACE HERE TO EXPRESS
I LOVE YOU ALL
© 1982 PAWS, INC. All Rights Reserved.
HAVE A HAPPY HOLIDAY. I'LL BE FUNNY AGAIN TOMORROW, TRUST ME
JIM DAVIS 12-25
CHRISTMAS DAY · 1982 ·

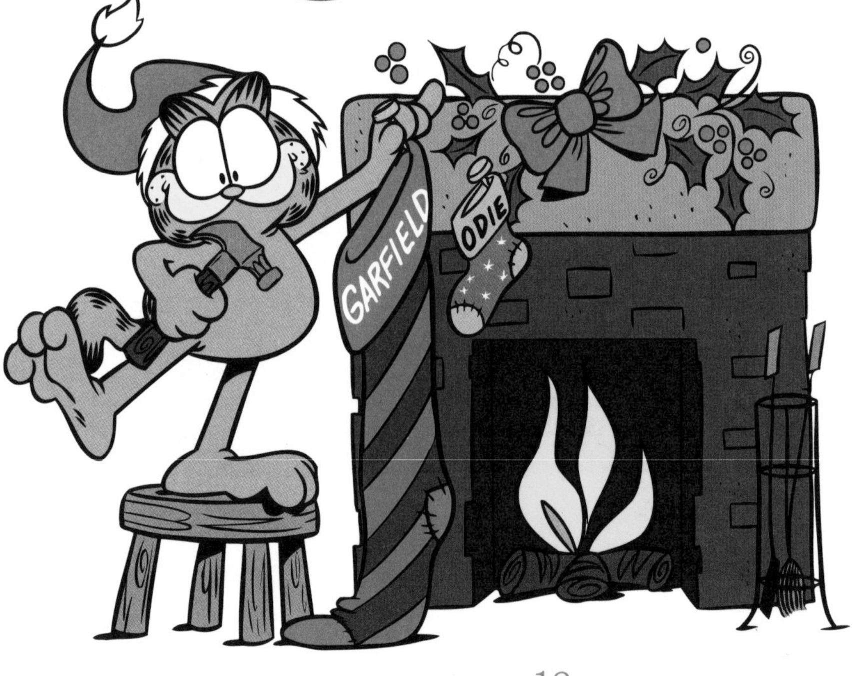
GARFIELD
ODIE

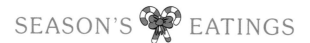

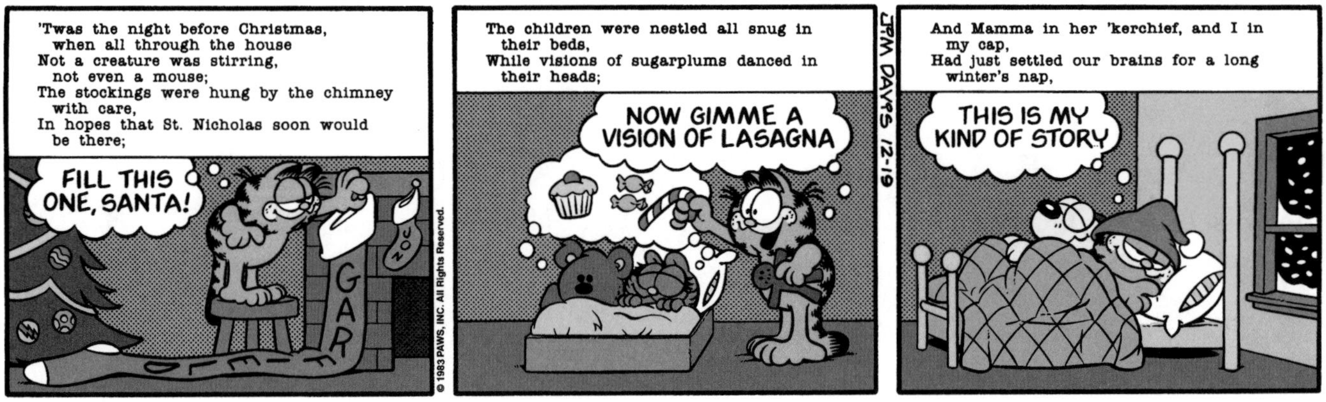
'Twas the night before Christmas,
when all through the house
Not a creature was stirring,
not even a mouse;
The stockings were hung by the chimney
with care,
In hopes that St. Nicholas soon would
be there;
FILL THIS ONE, SANTA!
GAR
© 1983 PAWS, INC. All Rights Reserved.
The children were nestled all snug in
their beds,
While visions of sugarplums danced in
their heads;
NOW GIMME A VISION OF LASAGNA
JPM DAVPS 12-19
And Mamma in her 'kerchief, and I in
my cap,
Had just settled our brains for a long
winter's nap,
THIS IS MY KIND OF STORY

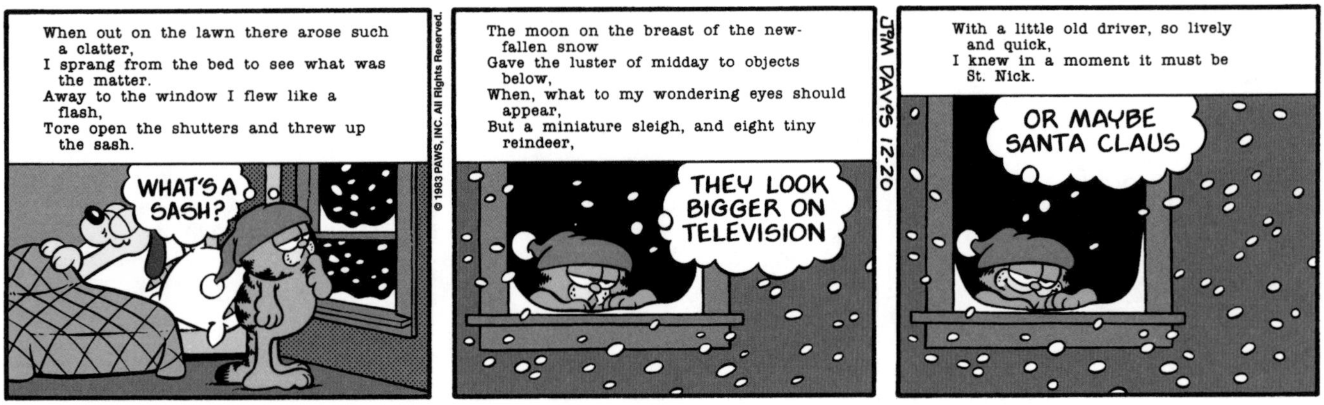
When out on the lawn there arose such
a clatter,
I sprang from the bed to see what was
the matter.
Away to the window I flew like a
flash,
Tore open the shutters and threw up
the sash.
WHAT'S A SASH?
© 1983 PAWS, INC. All Rights Reserved.
The moon on the breast of the new-
fallen snow
Gave the luster of midday to objects
below,
When, what to my wondering eyes should
appear,
But a miniature sleigh, and eight tiny
reindeer,
THEY LOOK BIGGER ON TELEVISION
JPM DAVPS 12-20
With a little old driver, so lively
and quick,
I knew in a moment it must be
St. Nick.
OR MAYBE SANTA CLAUS

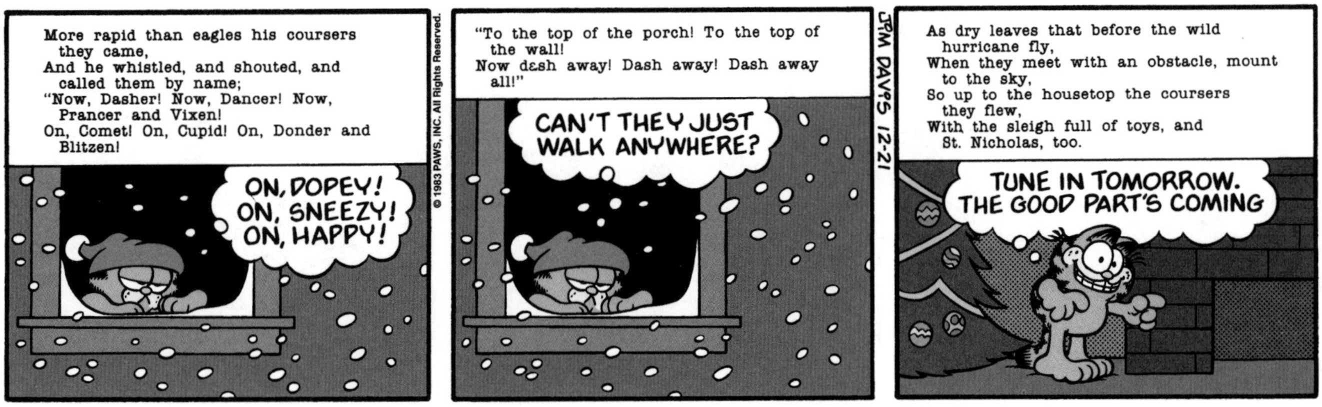
More rapid than eagles his coursers
they came,
And he whistled, and shouted, and
called them by name;
"Now, Dasher! Now, Dancer! Now,
Prancer and Vixen!
On, Comet! On, Cupid! On, Donder and
Blitzen!
ON, DOPEY! ON, SNEEZY! ON, HAPPY!
© 1983 PAWS, INC. All Rights Reserved.
"To the top of the porch! To the top of
the wall!
Now dash away! Dash away! Dash away
all!"
CAN'T THEY JUST WALK ANYWHERE?
JPM DAVPS 12-21
As dry leaves that before the wild
hurricane fly,
When they meet with an obstacle, mount
to the sky,
So up to the housetop the coursers
they flew,
With the sleigh full of toys, and
St. Nicholas, too.
TUNE IN TOMORROW. THE GOOD PART'S COMING

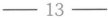

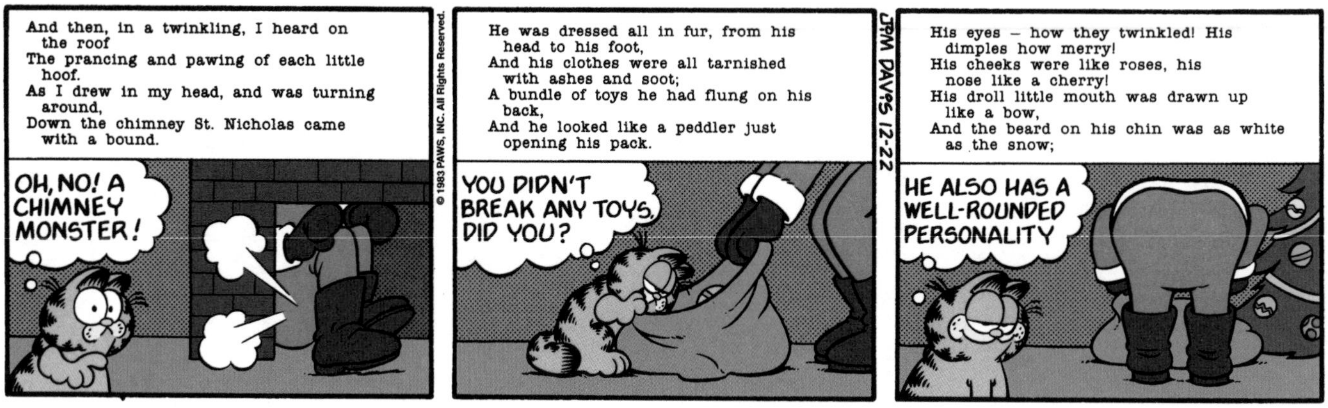
And then, in a twinkling, I heard on the roof
The prancing and pawing of each little hoof.
As I drew in my head, and was turning around,
Down the chimney St. Nicholas came with a bound.
OH, NO! A CHIMNEY MONSTER!
© 1983 PAWS, INC. All Rights Reserved.
He was dressed all in fur, from his head to his foot,
And his clothes were all tarnished with ashes and soot;
A bundle of toys he had flung on his back,
And he looked like a peddler just opening his pack.
YOU DIDN'T BREAK ANY TOYS, DID YOU?
JPM DAVPS 12-22
His eyes – how they twinkled! His dimples how merry!
His cheeks were like roses, his nose like a cherry!
His droll little mouth was drawn up like a bow,
And the beard on his chin was as white as the snow;
HE ALSO HAS A WELL-ROUNDED PERSONALITY

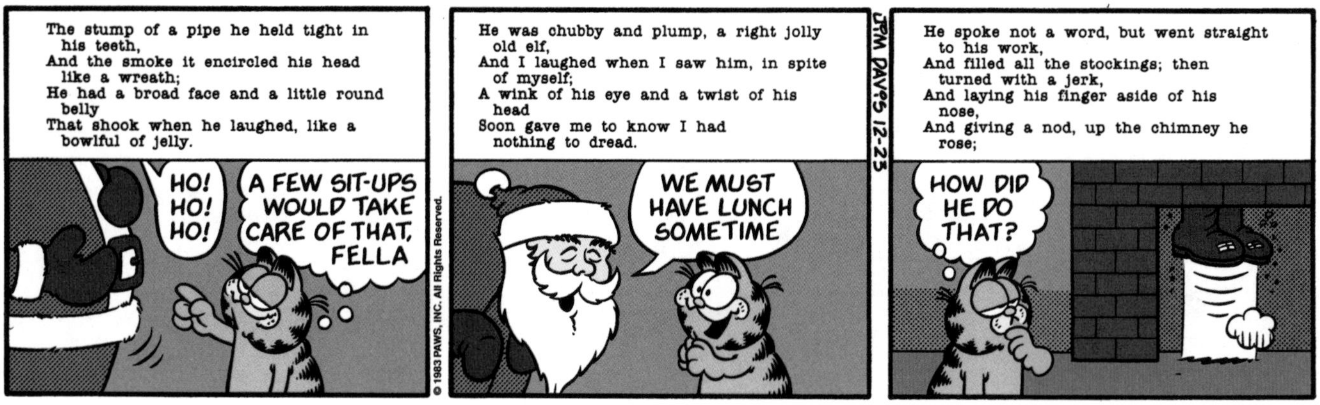
The stump of a pipe he held tight in his teeth,
And the smoke it encircled his head like a wreath;
He had a broad face and a little round belly
That shook when he laughed, like a bowlful of jelly.
HO! HO! HO!
A FEW SIT-UPS WOULD TAKE CARE OF THAT, FELLA
© 1983 PAWS, INC. All Rights Reserved.
He was chubby and plump, a right jolly old elf,
And I laughed when I saw him, in spite of myself;
A wink of his eye and a twist of his head
Soon gave me to know I had nothing to dread.
WE MUST HAVE LUNCH SOMETIME
JPM DAVPS 12-23
He spoke not a word, but went straight to his work,
And filled all the stockings; then turned with a jerk,
And laying his finger aside of his nose,
And giving a nod, up the chimney he rose;
HOW DID HE DO THAT?

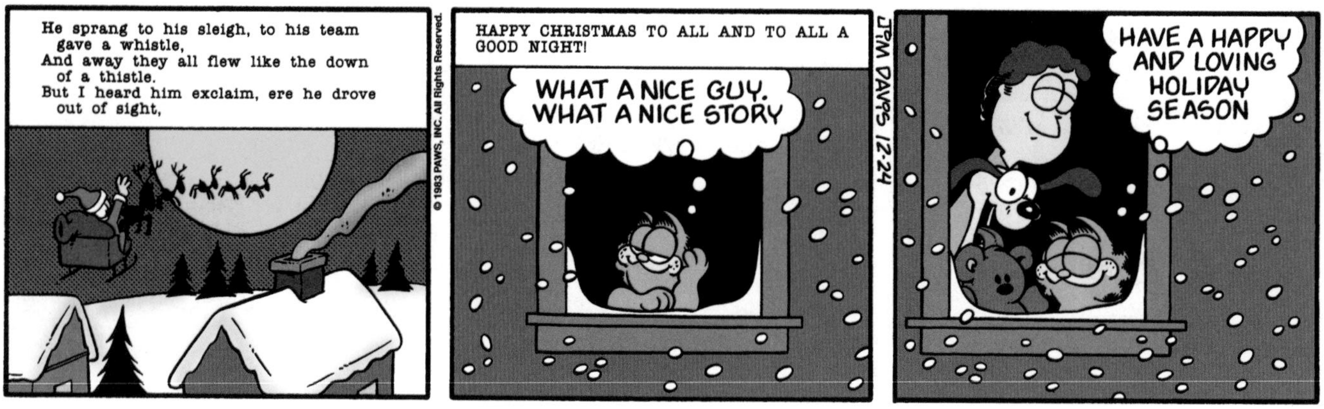
He sprang to his sleigh, to his team gave a whistle,
And away they all flew like the down of a thistle.
But I heard him exclaim, ere he drove out of sight,
© 1983 PAWS, INC. All Rights Reserved.
HAPPY CHRISTMAS TO ALL AND TO ALL A GOOD NIGHT!
WHAT A NICE GUY. WHAT A NICE STORY
JPM DAVPS 12-24
HAVE A HAPPY AND LOVING HOLIDAY SEASON

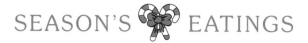

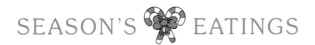

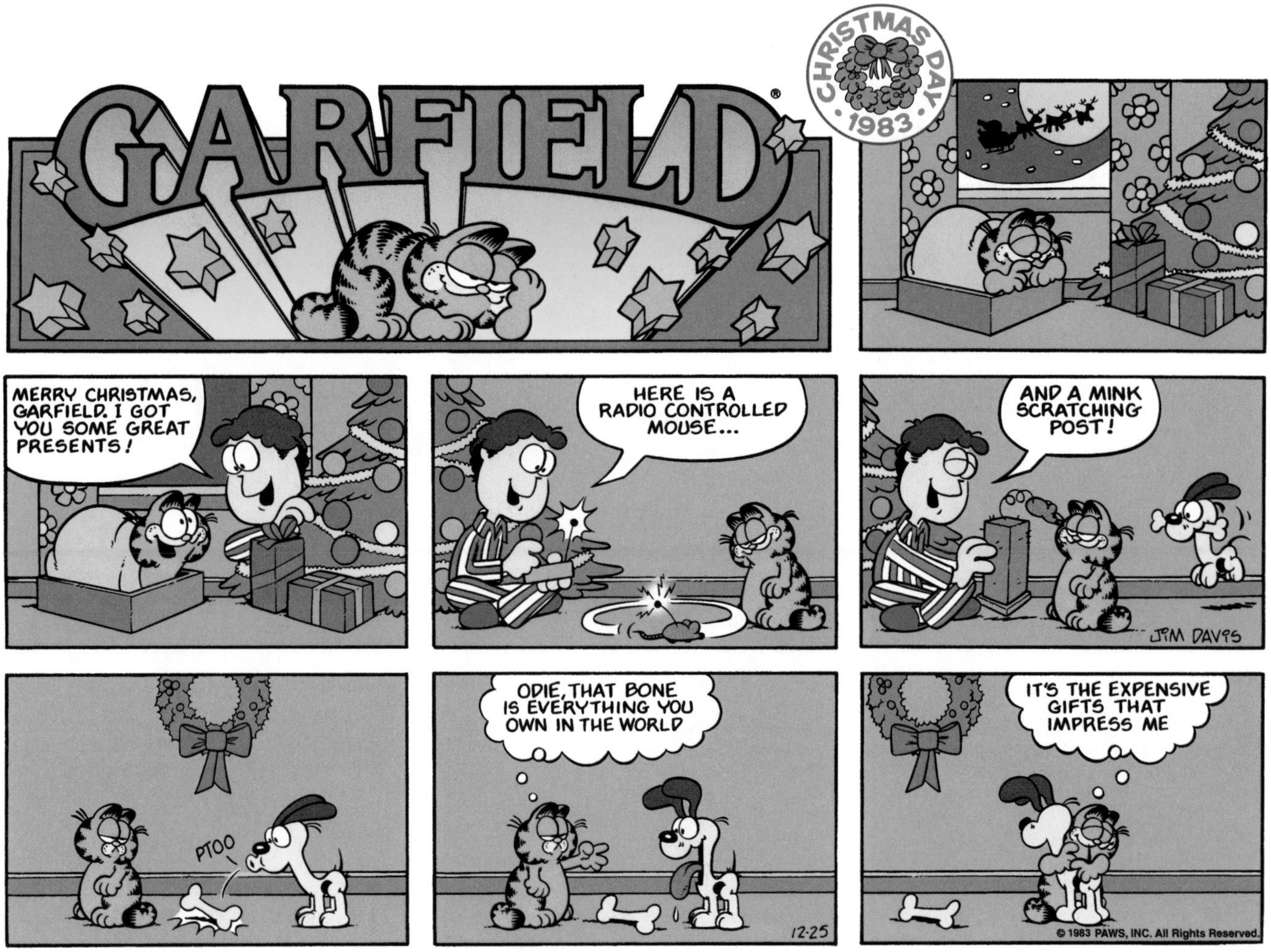
GARFIELD®
CHRISTMAS DAY 1983
MERRY CHRISTMAS, GARFIELD. I GOT YOU SOME GREAT PRESENTS!
HERE IS A RADIO CONTROLLED MOUSE...
AND A MINK SCRATCHING POST!
JIM DAVIS
PTOO
ODIE, THAT BONE IS EVERYTHING YOU OWN IN THE WORLD
12-25
IT'S THE EXPENSIVE GIFTS THAT IMPRESS ME
© 1983 PAWS, INC. All Rights Reserved.

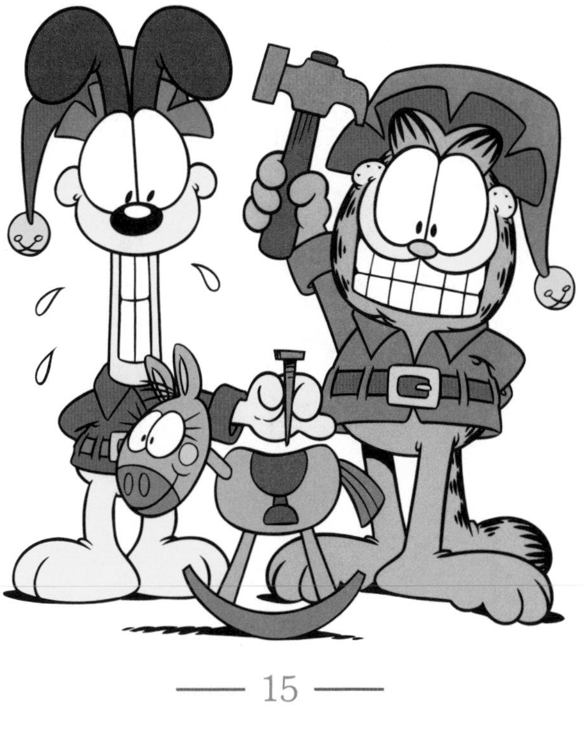

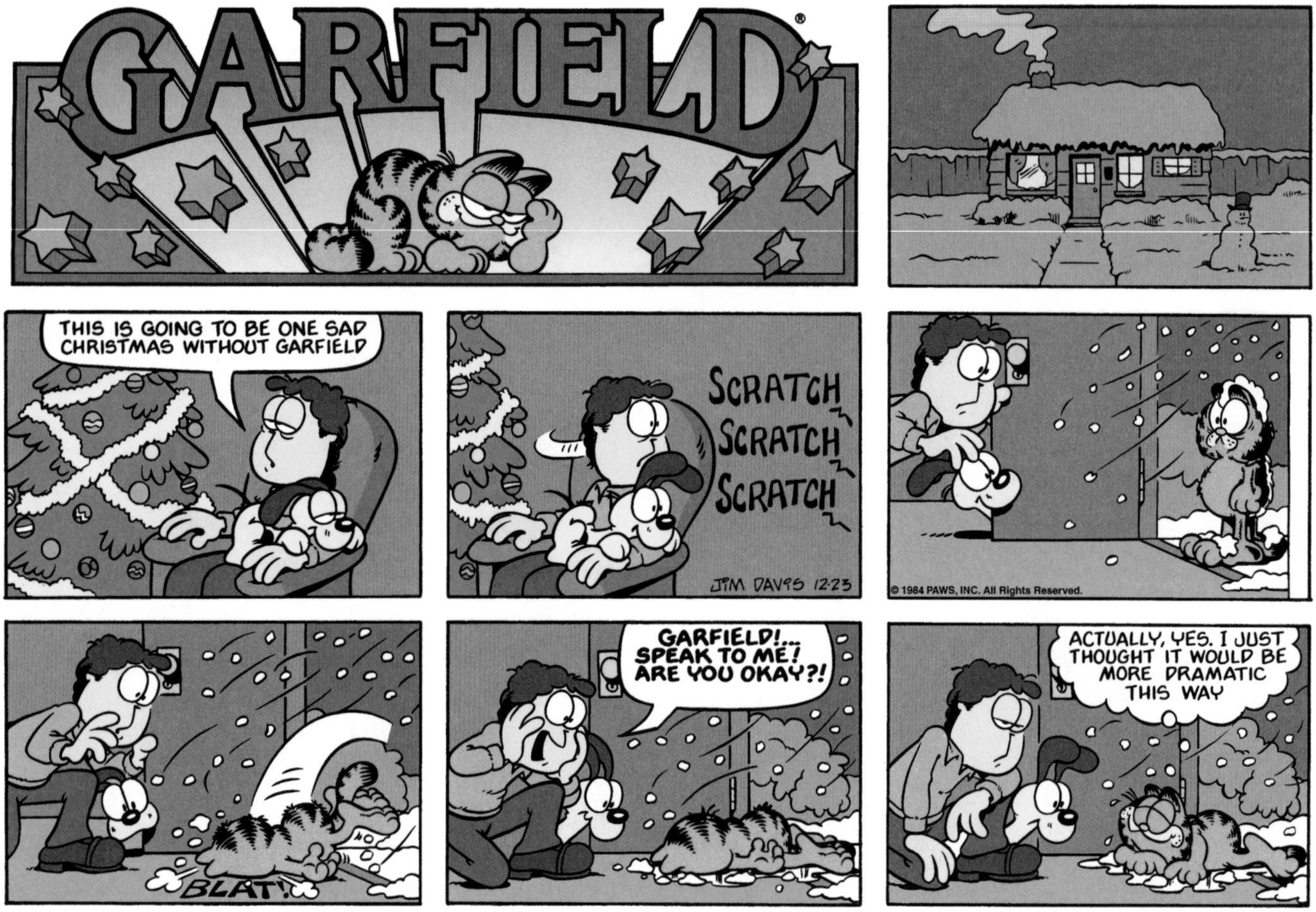
GARFIELD®
THIS IS GOING TO BE ONE SAD CHRISTMAS WITHOUT GARFIELD
SCRATCH
SCRATCH
SCRATCH
JIM DAVIS 12-23
© 1984 PAWS, INC. All Rights Reserved.
BLAT!
GARFIELD!... SPEAK TO ME! ARE YOU OKAY?!
ACTUALLY, YES. I JUST THOUGHT IT WOULD BE MORE DRAMATIC THIS WAY

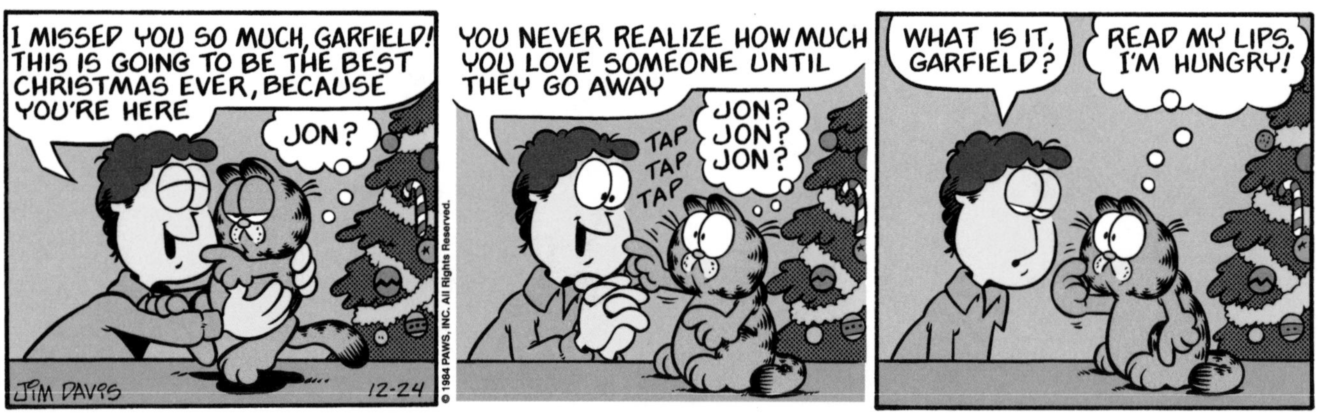
I MISSED YOU SO MUCH, GARFIELD! THIS IS GOING TO BE THE BEST CHRISTMAS EVER, BECAUSE YOU'RE HERE
JON?
JIM DAVIS 12-24
© 1984 PAWS, INC. All Rights Reserved.
YOU NEVER REALIZE HOW MUCH YOU LOVE SOMEONE UNTIL THEY GO AWAY
TAP
TAP
TAP
JON? JON? JON?
WHAT IS IT, GARFIELD?
READ MY LIPS. I'M HUNGRY!

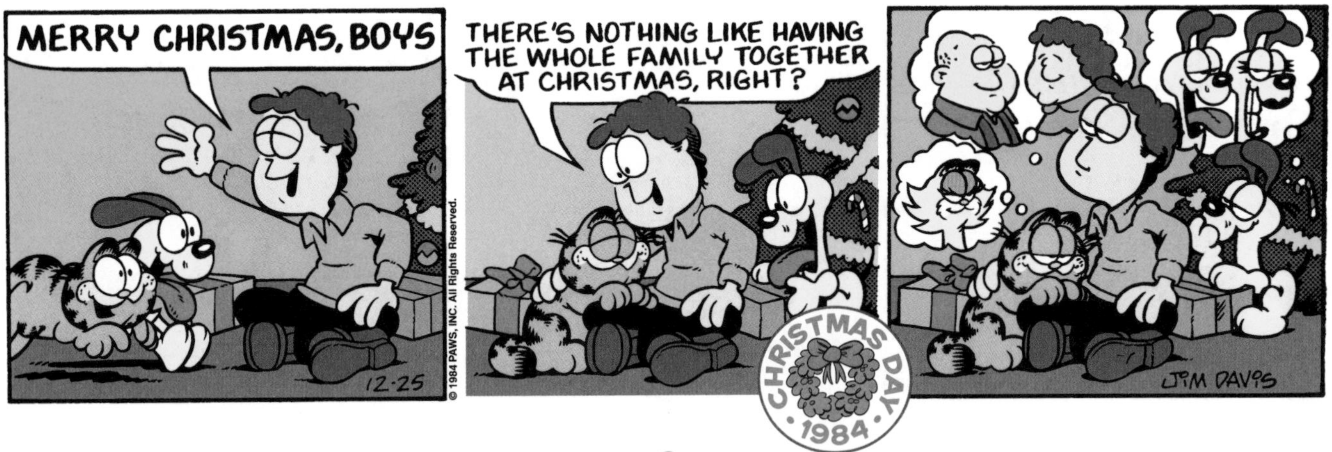
MERRY CHRISTMAS, BOYS
12-25
© 1984 PAWS, INC. All Rights Reserved.
THERE'S NOTHING LIKE HAVING THE WHOLE FAMILY TOGETHER AT CHRISTMAS, RIGHT?
CHRISTMAS DAY 1984
JIM DAVIS

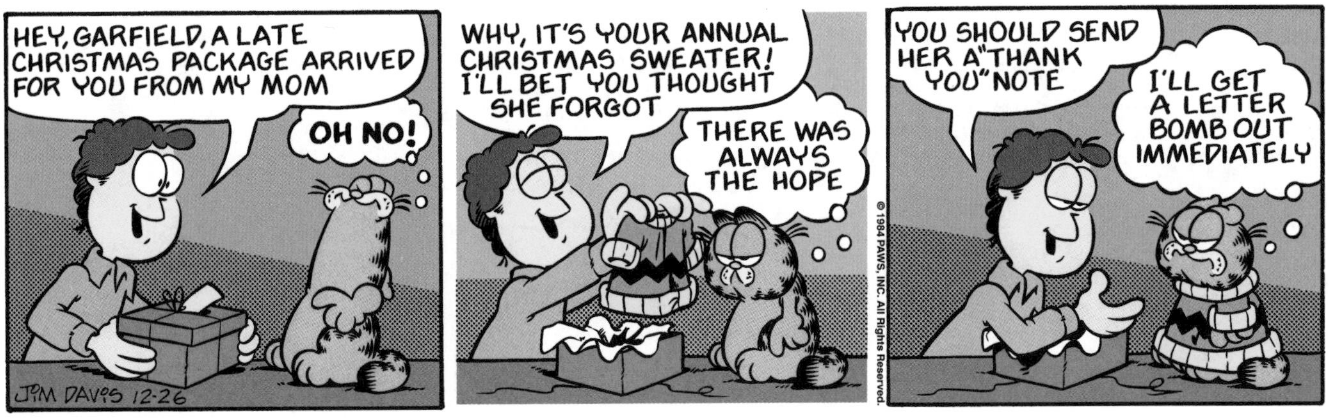
HEY, GARFIELD, A LATE CHRISTMAS PACKAGE ARRIVED FOR YOU FROM MY MOM
OH NO!
JIM DAVIS 12-26
WHY, IT'S YOUR ANNUAL CHRISTMAS SWEATER! I'LL BET YOU THOUGHT SHE FORGOT
THERE WAS ALWAYS THE HOPE
© 1984 PAWS, INC. All Rights Reserved.
YOU SHOULD SEND HER A "THANK YOU" NOTE
I'LL GET A LETTER BOMB OUT IMMEDIATELY

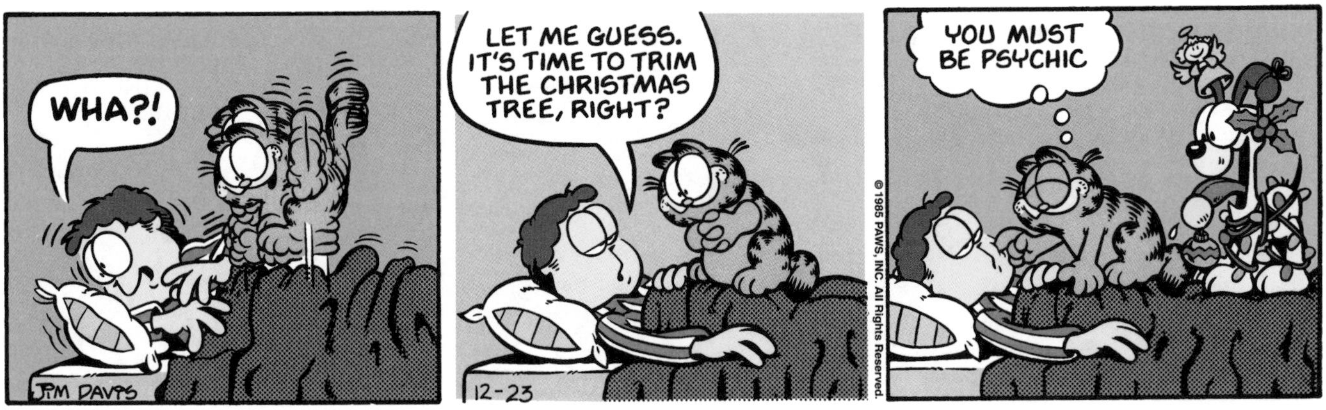
WHA?!
JIM DAVIS
LET ME GUESS. IT'S TIME TO TRIM THE CHRISTMAS TREE, RIGHT?
12-23
© 1985 PAWS, INC. All Rights Reserved.
YOU MUST BE PSYCHIC

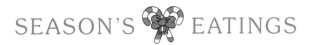

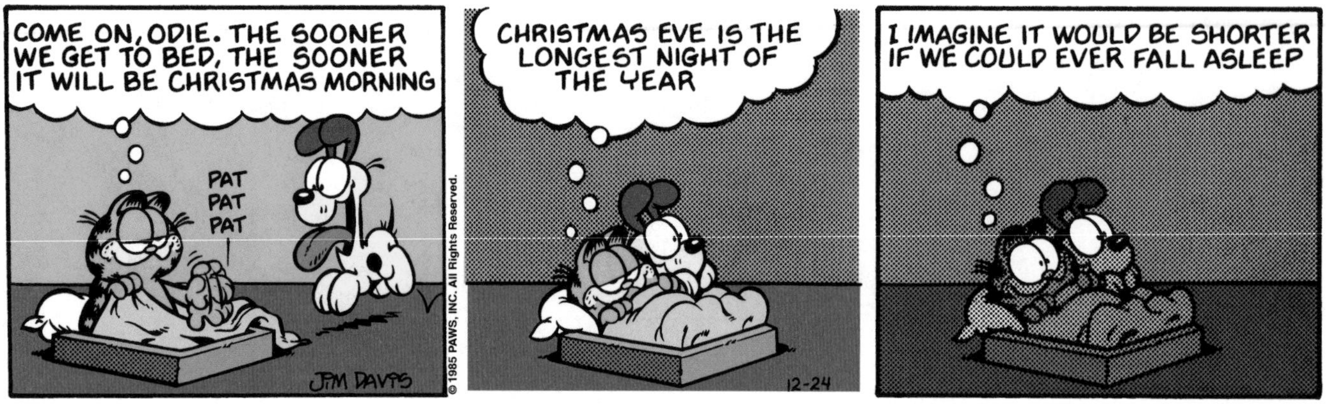
COME ON, ODIE. THE SOONER WE GET TO BED, THE SOONER IT WILL BE CHRISTMAS MORNING
PAT PAT PAT
JIM DAVIS
© 1985 PAWS, INC. All Rights Reserved.
CHRISTMAS EVE IS THE LONGEST NIGHT OF THE YEAR
12-24
I IMAGINE IT WOULD BE SHORTER IF WE COULD EVER FALL ASLEEP

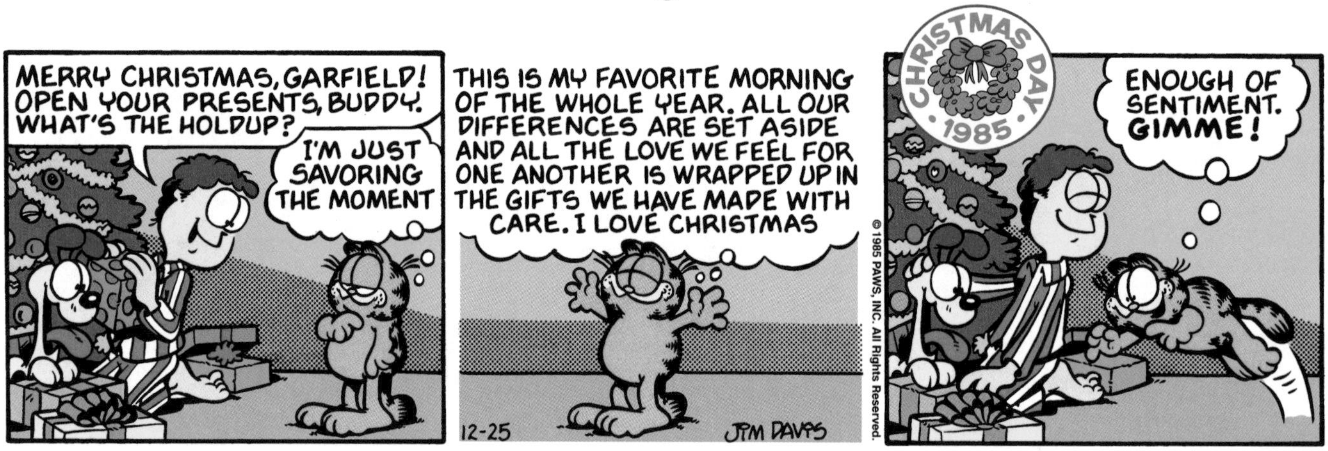
MERRY CHRISTMAS, GARFIELD! OPEN YOUR PRESENTS, BUDDY. WHAT'S THE HOLDUP?
I'M JUST SAVORING THE MOMENT
THIS IS MY FAVORITE MORNING OF THE WHOLE YEAR. ALL OUR DIFFERENCES ARE SET ASIDE AND ALL THE LOVE WE FEEL FOR ONE ANOTHER IS WRAPPED UP IN THE GIFTS WE HAVE MADE WITH CARE. I LOVE CHRISTMAS
12-25
JIM DAVIS
© 1985 PAWS, INC. All Rights Reserved.
CHRISTMAS DAY 1985
ENOUGH OF SENTIMENT. GIMME!

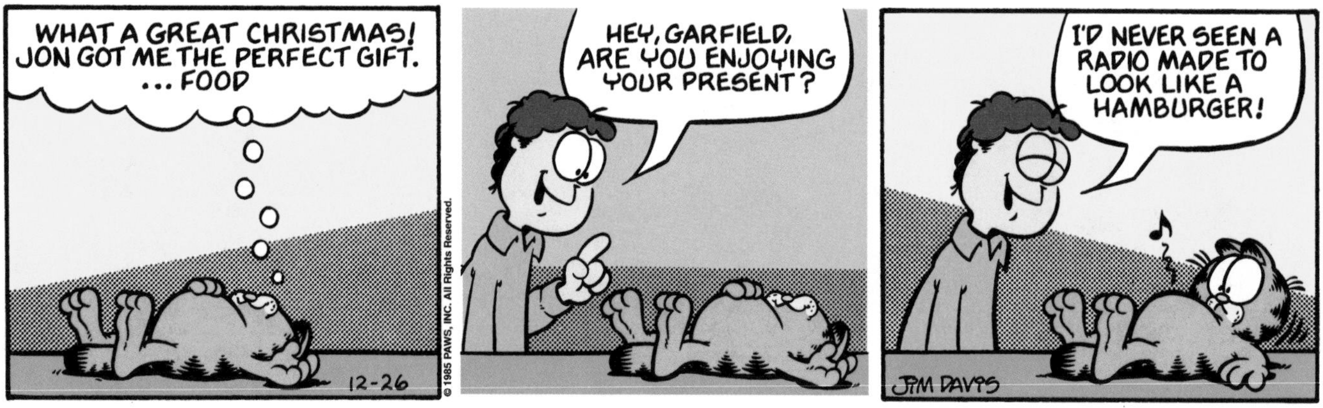
WHAT A GREAT CHRISTMAS! JON GOT ME THE PERFECT GIFT. ... FOOD
12-26
© 1985 PAWS, INC. All Rights Reserved.
HEY, GARFIELD, ARE YOU ENJOYING YOUR PRESENT?
I'D NEVER SEEN A RADIO MADE TO LOOK LIKE A HAMBURGER!
JIM DAVIS

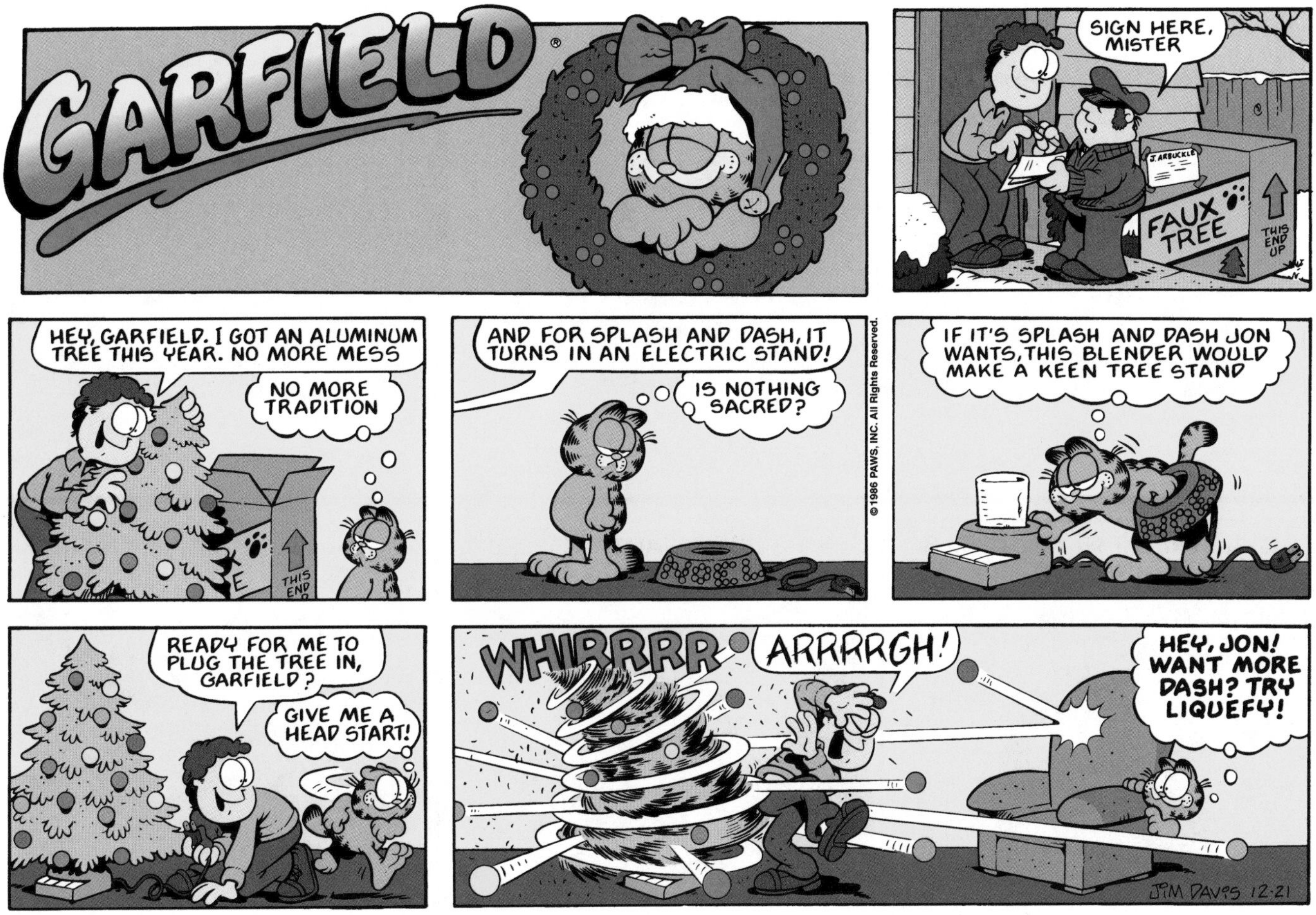
GARFIELD
SIGN HERE, MISTER
J ARBUCKLE
FAUX TREE
THIS END UP
HEY, GARFIELD. I GOT AN ALUMINUM TREE THIS YEAR. NO MORE MESS
NO MORE TRADITION
AND FOR SPLASH AND DASH, IT TURNS IN AN ELECTRIC STAND!
IS NOTHING SACRED?
© 1986 PAWS, INC. All Rights Reserved.
IF IT'S SPLASH AND DASH JON WANTS, THIS BLENDER WOULD MAKE A KEEN TREE STAND
READY FOR ME TO PLUG THE TREE IN, GARFIELD?
GIVE ME A HEAD START!
WHIRRRRR
ARRRRGH!
HEY, JON! WANT MORE DASH? TRY LIQUEFY!
JIM DAVIS 12-21

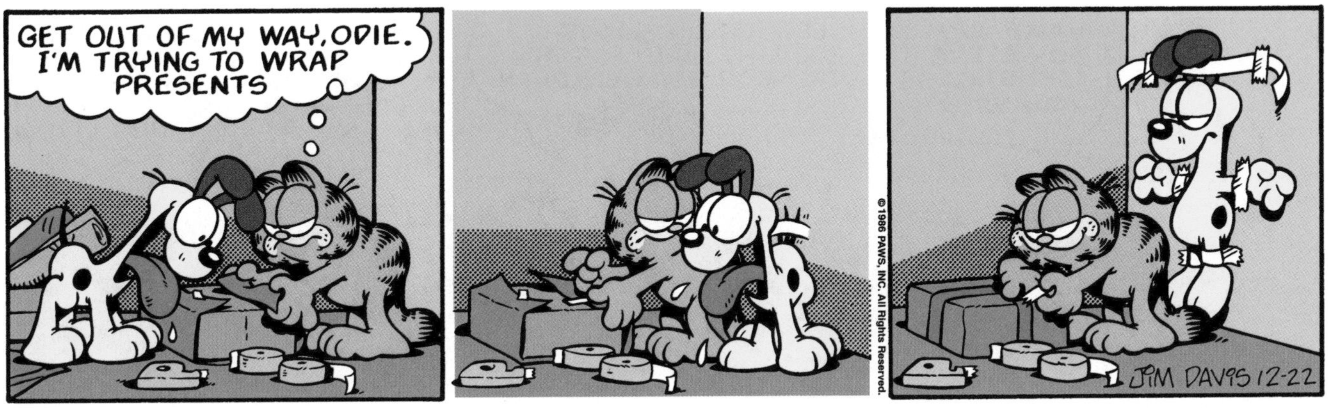
GET OUT OF MY WAY, ODIE. I'M TRYING TO WRAP PRESENTS
© 1986 PAWS, INC. All Rights Reserved.
JIM DAVIS 12-22

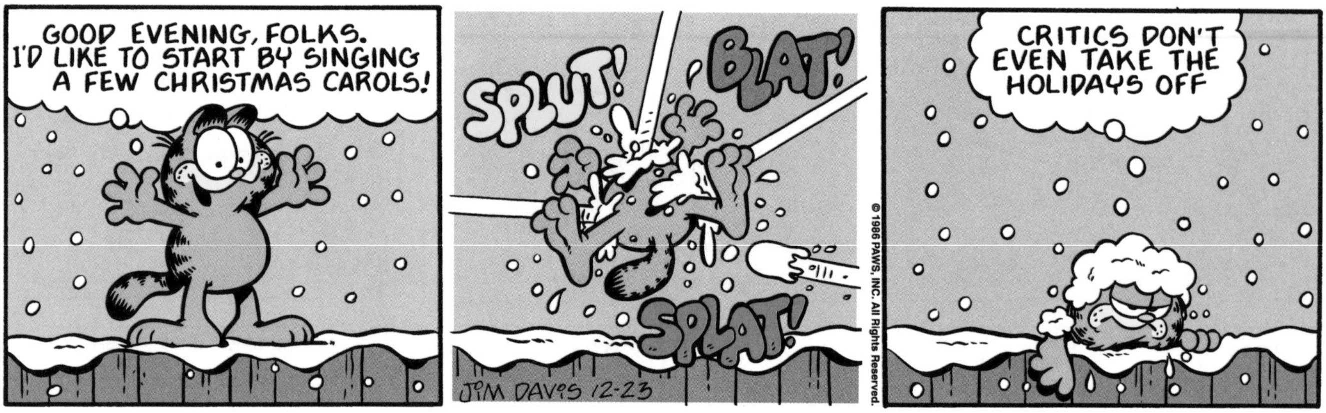
GOOD EVENING, FOLKS. I'D LIKE TO START BY SINGING A FEW CHRISTMAS CAROLS!
SPLUT!
BLAT!
SPLAT!
JIM DAVIS 12-23
© 1986 PAWS, INC. All Rights Reserved.
CRITICS DON'T EVEN TAKE THE HOLIDAYS OFF

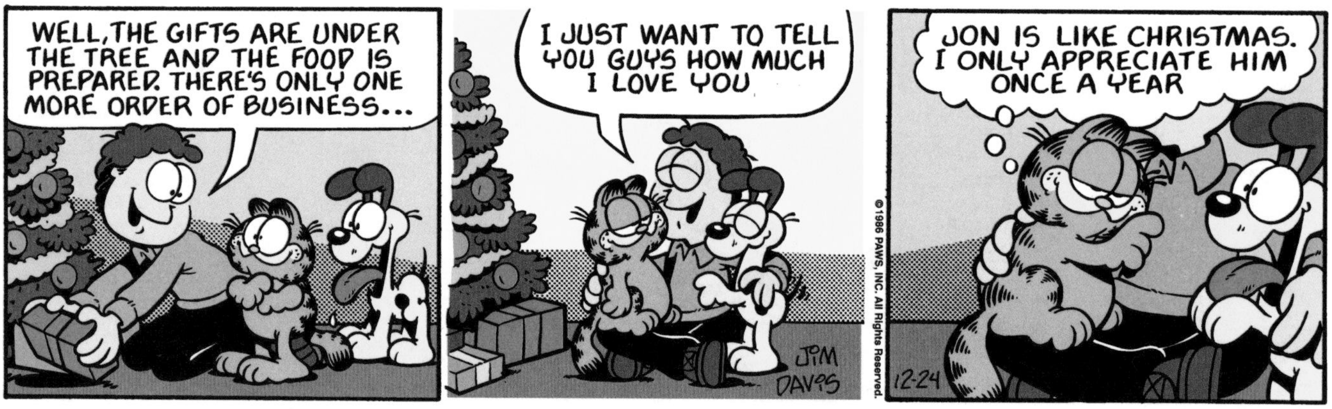
WELL, THE GIFTS ARE UNDER THE TREE AND THE FOOD IS PREPARED. THERE'S ONLY ONE MORE ORDER OF BUSINESS...
I JUST WANT TO TELL YOU GUYS HOW MUCH I LOVE YOU
JIM DAVIS
© 1986 PAWS, INC. All Rights Reserved.
JON IS LIKE CHRISTMAS. I ONLY APPRECIATE HIM ONCE A YEAR
12-24

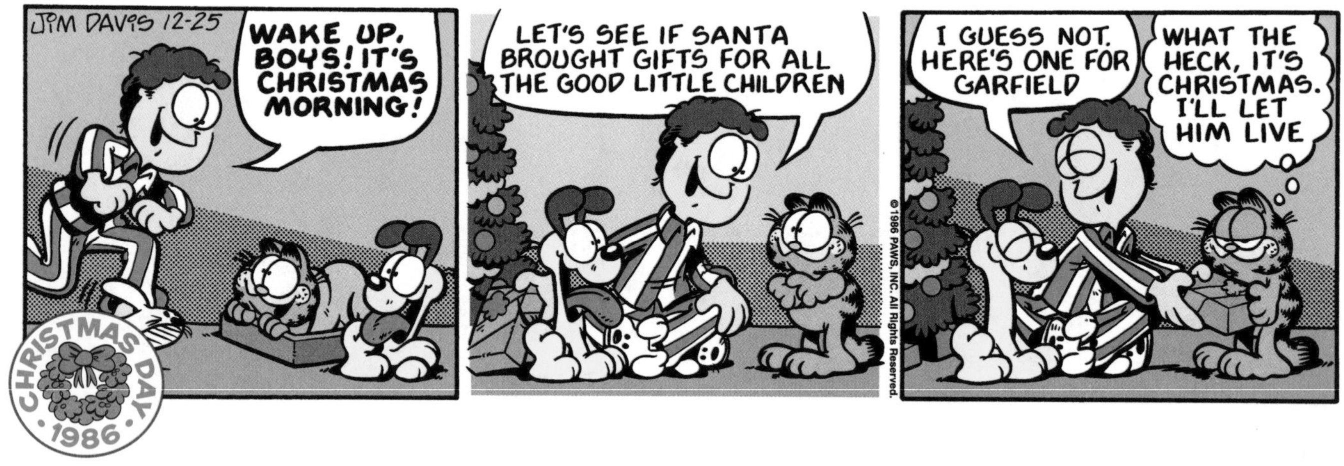
JIM DAVIS 12-25
WAKE UP, BOYS! IT'S CHRISTMAS MORNING!
CHRISTMAS DAY 1986
LET'S SEE IF SANTA BROUGHT GIFTS FOR ALL THE GOOD LITTLE CHILDREN
© 1986 PAWS, INC. All Rights Reserved.
I GUESS NOT. HERE'S ONE FOR GARFIELD
WHAT THE HECK, IT'S CHRISTMAS. I'LL LET HIM LIVE

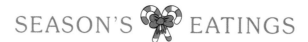

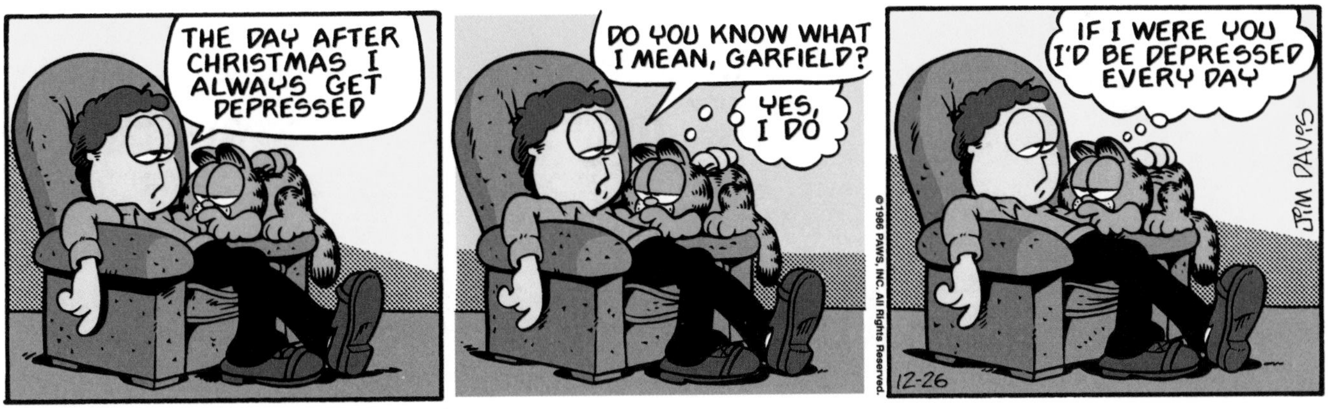
THE DAY AFTER CHRISTMAS I ALWAYS GET DEPRESSED
DO YOU KNOW WHAT I MEAN, GARFIELD?
YES, I DO
IF I WERE YOU I'D BE DEPRESSED EVERY DAY
© 1986 PAWS, INC. All Rights Reserved.
JIM DAVIS
12-26

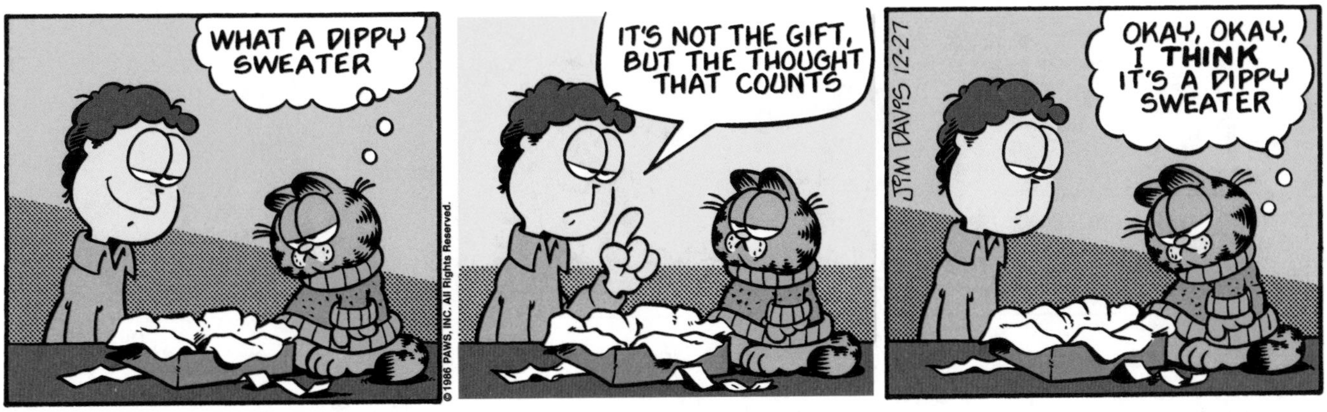
WHAT A DIPPY SWEATER
© 1986 PAWS, INC. All Rights Reserved.
IT'S NOT THE GIFT, BUT THE THOUGHT THAT COUNTS
JIM DAVIS 12-27
OKAY, OKAY, I **THINK** IT'S A DIPPY SWEATER

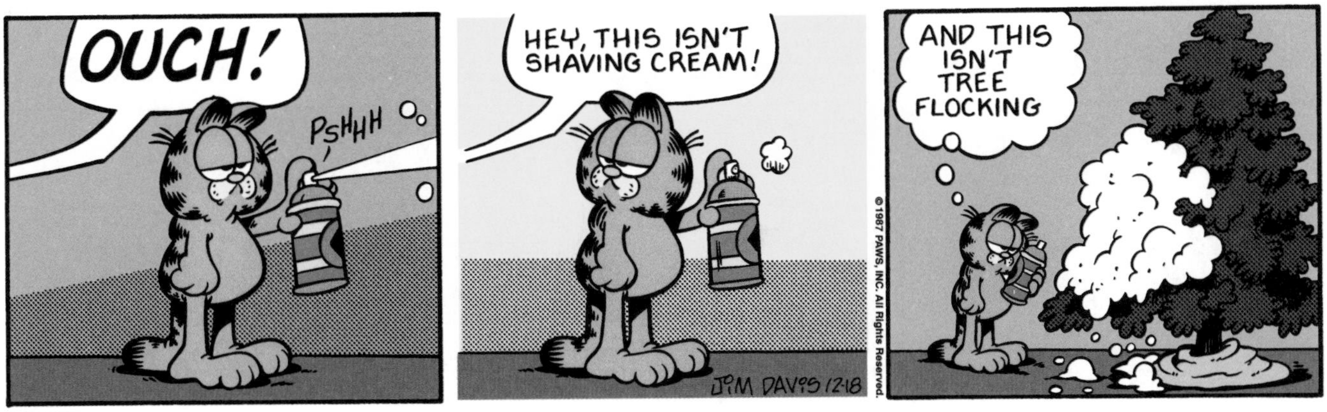
OUCH!
PSHHH
HEY, THIS ISN'T SHAVING CREAM!
JIM DAVIS 12-18
© 1987 PAWS, INC. All Rights Reserved.
AND THIS ISN'T TREE FLOCKING

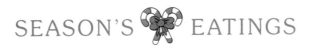

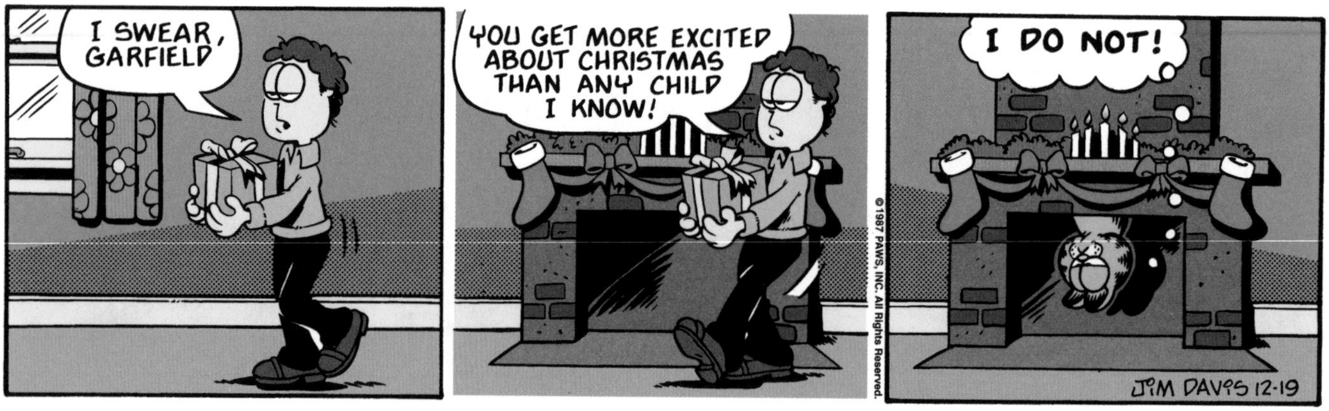
I SWEAR, GARFIELD
YOU GET MORE EXCITED ABOUT CHRISTMAS THAN ANY CHILD I KNOW!
I DO NOT!
© 1987 PAWS, INC. All Rights Reserved.
JIM DAVIS 12-19

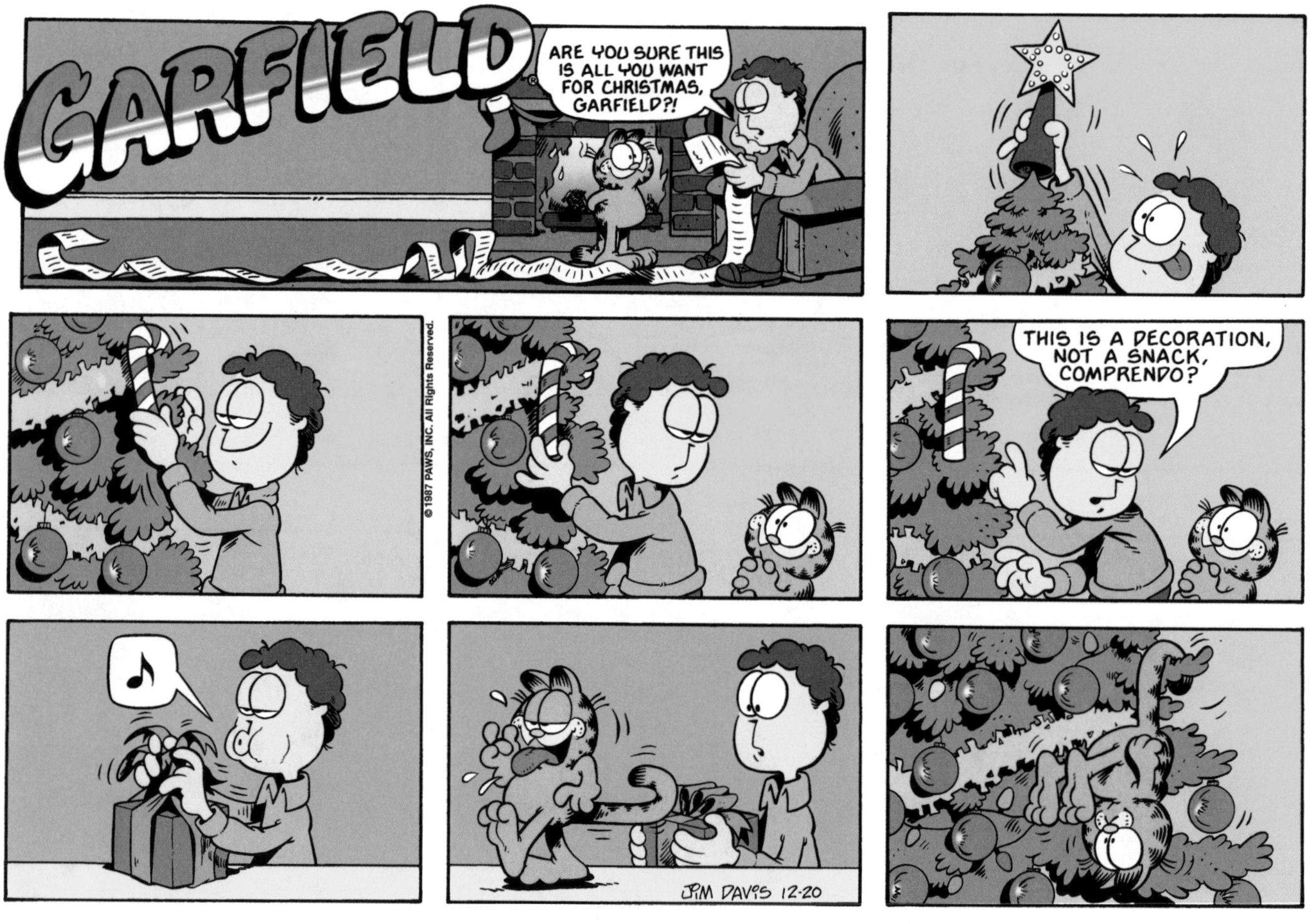
GARFIELD®
ARE YOU SURE THIS IS ALL YOU WANT FOR CHRISTMAS, GARFIELD?!
© 1987 PAWS, INC. All Rights Reserved.
THIS IS A DECORATION, NOT A SNACK, COMPRENDO?
♪
JIM DAVIS 12-20

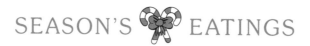

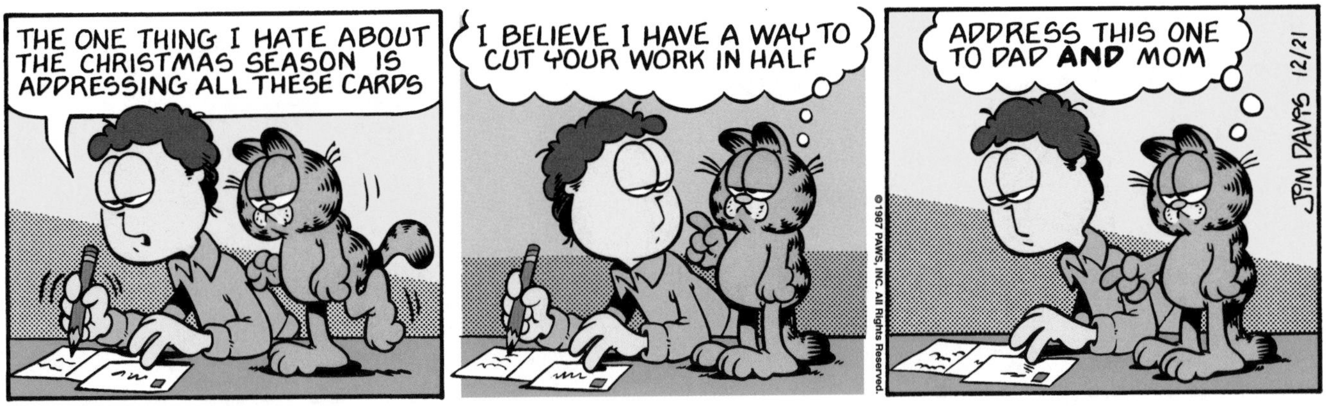
THE ONE THING I HATE ABOUT THE CHRISTMAS SEASON IS ADDRESSING ALL THESE CARDS
I BELIEVE I HAVE A WAY TO CUT YOUR WORK IN HALF
ADDRESS THIS ONE TO DAD **AND** MOM
JIM DAVIS 12/21
© 1987 PAWS, INC. All Rights Reserved.

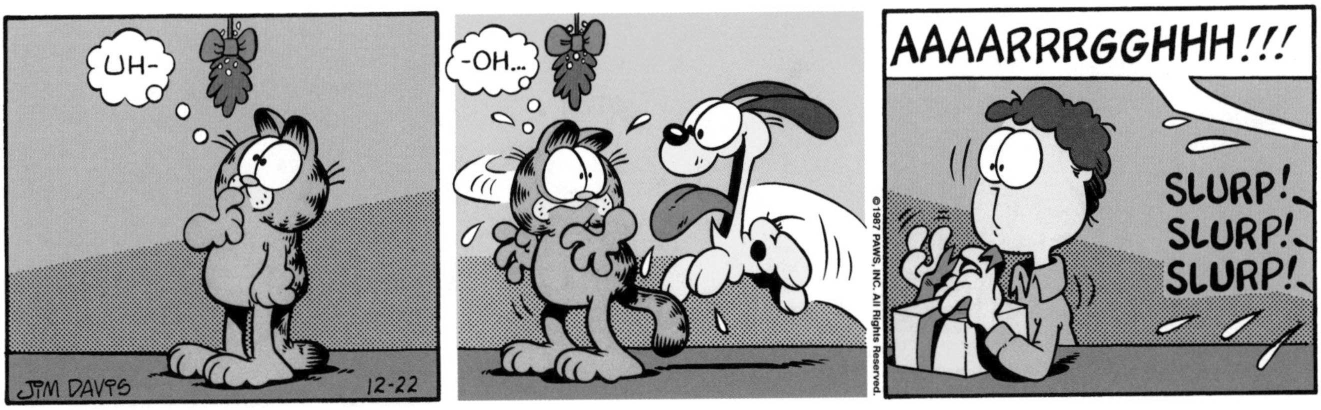
UH-
JIM DAVIS 12-22
-OH...
AAAARRRGGHHH!!!
SLURP!
SLURP!
SLURP!
© 1987 PAWS, INC. All Rights Reserved.

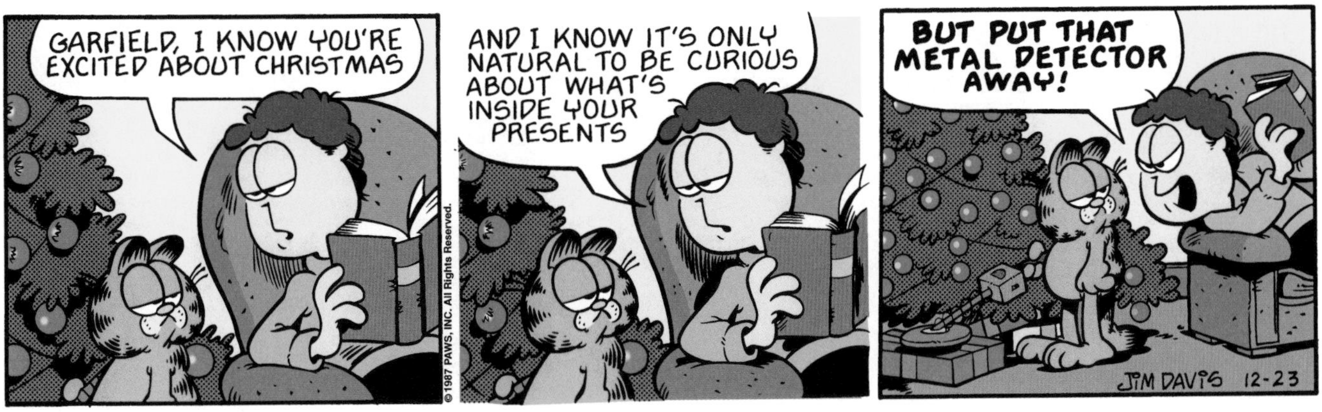
GARFIELD, I KNOW YOU'RE EXCITED ABOUT CHRISTMAS
AND I KNOW IT'S ONLY NATURAL TO BE CURIOUS ABOUT WHAT'S INSIDE YOUR PRESENTS
BUT PUT THAT METAL DETECTOR AWAY!
JIM DAVIS 12-23
© 1987 PAWS, INC. All Rights Reserved.

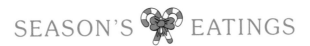

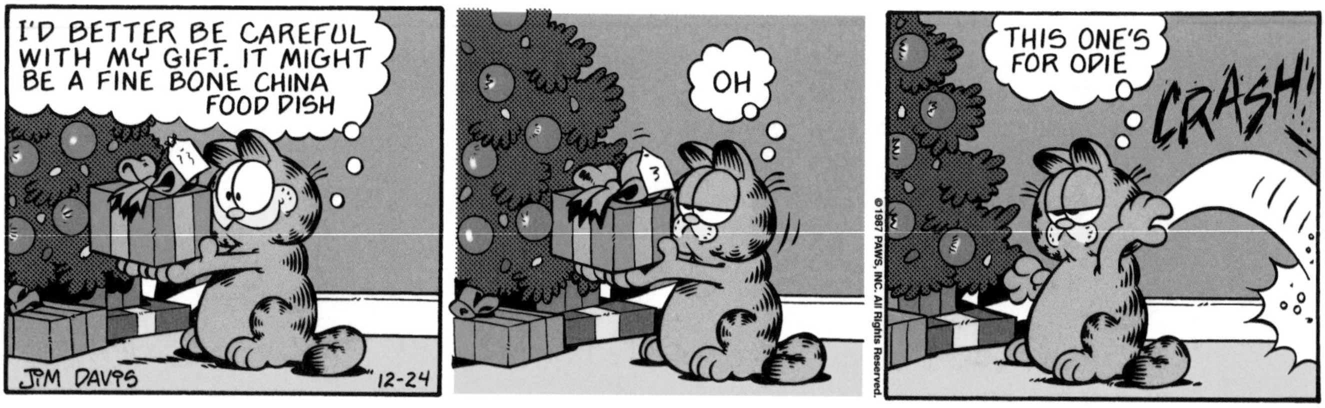
I'D BETTER BE CAREFUL WITH MY GIFT. IT MIGHT BE A FINE BONE CHINA FOOD DISH
JIM DAVIS
12-24
OH
THIS ONE'S FOR ODIE
CRASH!
© 1987 PAWS, INC. All Rights Reserved.

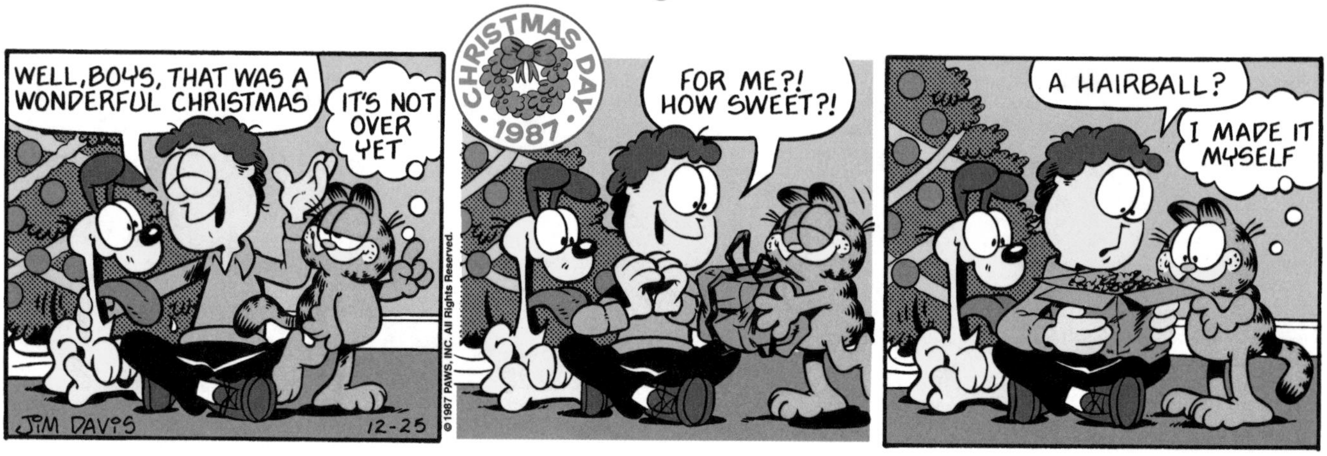
WELL, BOYS, THAT WAS A WONDERFUL CHRISTMAS
IT'S NOT OVER YET
JIM DAVIS
12-25
© 1987 PAWS, INC. All Rights Reserved.
CHRISTMAS DAY 1987
FOR ME?! HOW SWEET?!
A HAIRBALL?
I MADE IT MYSELF

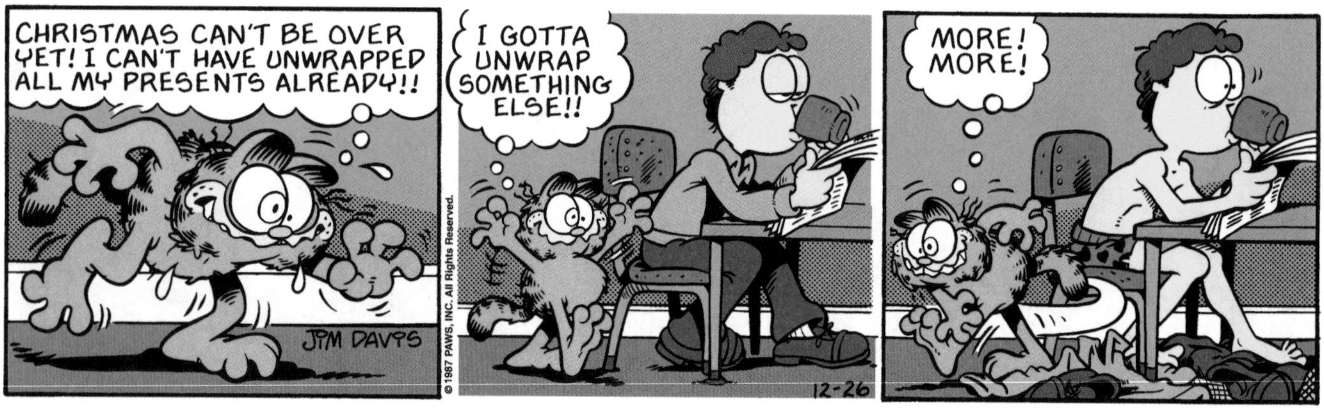
CHRISTMAS CAN'T BE OVER YET! I CAN'T HAVE UNWRAPPED ALL MY PRESENTS ALREADY!!
JIM DAVIS
© 1987 PAWS, INC. All Rights Reserved.
I GOTTA UNWRAP SOMETHING ELSE!!
12-26
MORE! MORE!

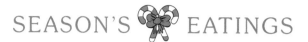

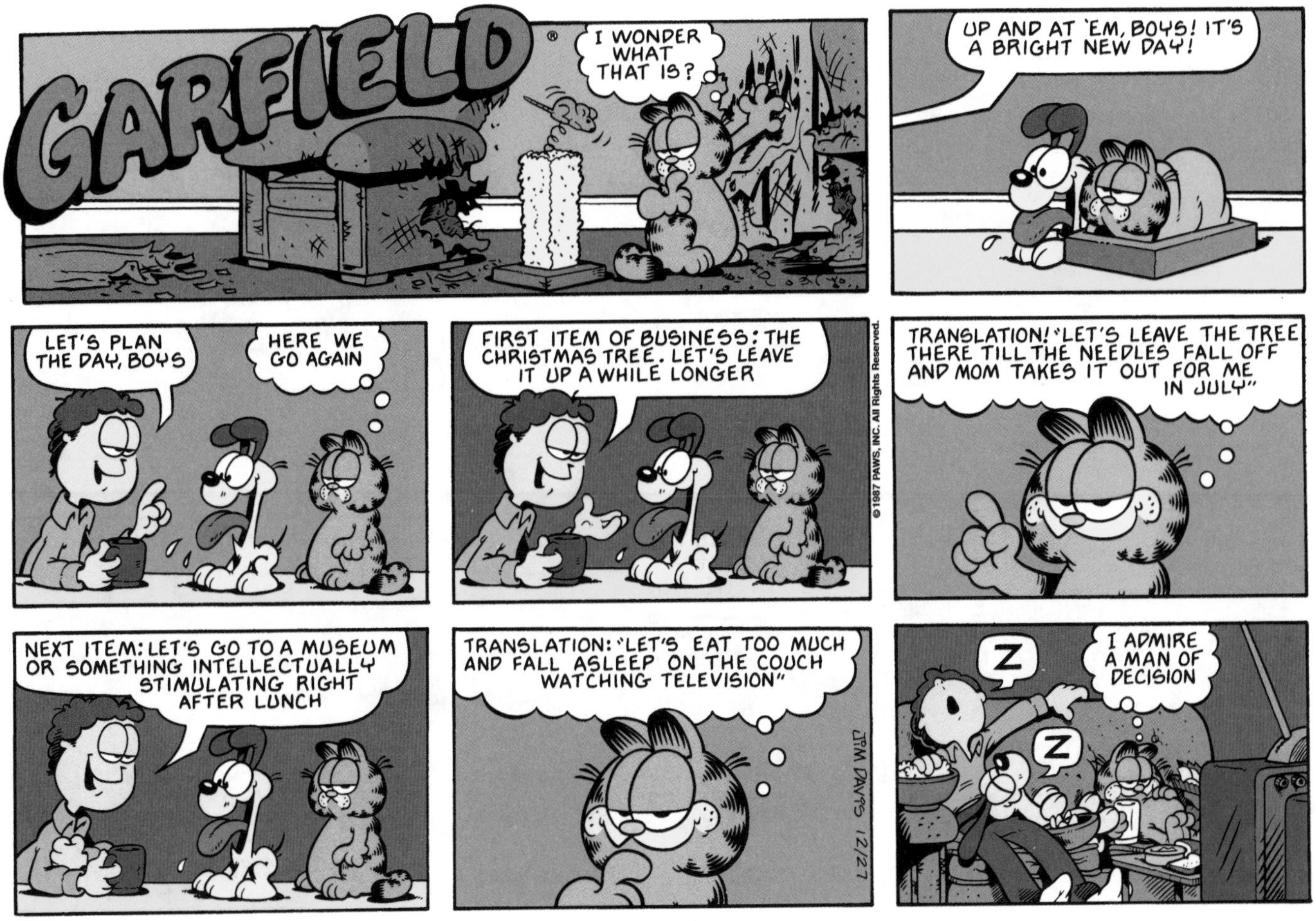
GARFIELD®
I WONDER WHAT THAT IS?
UP AND AT 'EM, BOYS! IT'S A BRIGHT NEW DAY!
LET'S PLAN THE DAY, BOYS
HERE WE GO AGAIN
FIRST ITEM OF BUSINESS: THE CHRISTMAS TREE. LET'S LEAVE IT UP A WHILE LONGER
© 1987 PAWS, INC. All Rights Reserved.
TRANSLATION! "LET'S LEAVE THE TREE THERE TILL THE NEEDLES FALL OFF AND MOM TAKES IT OUT FOR ME IN JULY"
NEXT ITEM: LET'S GO TO A MUSEUM OR SOMETHING INTELLECTUALLY STIMULATING RIGHT AFTER LUNCH
TRANSLATION: "LET'S EAT TOO MUCH AND FALL ASLEEP ON THE COUCH WATCHING TELEVISION"
JIM DAVIS 12/27
Z
Z
I ADMIRE A MAN OF DECISION

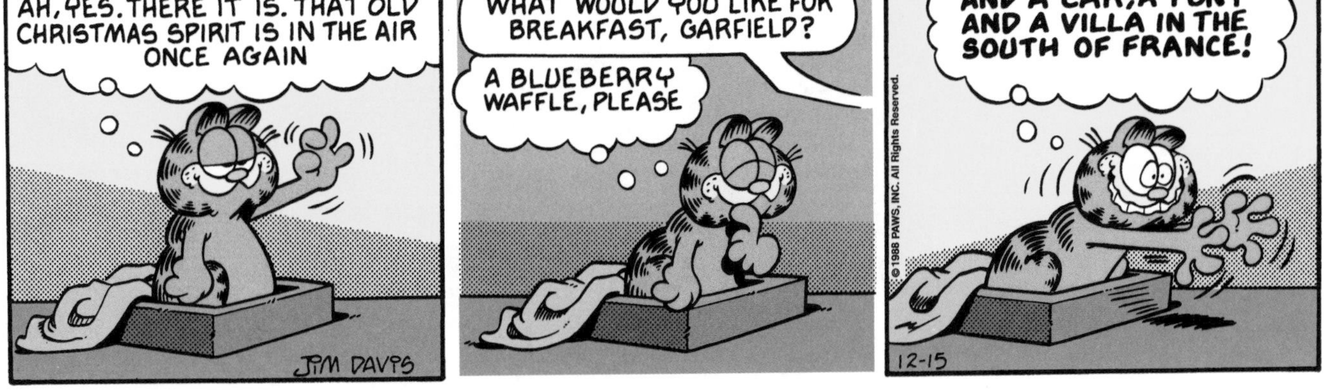
AH, YES. THERE IT IS. THAT OLD CHRISTMAS SPIRIT IS IN THE AIR ONCE AGAIN
JIM DAVIS
WHAT WOULD YOU LIKE FOR BREAKFAST, GARFIELD?
A BLUEBERRY WAFFLE, PLEASE
© 1988 PAWS, INC. All Rights Reserved.
AND A CAR, A PONY AND A VILLA IN THE SOUTH OF FRANCE!
12-15

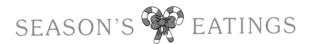

THAT'S RIGHT. STAY JUST LIKE THAT, ODIE
12-16
OH, JOOOON
JIM DAVIS
©1988 PAWS, INC. All Rights Reserved.
I GET THE HINT, GARFIELD
SUBTLE AS IT IS

LOOK, ODIE. WE MAY HAVE A WHITE CHRISTMAS AFTER ALL
JIM DAVIS
WAIT A MINUTE! THAT LOOKS LIKE FEATHERS!
©1988 PAWS, INC. All Rights Reserved.
12-17
MY PILLOW!
SCROOGE

BAH, HUMBUG!

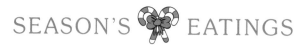

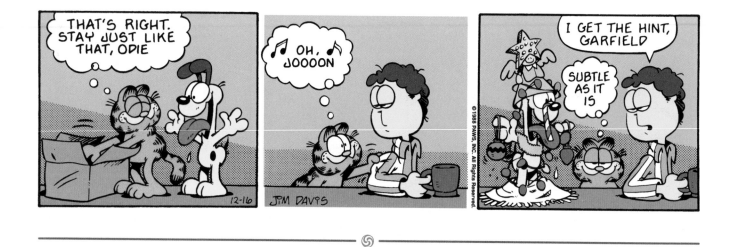

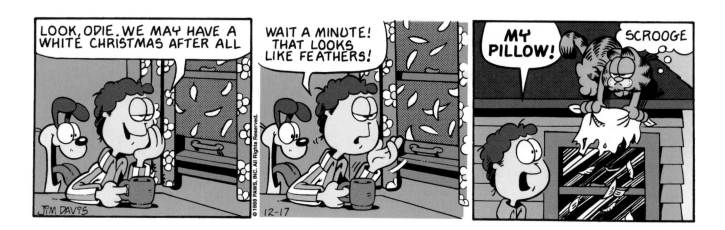

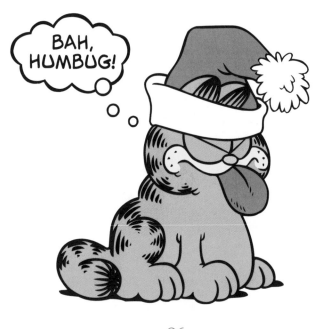

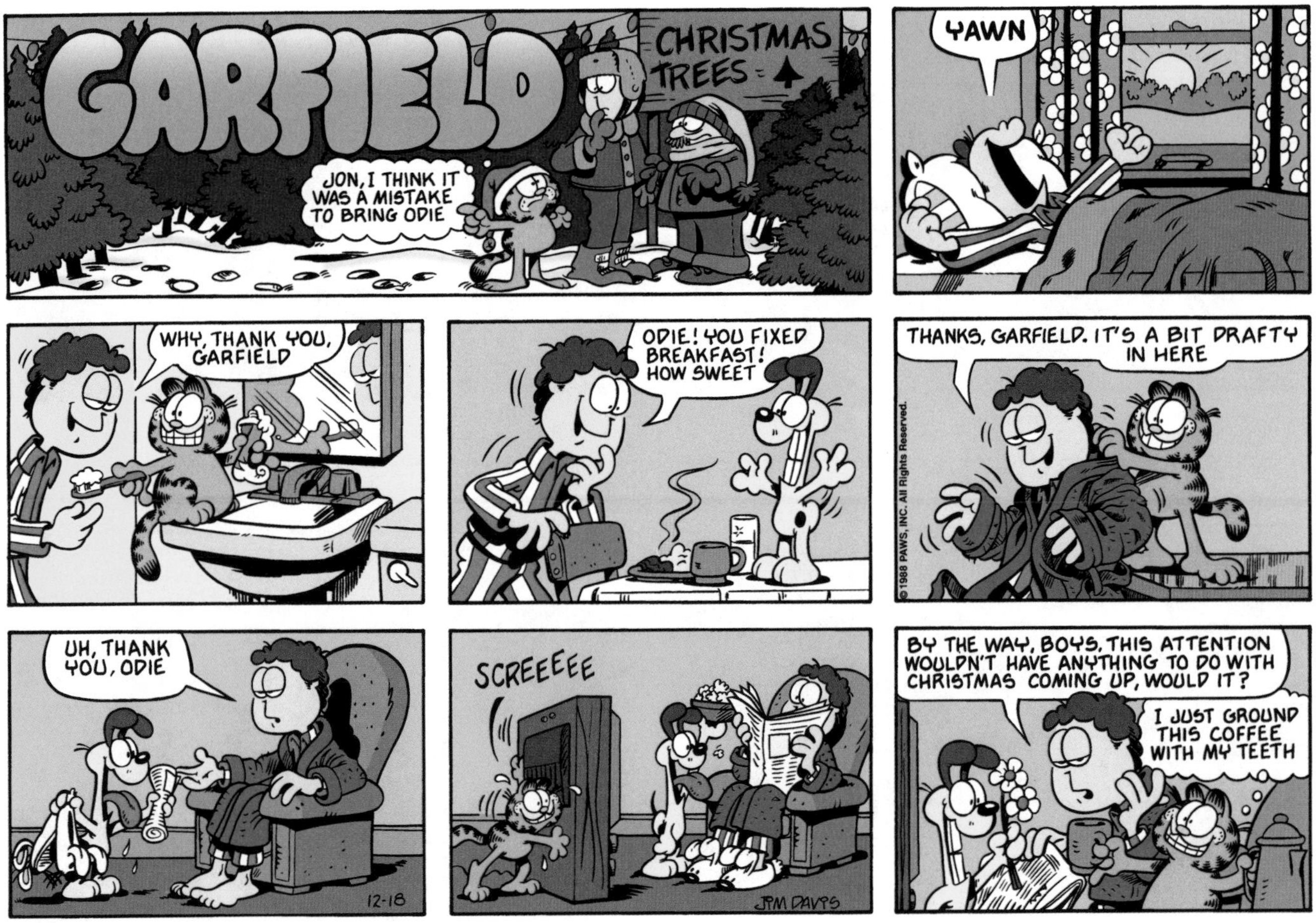
GARFIELD
CHRISTMAS TREES
JON, I THINK IT WAS A MISTAKE TO BRING ODIE
YAWN
WHY, THANK YOU, GARFIELD
ODIE! YOU FIXED BREAKFAST! HOW SWEET
THANKS, GARFIELD. IT'S A BIT DRAFTY IN HERE
© 1988 PAWS, INC. All Rights Reserved.
UH, THANK YOU, ODIE
12-18
SCREEEEE
JIM DAVIS
BY THE WAY, BOYS, THIS ATTENTION WOULDN'T HAVE ANYTHING TO DO WITH CHRISTMAS COMING UP, WOULD IT?
I JUST GROUND THIS COFFEE WITH MY TEETH

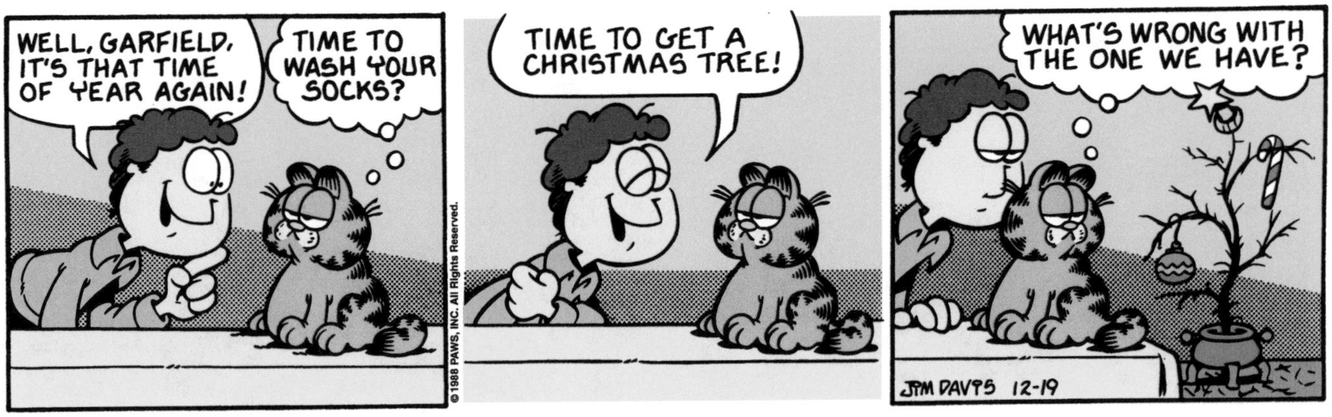
WELL, GARFIELD, IT'S THAT TIME OF YEAR AGAIN!
TIME TO WASH YOUR SOCKS?
© 1988 PAWS, INC. All Rights Reserved.
TIME TO GET A CHRISTMAS TREE!
WHAT'S WRONG WITH THE ONE WE HAVE?
JIM DAVIS 12-19

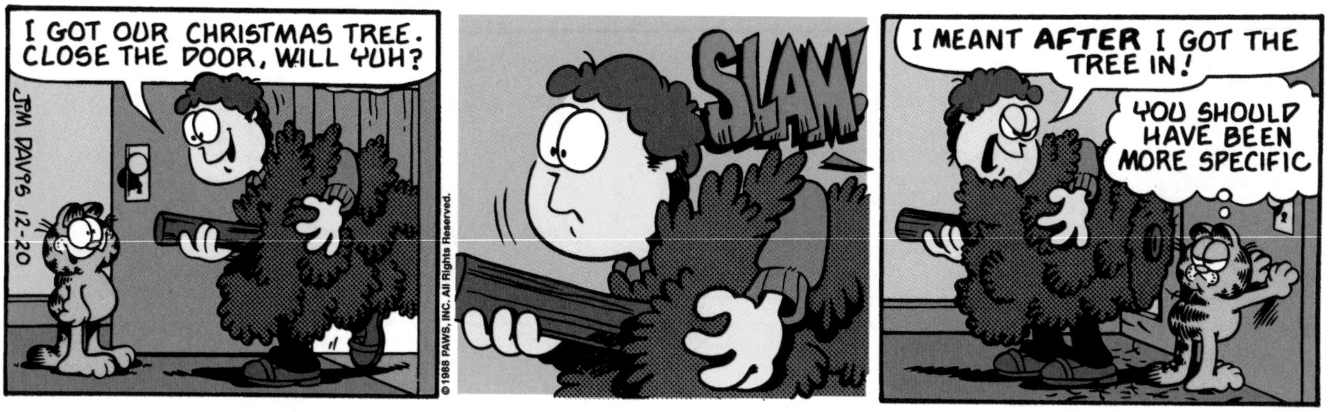
I GOT OUR CHRISTMAS TREE. CLOSE THE DOOR, WILL YUH?
JIM DAVIS 12-20
SLAM!
© 1988 PAWS, INC. All Rights Reserved.
I MEANT **AFTER** I GOT THE TREE IN!
YOU SHOULD HAVE BEEN MORE SPECIFIC

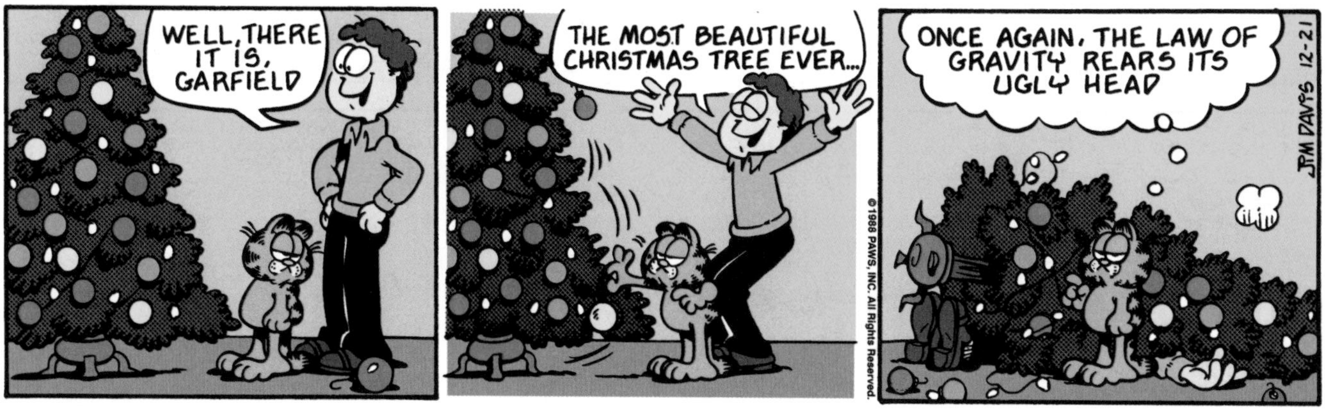
WELL, THERE IT IS, GARFIELD
THE MOST BEAUTIFUL CHRISTMAS TREE EVER...
© 1988 PAWS, INC. All Rights Reserved.
ONCE AGAIN, THE LAW OF GRAVITY REARS ITS UGLY HEAD
JIM DAVIS 12-21

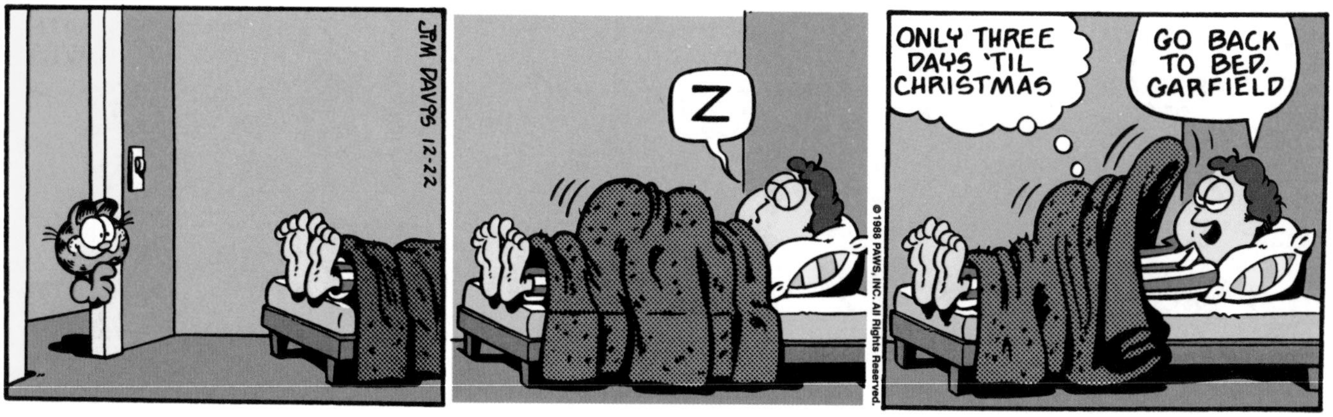
JIM DAVIS 12-22
Z
© 1988 PAWS, INC. All Rights Reserved.
ONLY THREE DAYS 'TIL CHRISTMAS
GO BACK TO BED, GARFIELD

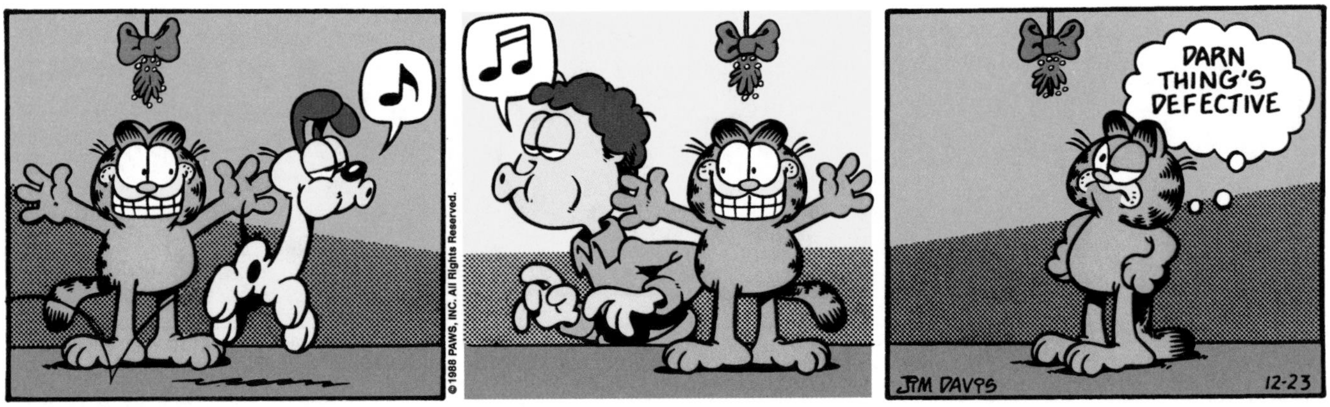
♪
©1988 PAWS, INC. All Rights Reserved.
♫
DARN THING'S DEFECTIVE
JIM DAVIS 12-23

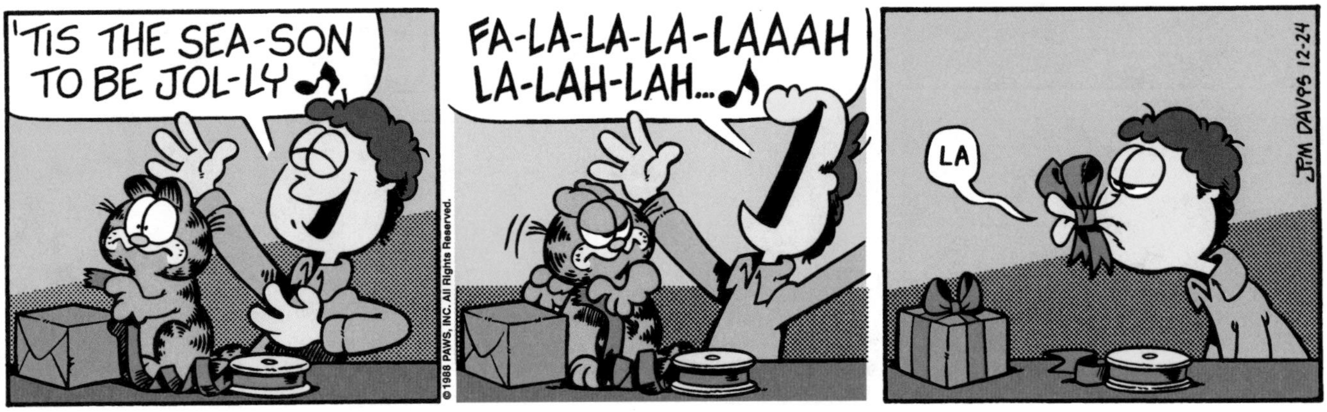
'TIS THE SEA-SON TO BE JOL-LY ♪
©1988 PAWS, INC. All Rights Reserved.
FA-LA-LA-LA-LAAAH LA-LAH-LAH... ♪
LA
JIM DAVIS 12-24

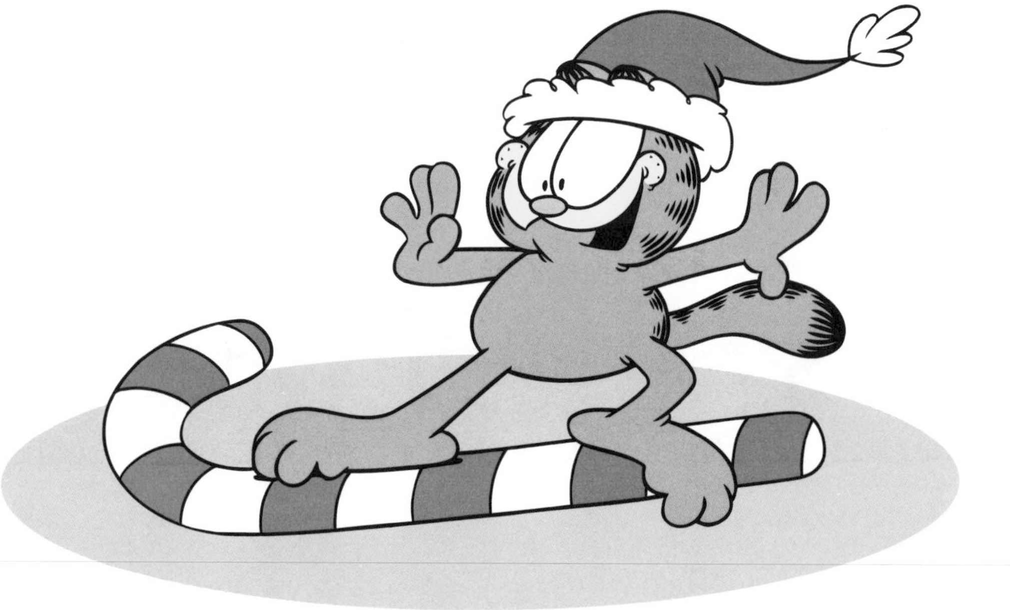

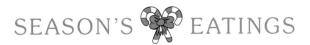

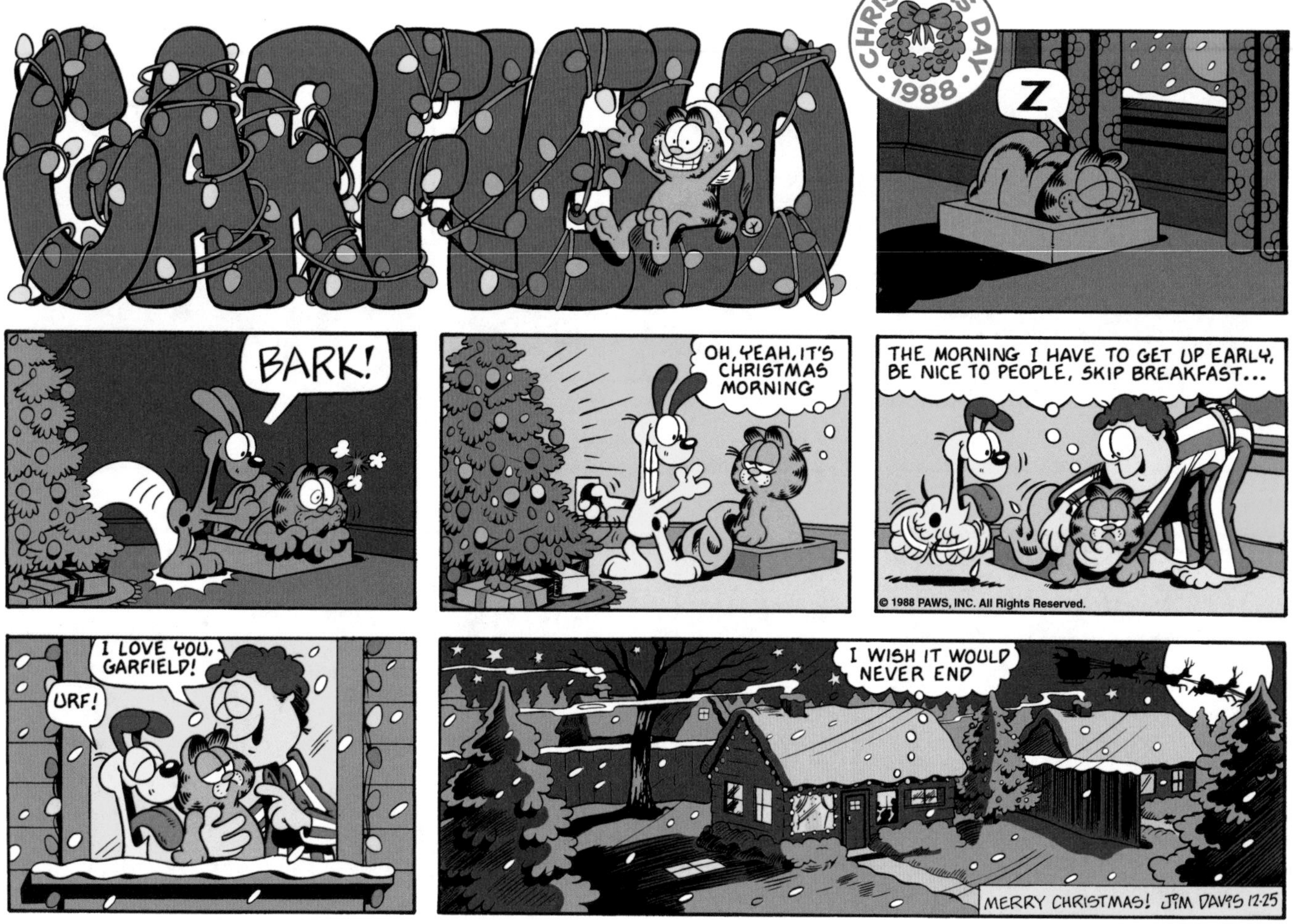
GARFIELD
CHRISTMAS DAY 1988
Z
BARK!
OH, YEAH, IT'S CHRISTMAS MORNING
THE MORNING I HAVE TO GET UP EARLY, BE NICE TO PEOPLE, SKIP BREAKFAST...
© 1988 PAWS, INC. All Rights Reserved.
I LOVE YOU, GARFIELD!
URF!
I WISH IT WOULD NEVER END
MERRY CHRISTMAS! JIM DAVIS 12-25

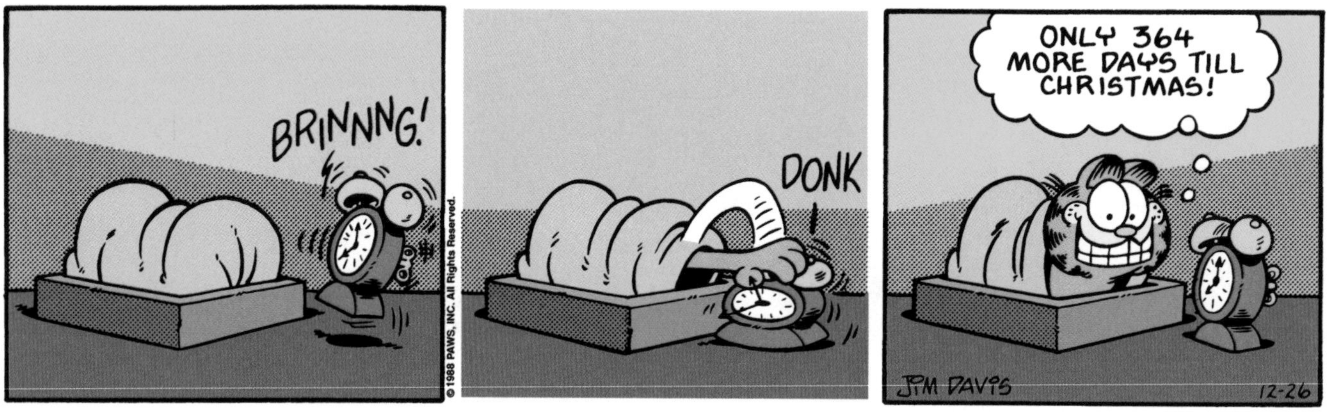
BRINNNG!
© 1988 PAWS, INC. All Rights Reserved.
DONK
ONLY 364 MORE DAYS TILL CHRISTMAS!
JIM DAVIS
12-26

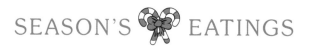

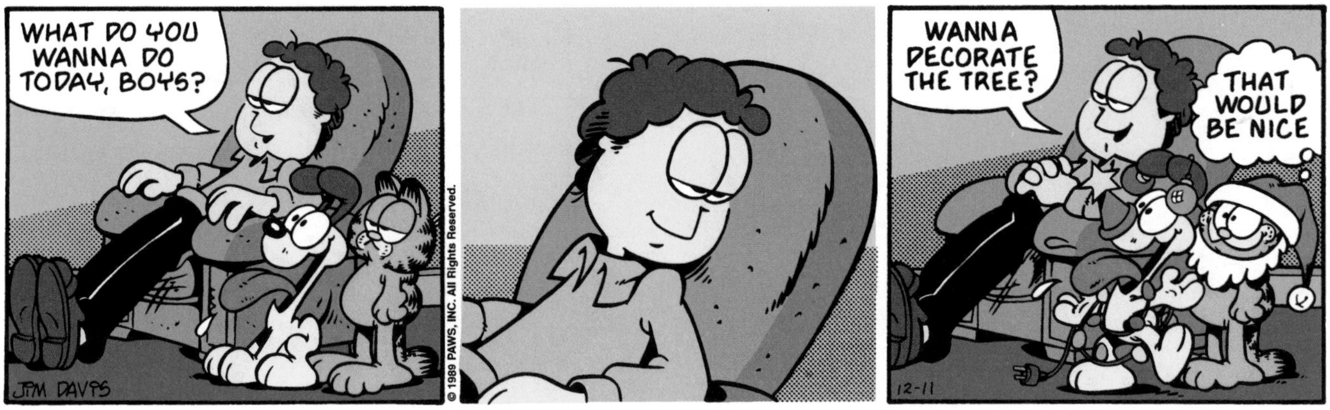
WHAT DO YOU WANNA DO TODAY, BOYS?
JIM DAVIS
© 1989 PAWS, INC. All Rights Reserved.
WANNA DECORATE THE TREE?
THAT WOULD BE NICE
12-11

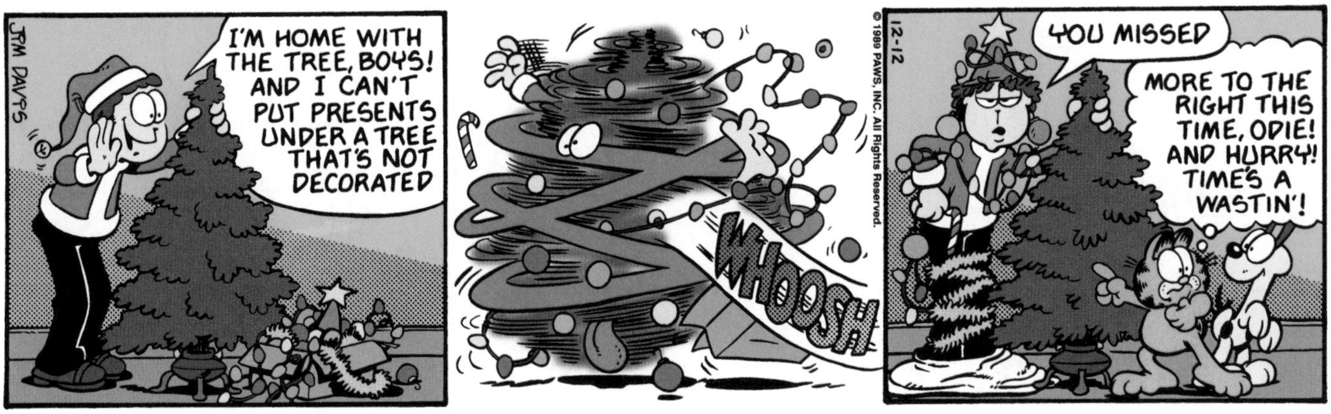
JIM DAVIS
I'M HOME WITH THE TREE, BOYS! AND I CAN'T PUT PRESENTS UNDER A TREE THAT'S NOT DECORATED
WHOOSH
© 1989 PAWS, INC. All Rights Reserved.
12-12
YOU MISSED
MORE TO THE RIGHT THIS TIME, ODIE! AND HURRY! TIME'S A WASTIN'!

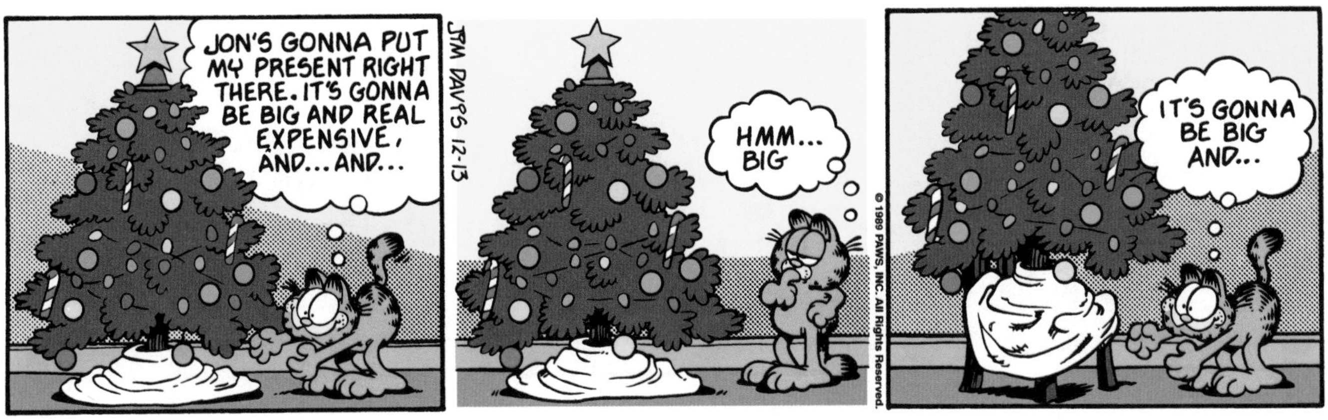
JON'S GONNA PUT MY PRESENT RIGHT THERE. IT'S GONNA BE BIG AND REAL EXPENSIVE, AND... AND...
JIM DAVIS 12-13
HMM... BIG
© 1989 PAWS, INC. All Rights Reserved.
IT'S GONNA BE BIG AND...

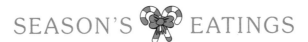

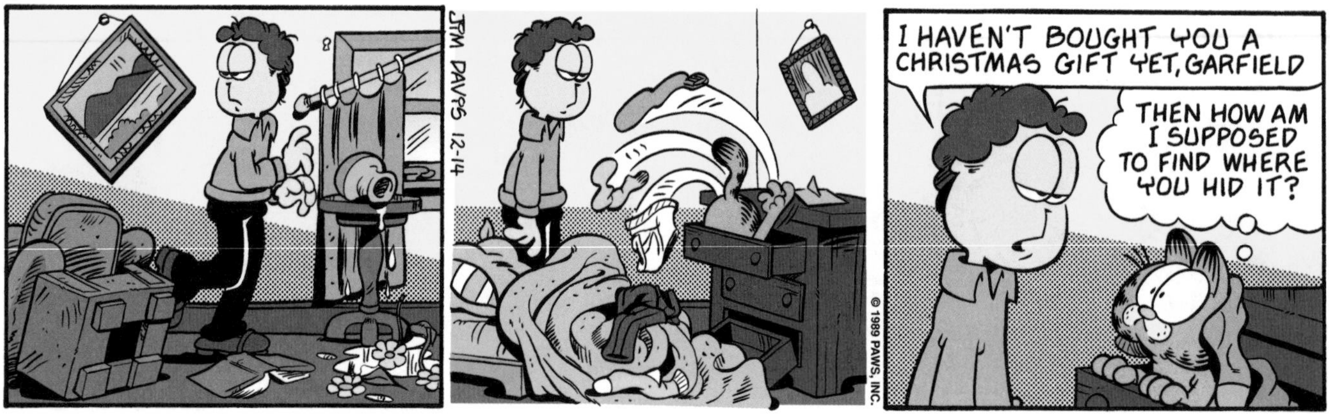
JIM DAVIS 12-14
© 1989 PAWS, INC.
I HAVEN'T BOUGHT YOU A CHRISTMAS GIFT YET, GARFIELD
THEN HOW AM I SUPPOSED TO FIND WHERE YOU HID IT?

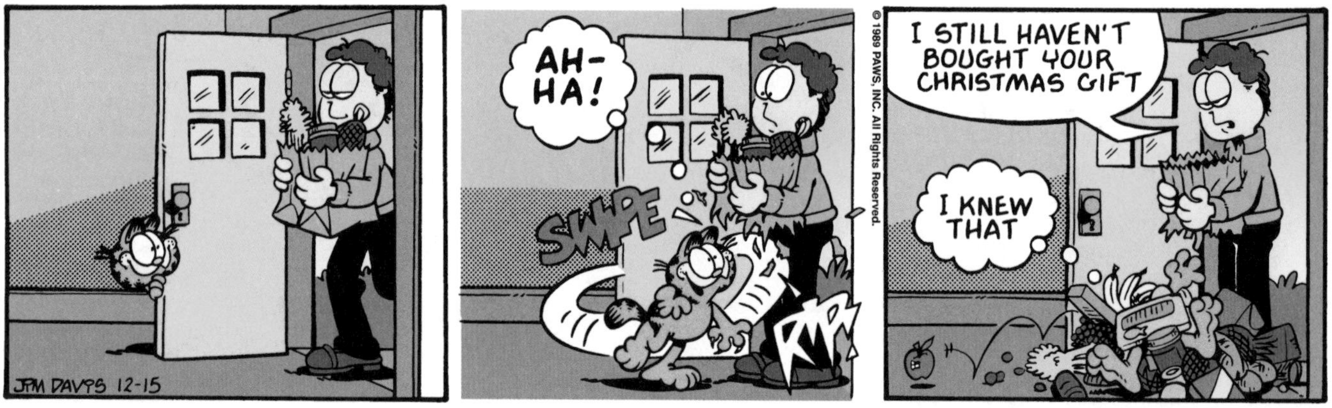
JIM DAVIS 12-15
AH-HA!
SWIPE
RIP
© 1989 PAWS, INC. All Rights Reserved.
I STILL HAVEN'T BOUGHT YOUR CHRISTMAS GIFT
I KNEW THAT

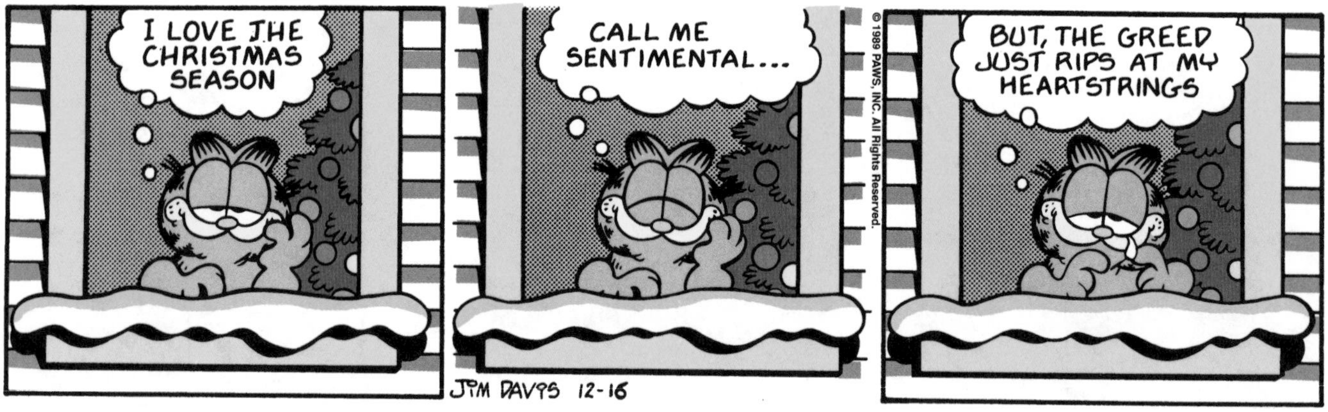
I LOVE THE CHRISTMAS SEASON
CALL ME SENTIMENTAL...
© 1989 PAWS, INC. All Rights Reserved.
BUT, THE GREED JUST RIPS AT MY HEARTSTRINGS
JIM DAVIS 12-16

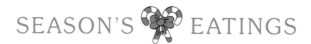

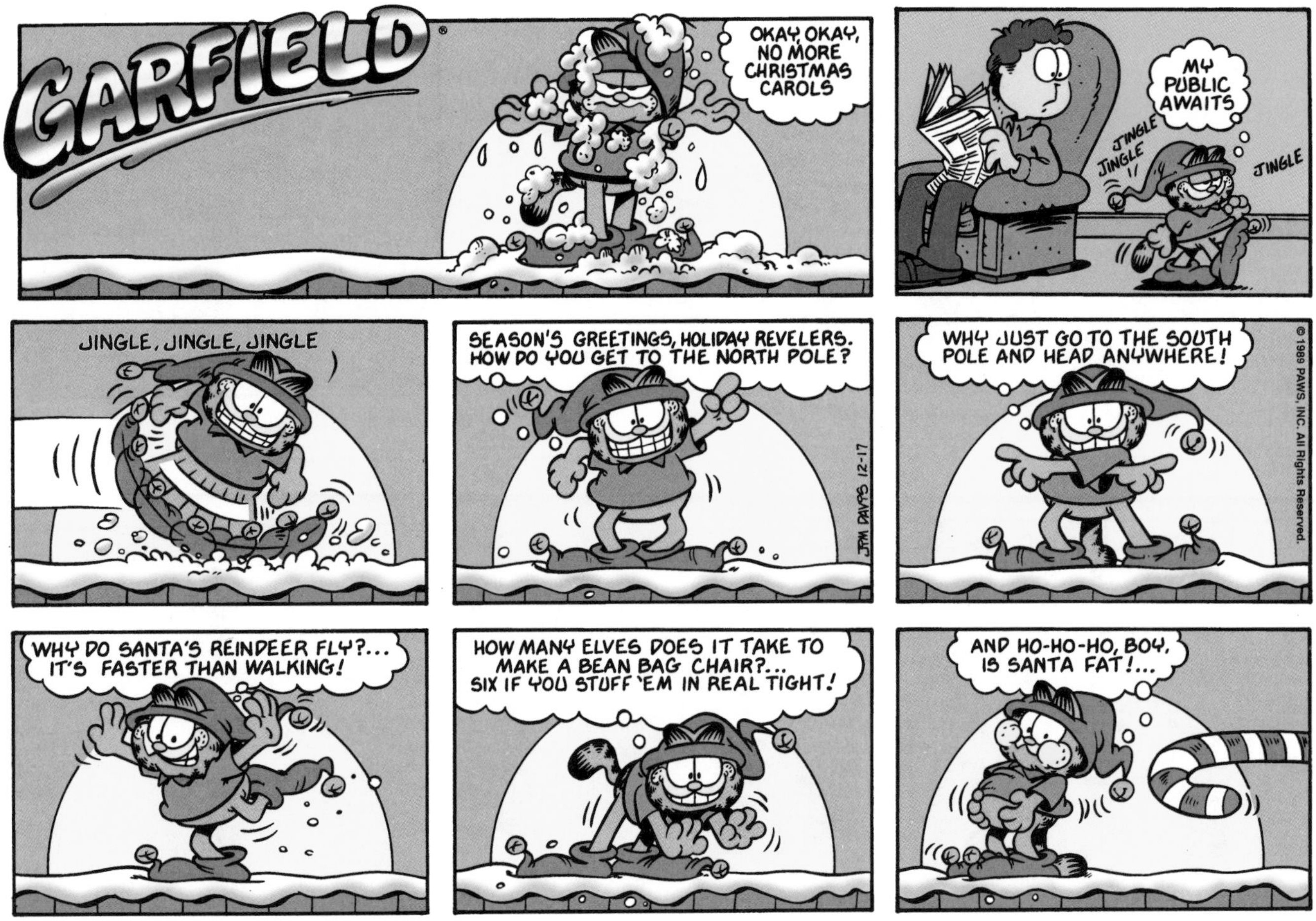
GARFIELD
OKAY, OKAY, NO MORE CHRISTMAS CAROLS
MY PUBLIC AWAITS
JINGLE JINGLE
JINGLE
JINGLE, JINGLE, JINGLE
SEASON'S GREETINGS, HOLIDAY REVELERS. HOW DO YOU GET TO THE NORTH POLE?
JPM DAVIS 12-17
WHY JUST GO TO THE SOUTH POLE AND HEAD ANYWHERE!
© 1989 PAWS, INC. All Rights Reserved.
WHY DO SANTA'S REINDEER FLY?... IT'S FASTER THAN WALKING!
HOW MANY ELVES DOES IT TAKE TO MAKE A BEAN BAG CHAIR?... SIX IF YOU STUFF 'EM IN REAL TIGHT!
AND HO-HO-HO, BOY, IS SANTA FAT!...

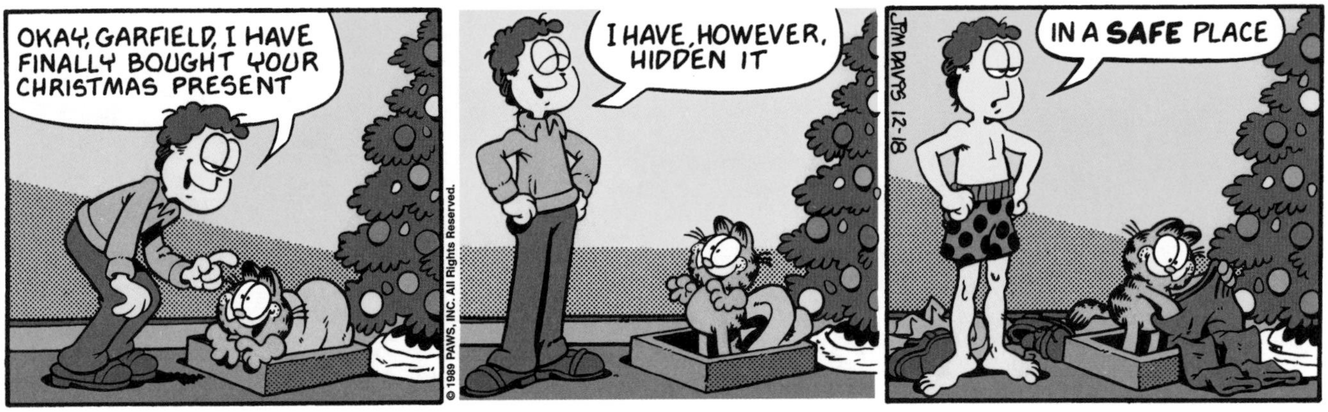
OKAY, GARFIELD, I HAVE FINALLY BOUGHT YOUR CHRISTMAS PRESENT
© 1989 PAWS, INC. All Rights Reserved.
I HAVE, HOWEVER, HIDDEN IT
JPM DAVIS 12-18
IN A SAFE PLACE

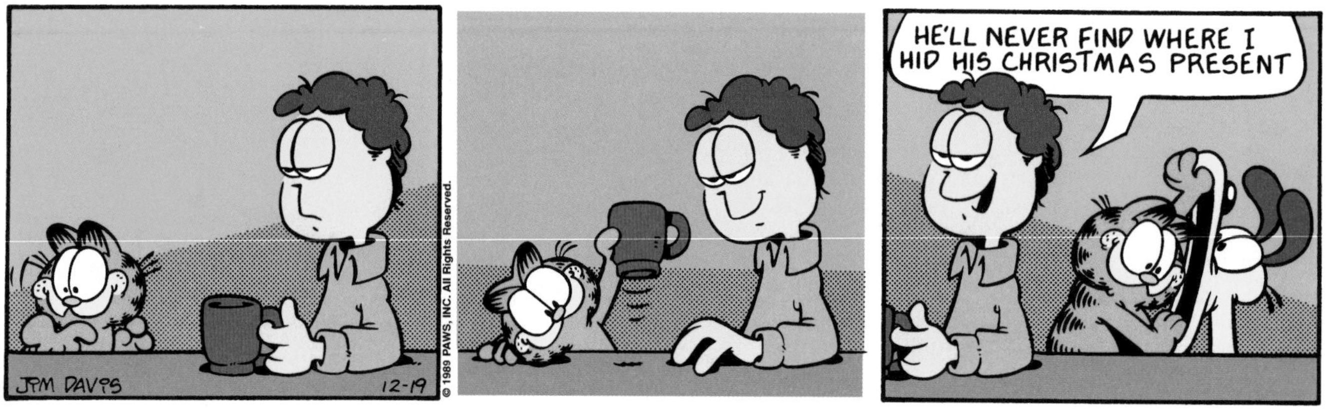
JIM DAVIS
12-19
© 1989 PAWS, INC. All Rights Reserved.
HE'LL NEVER FIND WHERE I HID HIS CHRISTMAS PRESENT

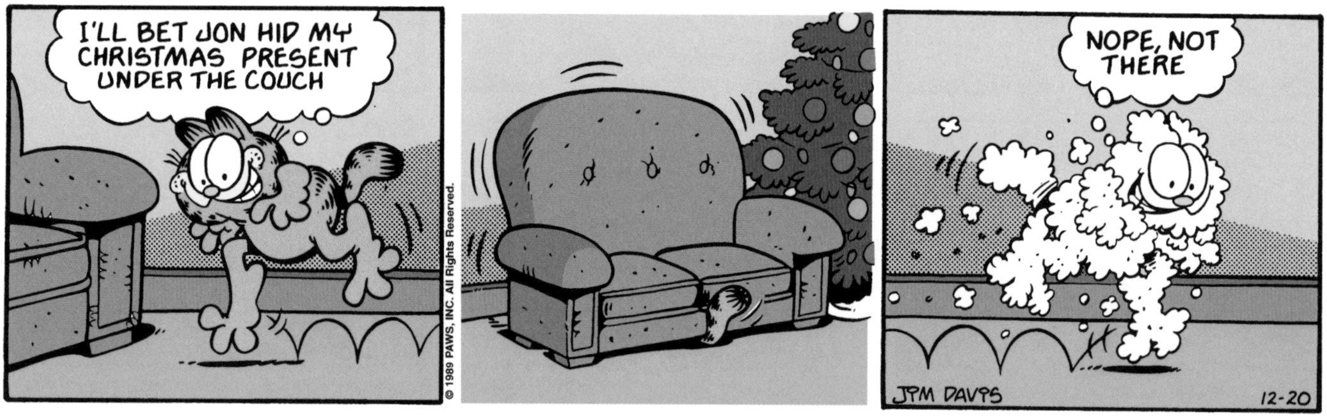
I'LL BET JON HID MY CHRISTMAS PRESENT UNDER THE COUCH
© 1989 PAWS, INC. All Rights Reserved.
NOPE, NOT THERE
JIM DAVIS
12-20

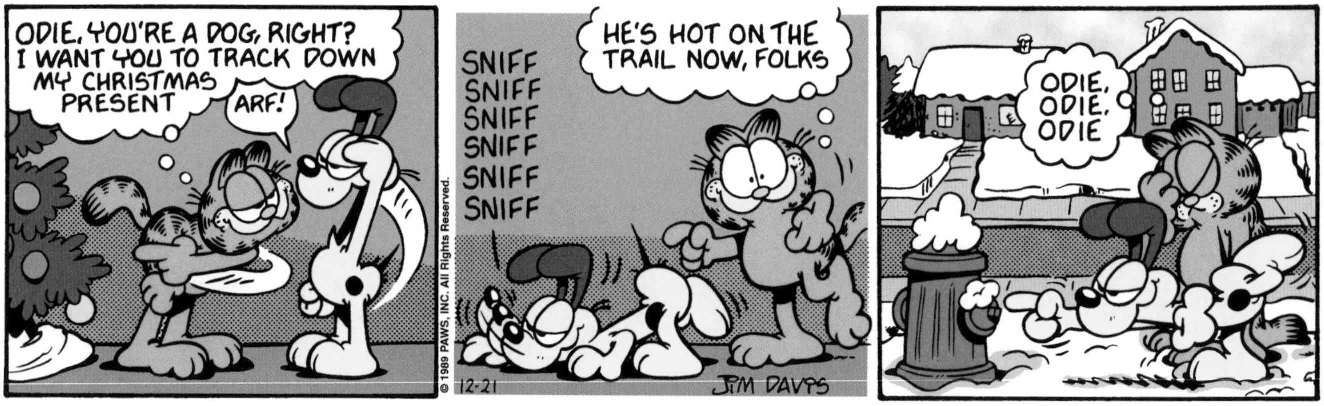
ODIE, YOU'RE A DOG, RIGHT? I WANT YOU TO TRACK DOWN MY CHRISTMAS PRESENT
ARF!
© 1989 PAWS, INC. All Rights Reserved.
SNIFF SNIFF SNIFF SNIFF SNIFF SNIFF
HE'S HOT ON THE TRAIL NOW, FOLKS
12-21
JIM DAVIS
ODIE, ODIE, ODIE

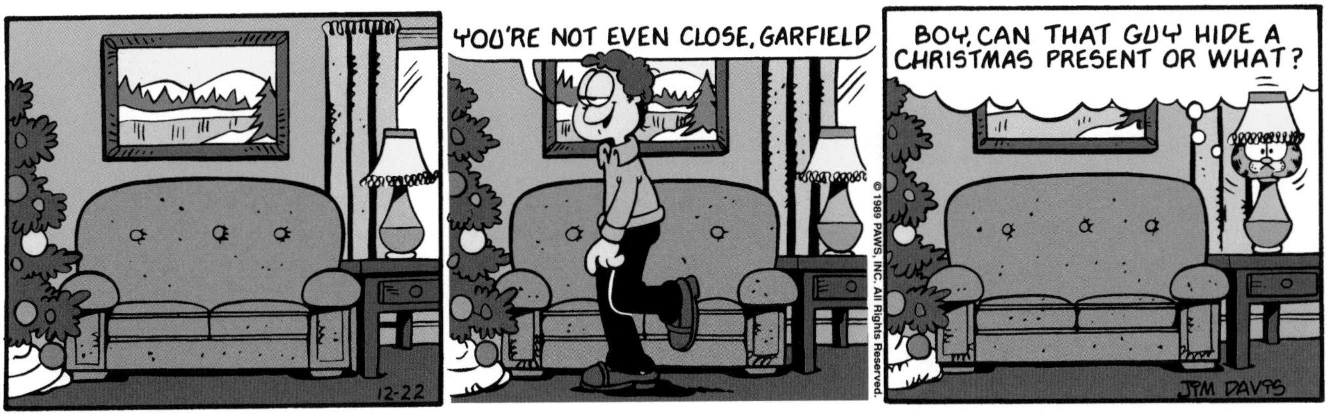
12-22
YOU'RE NOT EVEN CLOSE, GARFIELD
© 1989 PAWS, INC. All Rights Reserved.
BOY, CAN THAT GUY HIDE A CHRISTMAS PRESENT OR WHAT?
JIM DAVIS

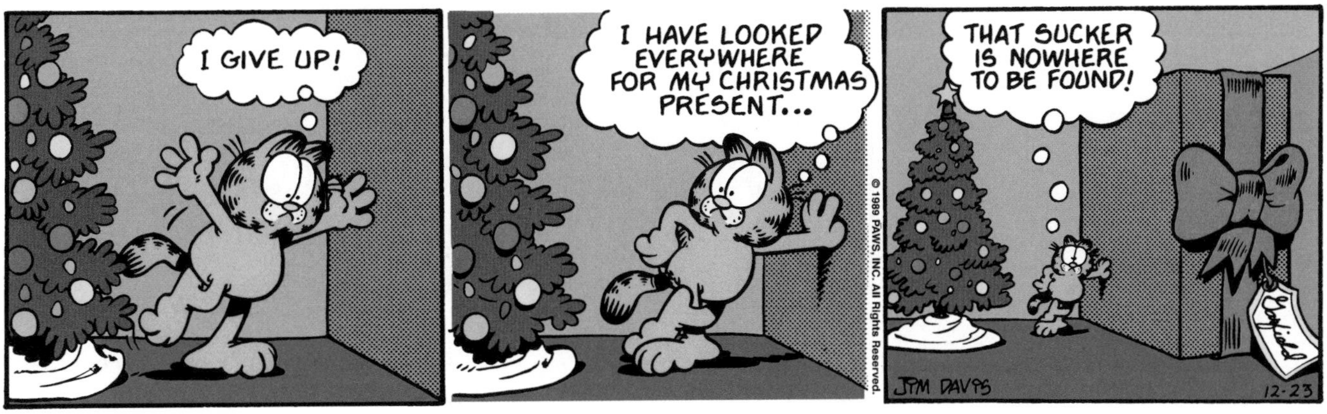
I GIVE UP!
I HAVE LOOKED EVERYWHERE FOR MY CHRISTMAS PRESENT...
© 1989 PAWS, INC. All Rights Reserved.
THAT SUCKER IS NOWHERE TO BE FOUND!
JIM DAVIS
12-23

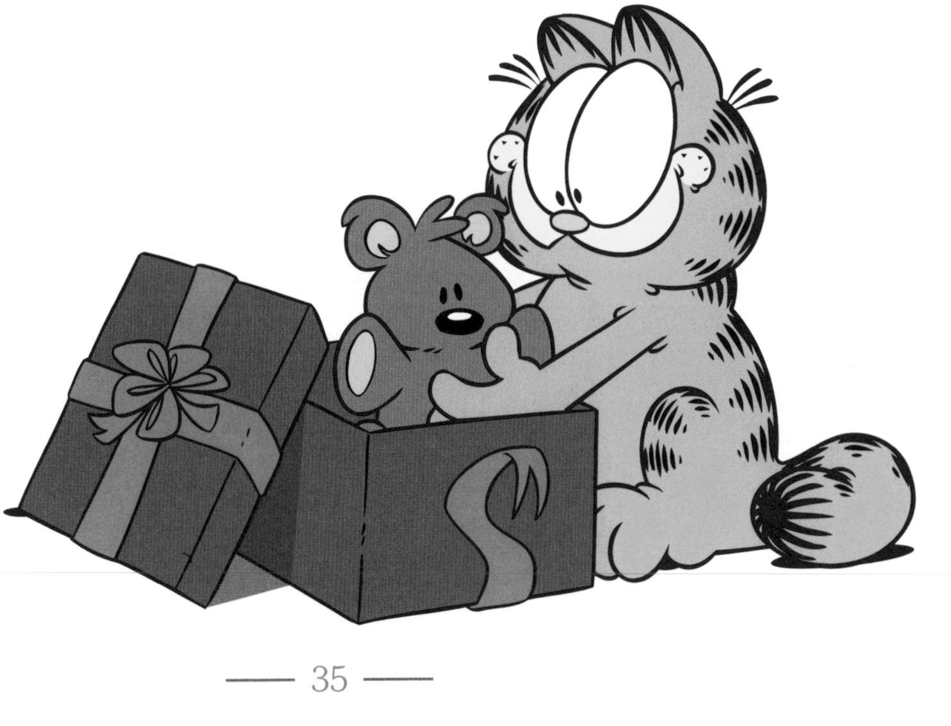

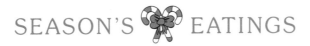

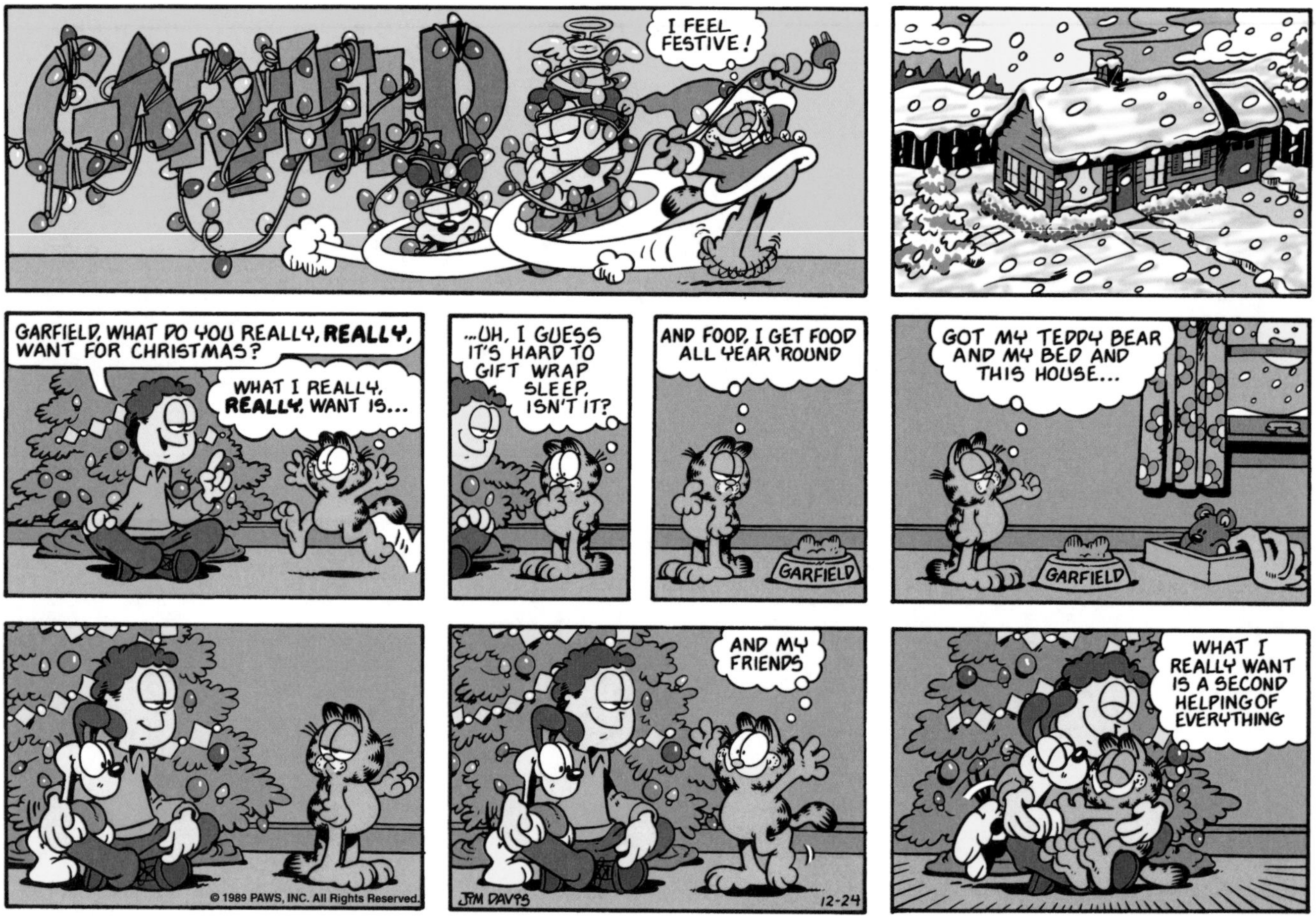
I FEEL FESTIVE!
GARFIELD, WHAT DO YOU REALLY, **REALLY**, WANT FOR CHRISTMAS?
WHAT I REALLY, **REALLY**, WANT IS...
...UH, I GUESS IT'S HARD TO GIFT WRAP SLEEP, ISN'T IT?
AND FOOD, I GET FOOD ALL YEAR 'ROUND
GOT MY TEDDY BEAR AND MY BED AND THIS HOUSE...
GARFIELD
GARFIELD
AND MY FRIENDS
WHAT I REALLY WANT IS A SECOND HELPING OF EVERYTHING
© 1989 PAWS, INC. All Rights Reserved.
JIM DAVIS
12-24

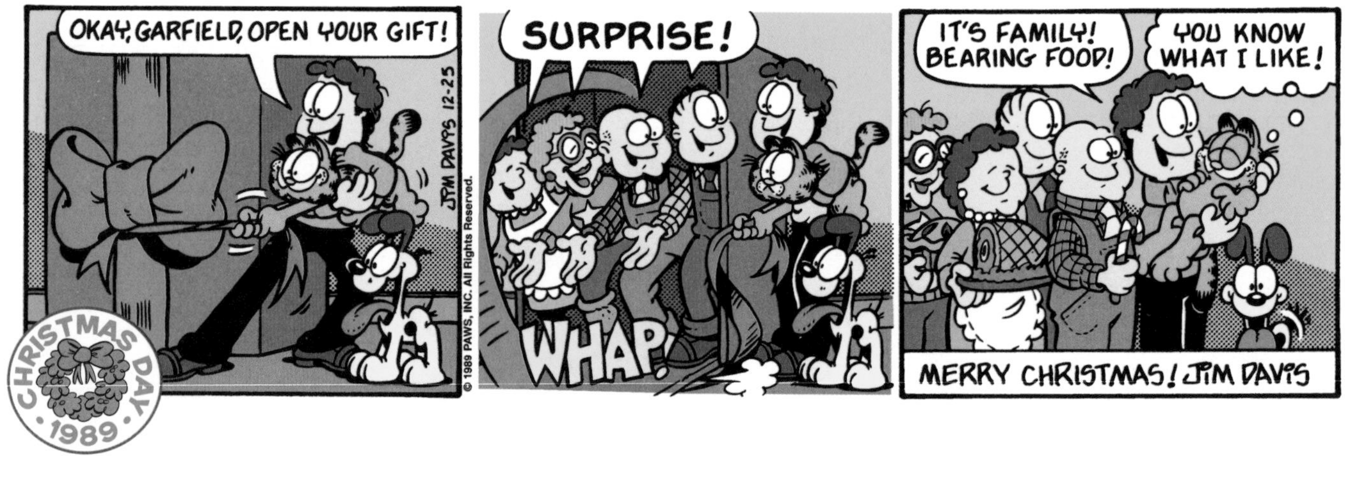
OKAY, GARFIELD, OPEN YOUR GIFT!
JIM DAVIS 12-25
© 1989 PAWS, INC. All Rights Reserved.
SURPRISE!
WHAP!
IT'S FAMILY! BEARING FOOD!
YOU KNOW WHAT I LIKE!
MERRY CHRISTMAS! JIM DAVIS
CHRISTMAS DAY 1989

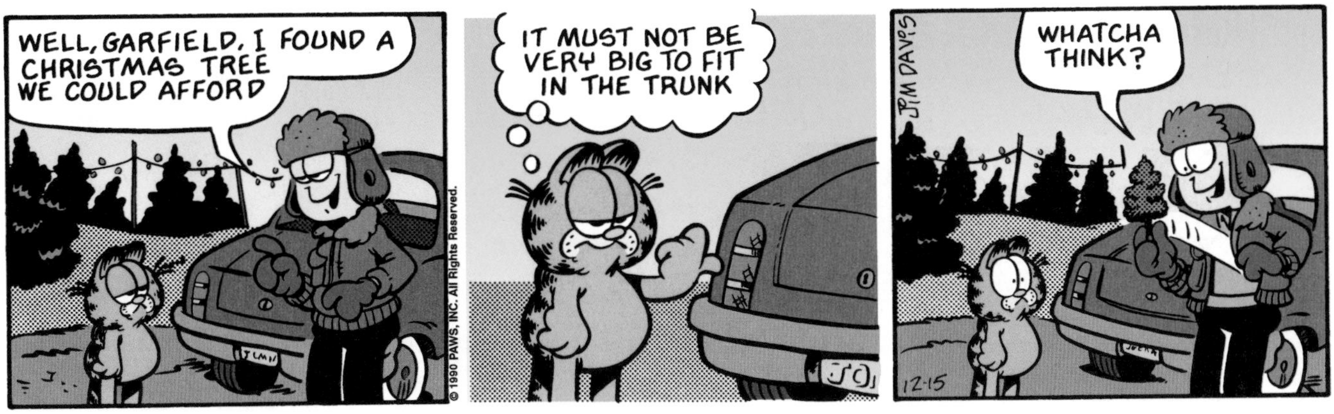
WELL, GARFIELD, I FOUND A CHRISTMAS TREE WE COULD AFFORD
© 1990 PAWS, INC. All Rights Reserved.
IT MUST NOT BE VERY BIG TO FIT IN THE TRUNK
JIM DAVIS
WHATCHA THINK?
12-15

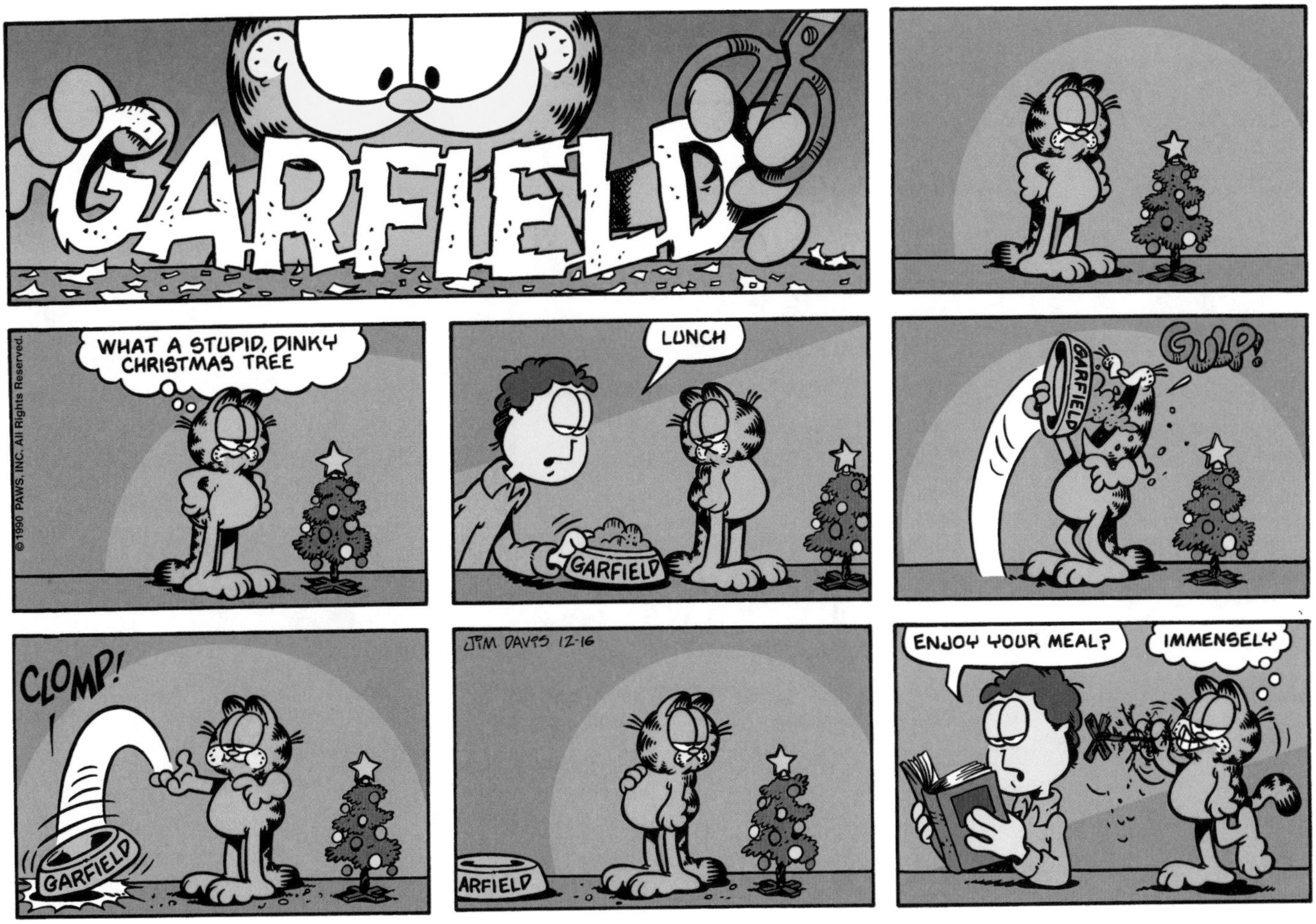
GARFIELD
© 1990 PAWS, INC. All Rights Reserved.
WHAT A STUPID, DINKY CHRISTMAS TREE
LUNCH
GARFIELD
GARFIELD
GULP!
CLOMP!
GARFIELD
JIM DAVIS 12-16
ARFIELD
ENJOY YOUR MEAL?
IMMENSELY

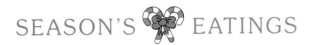

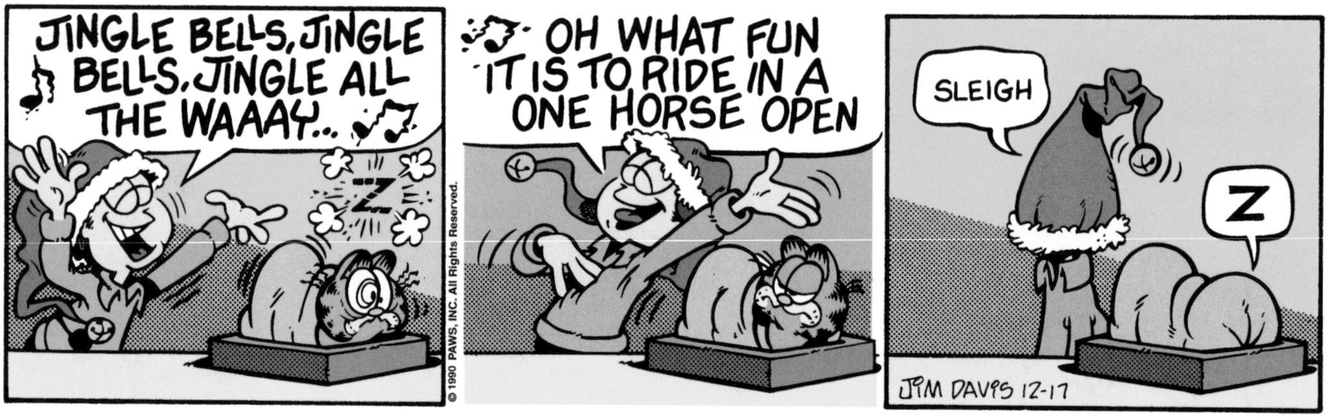
JINGLE BELLS, JINGLE BELLS, JINGLE ALL THE WAAAY...
Z
OH WHAT FUN IT IS TO RIDE IN A ONE HORSE OPEN
SLEIGH
Z
© 1990 PAWS, INC. All Rights Reserved.
JIM DAVIS 12-17

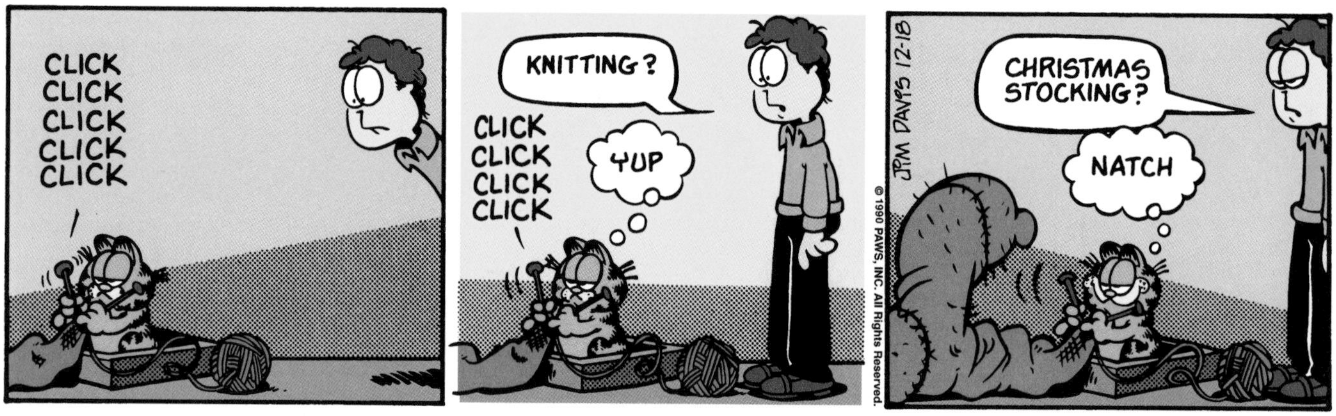
CLICK CLICK CLICK CLICK CLICK
KNITTING?
CLICK CLICK CLICK CLICK
YUP
CHRISTMAS STOCKING?
NATCH
JIM DAVIS 12-18
© 1990 PAWS, INC. All Rights Reserved.

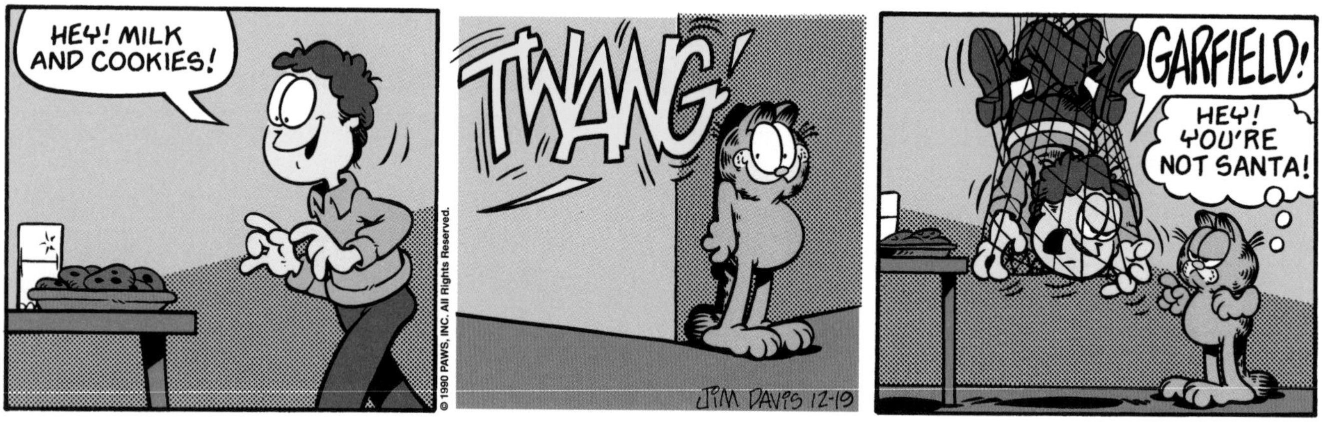
HEY! MILK AND COOKIES!
© 1990 PAWS, INC. All Rights Reserved.
TWANG!
JIM DAVIS 12-19
GARFIELD!
HEY! YOU'RE NOT SANTA!

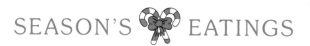

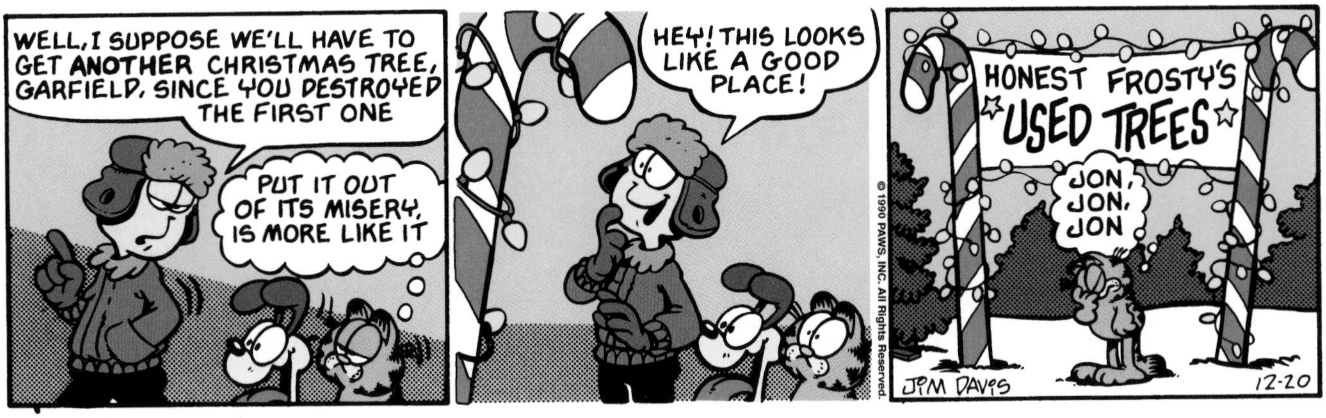
WELL, I SUPPOSE WE'LL HAVE TO GET ANOTHER CHRISTMAS TREE, GARFIELD, SINCE YOU DESTROYED THE FIRST ONE
PUT IT OUT OF ITS MISERY, IS MORE LIKE IT
HEY! THIS LOOKS LIKE A GOOD PLACE!
© 1990 PAWS, INC. All Rights Reserved.
HONEST FROSTY'S
USED TREES
JON, JON, JON
JIM DAVIS 12-20

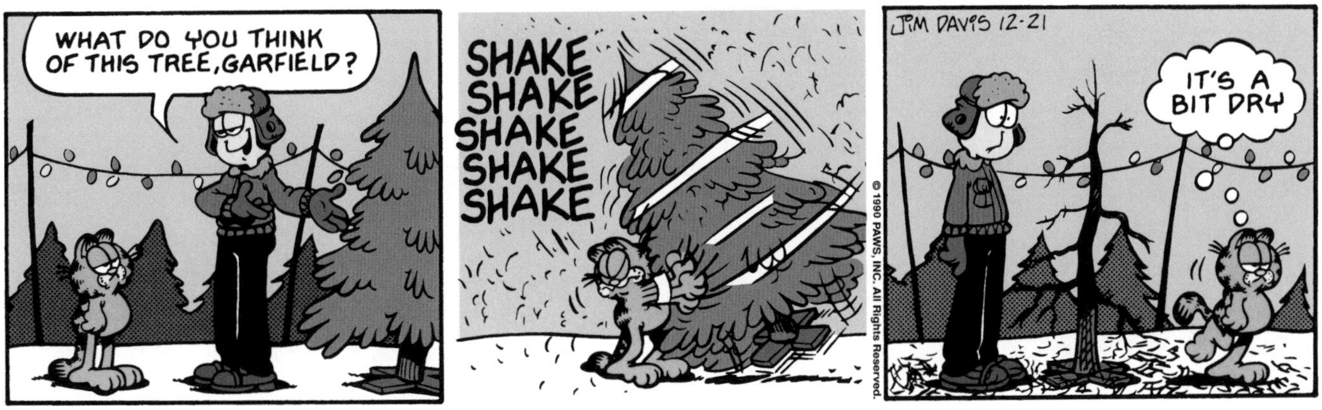
WHAT DO YOU THINK OF THIS TREE, GARFIELD?
SHAKE SHAKE SHAKE SHAKE SHAKE
© 1990 PAWS, INC. All Rights Reserved.
JIM DAVIS 12-21
IT'S A BIT DRY

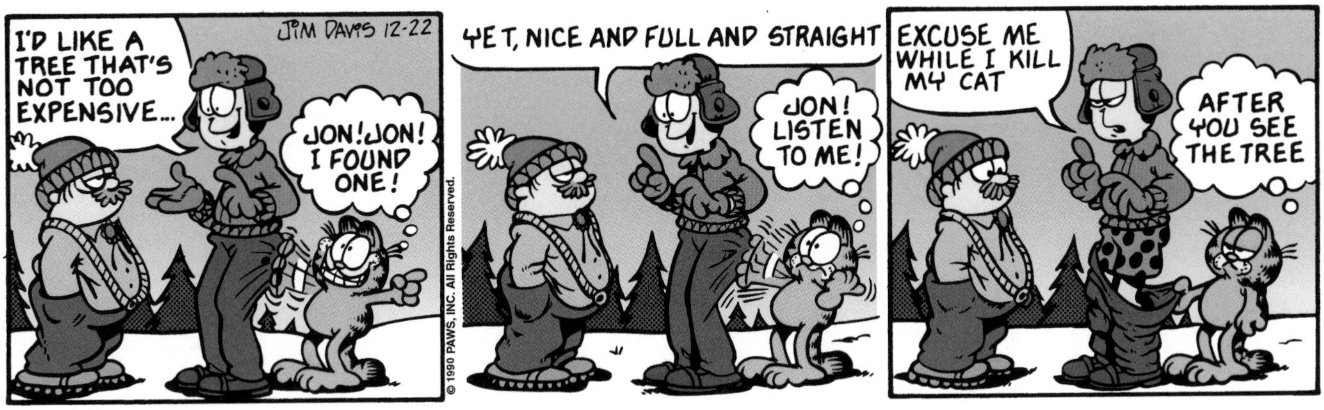
JIM DAVIS 12-22
I'D LIKE A TREE THAT'S NOT TOO EXPENSIVE...
JON! JON! I FOUND ONE!
© 1990 PAWS, INC. All Rights Reserved.
YET, NICE AND FULL AND STRAIGHT
JON! LISTEN TO ME!
EXCUSE ME WHILE I KILL MY CAT
AFTER YOU SEE THE TREE

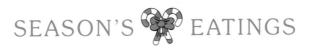

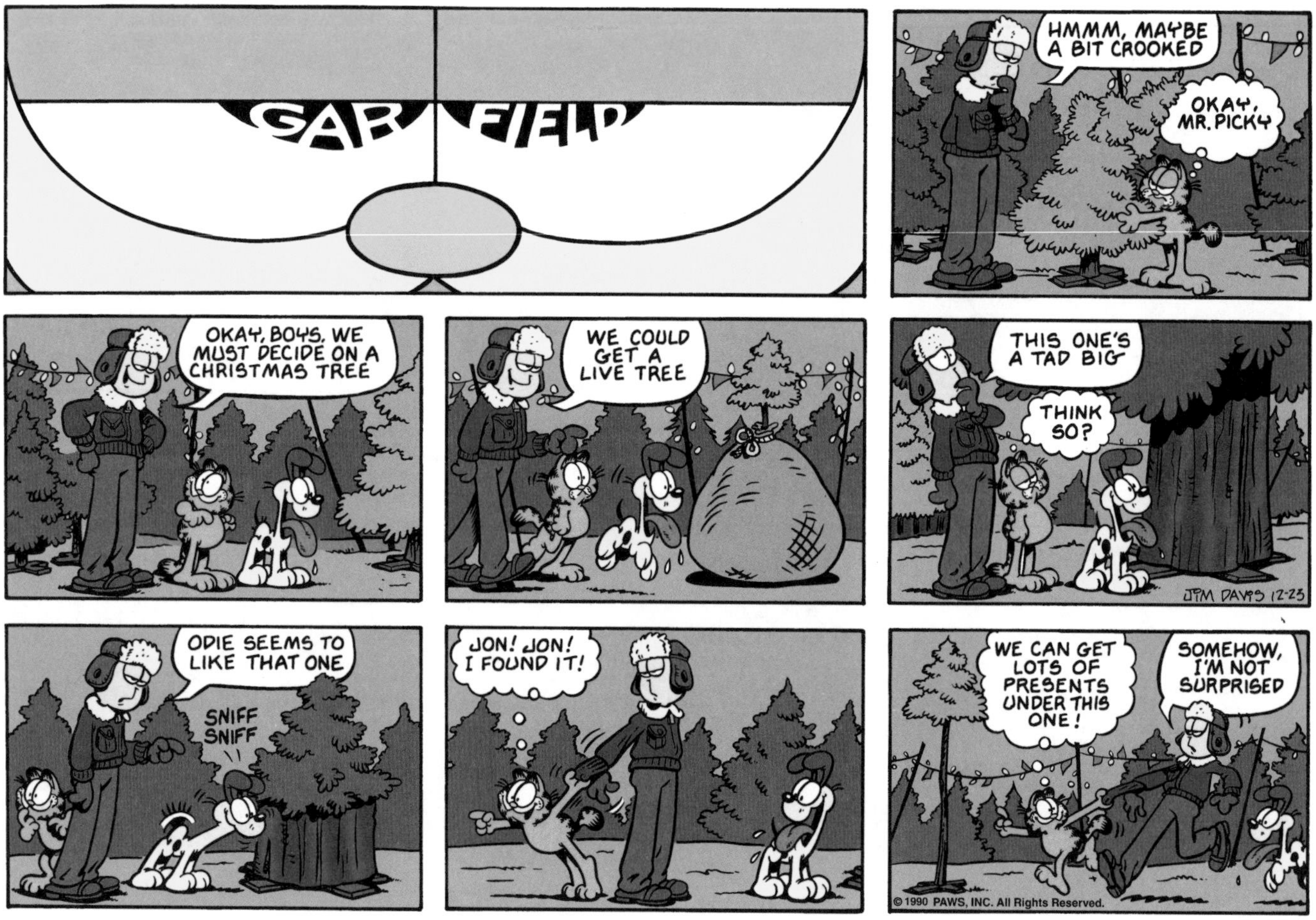
GARFIELD
HMMM, MAYBE A BIT CROOKED
OKAY, MR. PICKY
OKAY, BOYS, WE MUST DECIDE ON A CHRISTMAS TREE
WE COULD GET A LIVE TREE
THIS ONE'S A TAD BIG
THINK SO?
JIM DAVIS 12-23
ODIE SEEMS TO LIKE THAT ONE
SNIFF SNIFF
JON! JON! I FOUND IT!
WE CAN GET LOTS OF PRESENTS UNDER THIS ONE!
SOMEHOW, I'M NOT SURPRISED
© 1990 PAWS, INC. All Rights Reserved.

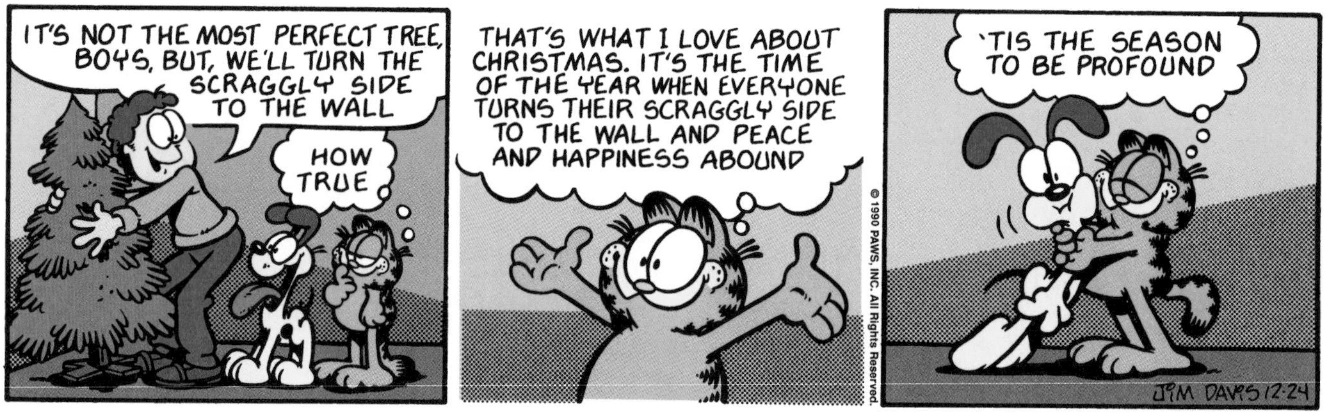
IT'S NOT THE MOST PERFECT TREE, BOYS, BUT, WE'LL TURN THE SCRAGGLY SIDE TO THE WALL
HOW TRUE
THAT'S WHAT I LOVE ABOUT CHRISTMAS. IT'S THE TIME OF THE YEAR WHEN EVERYONE TURNS THEIR SCRAGGLY SIDE TO THE WALL AND PEACE AND HAPPINESS ABOUND
© 1990 PAWS, INC. All Rights Reserved.
'TIS THE SEASON TO BE PROFOUND
JIM DAVIS 12-24

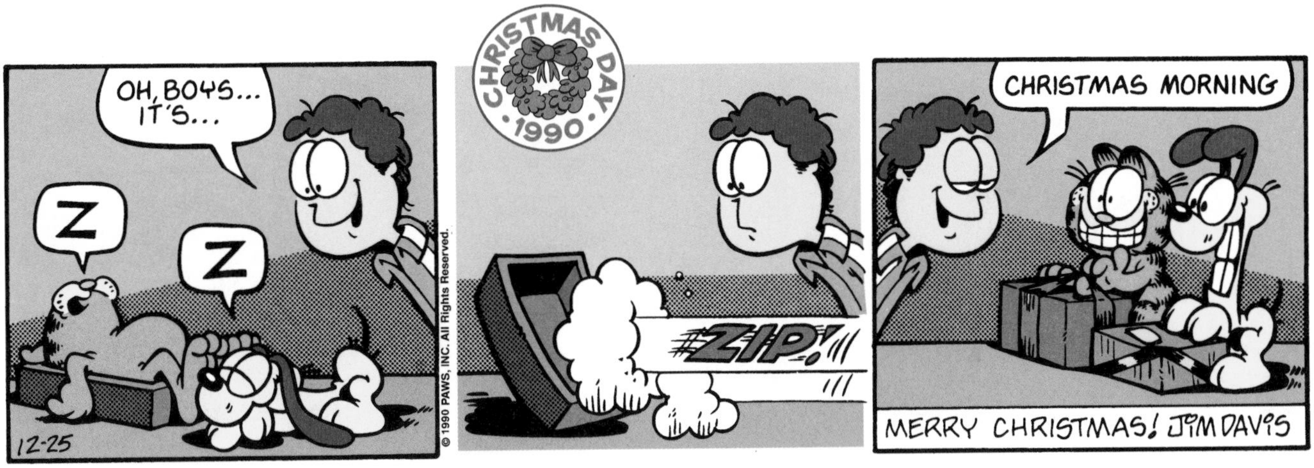
CHRISTMAS DAY 1990
OH, BOYS... IT'S...
Z
Z
12-25
© 1990 PAWS, INC. All Rights Reserved.
ZIP!
CHRISTMAS MORNING
MERRY CHRISTMAS! JIM DAVIS

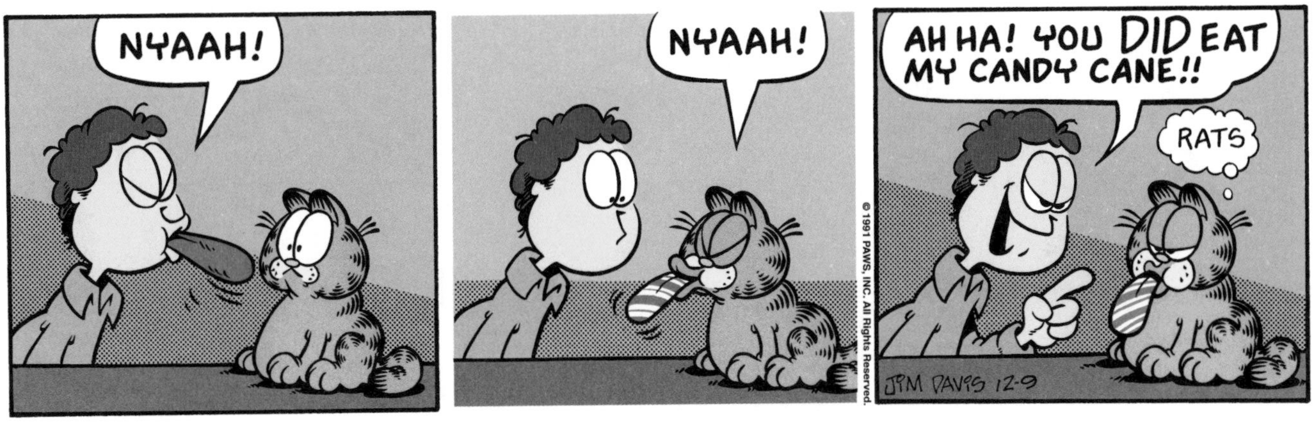
NYAAH!
NYAAH!
© 1991 PAWS, INC. All Rights Reserved.
AH HA! YOU DID EAT MY CANDY CANE!!
RATS
JIM DAVIS 12-9

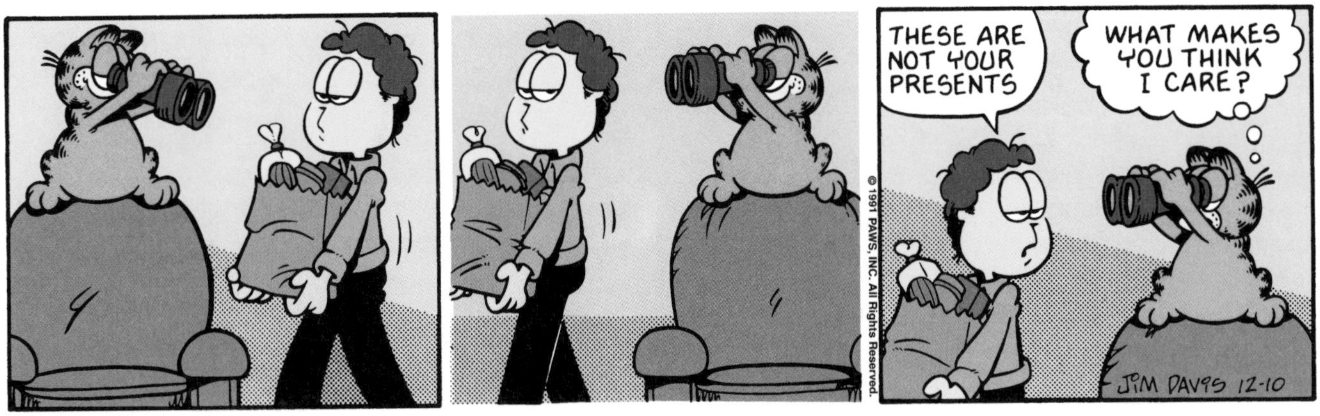
© 1991 PAWS, INC. All Rights Reserved.
THESE ARE NOT YOUR PRESENTS
WHAT MAKES YOU THINK I CARE?
JIM DAVIS 12-10

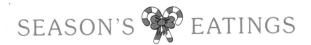

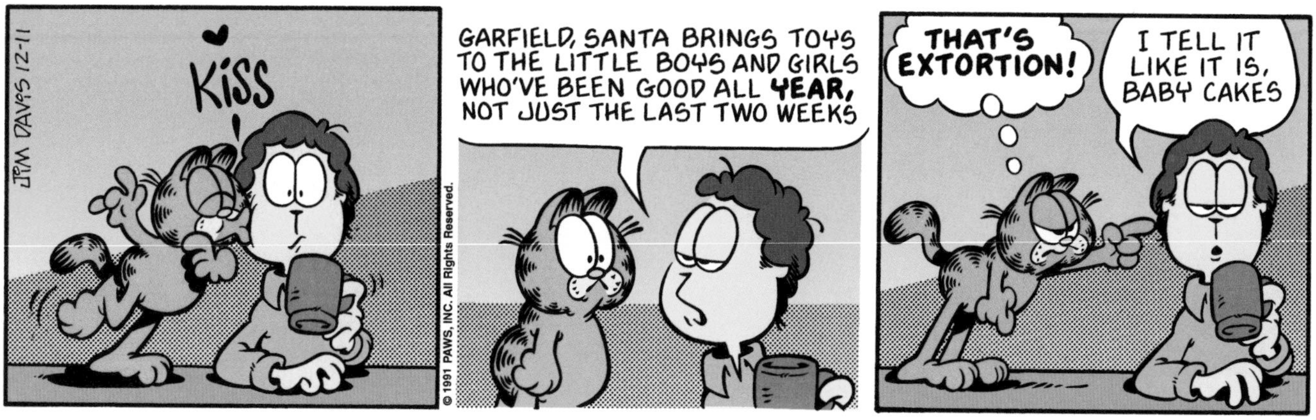
JIM DAVIS 12-11
KISS
GARFIELD, SANTA BRINGS TOYS TO THE LITTLE BOYS AND GIRLS WHO'VE BEEN GOOD ALL **YEAR**, NOT JUST THE LAST TWO WEEKS
© 1991 PAWS, INC. All Rights Reserved.
THAT'S EXTORTION!
I TELL IT LIKE IT IS, BABY CAKES

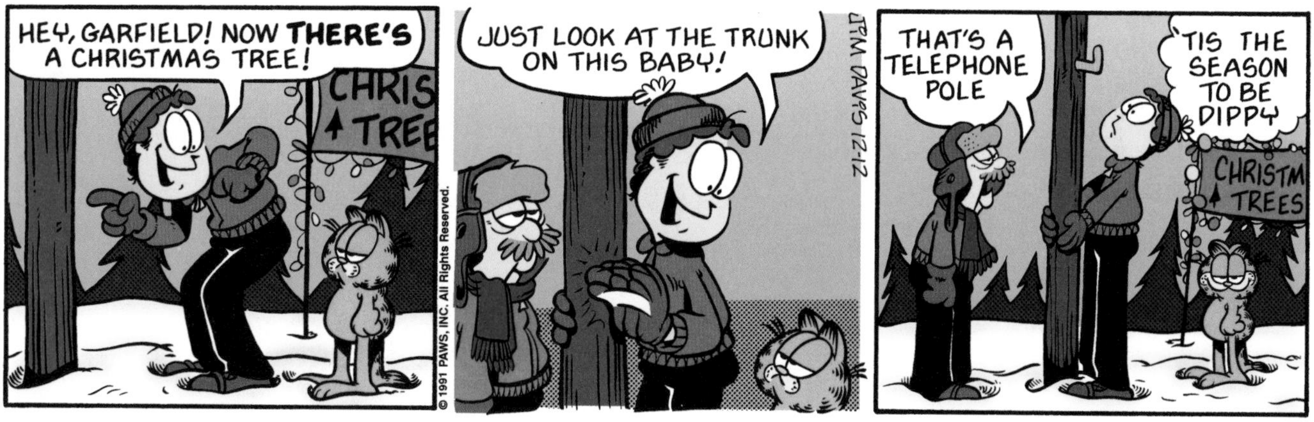
HEY, GARFIELD! NOW **THERE'S** A CHRISTMAS TREE!
CHRIS TREE
© 1991 PAWS, INC. All Rights Reserved.
JUST LOOK AT THE TRUNK ON THIS BABY!
JIM DAVIS 12-12
THAT'S A TELEPHONE POLE
'TIS THE SEASON TO BE DIPPY
CHRISTM TREES

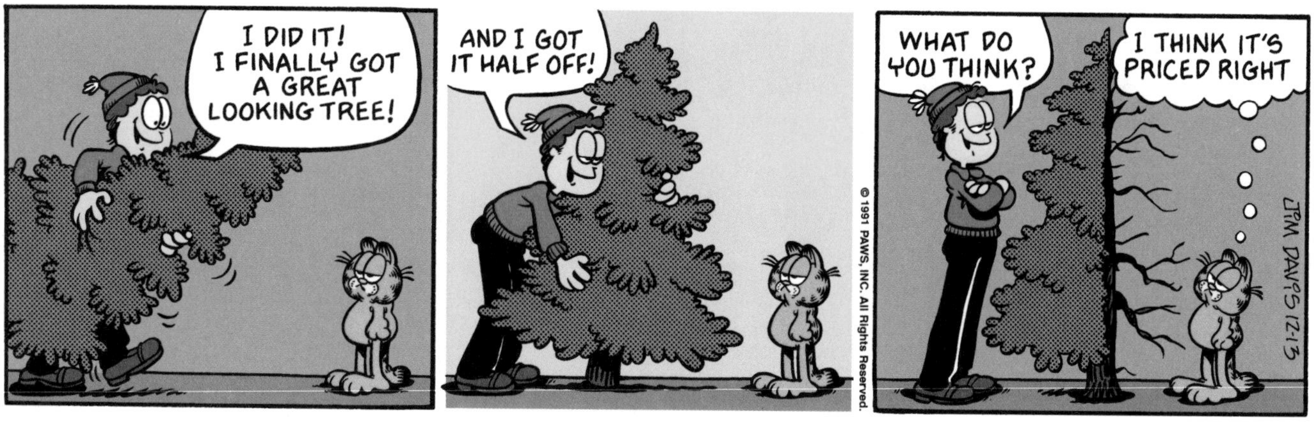
I DID IT! I FINALLY GOT A GREAT LOOKING TREE!
AND I GOT IT HALF OFF!
© 1991 PAWS, INC. All Rights Reserved.
WHAT DO YOU THINK?
I THINK IT'S PRICED RIGHT
JIM DAVIS 12-13

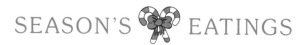

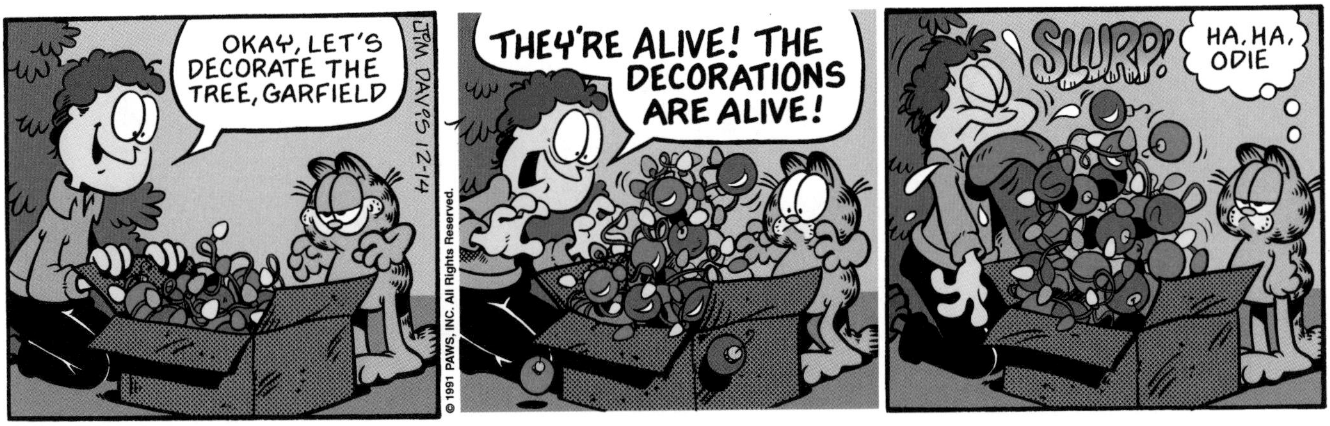
OKAY, LET'S DECORATE THE TREE, GARFIELD
JIM DAVIS 12-14
© 1991 PAWS, INC. All Rights Reserved.
THEY'RE ALIVE! THE DECORATIONS ARE ALIVE!
SLURP!
HA, HA, ODIE

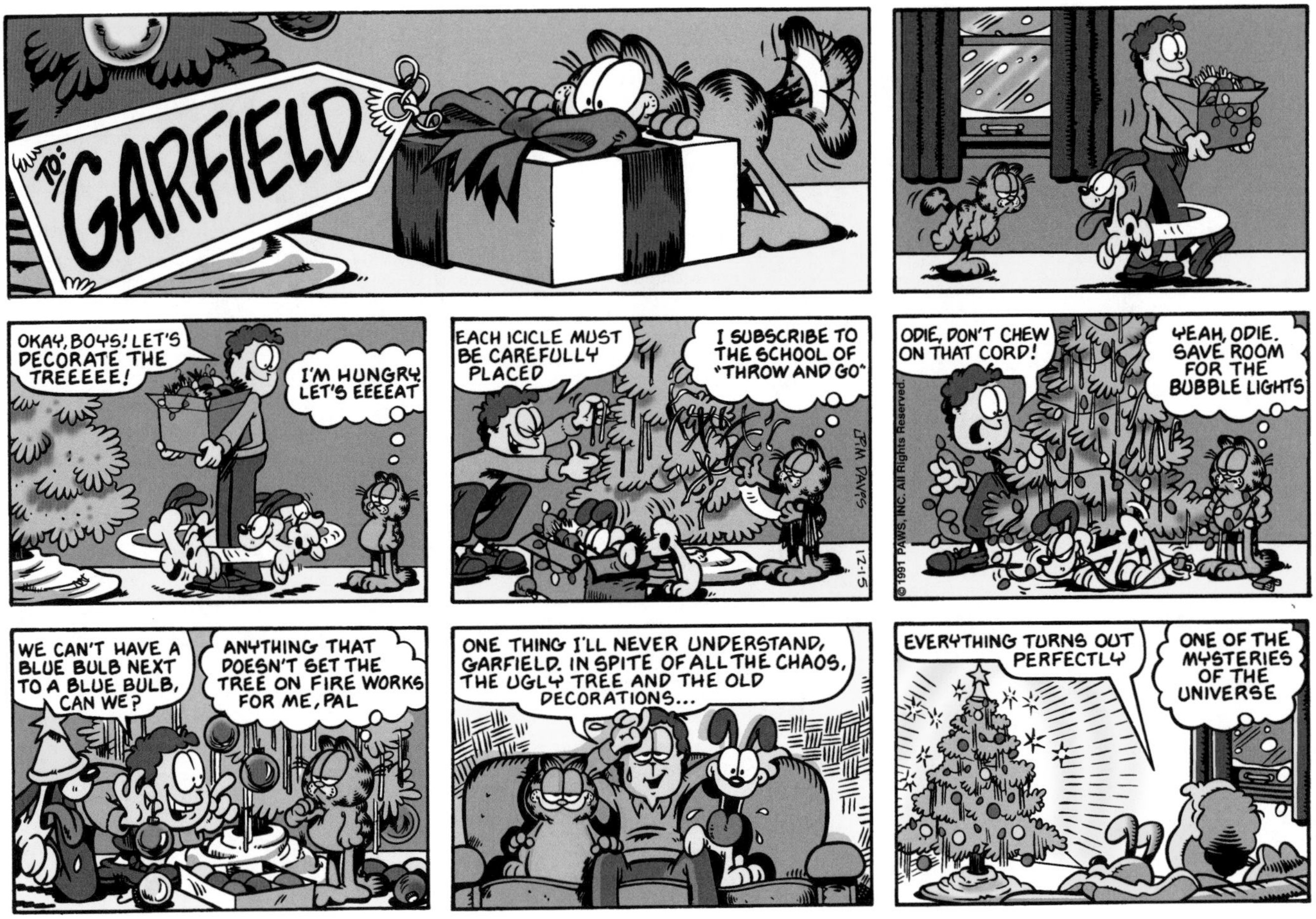
TO: GARFIELD
OKAY, BOYS! LET'S DECORATE THE TREEEEE!
I'M HUNGRY. LET'S EEEEAT
EACH ICICLE MUST BE CAREFULLY PLACED
I SUBSCRIBE TO THE SCHOOL OF "THROW AND GO"
JIM DAVIS 12-15
© 1991 PAWS, INC. All Rights Reserved.
ODIE, DON'T CHEW ON THAT CORD!
YEAH, ODIE. SAVE ROOM FOR THE BUBBLE LIGHTS
WE CAN'T HAVE A BLUE BULB NEXT TO A BLUE BULB, CAN WE?
ANYTHING THAT DOESN'T SET THE TREE ON FIRE WORKS FOR ME, PAL
ONE THING I'LL NEVER UNDERSTAND, GARFIELD. IN SPITE OF ALL THE CHAOS, THE UGLY TREE AND THE OLD DECORATIONS...
EVERYTHING TURNS OUT PERFECTLY
ONE OF THE MYSTERIES OF THE UNIVERSE

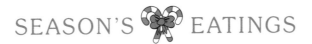

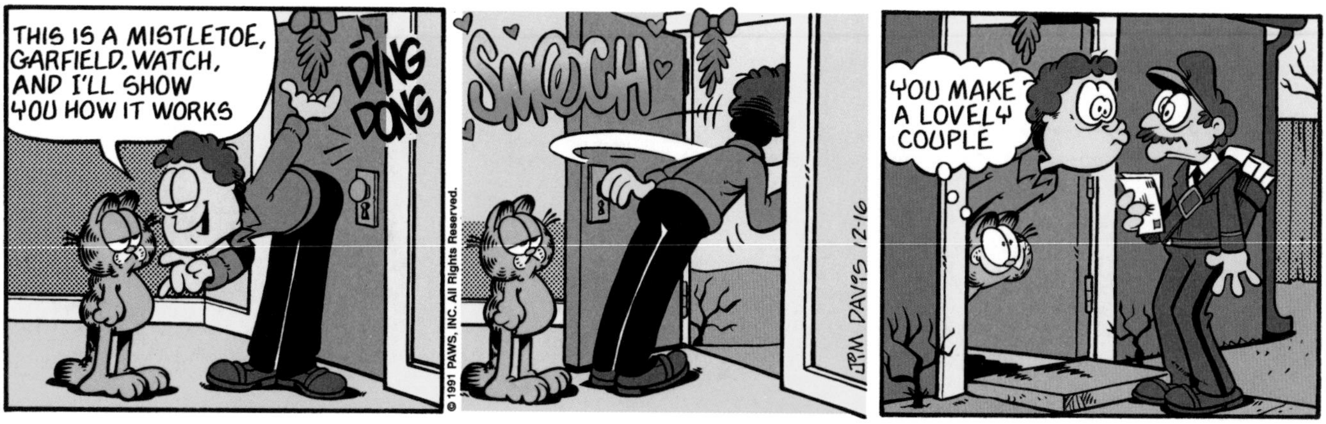
THIS IS A MISTLETOE, GARFIELD. WATCH, AND I'LL SHOW YOU HOW IT WORKS
DING DONG
SMOOCH
YOU MAKE A LOVELY COUPLE
© 1991 PAWS, INC. All Rights Reserved.
JIM DAVIS 12-16

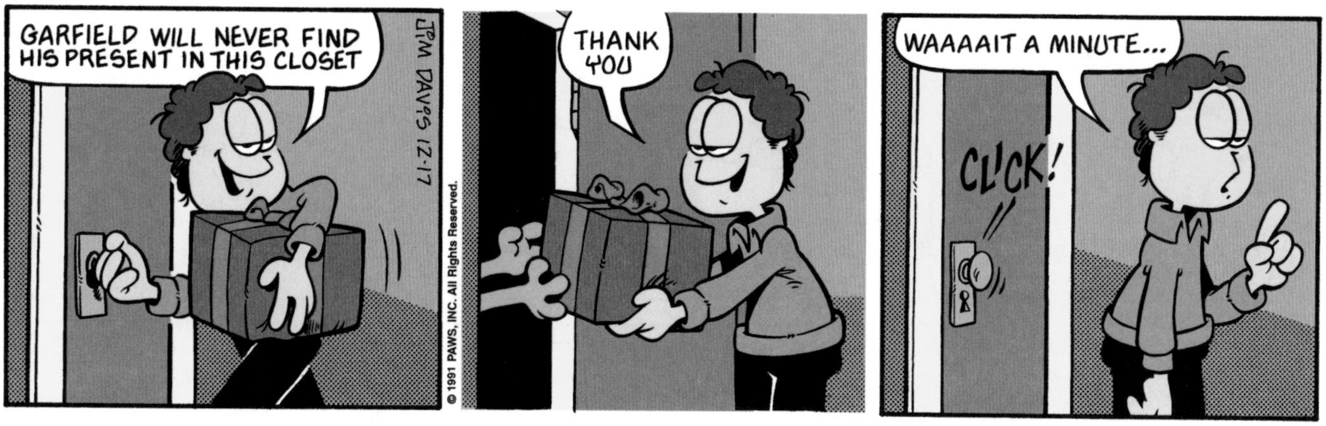
GARFIELD WILL NEVER FIND HIS PRESENT IN THIS CLOSET
JIM DAVIS 12-17
© 1991 PAWS, INC. All Rights Reserved.
THANK YOU
WAAAAIT A MINUTE...
CLICK!

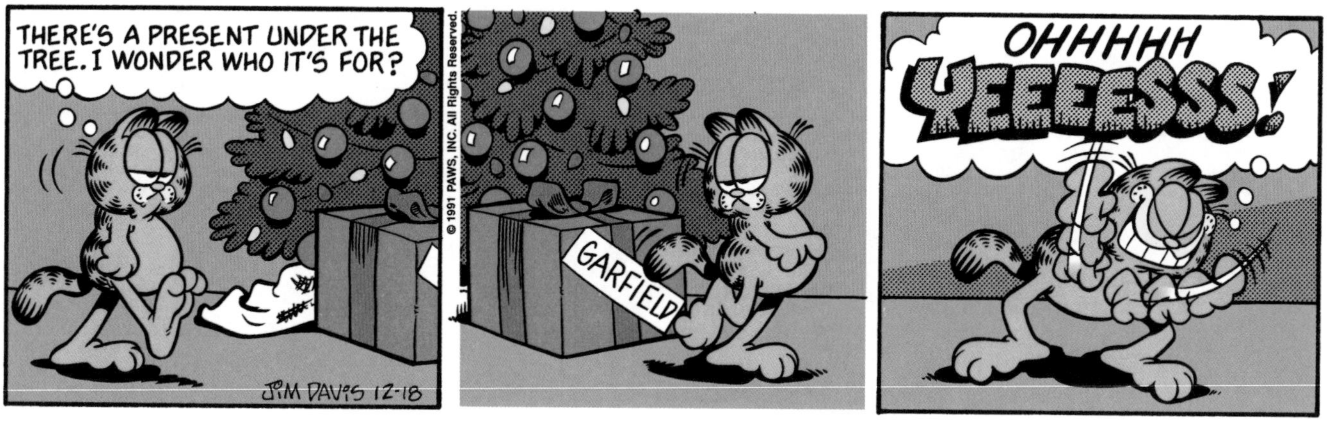
THERE'S A PRESENT UNDER THE TREE. I WONDER WHO IT'S FOR?
JIM DAVIS 12-18
© 1991 PAWS, INC. All Rights Reserved.
GARFIELD
OHHHHH
YEEEESSS!

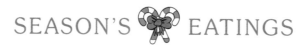

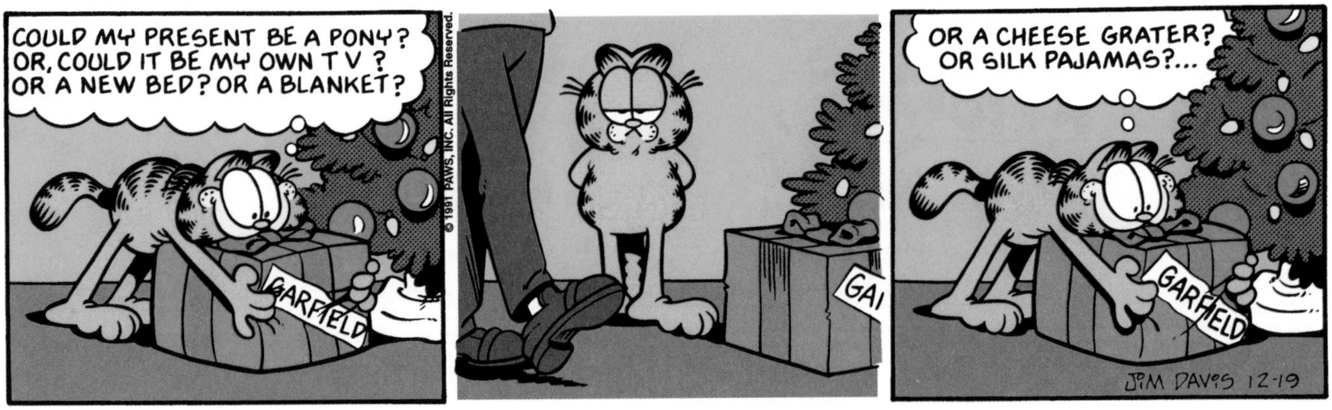
COULD MY PRESENT BE A PONY? OR, COULD IT BE MY OWN T V ? OR A NEW BED? OR A BLANKET?
© 1991 PAWS, INC. All Rights Reserved.
GARFIELD
GA
OR A CHEESE GRATER? OR SILK PAJAMAS?...
GARFIELD
JIM DAVIS 12-19

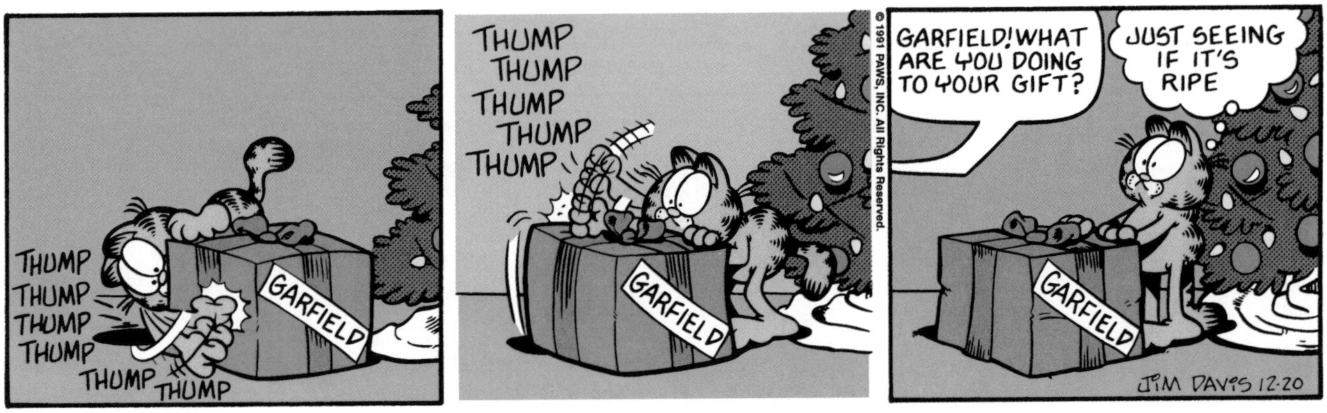
THUMP THUMP THUMP THUMP THUMP THUMP
GARFIELD
THUMP THUMP THUMP THUMP THUMP
GARFIELD
© 1991 PAWS, INC. All Rights Reserved.
GARFIELD! WHAT ARE YOU DOING TO YOUR GIFT?
JUST SEEING IF IT'S RIPE
GARFIELD
JIM DAVIS 12-20

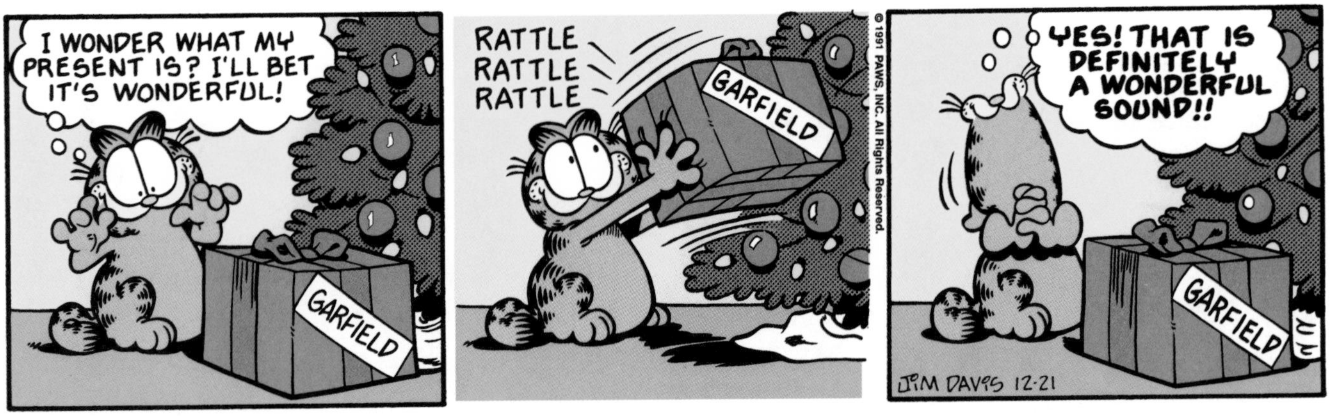
I WONDER WHAT MY PRESENT IS? I'LL BET IT'S WONDERFUL!
GARFIELD
RATTLE RATTLE RATTLE
GARFIELD
© 1991 PAWS, INC. All Rights Reserved.
YES! THAT IS DEFINITELY A WONDERFUL SOUND!!
GARFIELD
JIM DAVIS 12-21

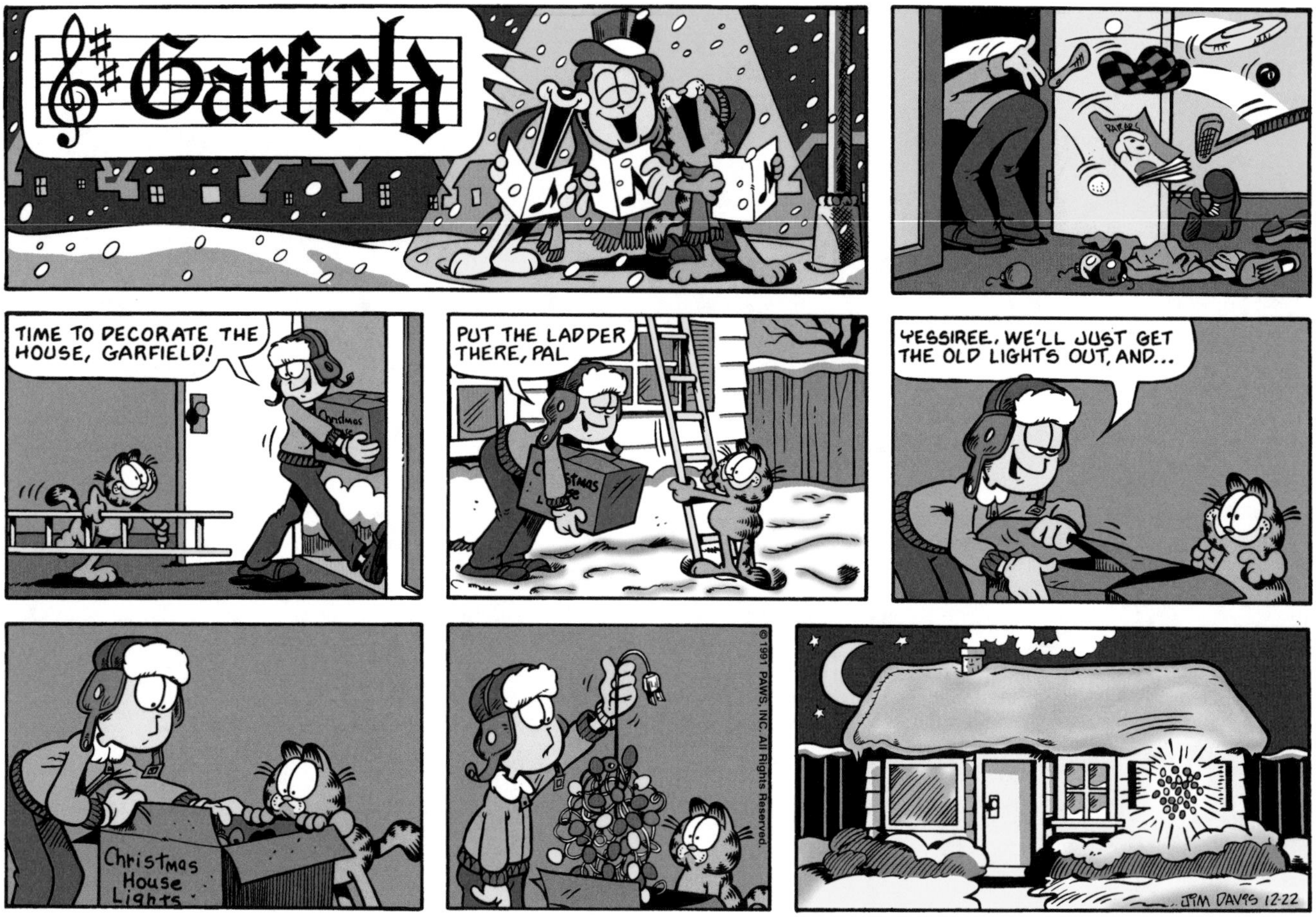
Garfield
TIME TO DECORATE THE HOUSE, GARFIELD!
PUT THE LADDER THERE, PAL
YESSIREE. WE'LL JUST GET THE OLD LIGHTS OUT, AND...
Christmas House Lights
© 1991 PAWS, INC. All Rights Reserved.
JIM DAVIS 12-22

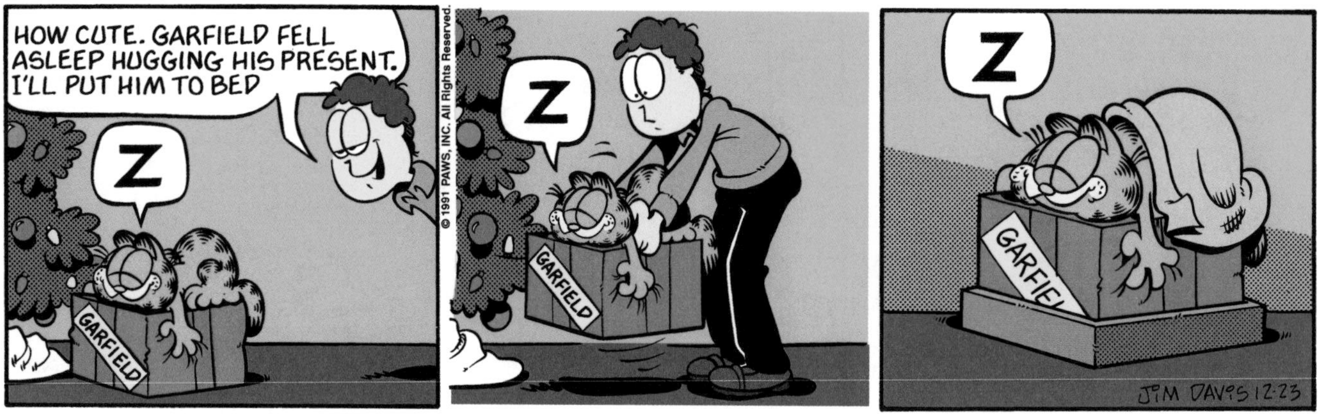
HOW CUTE. GARFIELD FELL ASLEEP HUGGING HIS PRESENT. I'LL PUT HIM TO BED
Z
GARFIELD
© 1991 PAWS, INC. All Rights Reserved.
Z
GARFIELD
Z
JIM DAVIS 12-23

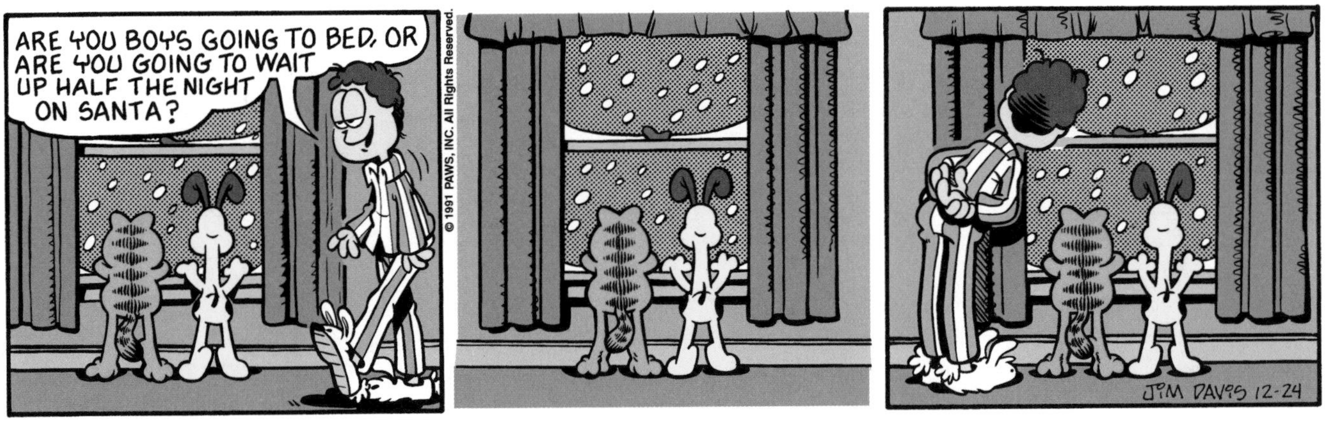
ARE YOU BOYS GOING TO BED, OR ARE YOU GOING TO WAIT UP HALF THE NIGHT ON SANTA?
© 1991 PAWS, INC. All Rights Reserved.
JIM DAVIS 12-24

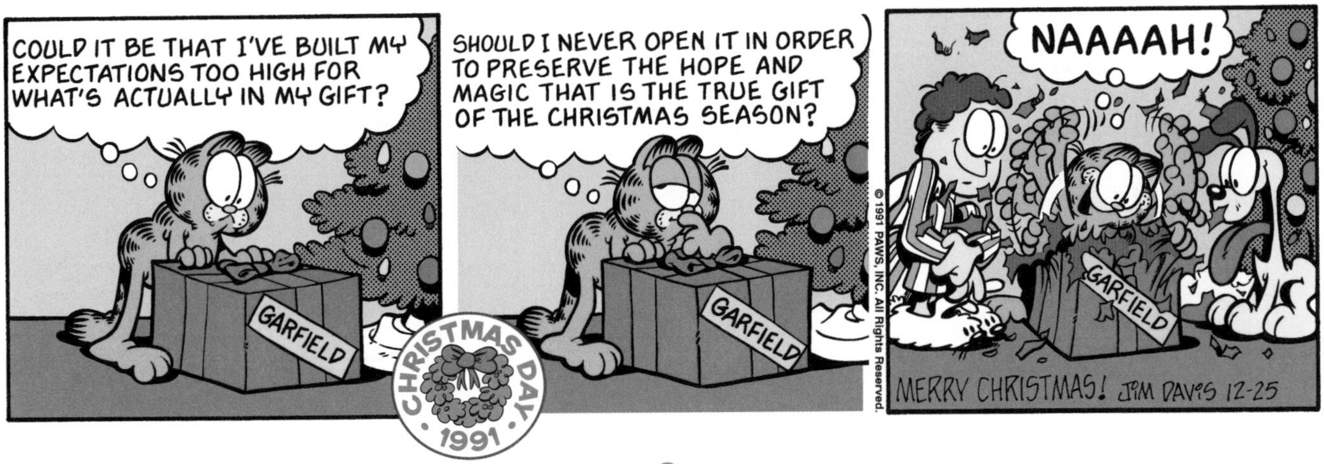
COULD IT BE THAT I'VE BUILT MY EXPECTATIONS TOO HIGH FOR WHAT'S ACTUALLY IN MY GIFT?
GARFIELD
CHRISTMAS DAY 1991
SHOULD I NEVER OPEN IT IN ORDER TO PRESERVE THE HOPE AND MAGIC THAT IS THE TRUE GIFT OF THE CHRISTMAS SEASON?
GARFIELD
© 1991 PAWS, INC. All Rights Reserved.
NAAAAH!
GARFIELD
MERRY CHRISTMAS! JIM DAVIS 12-25

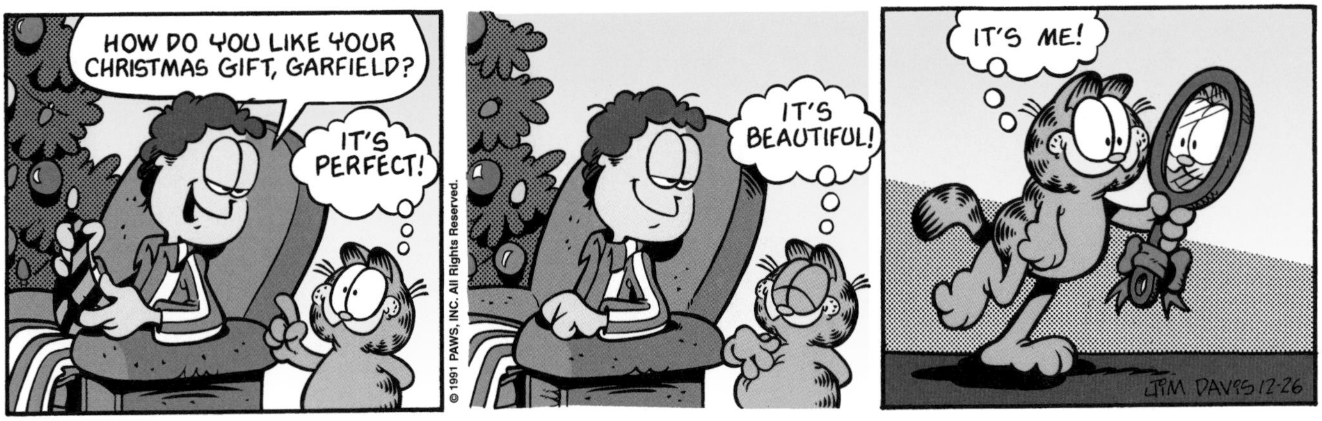
HOW DO YOU LIKE YOUR CHRISTMAS GIFT, GARFIELD?
IT'S PERFECT!
© 1991 PAWS, INC. All Rights Reserved.
IT'S BEAUTIFUL!
IT'S ME!
JIM DAVIS 12-26

I CALLED TO THANK YOU FOR THE CHRISTMAS GIFT, MOM
YOU REALLY OUTDID YOURSELF THIS TIME
I DIDN'T KNOW YOU COULD CROCHET A SUIT
SOMEONE SHOULD STOP HER
© 1991 PAWS, INC. All Rights Reserved.
JIM DAVIS 12-27

GUESS WHAT, MOM...
I THINK GARFIELD ACTUALLY LIKES THE SWEATER YOU MADE HIM
THE SHOULDER PADS WON ME OVER
© 1991 PAWS, INC. All Rights Reserved.
JIM DAVIS 12-28

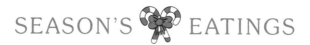

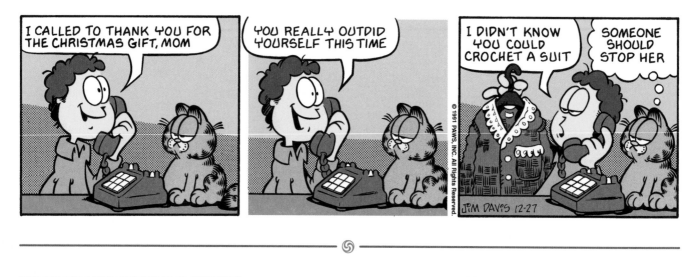

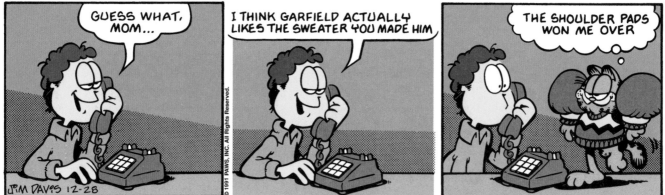

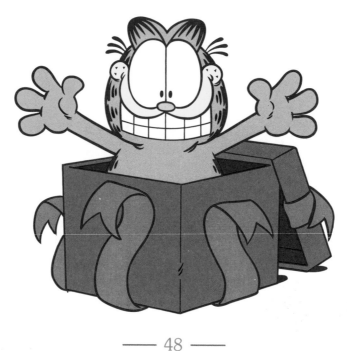

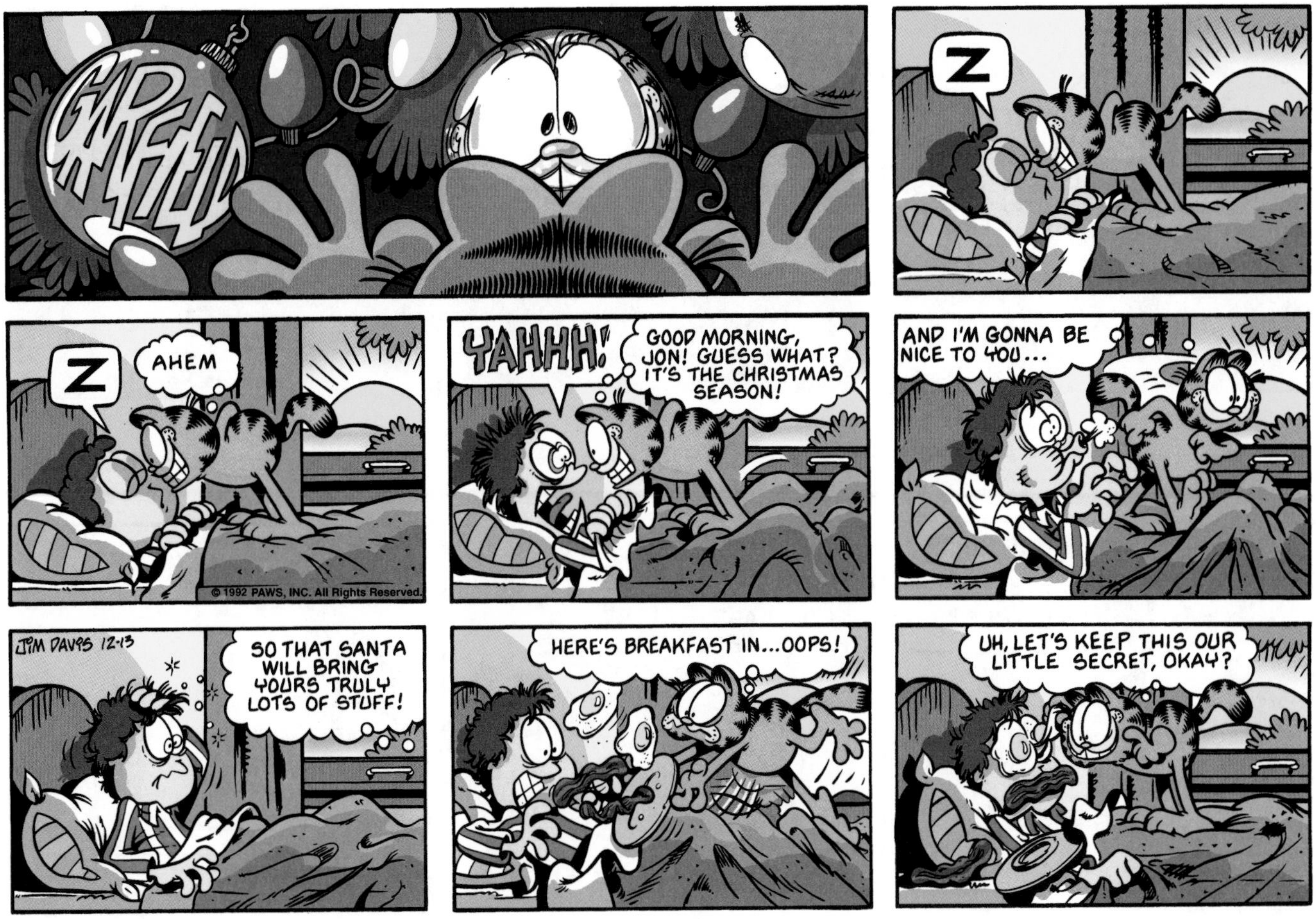
GARFIELD
Z
Z
AHEM
© 1992 PAWS, INC. All Rights Reserved.
YAHHH!
GOOD MORNING, JON! GUESS WHAT? IT'S THE CHRISTMAS SEASON!
AND I'M GONNA BE NICE TO YOU...
JIM DAVIS 12-13
SO THAT SANTA WILL BRING YOURS TRULY LOTS OF STUFF!
HERE'S BREAKFAST IN...OOPS!
UH, LET'S KEEP THIS OUR LITTLE SECRET, OKAY?

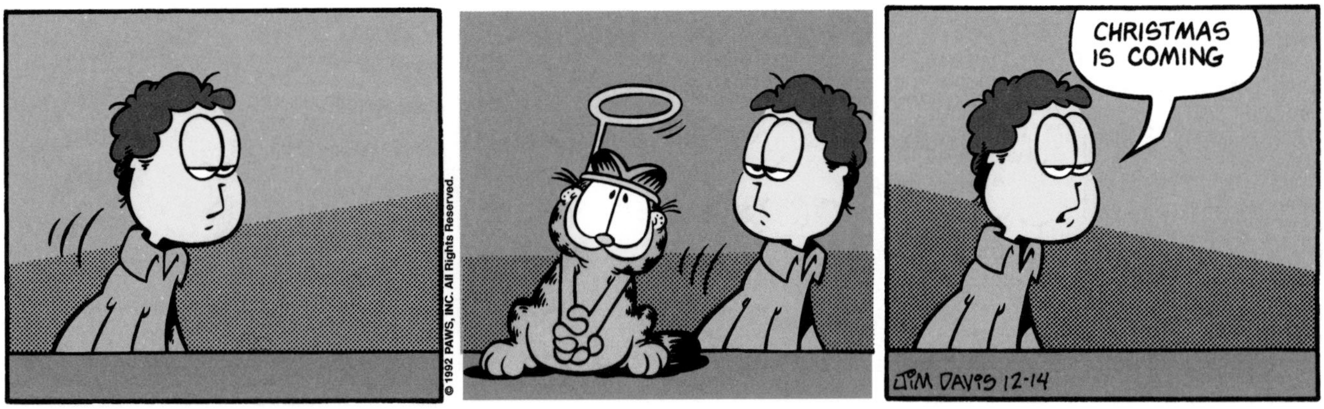
© 1992 PAWS, INC. All Rights Reserved.
CHRISTMAS IS COMING
JIM DAVIS 12-14

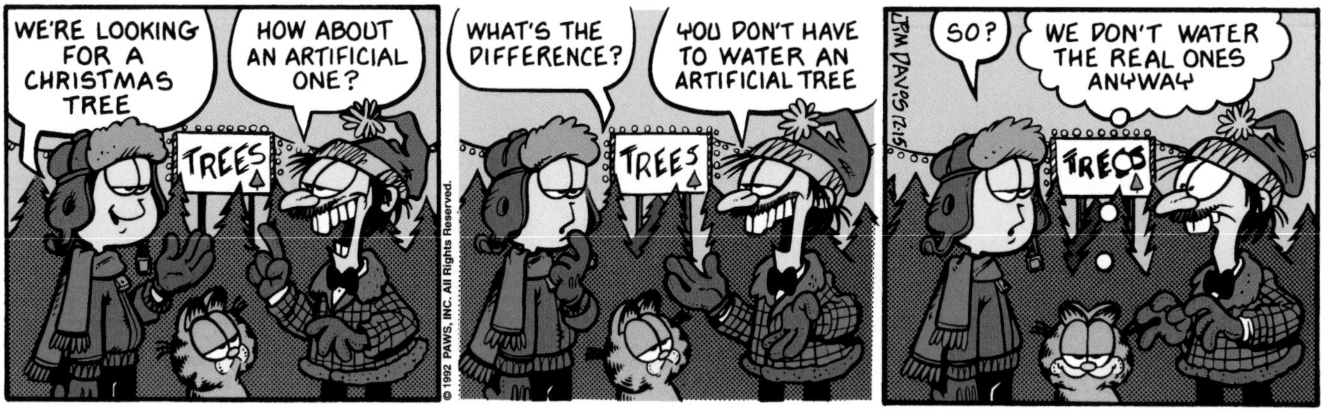
WE'RE LOOKING FOR A CHRISTMAS TREE
HOW ABOUT AN ARTIFICIAL ONE?
TREES
© 1992 PAWS, INC. All Rights Reserved.
WHAT'S THE DIFFERENCE?
YOU DON'T HAVE TO WATER AN ARTIFICIAL TREE
TREES
JIM DAVIS 12-15
SO?
WE DON'T WATER THE REAL ONES ANYWAY

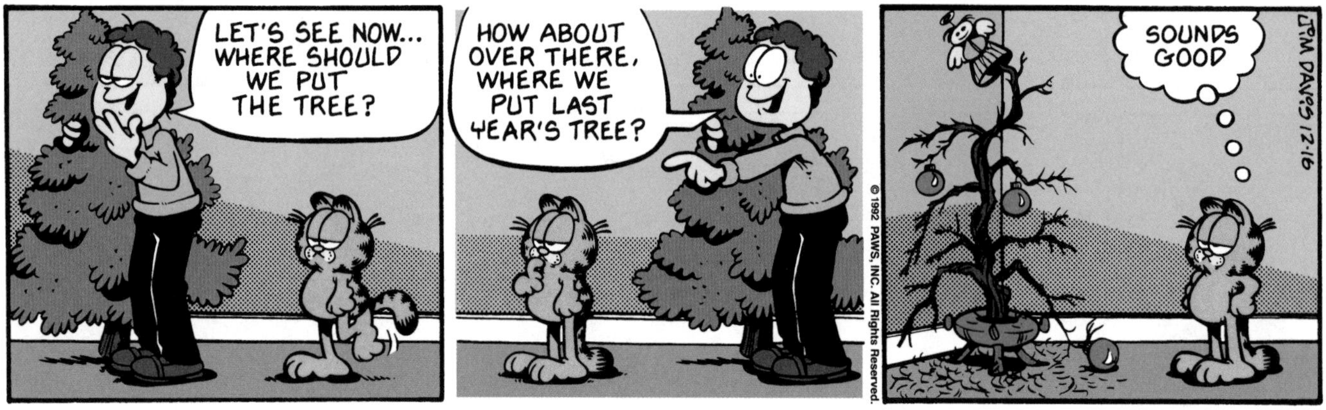
LET'S SEE NOW... WHERE SHOULD WE PUT THE TREE?
HOW ABOUT OVER THERE, WHERE WE PUT LAST YEAR'S TREE?
© 1992 PAWS, INC. All Rights Reserved.
SOUNDS GOOD
JIM DAVIS 12-16

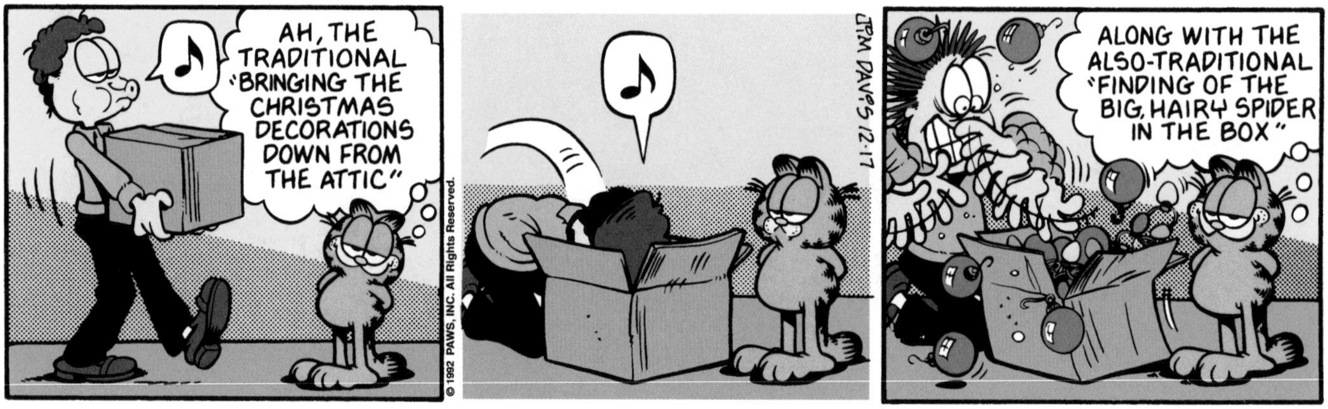
♪
AH, THE TRADITIONAL "BRINGING THE CHRISTMAS DECORATIONS DOWN FROM THE ATTIC"
© 1992 PAWS, INC. All Rights Reserved.
♪
JIM DAVIS 12-17
ALONG WITH THE ALSO-TRADITIONAL "FINDING OF THE BIG, HAIRY SPIDER IN THE BOX"

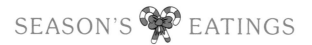

JOIN US NOW, WON'T YOU?
JIM DAVIS 12-18
IN OUR TRADITIONAL HOLIDAY SEARCH...
FOR THE ONE BAD BULB IN A STRING OF FIVE ZILLION THAT MAKES THE OTHERS GO OUT
© 1992 PAWS, INC. All Rights Reserved.

CHRISTMAS IS A TIME OF TRADITIONS
JIM DAVIS 12-19
© 1992 PAWS, INC. All Rights Reserved.
SOME OLD, SOME NEW, SOME UNIVERSAL...
AND SOME FROM THE LUNATIC FRINGE
C'MON, GARFIELD! PUT YOURS ON!

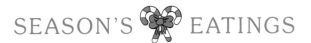

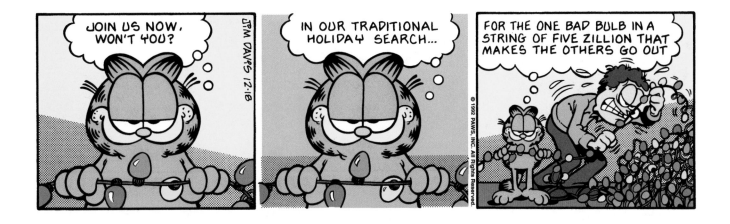

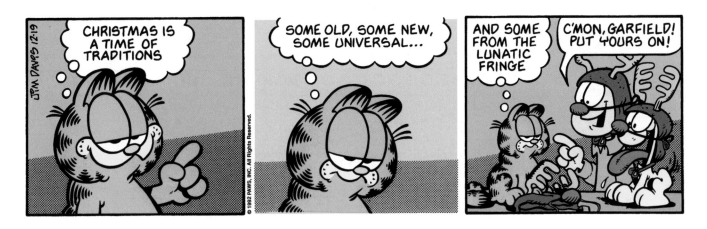

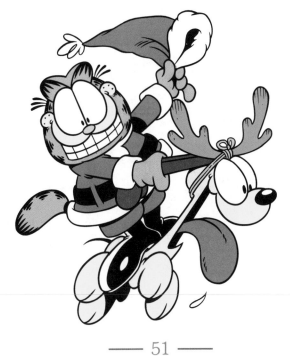

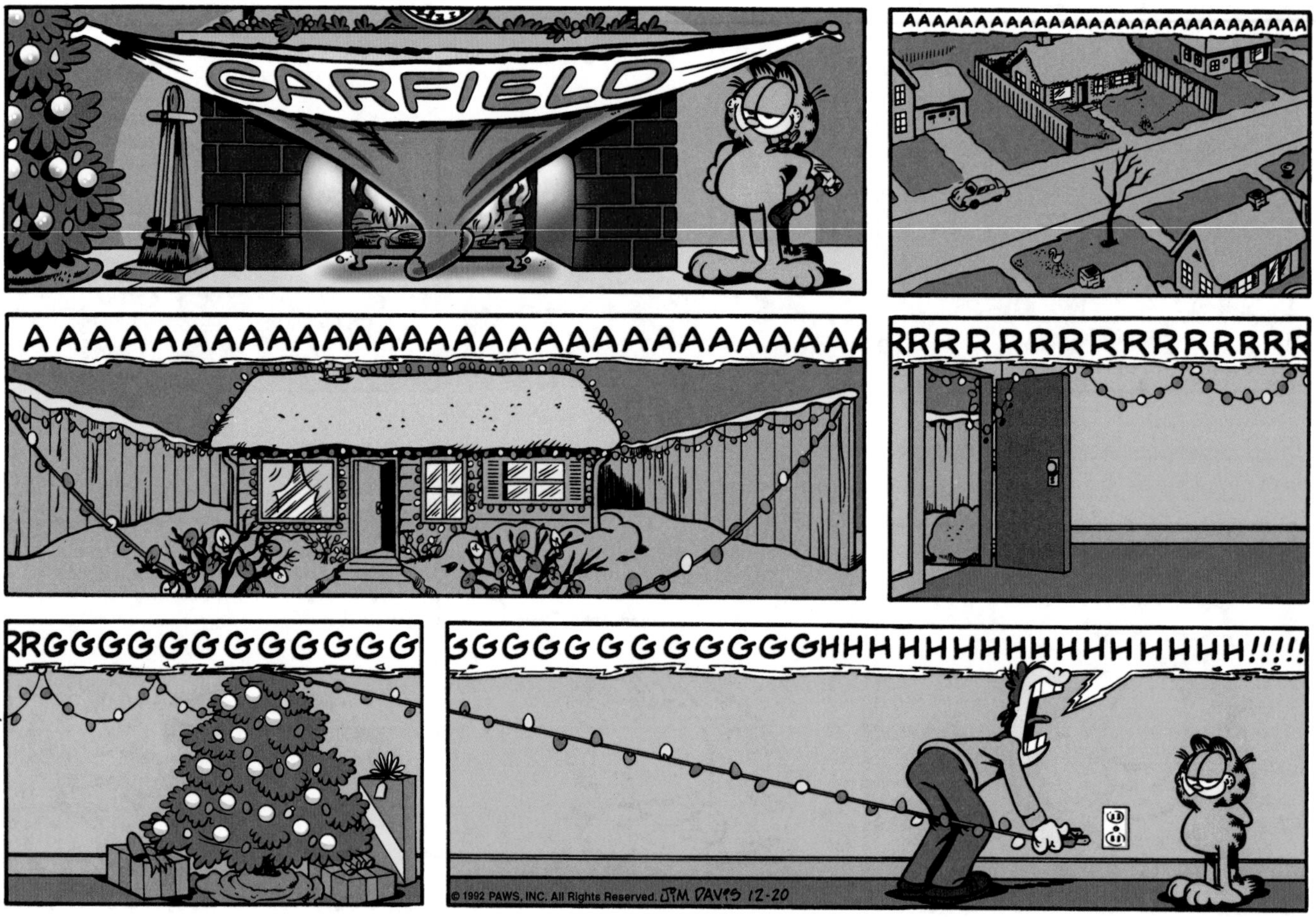
GARFIELD
AAAAAAAAAAAAAAAAAAAAAAAAAAAAA
AAAAAAAAAAAAAAAAAAAAAAAAAAAAAAAA
RRRRRRRRRRRRRRRR
RRGGGGGGGGGGGGG
GGGGGGGGGGGGGHHHHHHHHHHHHHHHHH!!!!!
© 1992 PAWS, INC. All Rights Reserved. JIM DAVIS 12-20

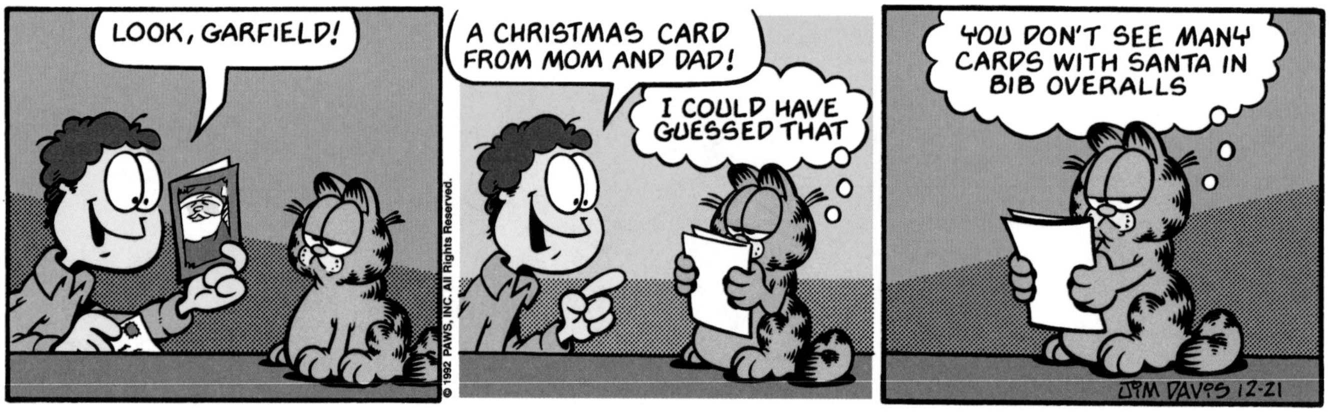
LOOK, GARFIELD!
© 1992 PAWS, INC. All Rights Reserved.
A CHRISTMAS CARD FROM MOM AND DAD!
I COULD HAVE GUESSED THAT
YOU DON'T SEE MANY CARDS WITH SANTA IN BIB OVERALLS
JIM DAVIS 12-21

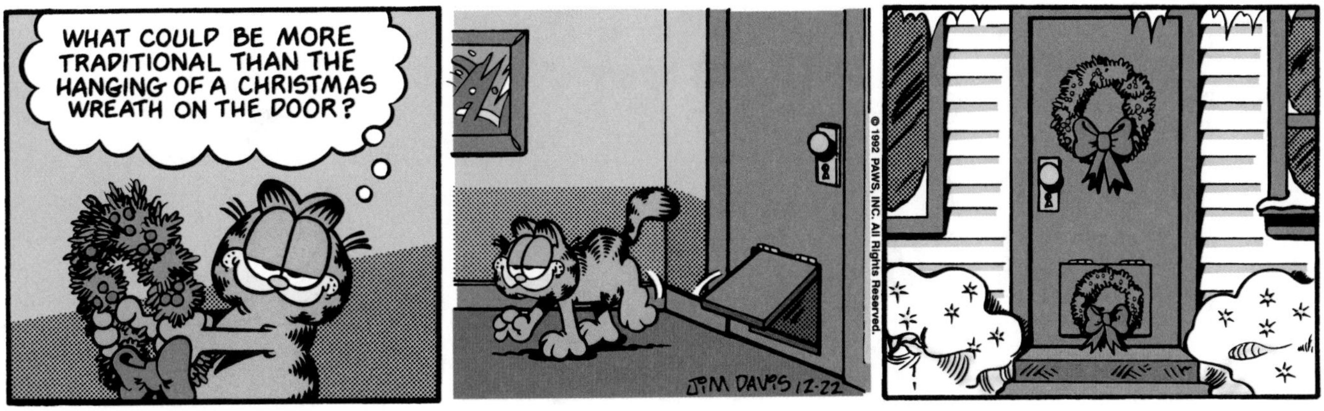
WHAT COULD BE MORE TRADITIONAL THAN THE HANGING OF A CHRISTMAS WREATH ON THE DOOR?
© 1992 PAWS, INC. All Rights Reserved.
JIM DAVIS 12-22

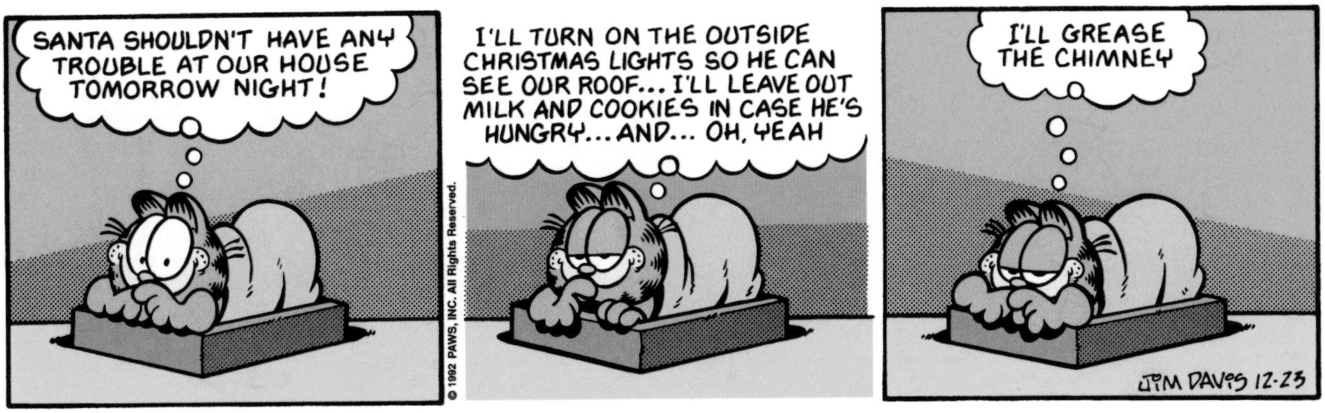
SANTA SHOULDN'T HAVE ANY TROUBLE AT OUR HOUSE TOMORROW NIGHT!
© 1992 PAWS, INC. All Rights Reserved.
I'LL TURN ON THE OUTSIDE CHRISTMAS LIGHTS SO HE CAN SEE OUR ROOF... I'LL LEAVE OUT MILK AND COOKIES IN CASE HE'S HUNGRY... AND... OH, YEAH
I'LL GREASE THE CHIMNEY
JIM DAVIS 12-23

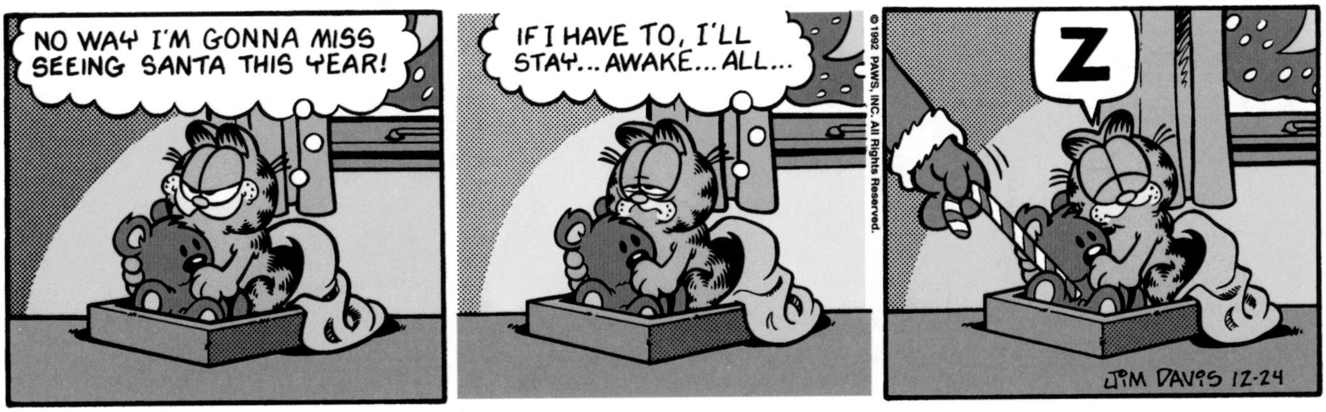
NO WAY I'M GONNA MISS SEEING SANTA THIS YEAR!
IF I HAVE TO, I'LL STAY... AWAKE... ALL...
© 1992 PAWS, INC. All Rights Reserved.
Z
JIM DAVIS 12-24

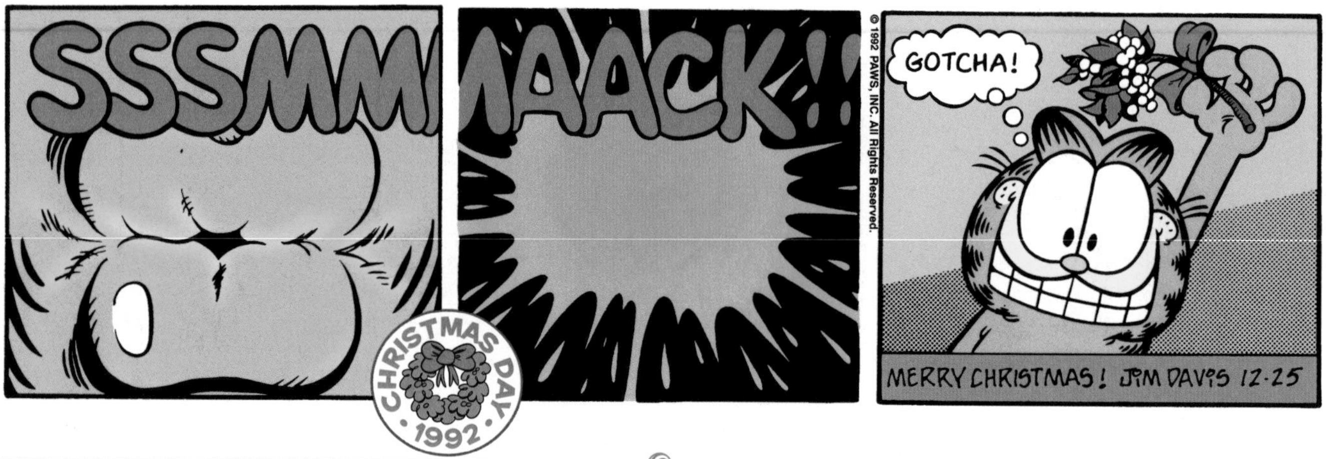
SSSMMMAACK!!
GOTCHA!
CHRISTMAS DAY 1992
MERRY CHRISTMAS! JIM DAVIS 12-25
© 1992 PAWS, INC. All Rights Reserved.

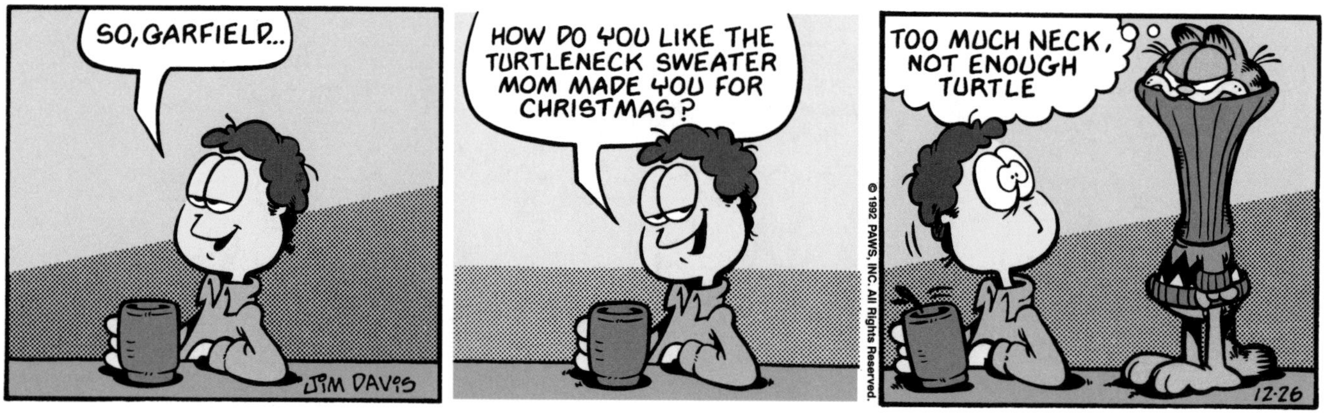
SO, GARFIELD...
HOW DO YOU LIKE THE TURTLENECK SWEATER MOM MADE YOU FOR CHRISTMAS?
TOO MUCH NECK, NOT ENOUGH TURTLE
JIM DAVIS
12-26
© 1992 PAWS, INC. All Rights Reserved.

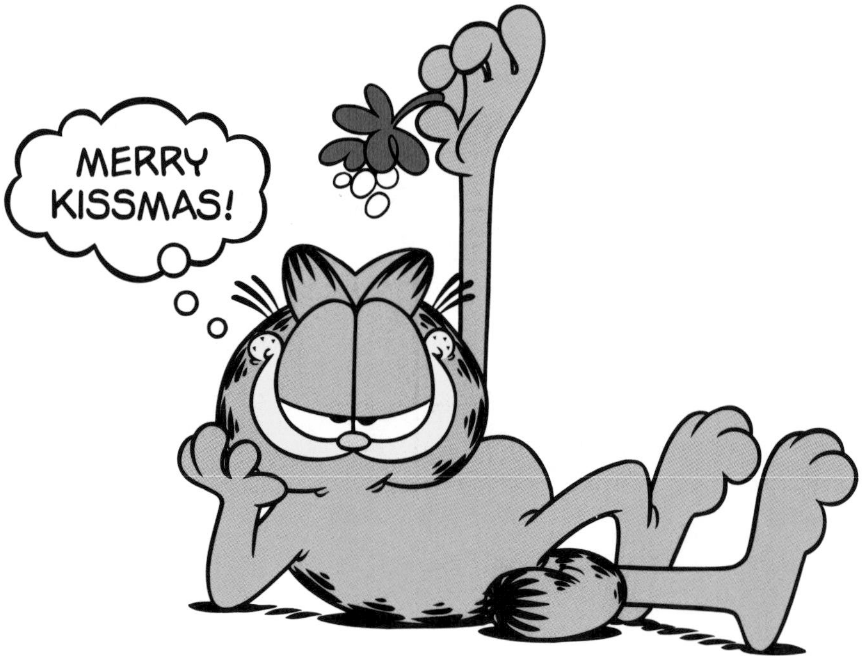
MERRY KISSMAS!

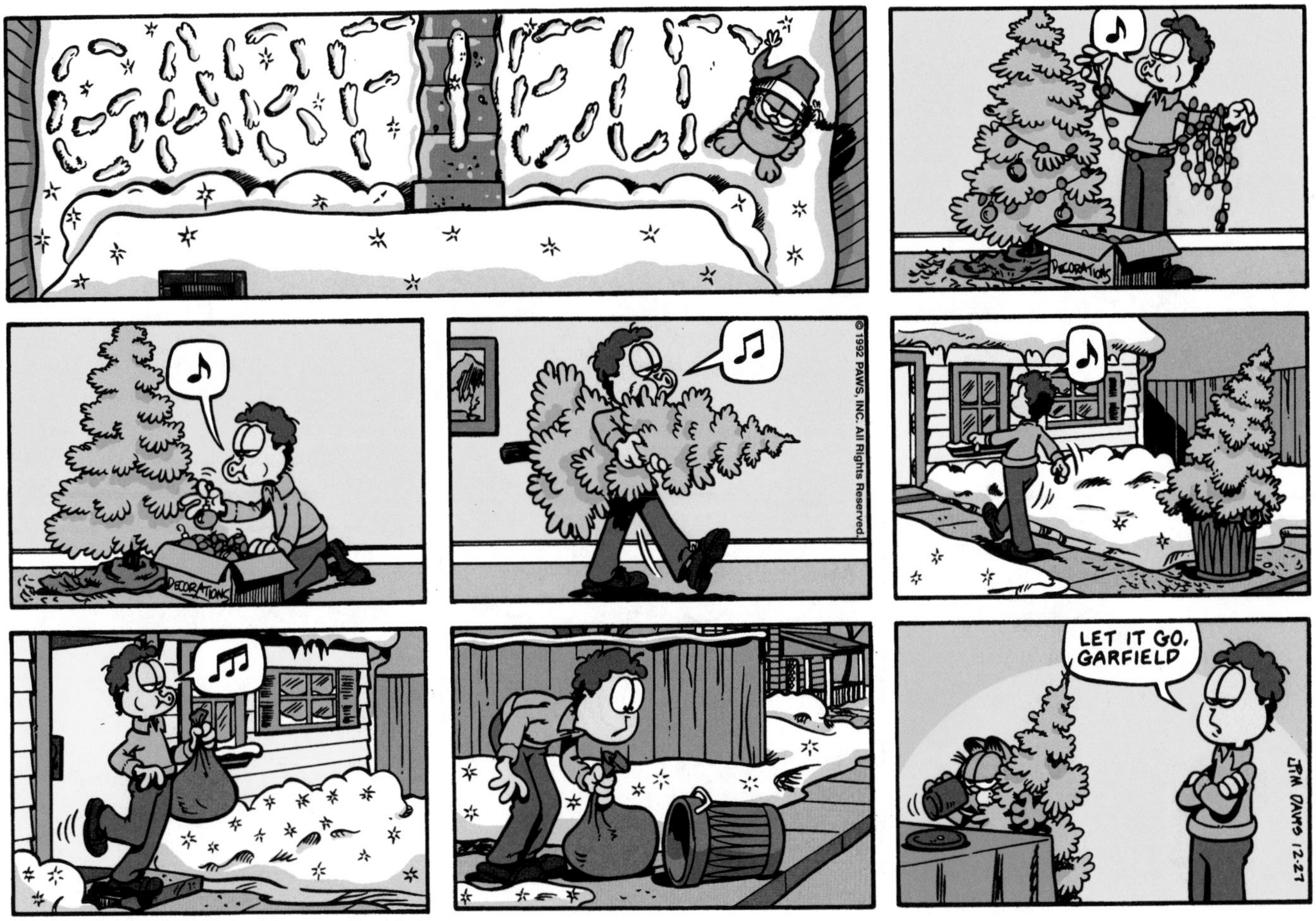
© 1992 PAWS, INC. All Rights Reserved.
LET IT GO, GARFIELD
JIM DAVIS 12-27

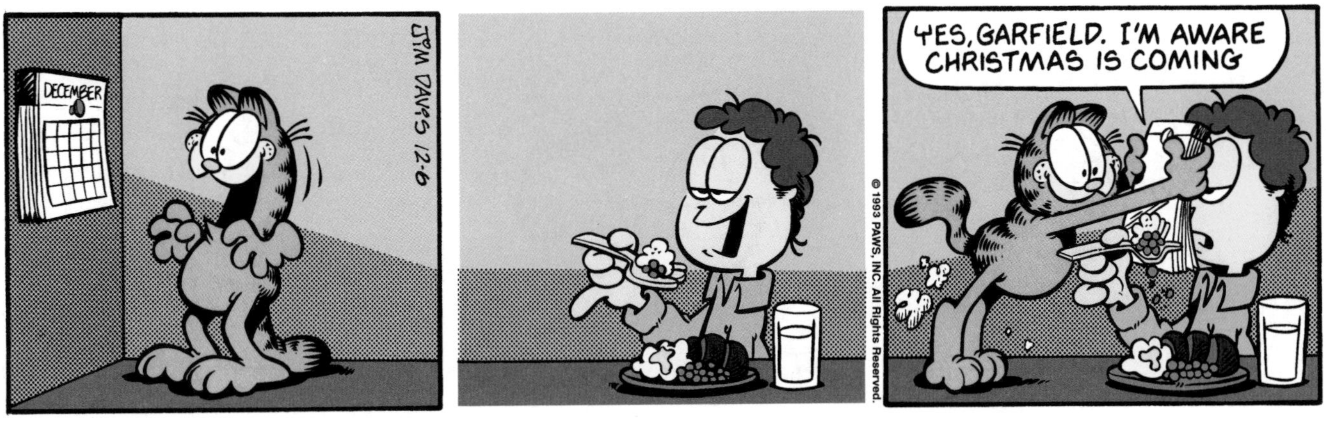
DECEMBER
JIM DAVIS 12-6
© 1993 PAWS, INC. All Rights Reserved.
YES, GARFIELD. I'M AWARE CHRISTMAS IS COMING

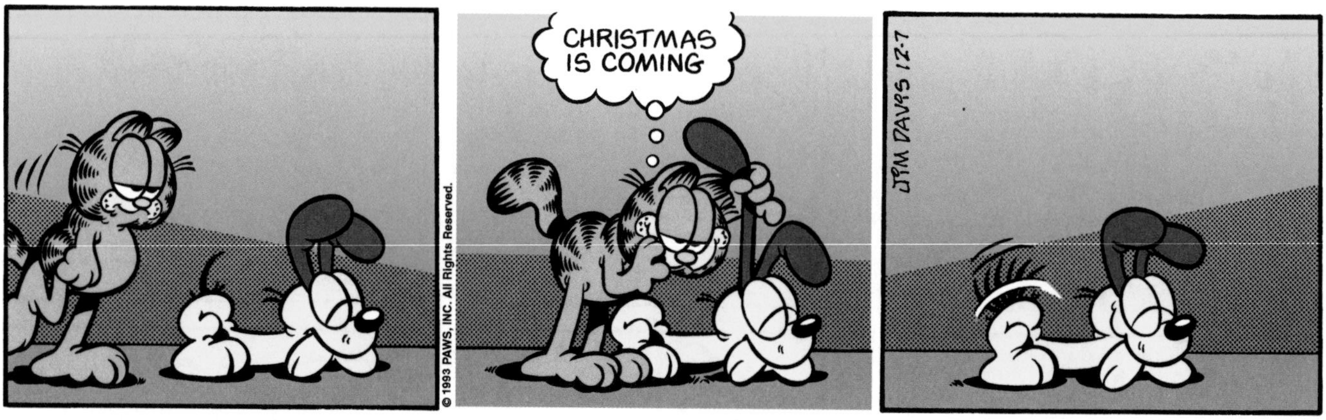
© 1993 PAWS, INC. All Rights Reserved.
CHRISTMAS IS COMING
JIM DAVIS 12-7

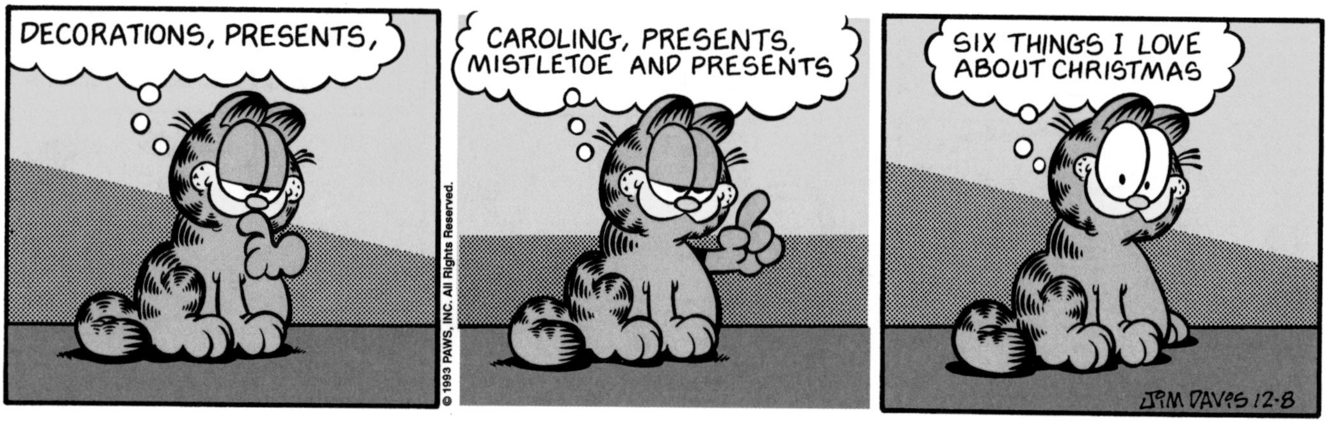
DECORATIONS, PRESENTS,
© 1993 PAWS, INC. All Rights Reserved.
CAROLING, PRESENTS, MISTLETOE AND PRESENTS
SIX THINGS I LOVE ABOUT CHRISTMAS
JIM DAVIS 12-8

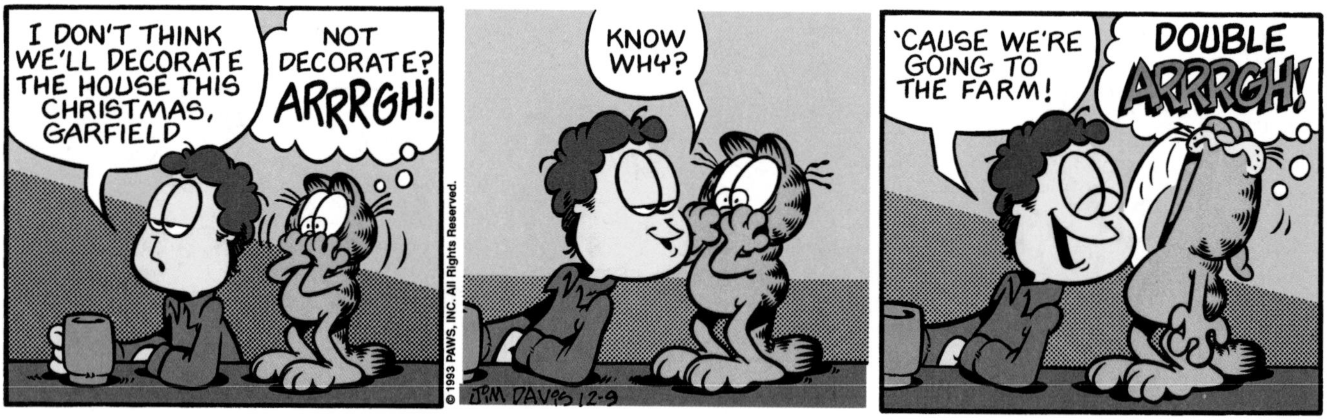
I DON'T THINK WE'LL DECORATE THE HOUSE THIS CHRISTMAS, GARFIELD
NOT DECORATE? ARRRGH!
© 1993 PAWS, INC. All Rights Reserved.
KNOW WHY?
JIM DAVIS 12-9
'CAUSE WE'RE GOING TO THE FARM!
DOUBLE ARRRGH!

GARFIELD, I KNOW YOU DON'T WANT TO GO TO THE FARM FOR CHRISTMAS, BUT WARM UP TO IT, OKAY?
JIM DAVIS 12-10
© 1993 PAWS, INC. All Rights Reserved.
HYUCK! HYUCK! HYUCK!
STOP THAT!

C'MON, GARFIELD! WE'RE LEAVING FOR THE FARM!
JUST A MINUTE...
JIM DAVIS 12-11
HURRY UP!
© 1993 PAWS, INC. All Rights Reserved.
WHAT WERE YOU DOING IN THERE?
LEAVING SANTA A FORWARDING ADDRESS

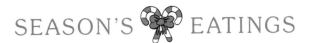

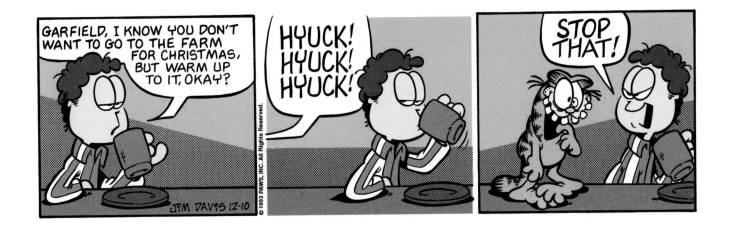

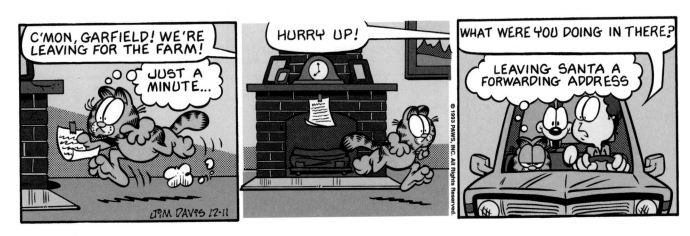

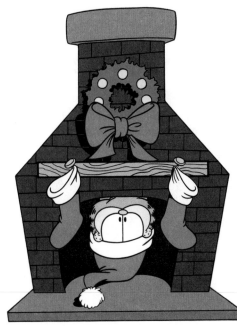

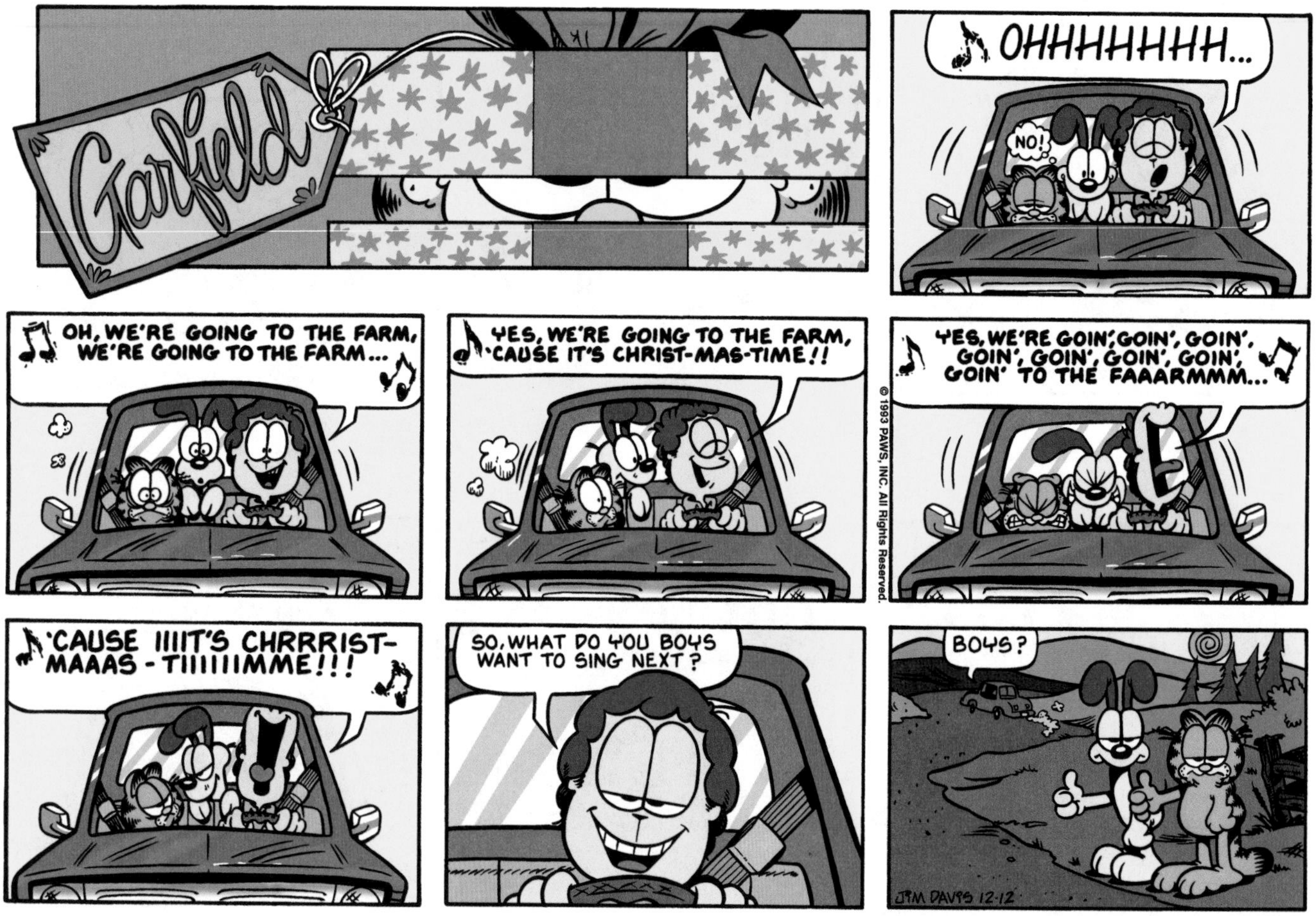
Garfield
OHHHHHHH...
NO!
OH, WE'RE GOING TO THE FARM, WE'RE GOING TO THE FARM...
YES, WE'RE GOING TO THE FARM, 'CAUSE IT'S CHRIST-MAS-TIME!!
YES, WE'RE GOIN', GOIN', GOIN', GOIN', GOIN', GOIN', GOIN', GOIN' TO THE FAAARMMM...
'CAUSE IIIIT'S CHRRRIST-MAAAS - TIIIIIIMME!!!
SO, WHAT DO YOU BOYS WANT TO SING NEXT?
BOYS?
© 1993 PAWS, INC. All Rights Reserved.
JIM DAVIS 12-12

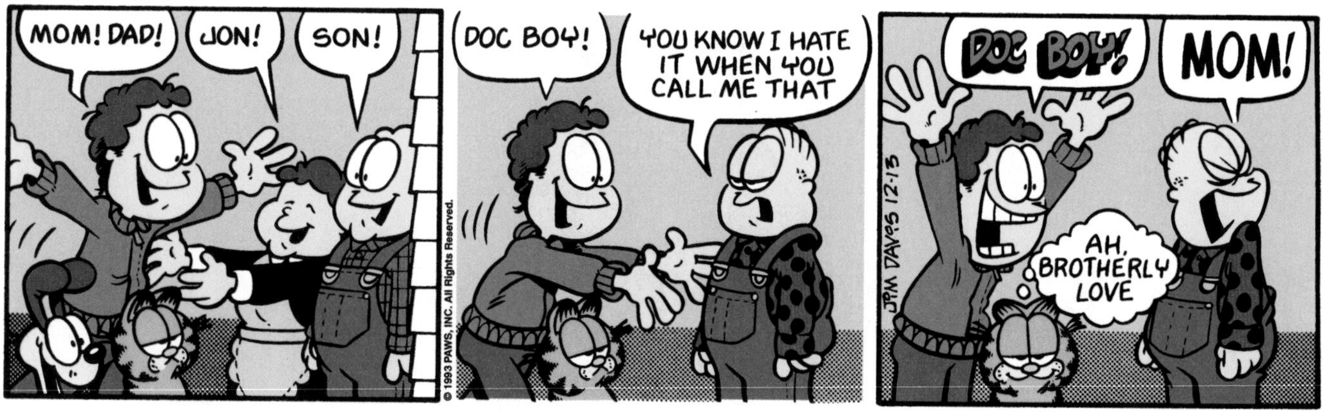
MOM! DAD!
JON!
SON!
DOC BOY!
YOU KNOW I HATE IT WHEN YOU CALL ME THAT
DOC BOY!
MOM!
AH, BROTHERLY LOVE
© 1993 PAWS, INC. All Rights Reserved.
JIM DAVIS 12-13

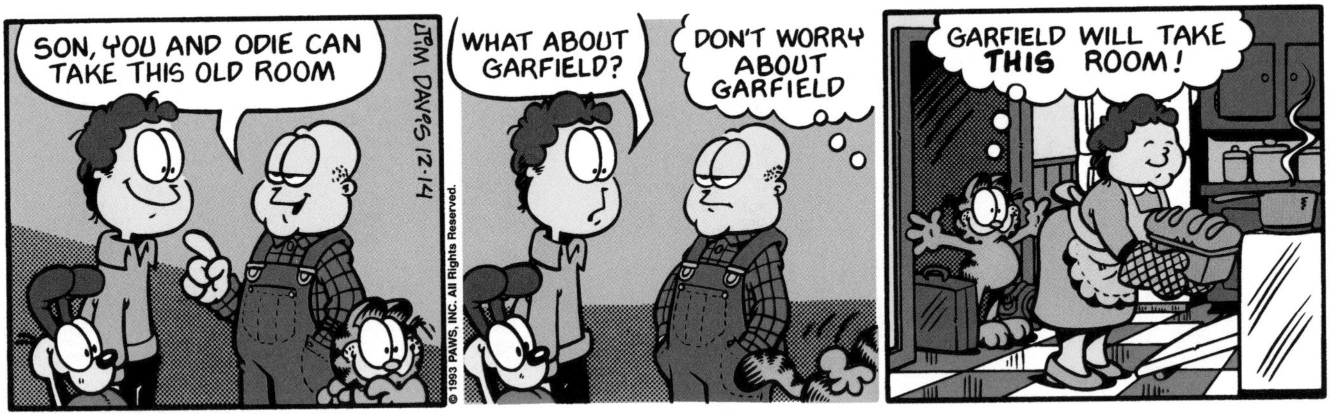
SON, YOU AND ODIE CAN TAKE THIS OLD ROOM
JIM DAVIS 12-14
© 1993 PAWS, INC. All Rights Reserved.
WHAT ABOUT GARFIELD?
DON'T WORRY ABOUT GARFIELD
GARFIELD WILL TAKE **THIS** ROOM!

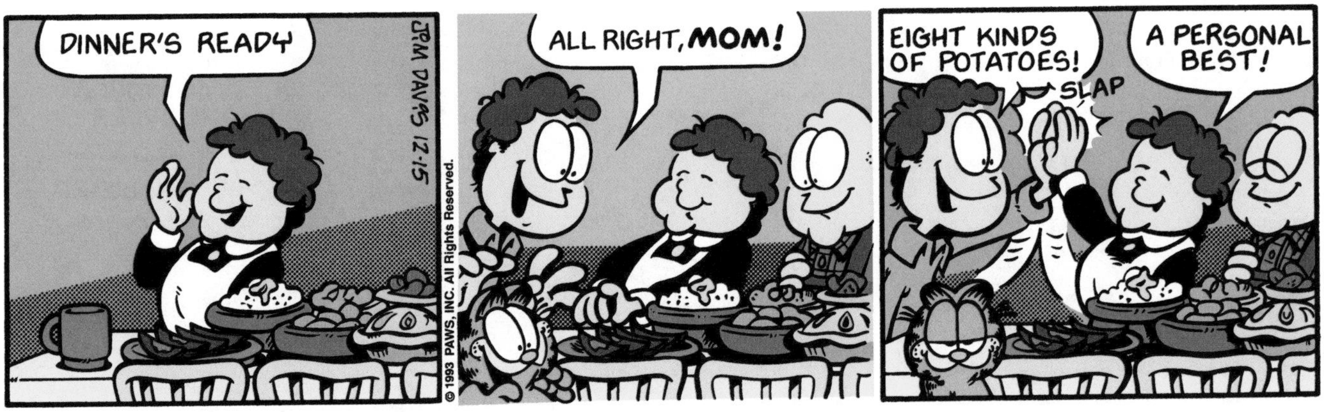
DINNER'S READY
JIM DAVIS 12-15
© 1993 PAWS, INC. All Rights Reserved.
ALL RIGHT, **MOM!**
EIGHT KINDS OF POTATOES!
SLAP
A PERSONAL BEST!

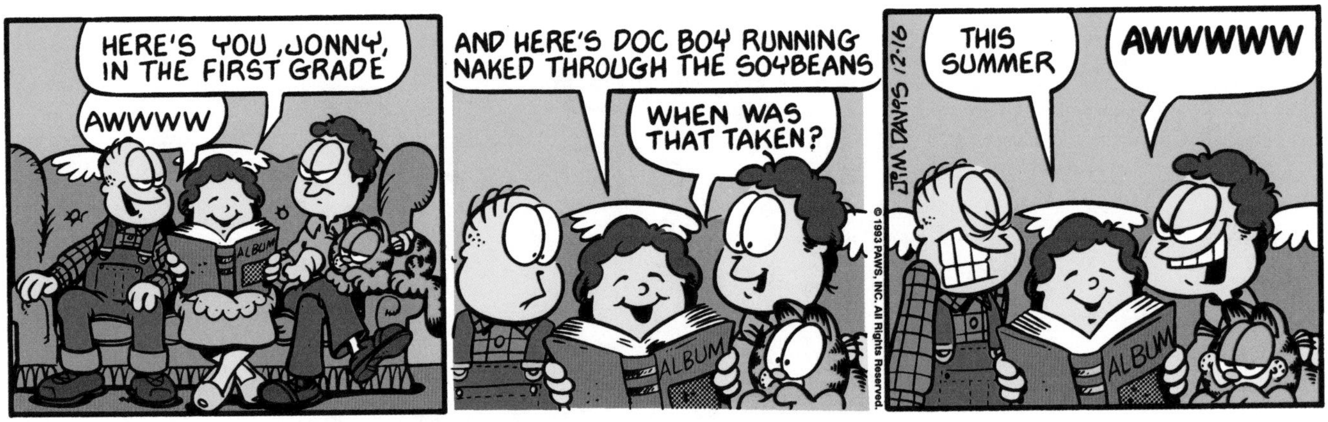
HERE'S YOU, JONNY, IN THE FIRST GRADE
AWWWW
AND HERE'S DOC BOY RUNNING NAKED THROUGH THE SOYBEANS
WHEN WAS THAT TAKEN?
JIM DAVIS 12-16
© 1993 PAWS, INC. All Rights Reserved.
THIS SUMMER
AWWWWW

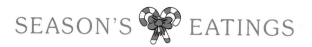

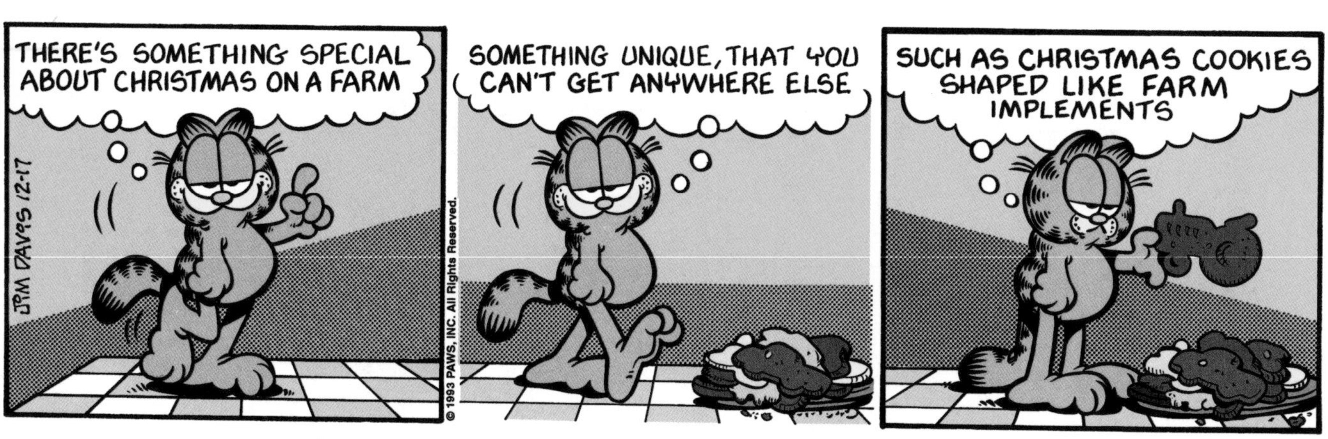
THERE'S SOMETHING SPECIAL ABOUT CHRISTMAS ON A FARM
SOMETHING UNIQUE, THAT YOU CAN'T GET ANYWHERE ELSE
SUCH AS CHRISTMAS COOKIES SHAPED LIKE FARM IMPLEMENTS
© 1993 PAWS, INC. All Rights Reserved.

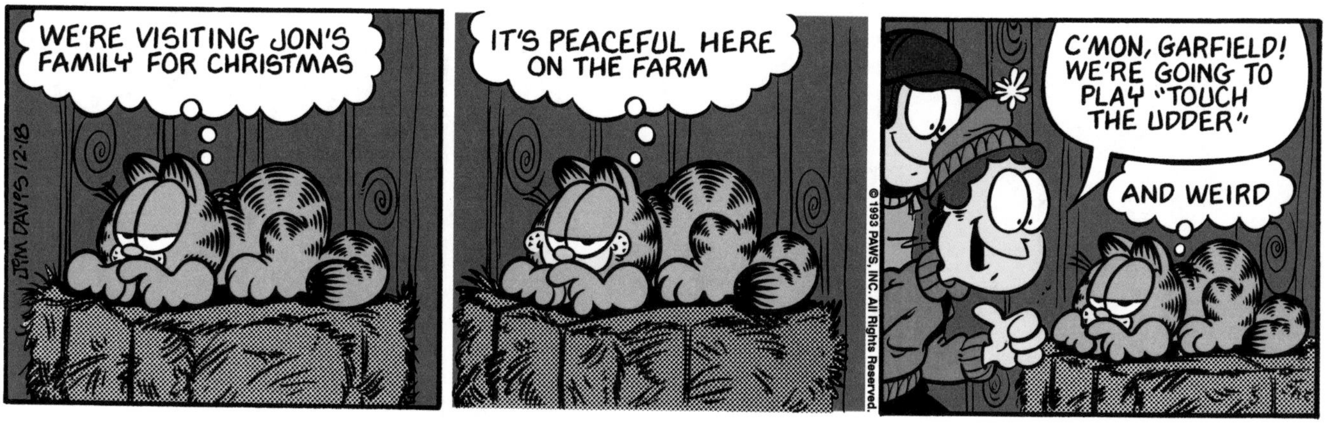
WE'RE VISITING JON'S FAMILY FOR CHRISTMAS
IT'S PEACEFUL HERE ON THE FARM
C'MON, GARFIELD! WE'RE GOING TO PLAY "TOUCH THE UDDER"
AND WEIRD
© 1993 PAWS, INC. All Rights Reserved.

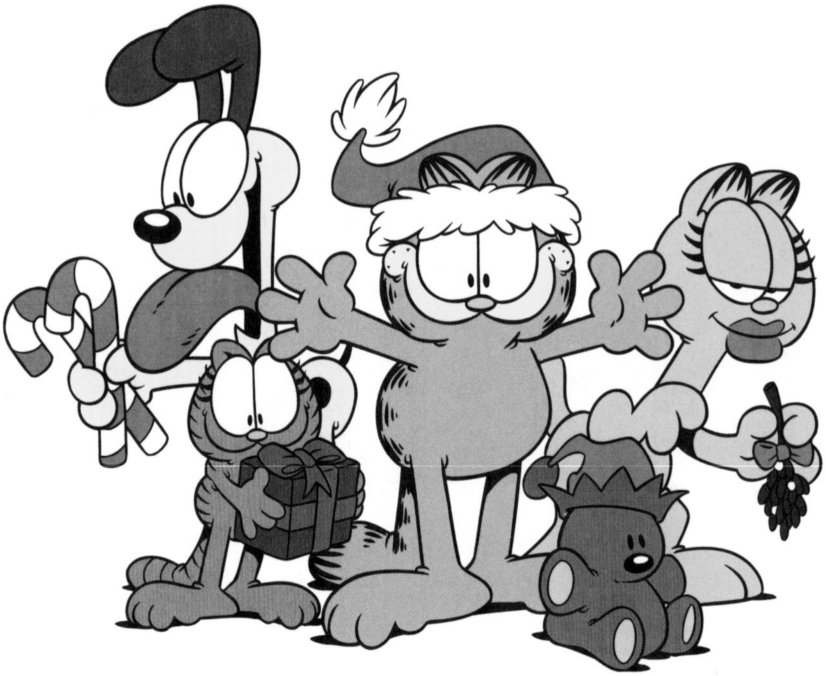

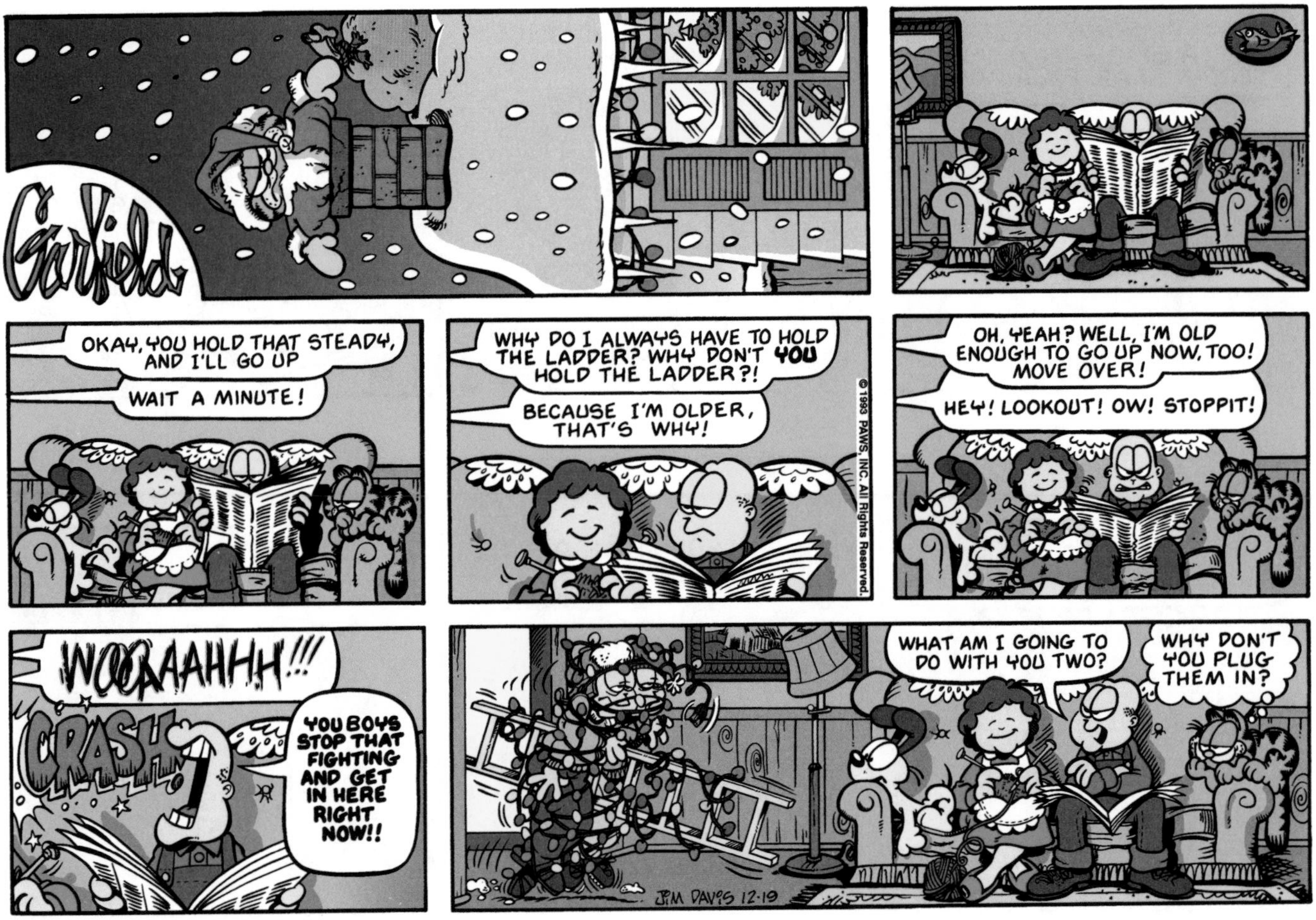
Garfield
OKAY, YOU HOLD THAT STEADY, AND I'LL GO UP
WAIT A MINUTE!
WHY DO I ALWAYS HAVE TO HOLD THE LADDER? WHY DON'T **YOU** HOLD THE LADDER?!
BECAUSE I'M OLDER, THAT'S WHY!
© 1993 PAWS, INC. All Rights Reserved.
OH, YEAH? WELL, I'M OLD ENOUGH TO GO UP NOW, TOO! MOVE OVER!
HEY! LOOKOUT! OW! STOPPIT!
WOOAAAHHH!!!
CRASH
YOU BOYS STOP THAT FIGHTING AND GET IN HERE RIGHT NOW!!
WHAT AM I GOING TO DO WITH YOU TWO?
WHY DON'T YOU PLUG THEM IN?
JIM DAVIS 12·19

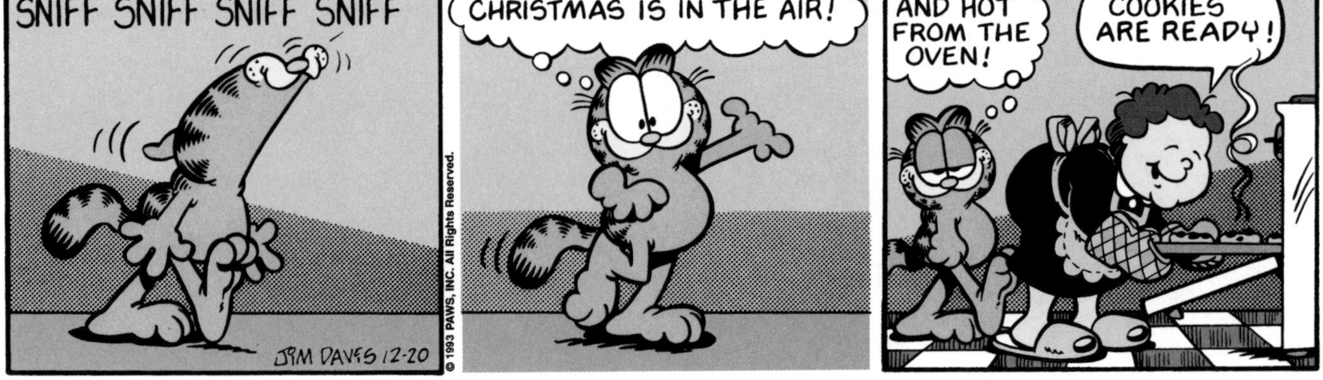
SNIFF SNIFF SNIFF SNIFF
JIM DAVIS 12-20
© 1993 PAWS, INC. All Rights Reserved.
CHRISTMAS IS IN THE AIR!
AND HOT FROM THE OVEN!
COOKIES ARE READY!

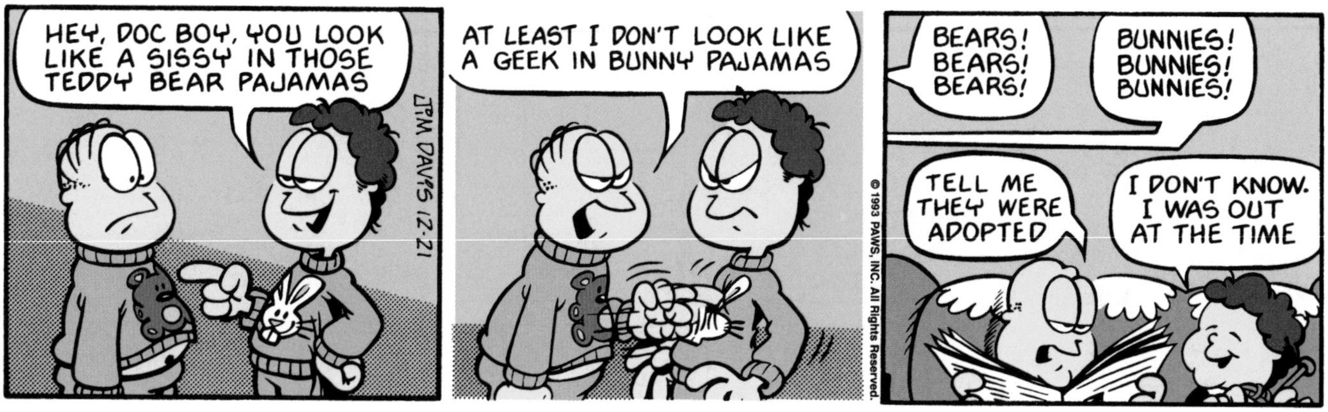
HEY, DOC BOY, YOU LOOK LIKE A SISSY IN THOSE TEDDY BEAR PAJAMAS
JIM DAVIS 12-21
AT LEAST I DON'T LOOK LIKE A GEEK IN BUNNY PAJAMAS
© 1993 PAWS, INC. All Rights Reserved.
BEARS! BEARS! BEARS!
BUNNIES! BUNNIES! BUNNIES!
TELL ME THEY WERE ADOPTED
I DON'T KNOW. I WAS OUT AT THE TIME

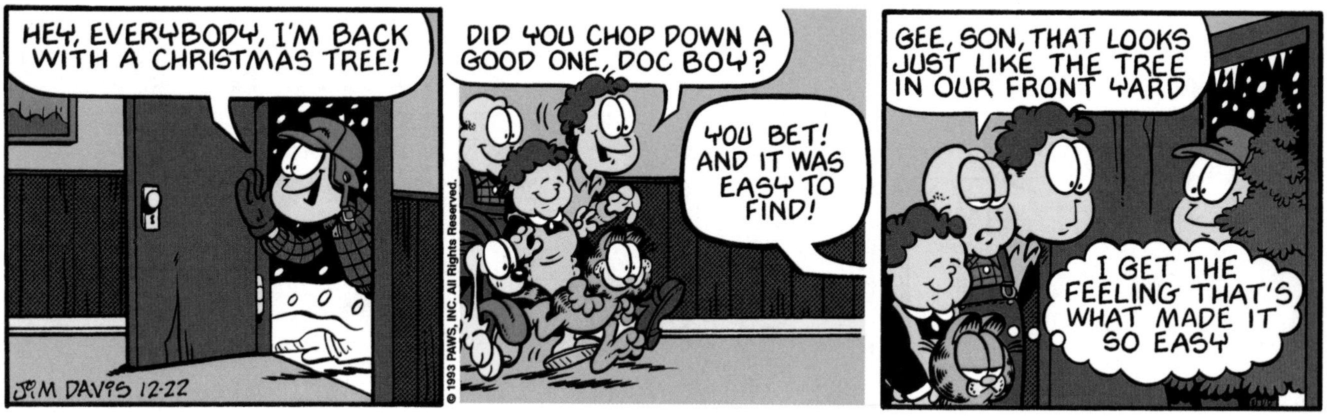
HEY, EVERYBODY, I'M BACK WITH A CHRISTMAS TREE!
JIM DAVIS 12-22
DID YOU CHOP DOWN A GOOD ONE, DOC BOY?
YOU BET! AND IT WAS EASY TO FIND!
© 1993 PAWS, INC. All Rights Reserved.
GEE, SON, THAT LOOKS JUST LIKE THE TREE IN OUR FRONT YARD
I GET THE FEELING THAT'S WHAT MADE IT SO EASY

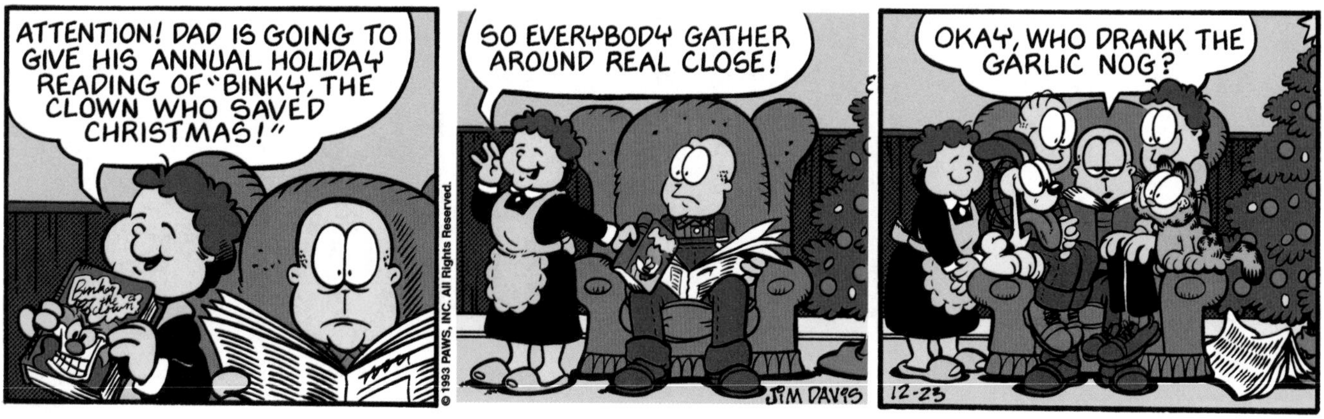
ATTENTION! DAD IS GOING TO GIVE HIS ANNUAL HOLIDAY READING OF "BINKY, THE CLOWN WHO SAVED CHRISTMAS!"
© 1993 PAWS, INC. All Rights Reserved.
SO EVERYBODY GATHER AROUND REAL CLOSE!
JIM DAVIS
OKAY, WHO DRANK THE GARLIC NOG?
12-23

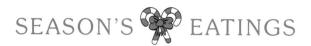

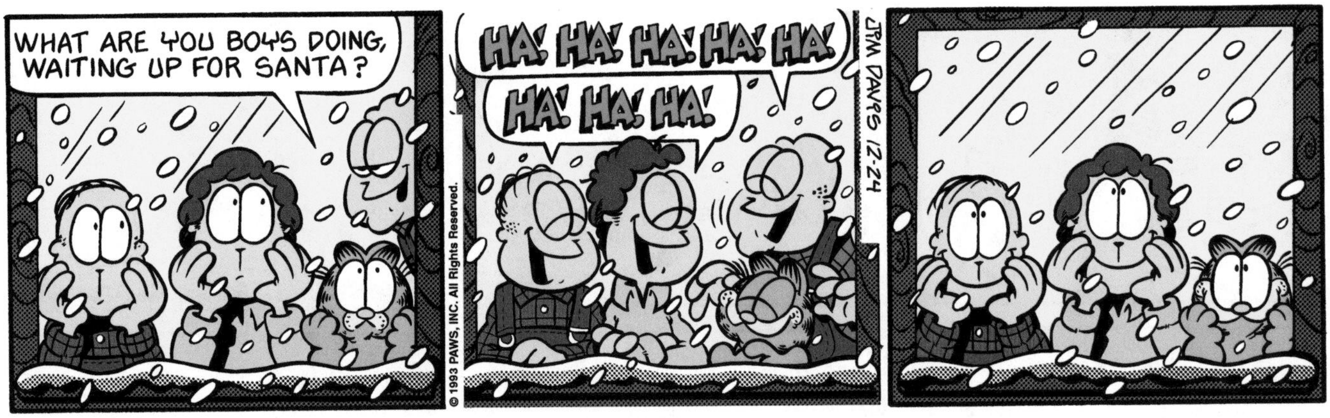
WHAT ARE YOU BOYS DOING, WAITING UP FOR SANTA?
HA! HA! HA! HA! HA!
HA! HA! HA!
JIM DAVIS 12-24
© 1993 PAWS, INC. All Rights Reserved.

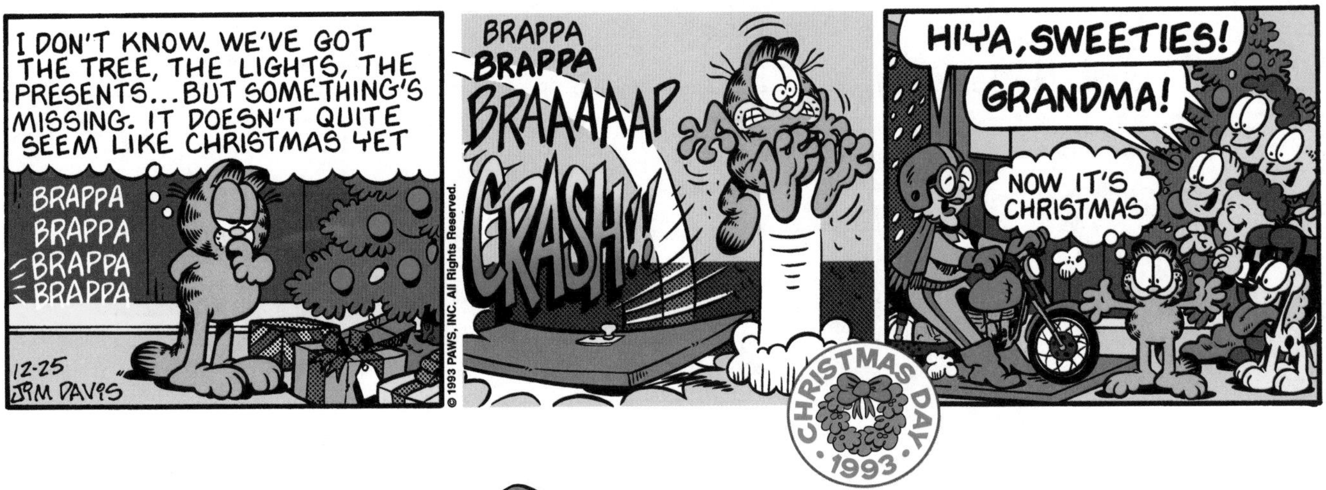
I DON'T KNOW. WE'VE GOT THE TREE, THE LIGHTS, THE PRESENTS... BUT SOMETHING'S MISSING. IT DOESN'T QUITE SEEM LIKE CHRISTMAS YET
BRAPPA
BRAPPA
BRAPPA
BRAPPA
12-25
JIM DAVIS
BRAPPA
BRAPPA
BRAAAAAP
CRASH!!
© 1993 PAWS, INC. All Rights Reserved.
HIYA, SWEETIES!
GRANDMA!
NOW IT'S CHRISTMAS
CHRISTMAS DAY 1993

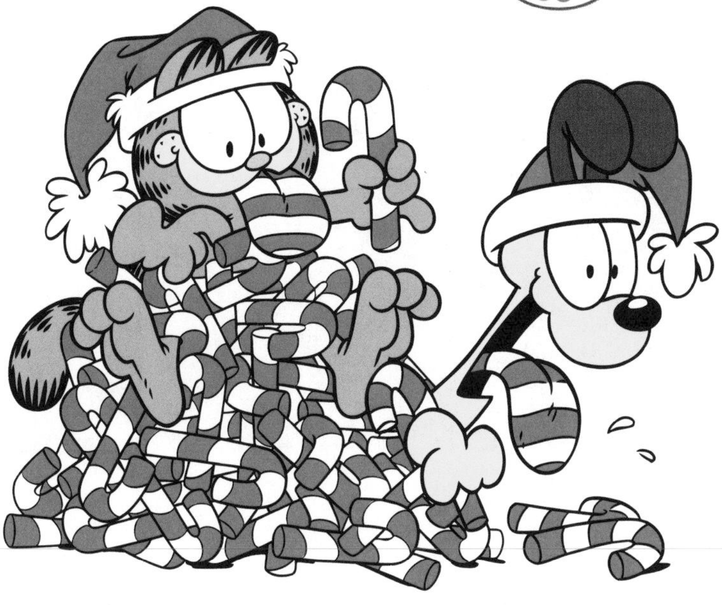

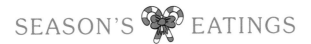

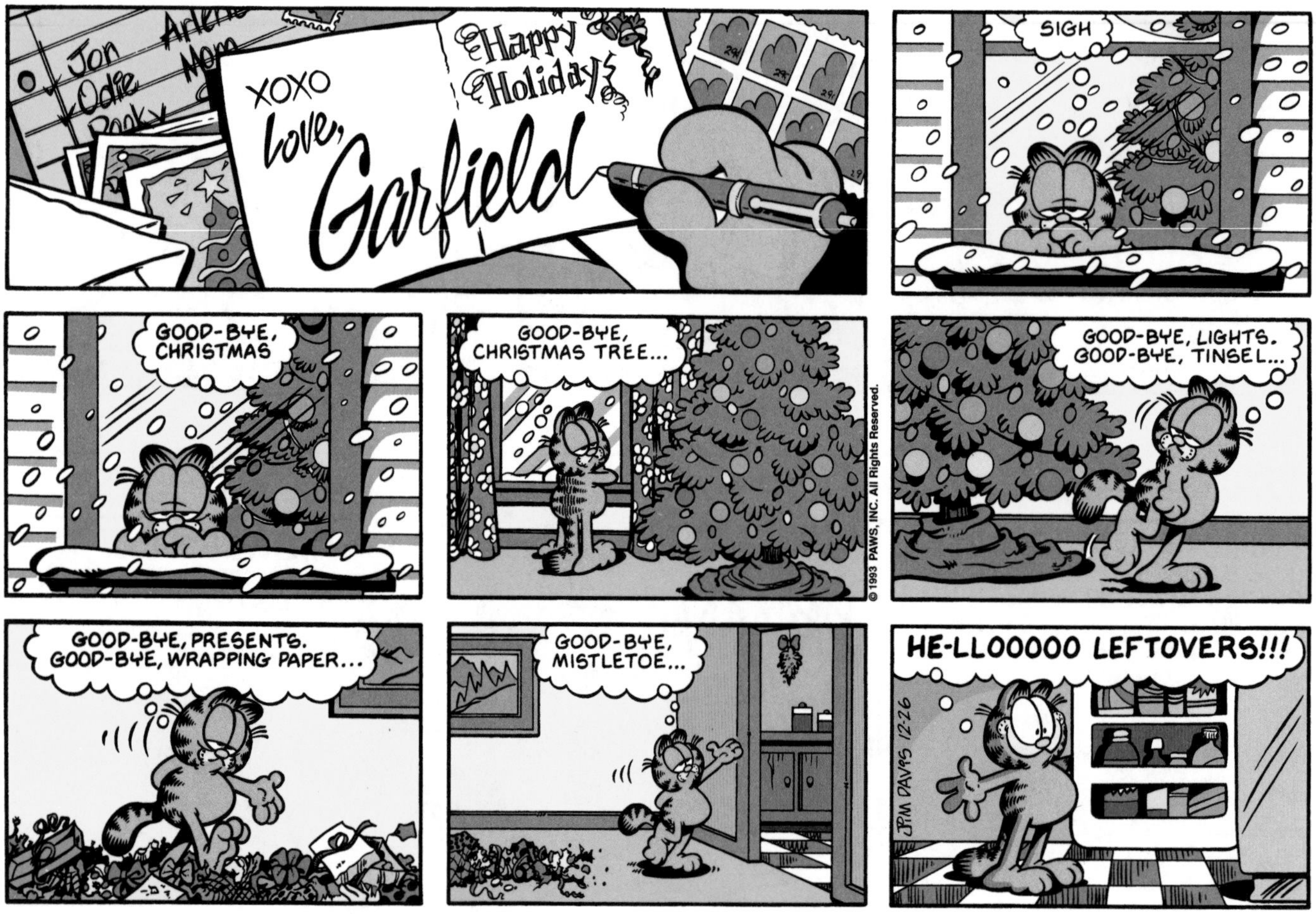
Jon
Odie
Arlene
Mom
XOXO
love,
Garfield
Happy Holidays
SIGH
GOOD-BYE, CHRISTMAS
GOOD-BYE, CHRISTMAS TREE...
© 1993 PAWS, INC. All Rights Reserved.
GOOD-BYE, LIGHTS. GOOD-BYE, TINSEL...
GOOD-BYE, PRESENTS. GOOD-BYE, WRAPPING PAPER...
GOOD-BYE, MISTLETOE...
HE-LLOOOOO LEFTOVERS!!!
JIM DAVIS 12-26

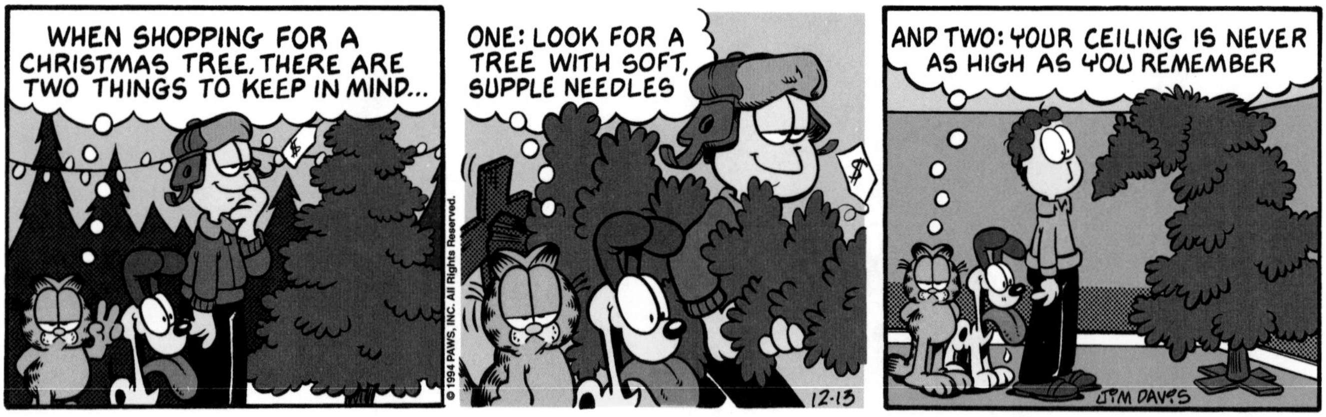
WHEN SHOPPING FOR A CHRISTMAS TREE, THERE ARE TWO THINGS TO KEEP IN MIND...
© 1994 PAWS, INC. All Rights Reserved.
ONE: LOOK FOR A TREE WITH SOFT, SUPPLE NEEDLES
12-13
AND TWO: YOUR CEILING IS NEVER AS HIGH AS YOU REMEMBER
JIM DAVIS

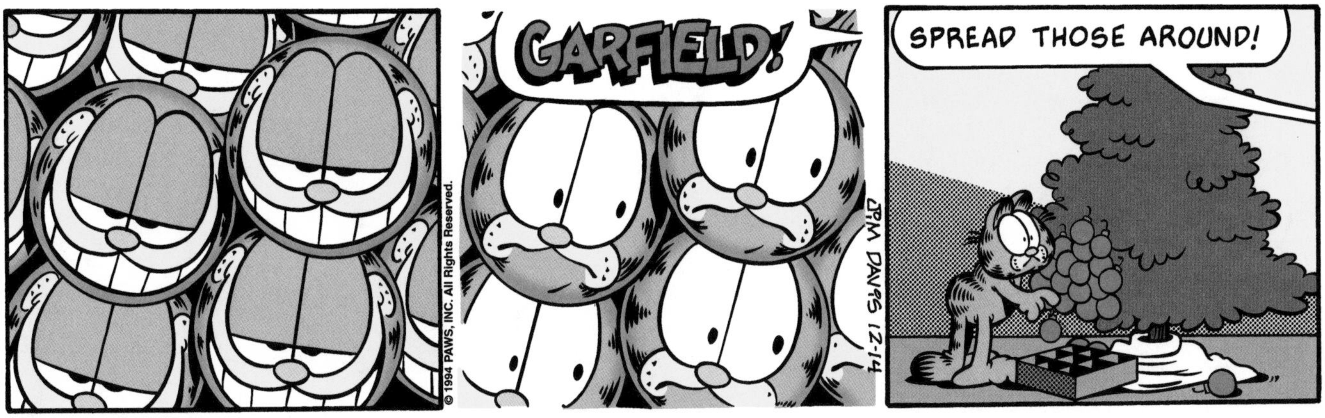

GARFIELD!
SPREAD THOSE AROUND!
© 1994 PAWS, INC. All Rights Reserved.
JIM DAVIS 12-14

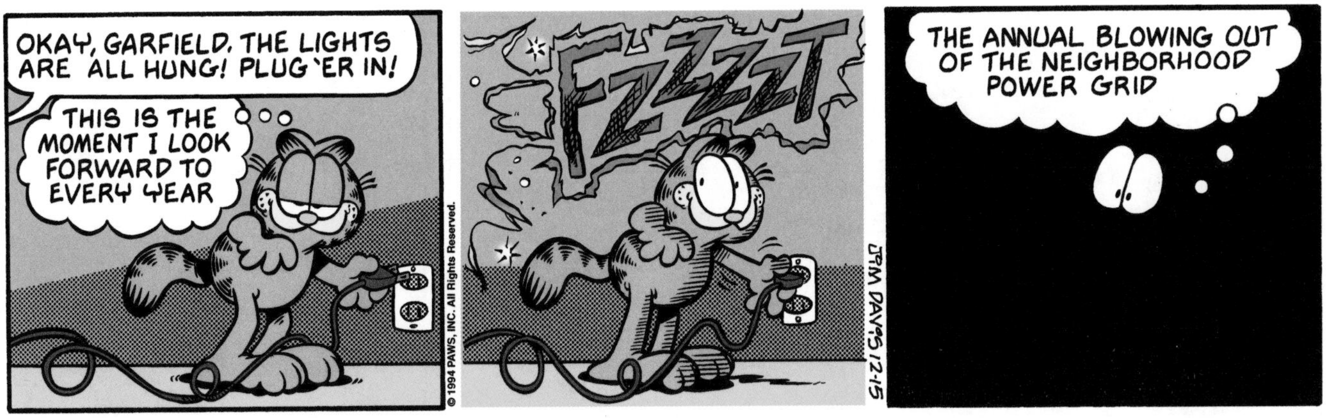

OKAY, GARFIELD, THE LIGHTS ARE ALL HUNG! PLUG'ER IN!
THIS IS THE MOMENT I LOOK FORWARD TO EVERY YEAR
FZZZZT
THE ANNUAL BLOWING OUT OF THE NEIGHBORHOOD POWER GRID
© 1994 PAWS, INC. All Rights Reserved.
JIM DAVIS 12-15

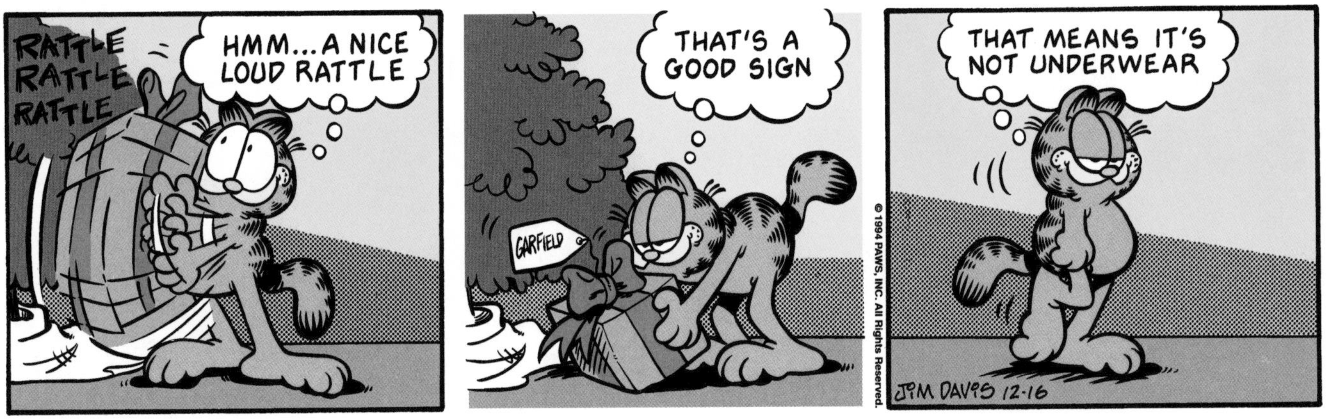

RATTLE RATTLE RATTLE
HMM... A NICE LOUD RATTLE
THAT'S A GOOD SIGN
GARFIELD
THAT MEANS IT'S NOT UNDERWEAR
© 1994 PAWS, INC. All Rights Reserved.
JIM DAVIS 12-16

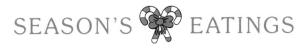

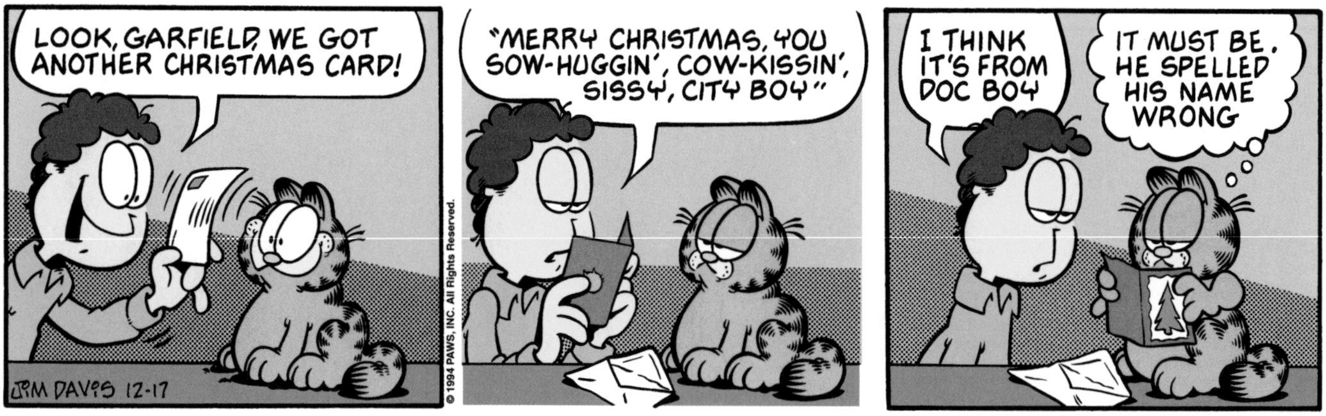
LOOK, GARFIELD, WE GOT ANOTHER CHRISTMAS CARD!
JIM DAVIS 12-17
"MERRY CHRISTMAS, YOU SOW-HUGGIN', COW-KISSIN', SISSY, CITY BOY"
© 1994 PAWS, INC. All Rights Reserved.
I THINK IT'S FROM DOC BOY
IT MUST BE. HE SPELLED HIS NAME WRONG

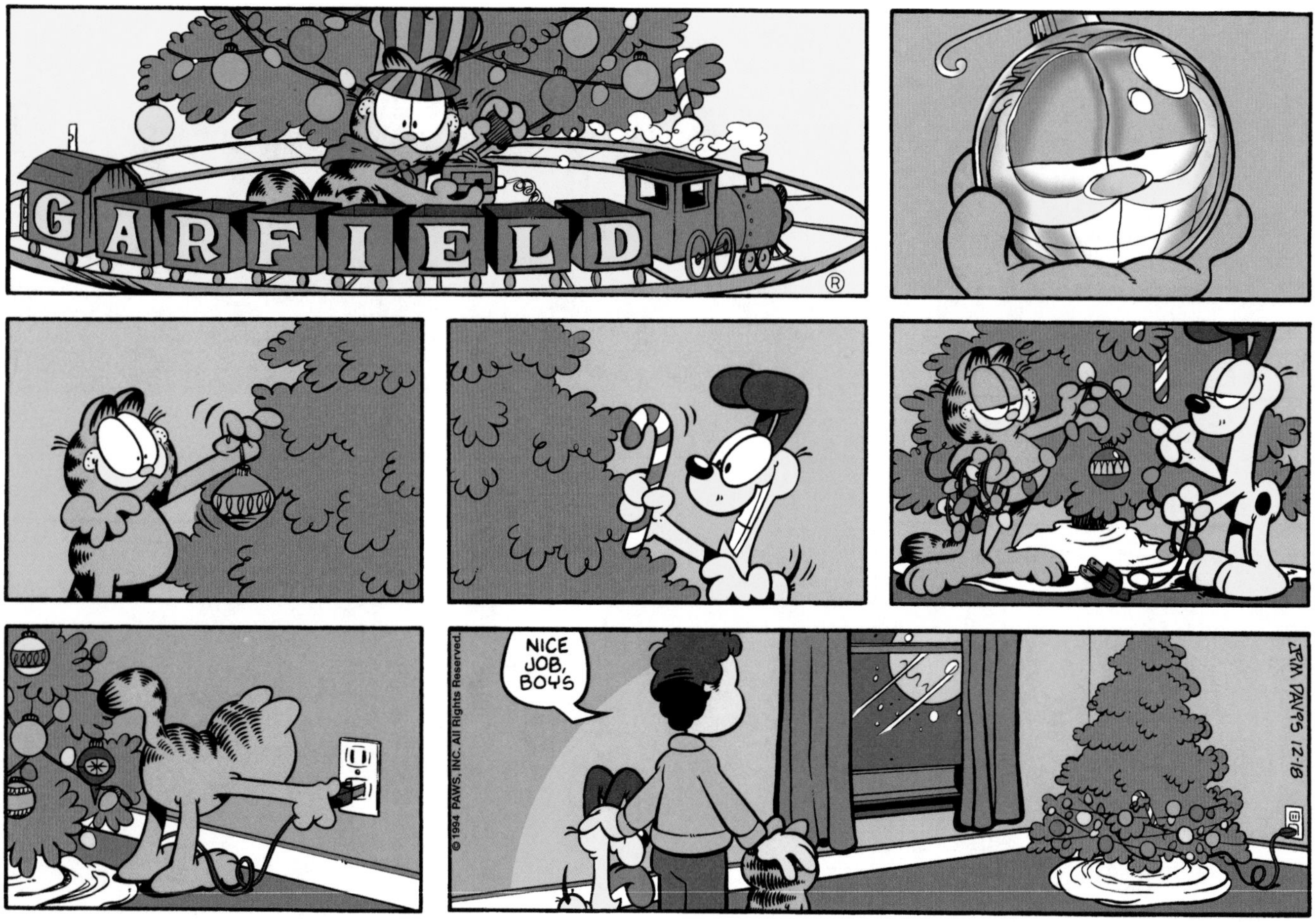
GARFIELD
®
© 1994 PAWS, INC. All Rights Reserved.
NICE JOB, BOYS
JIM DAVIS 12-18

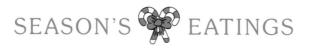

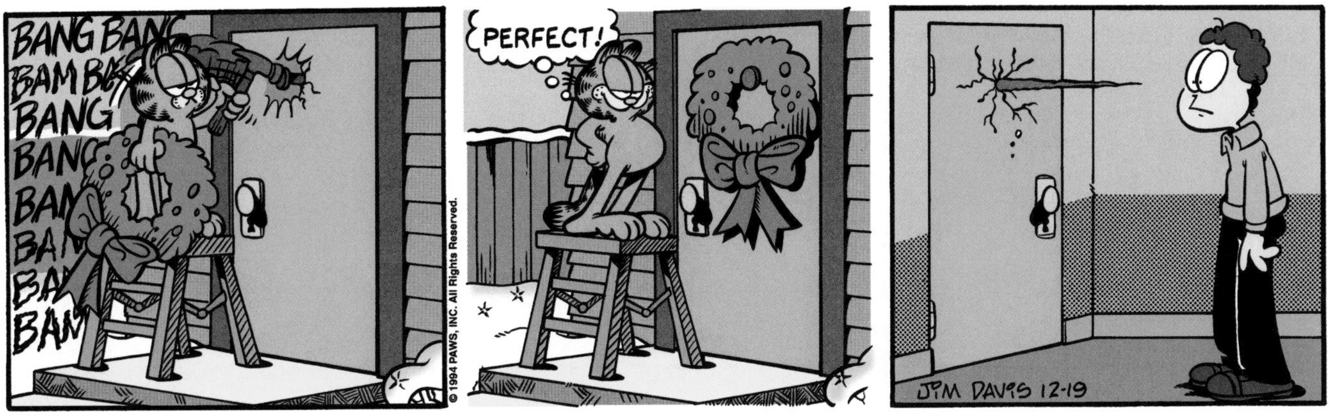
BANG BANG
BANG
PERFECT!
© 1994 PAWS, INC. All Rights Reserved.
JIM DAVIS 12-19

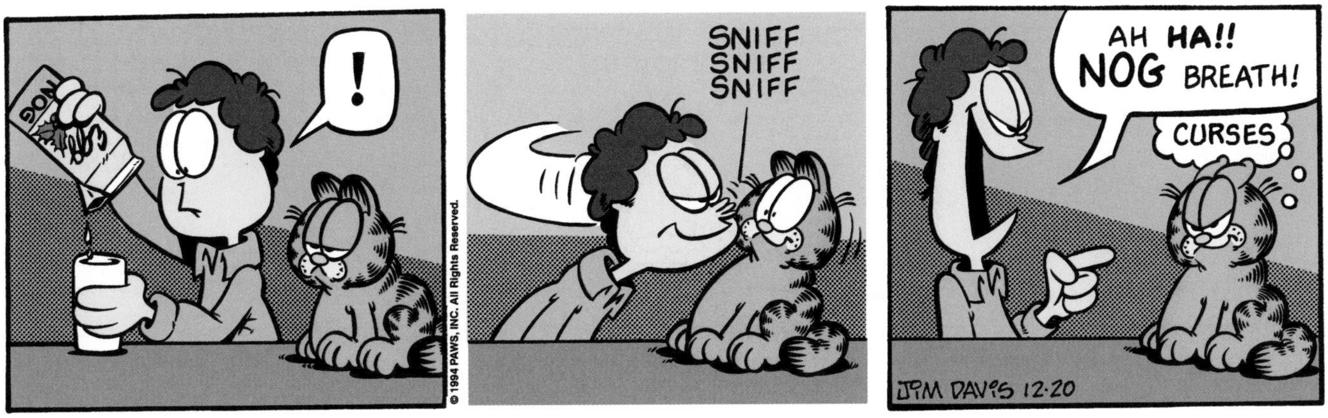
NOG
!
SNIFF
SNIFF
SNIFF
AH HA!! NOG BREATH!
CURSES
© 1994 PAWS, INC. All Rights Reserved.
JIM DAVIS 12-20

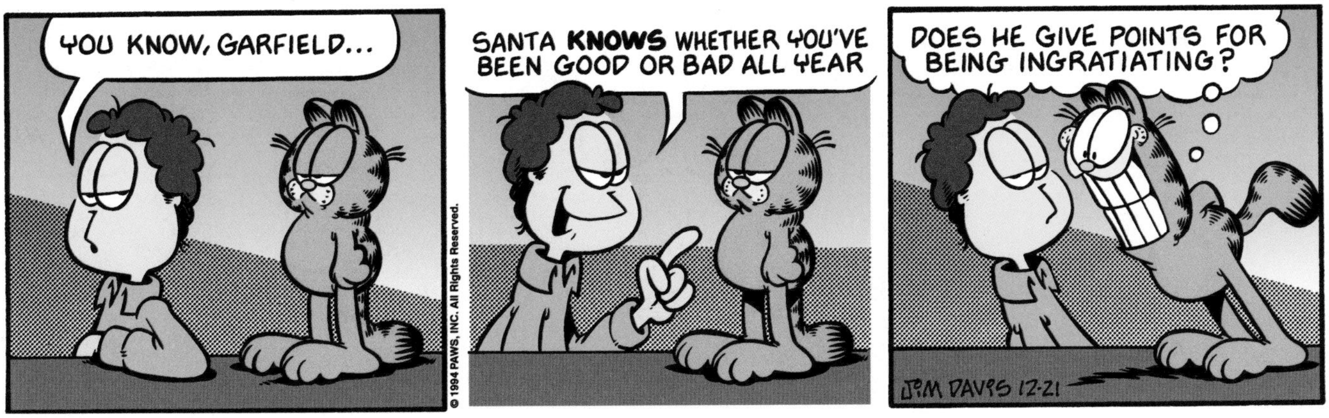
YOU KNOW, GARFIELD...
SANTA KNOWS WHETHER YOU'VE BEEN GOOD OR BAD ALL YEAR
DOES HE GIVE POINTS FOR BEING INGRATIATING?
© 1994 PAWS, INC. All Rights Reserved.
JIM DAVIS 12-21

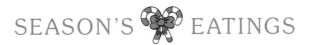

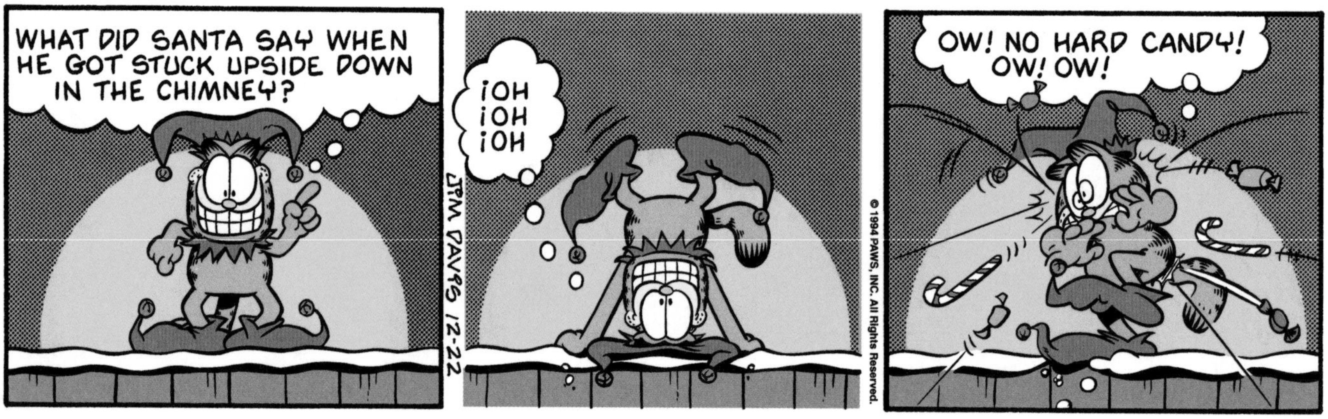
WHAT DID SANTA SAY WHEN HE GOT STUCK UPSIDE DOWN IN THE CHIMNEY?
¡OH ¡OH ¡OH
JIM DAVIS 12-22
© 1994 PAWS, INC. All Rights Reserved.
OW! NO HARD CANDY! OW! OW!

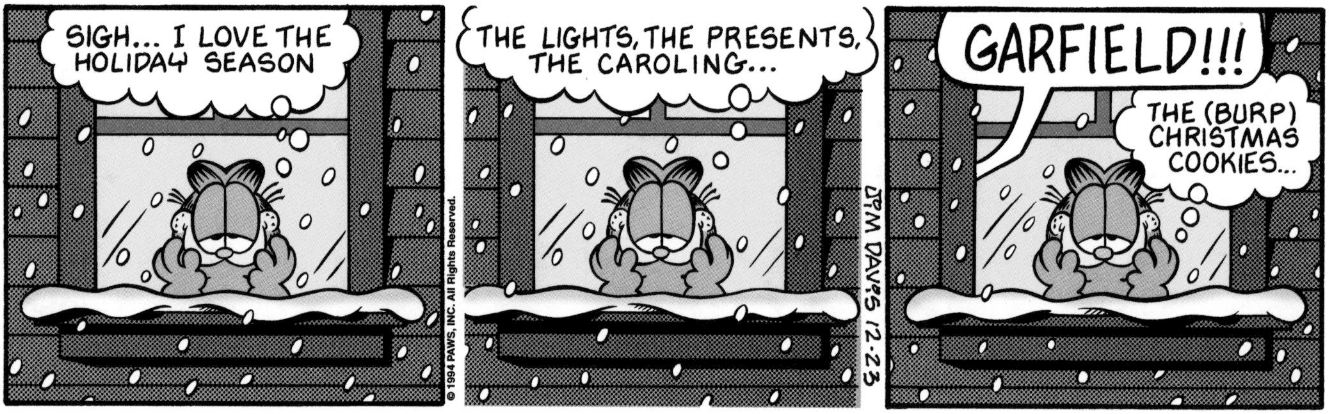
SIGH... I LOVE THE HOLIDAY SEASON
© 1994 PAWS, INC. All Rights Reserved.
THE LIGHTS, THE PRESENTS, THE CAROLING...
JIM DAVIS 12-23
GARFIELD!!!
THE (BURP) CHRISTMAS COOKIES...

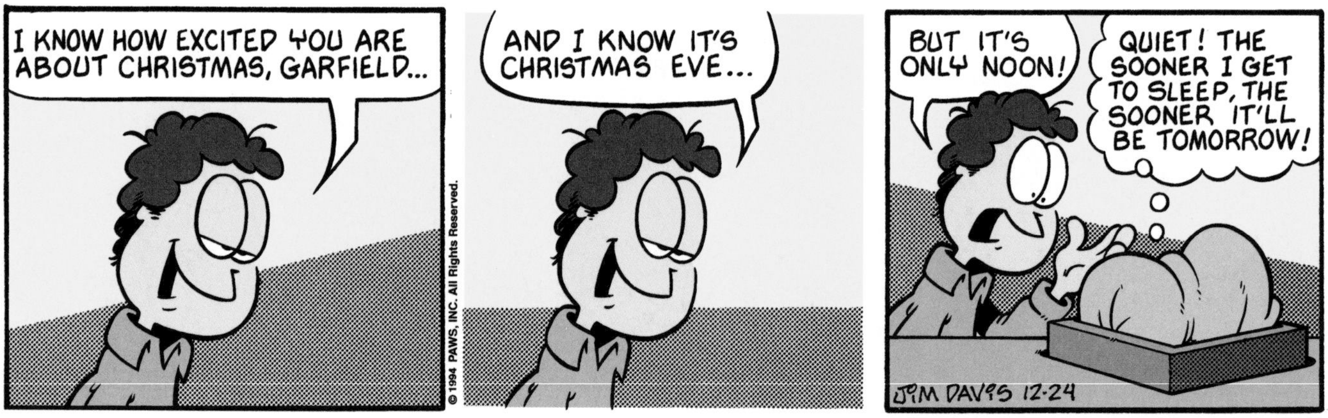
I KNOW HOW EXCITED YOU ARE ABOUT CHRISTMAS, GARFIELD...
© 1994 PAWS, INC. All Rights Reserved.
AND I KNOW IT'S CHRISTMAS EVE...
BUT IT'S ONLY NOON!
QUIET! THE SOONER I GET TO SLEEP, THE SOONER IT'LL BE TOMORROW!
JIM DAVIS 12-24

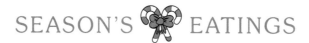

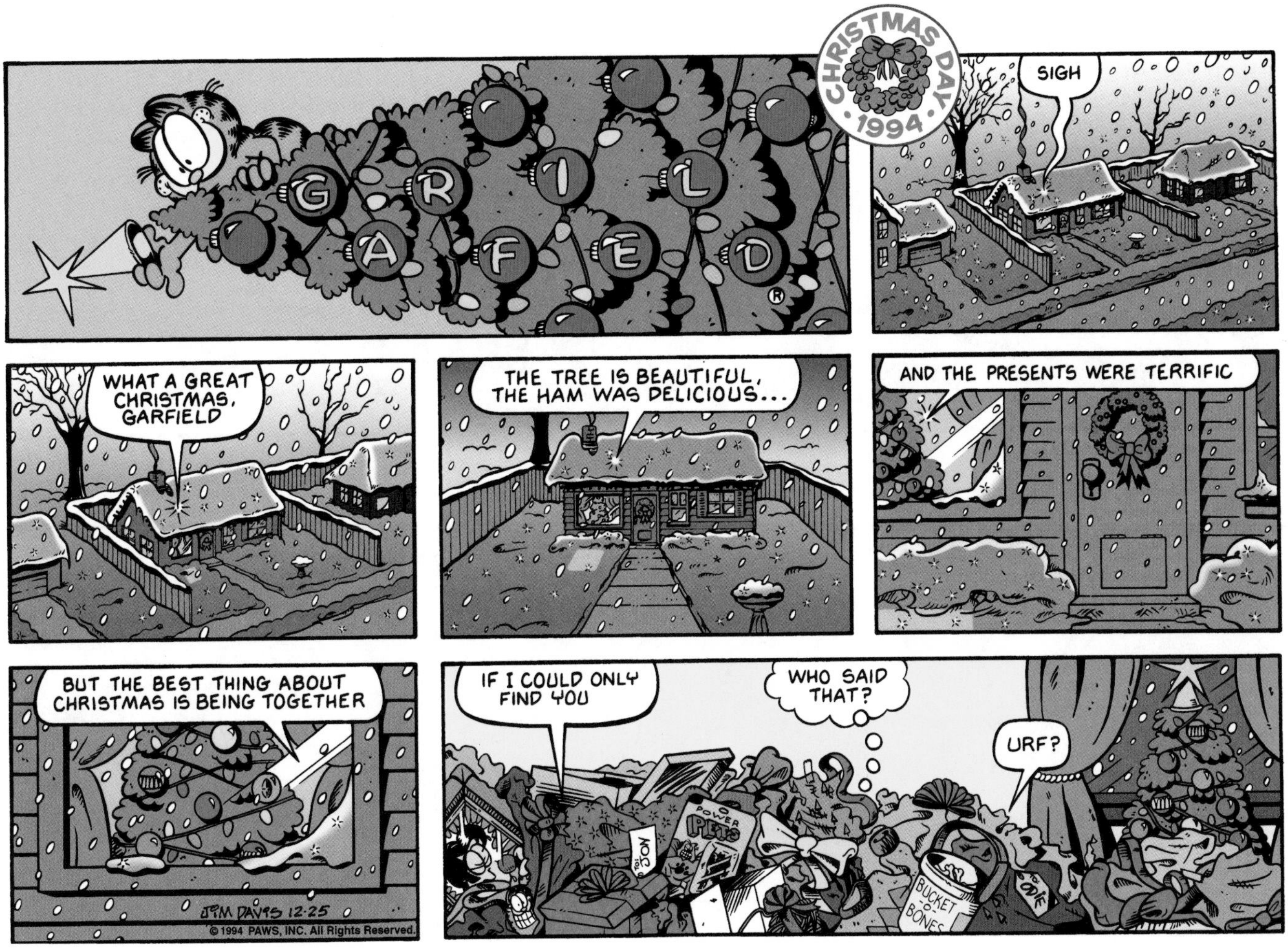
GARFIELD
CHRISTMAS DAY 1994
SIGH
WHAT A GREAT CHRISTMAS, GARFIELD
THE TREE IS BEAUTIFUL, THE HAM WAS DELICIOUS...
AND THE PRESENTS WERE TERRIFIC
BUT THE BEST THING ABOUT CHRISTMAS IS BEING TOGETHER
JIM DAVIS 12-25
© 1994 PAWS, INC. All Rights Reserved.
IF I COULD ONLY FIND YOU
WHO SAID THAT?
URF?
POWER PETS
TO: JON
BUCKET -O- BONES
ODIE

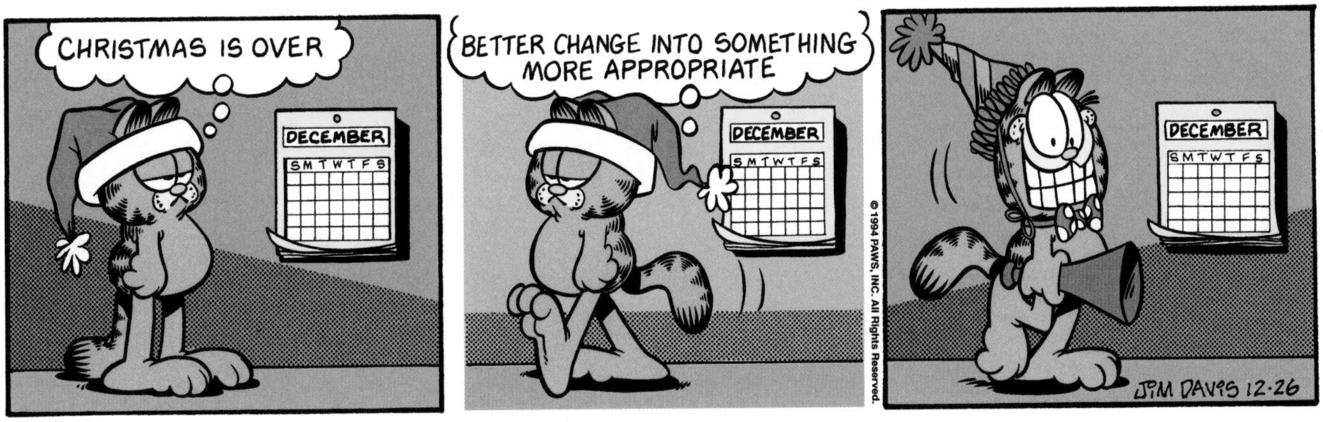
CHRISTMAS IS OVER
DECEMBER
S M T W T F S
BETTER CHANGE INTO SOMETHING MORE APPROPRIATE
DECEMBER
S M T W T F S
© 1994 PAWS, INC. All Rights Reserved.
DECEMBER
S M T W T F S
JIM DAVIS 12-26

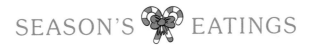

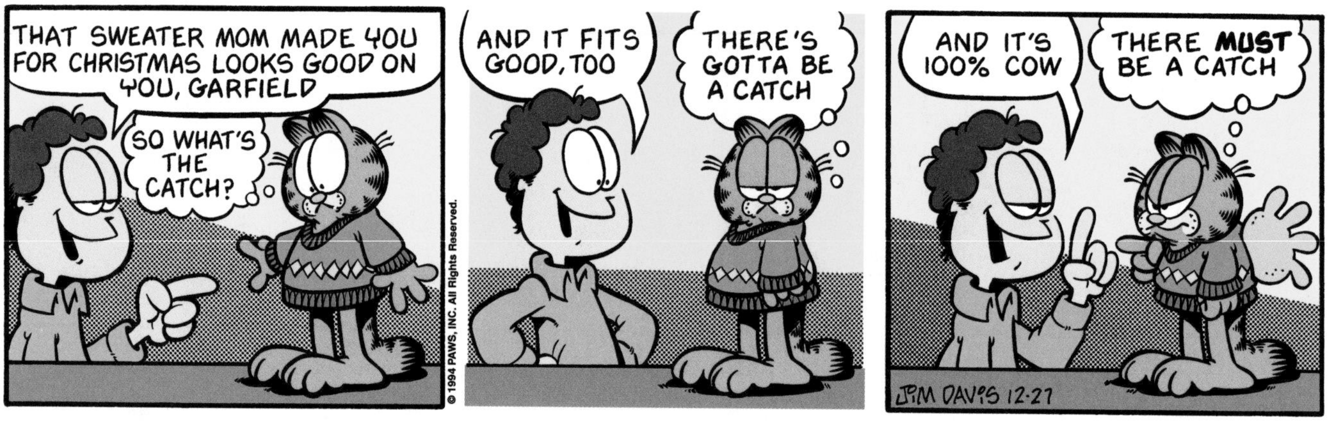
THAT SWEATER MOM MADE YOU FOR CHRISTMAS LOOKS GOOD ON YOU, GARFIELD
SO WHAT'S THE CATCH?
AND IT FITS GOOD, TOO
THERE'S GOTTA BE A CATCH
AND IT'S 100% COW
THERE MUST BE A CATCH
© 1994 PAWS, INC. All Rights Reserved.
JIM DAVIS 12-27

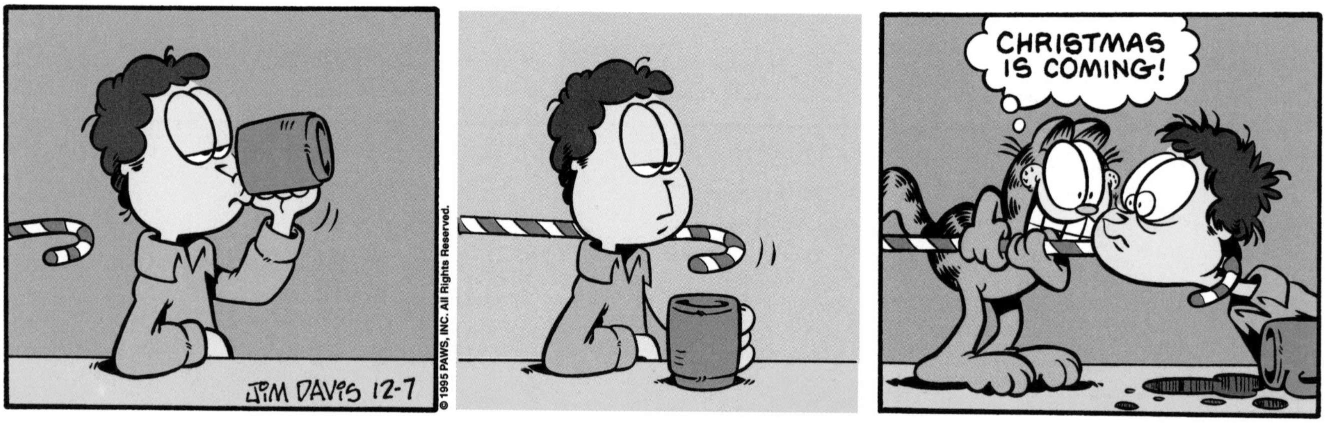
JIM DAVIS 12-7
© 1995 PAWS, INC. All Rights Reserved.
CHRISTMAS IS COMING!

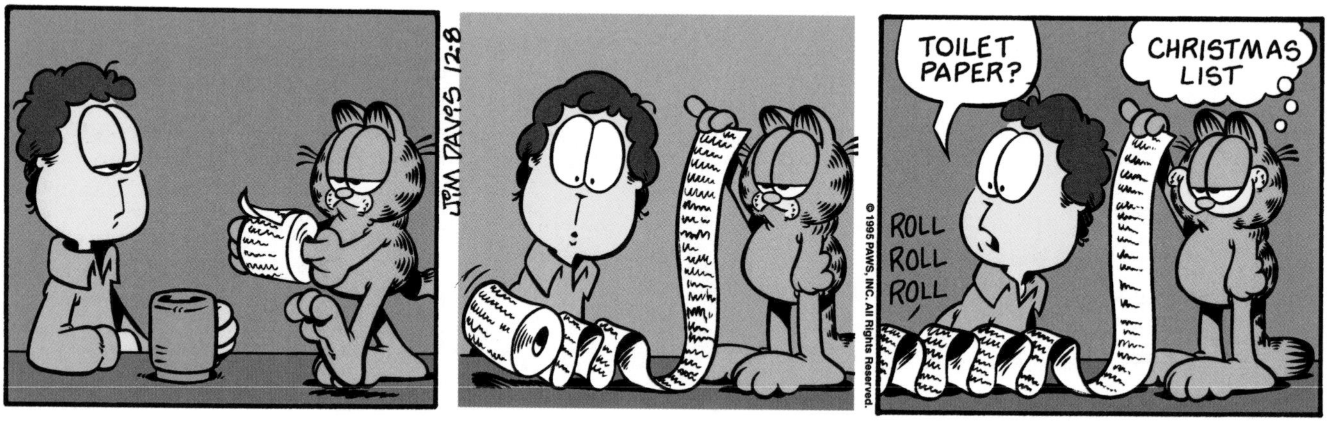
JIM DAVIS 12-8
TOILET PAPER?
CHRISTMAS LIST
ROLL
ROLL
ROLL
© 1995 PAWS, INC. All Rights Reserved.

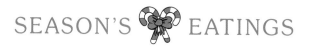

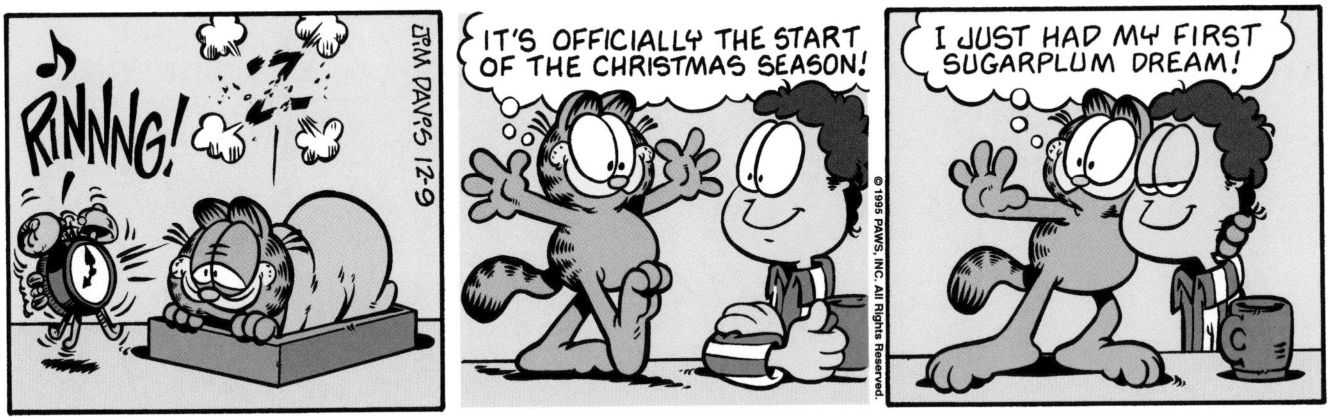
RINNNG!
JIM DAVIS 12-9
IT'S OFFICIALLY THE START OF THE CHRISTMAS SEASON!
© 1995 PAWS, INC. All Rights Reserved.
I JUST HAD MY FIRST SUGARPLUM DREAM!

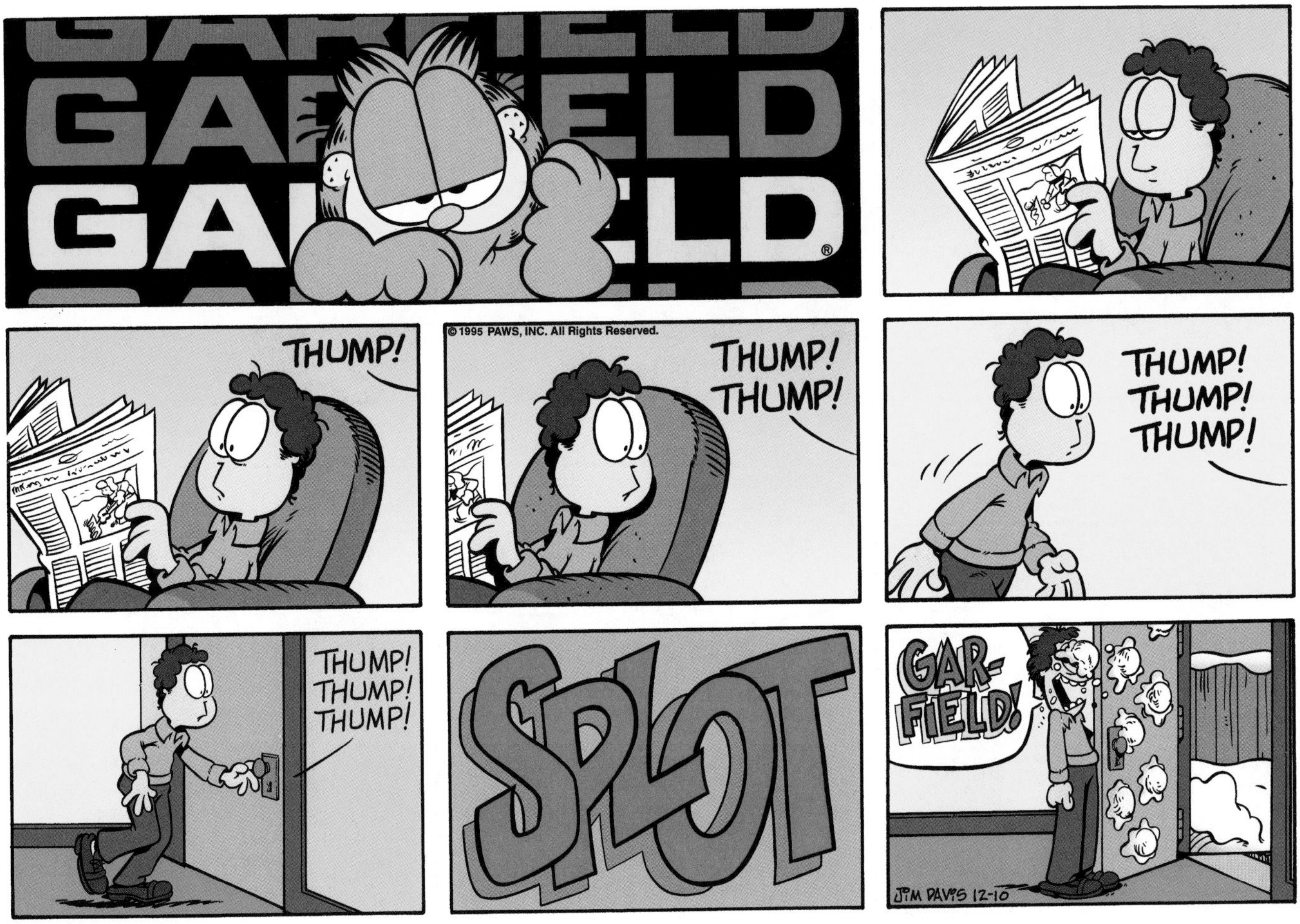
THUMP!
© 1995 PAWS, INC. All Rights Reserved.
THUMP! THUMP!
THUMP! THUMP! THUMP!
THUMP! THUMP! THUMP!
SPLOT
GAR-FIELD!
JIM DAVIS 12-10

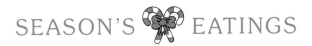

JON, GUESS WHAT I FOUND!
IT'S A CHRISTMAS STARTER KIT!
© 1995 PAWS, INC. All Rights Reserved.
JIM DAVIS 12-11
ALL YOU ADD IS THE TREE

THERE ARE SO MANY NICE TREES TO CHOOSE FROM
STMAS TREES
© 1995 PAWS, INC. All Rights Reserved.
I CAN'T DECIDE WHICH ONE I LIKE...
NEITHER CAN ODIE
JIM DAVIS
HE LIKES THEM ALL
12-12

ONE...TWO... THREE... PULL!
JIM DAVIS 12-13
MAYBE I SHOULD HAVE PULLED IT THROUGH THE DOOR THE OTHER WAY
© 1995 PAWS, INC. All Rights Reserved.
GEE, YOU THINK SO, EINSTEIN?

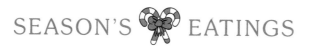

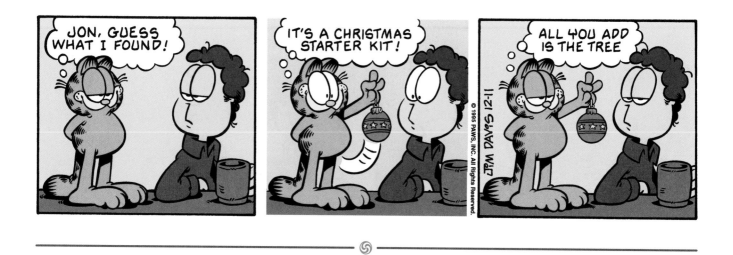

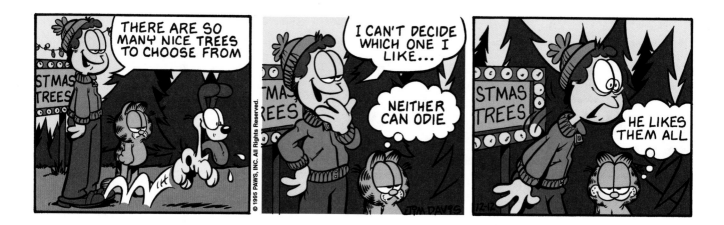

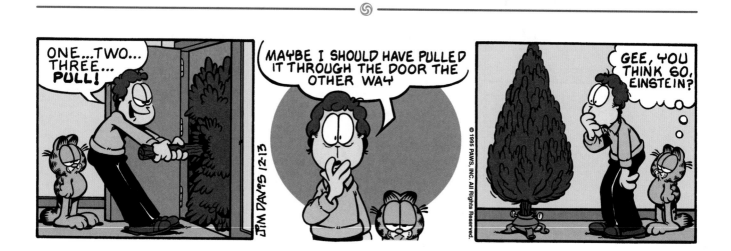

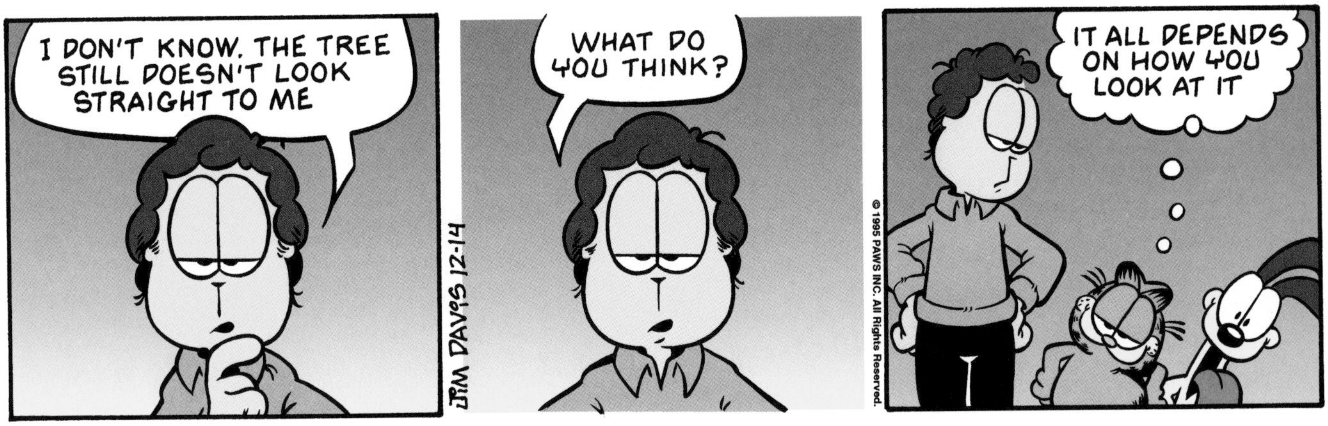
I DON'T KNOW. THE TREE STILL DOESN'T LOOK STRAIGHT TO ME
JIM DAVIS 12-14
WHAT DO YOU THINK?
© 1995 PAWS INC. All Rights Reserved.
IT ALL DEPENDS ON HOW YOU LOOK AT IT

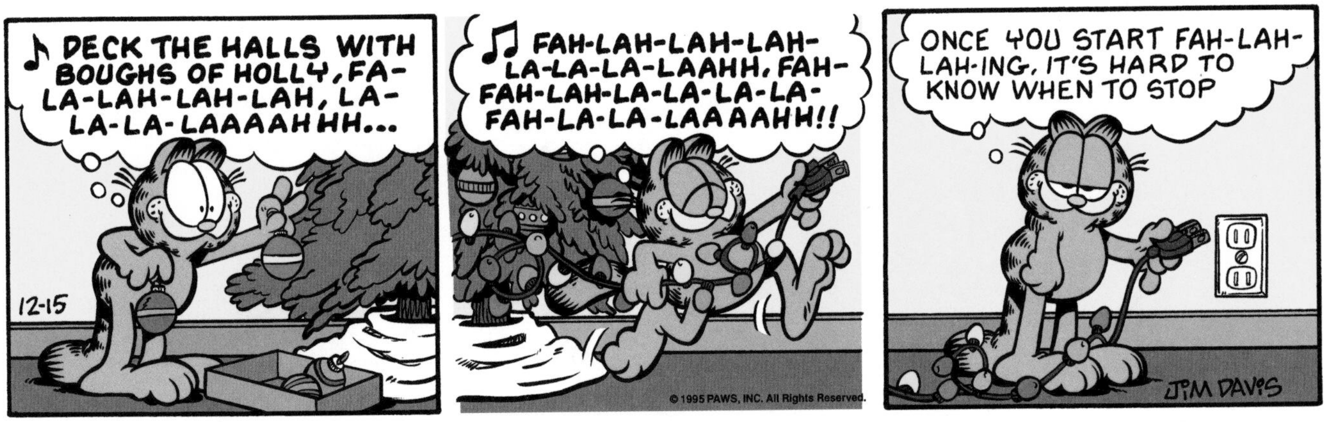
♪ DECK THE HALLS WITH BOUGHS OF HOLLY, FA-LA-LAH-LAH-LAH, LA-LA-LA-LAAAAHHH...
12-15
♫ FAH-LAH-LAH-LAH-LA-LA-LA-LAAHH, FAH-FAH-LAH-LA-LA-LA-LA-FAH-LA-LA-LAAAAHH!!
© 1995 PAWS, INC. All Rights Reserved.
ONCE YOU START FAH-LAH-LAH-ING, IT'S HARD TO KNOW WHEN TO STOP
JIM DAVIS

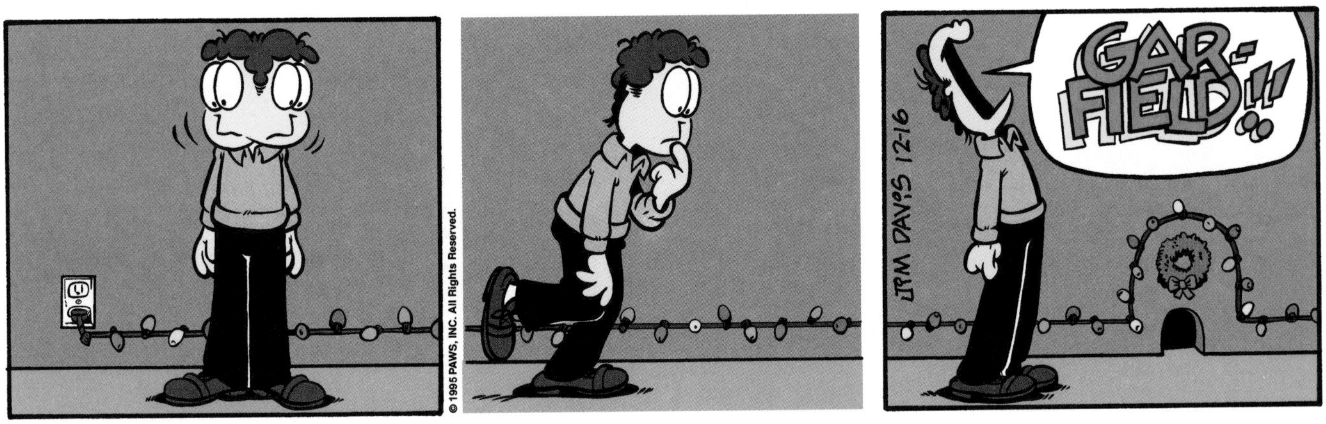
© 1995 PAWS, INC. All Rights Reserved.
JIM DAVIS 12-16
GAR-FIELD!!!

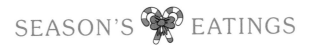

Top 10 Presents Garfield Wants for Christmas

10 **Combination** birdbath/deep fryer

9 **Keys to** Santa's sleigh

8 **Snoopy** dart board

7 **Wading pool** filled with gravy

6 **Tongue-reduction** surgery for Odie

5 **Remote-controlled** refrigerator

4 **Six-pack** of slave dogs

3 **His body** weight in catnip

2 **"Lassie Falls Down a** Mine Shaft" on DVD

1 **A partridge in a pear** tree, with a side of fries

Top 10 Presents Jon Wants for Christmas

10 Someone to kiss under the mistletoe besides Odie

9 Autographed photo of the Teletubbies

8 "Great Moments in Figure Skating" on DVD

7 Digital wireless nose-hair clippers

6 New pair of bunny slippers

5 Subscription to "Macho Stamp Collector Monthly" magazine

4 His mother's top-secret recipe for divinity fudge

3 Bigger Plexiglas container to hold belly-button lint collection

2 "Born 2B Wild" temporary tattoo

1 Accordion lessons for life

BIG FAT MERRY HOLIDAY TIPS

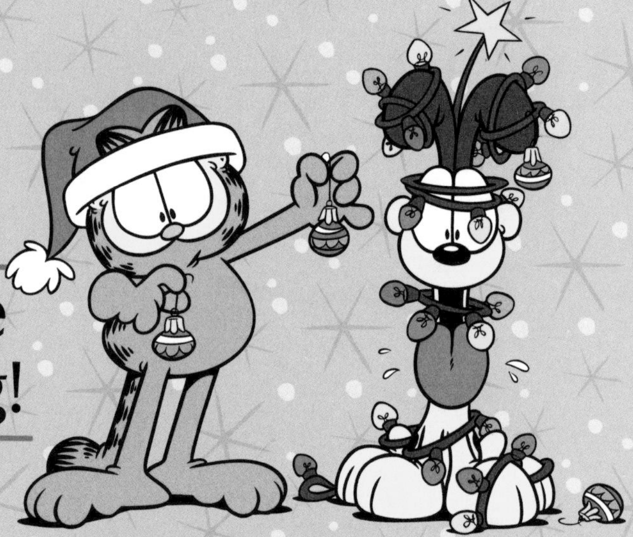

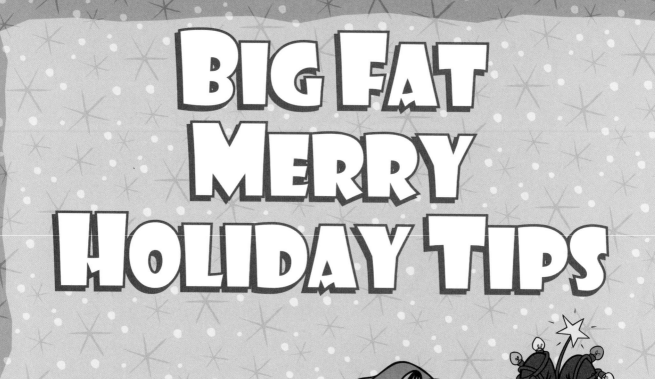

Don't just deck the halls...deck the dog!

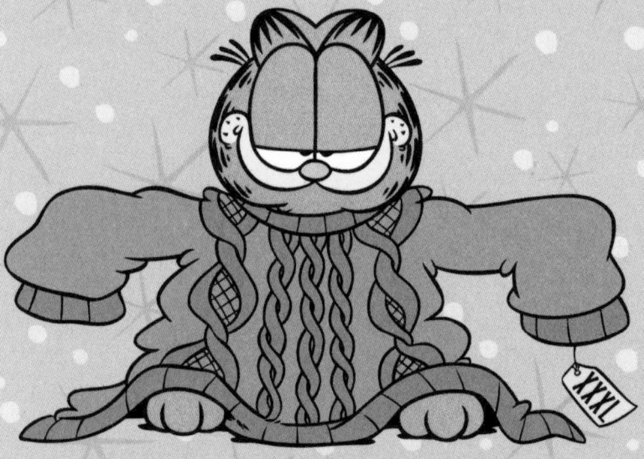
XXXL

Tell them your size!

Take a long winter's nap. Better yet, hibernate!

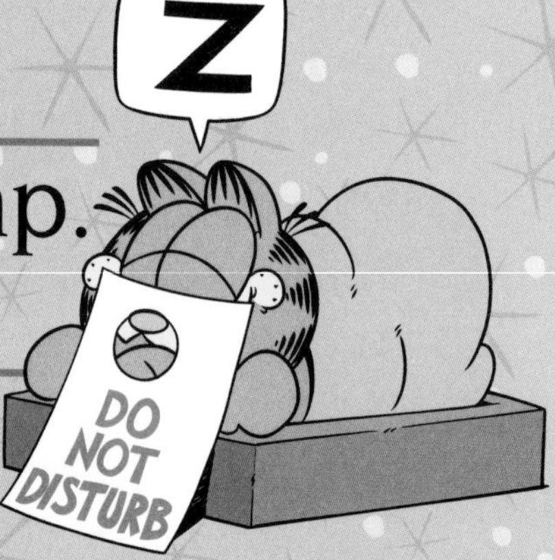
Z
DO NOT DISTURB

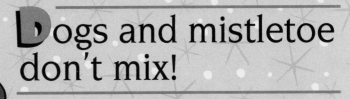

Dogs and mistletoe don't mix!

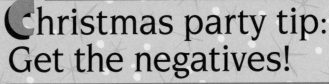

The best presents come gift-boxed!

Christmas party tip: Get the negatives!

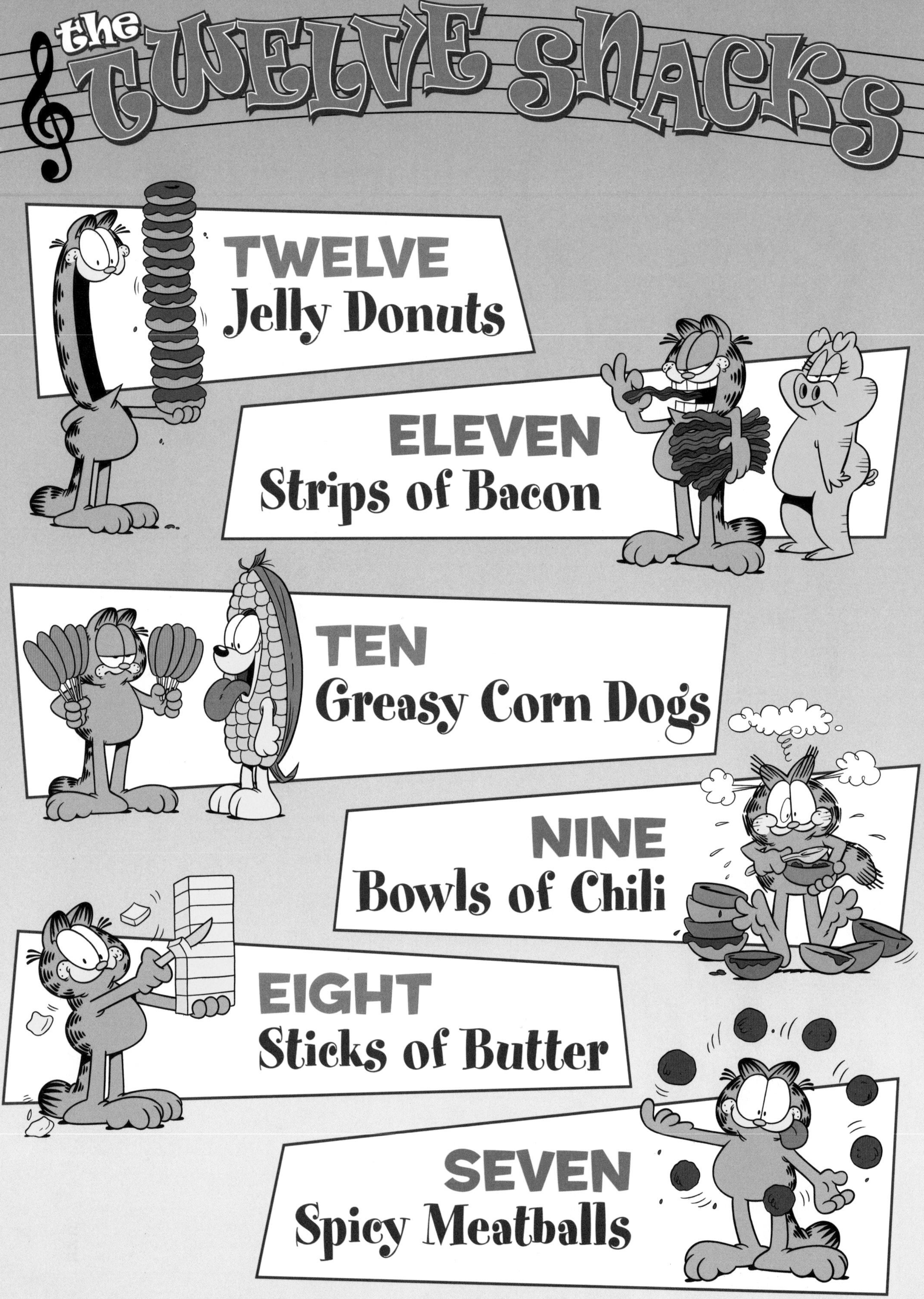
the TWELVE SNACKS
TWELVE
Jelly Donuts
ELEVEN
Strips of Bacon
TEN
Greasy Corn Dogs
NINE
Bowls of Chili
EIGHT
Sticks of Butter
SEVEN
Spicy Meatballs

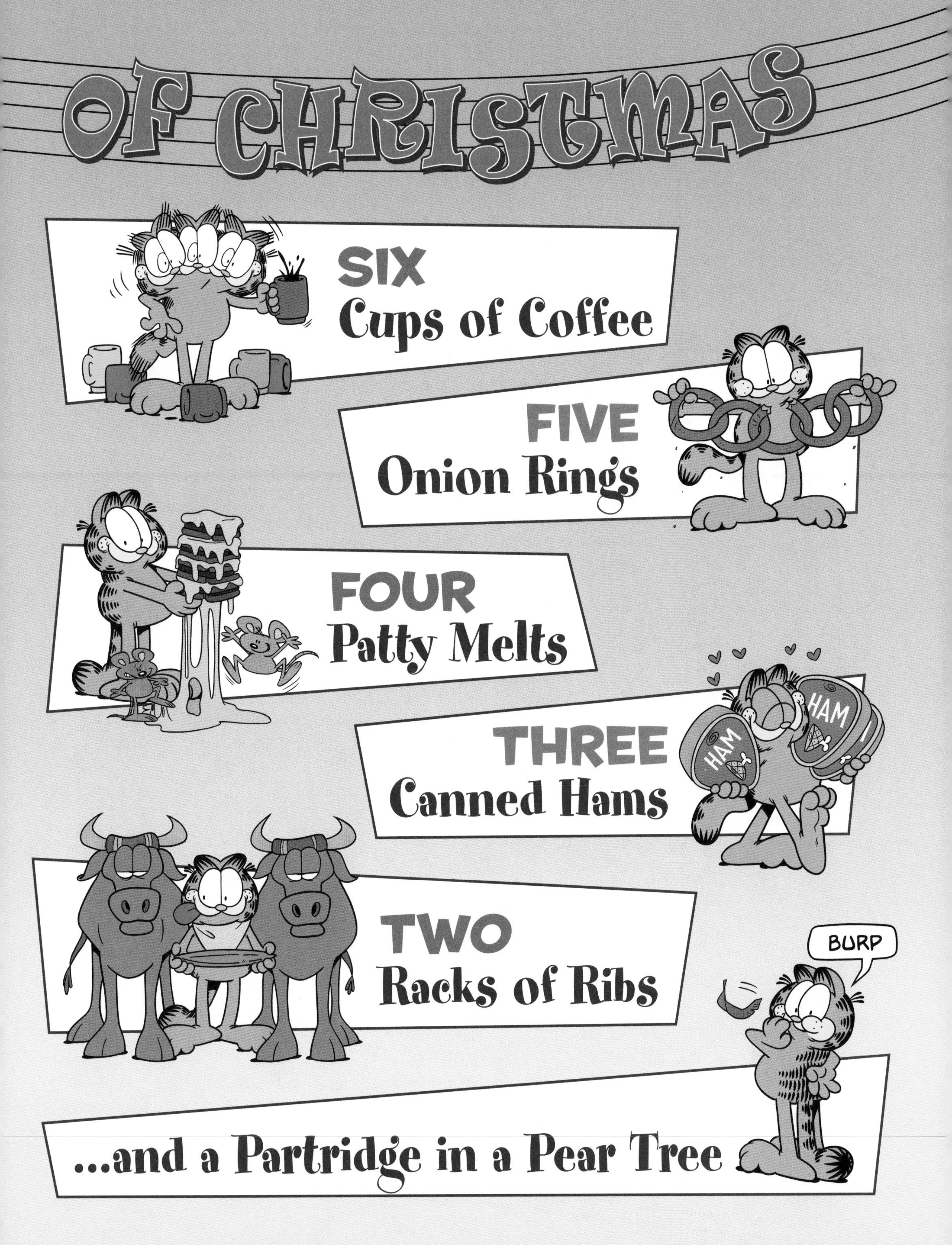
OF CHRISTMAS
SIX
Cups of Coffee
FIVE
Onion Rings
FOUR
Patty Melts
THREE
Canned Hams
HAM
HAM
TWO
Racks of Ribs
BURP
...and a Partridge in a Pear Tree

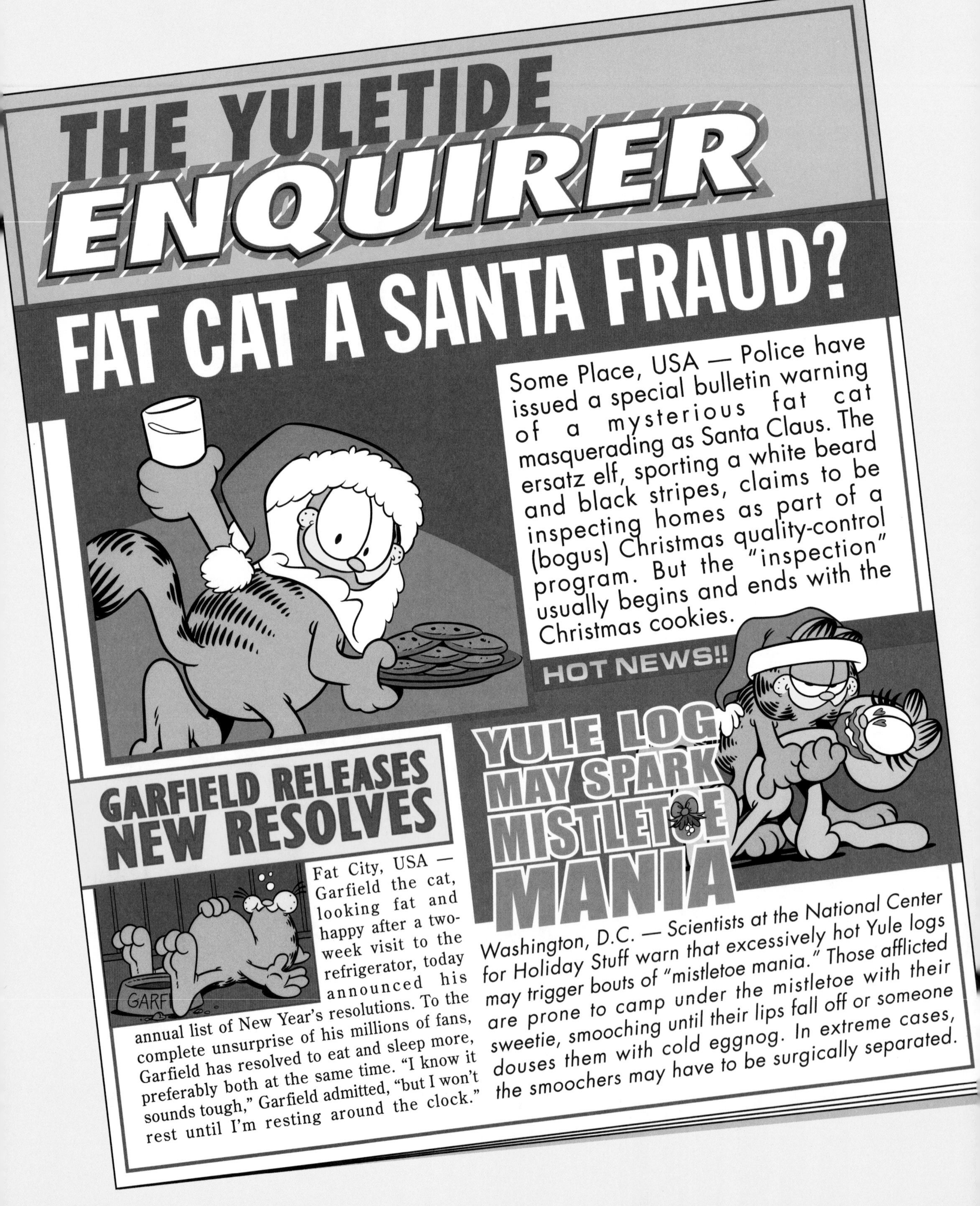

THE YULETIDE ENQUIRER

FAT CAT A SANTA FRAUD?

Some Place, USA — Police have issued a special bulletin warning of a mysterious fat cat masquerading as Santa Claus. The ersatz elf, sporting a white beard and black stripes, claims to be inspecting homes as part of a (bogus) Christmas quality-control program. But the "inspection" usually begins and ends with the Christmas cookies.

HOT NEWS!!

GARFIELD RELEASES NEW RESOLVES

Fat City, USA — Garfield the cat, looking fat and happy after a two-week visit to the refrigerator, today announced his annual list of New Year's resolutions. To the complete unsurprise of his millions of fans, Garfield has resolved to eat and sleep more, preferably both at the same time. "I know it sounds tough," Garfield admitted, "but I won't rest until I'm resting around the clock."

YULE LOG MAY SPARK MISTLETOE MANIA

Washington, D.C. — Scientists at the National Center for Holiday Stuff warn that excessively hot Yule logs may trigger bouts of "mistletoe mania." Those afflicted are prone to camp under the mistletoe with their sweetie, smooching until their lips fall off or someone douses them with cold eggnog. In extreme cases, the smoochers may have to be surgically separated.

MISTLETOE TATTLER

WE KISS AND TELL!

FRUITCAKE CONKS CAT

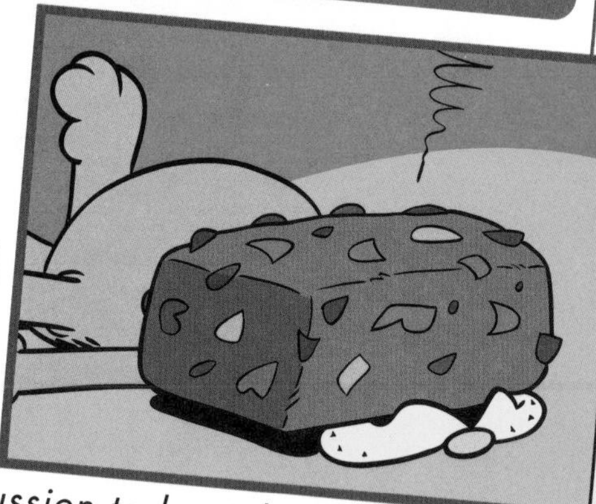

Muncie, IN — Garfield, a local feline, suffered a mild concussion today when he pulled a fruitcake off a table onto his head. "My aunt sends me a fruitcake every Christmas," explained Jon Arbuckle, the cat's owner. "Garfield mistook it for something edible."

Fruitcake, among the hardest substances known to man, causes numerous injuries every holiday season.

FARMER SPOTS RARE REINDOG

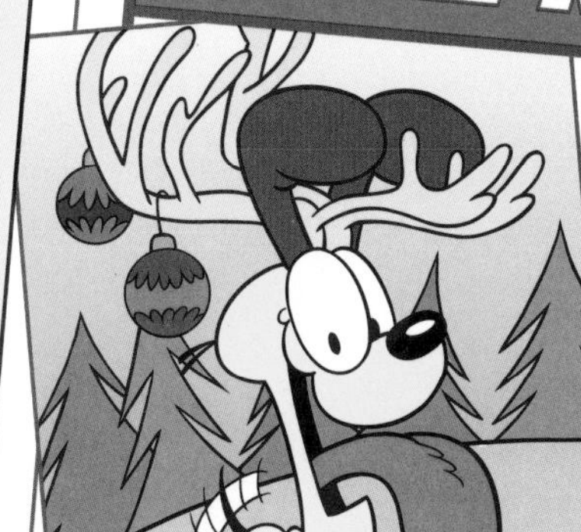

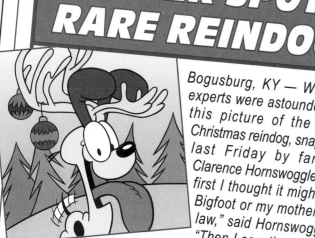

Bogusburg, KY — Wildlife experts were astounded by this picture of the rare Christmas reindog, snapped last Friday by farmer Clarence Hornswoggle. "At first I thought it might be Bigfoot or my mother-in-law," said Hornswoggle. "Then I saw the antlers. Wanna buy the movie rights?"

Reindogs are most often sighted in December. In the wee hours. After a lot of eggnog.

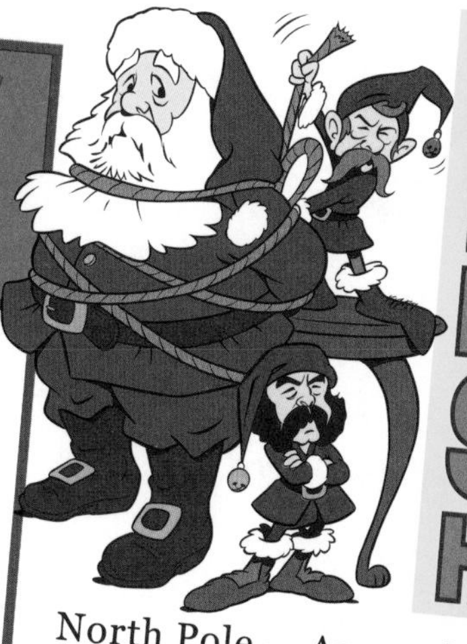

UNHAPPY ELVES HOLD SANTA HOSTAGE

North Pole — Angry elves took Santa Claus hostage today, barricading themselves inside their North Pole workshop. The elves are upset about next season's increased production quotas, and the fact that none of them can reach the new soap dispensers in the rest rooms. While they have not yet released an official list of demands, it is almost certain to be short.

IF GARFIELD REPLACED SANTA, GARFIELD WOULD...

Equip the sleigh with a snack bar and in-flight movies

Outlaw fruitcakes

Move operations from the North Pole to Miami Beach

Sell the names on his "naughty" list to telemarketers

Give those on his "nice" list a bonus canned ham

Turn Rudolph & Co. into reindeer stew

Call for the mandatory widening of all chimneys

Prefer you leave out a T-bone steak and curly fries instead of milk and cookies

Least Favorite Christmas Books

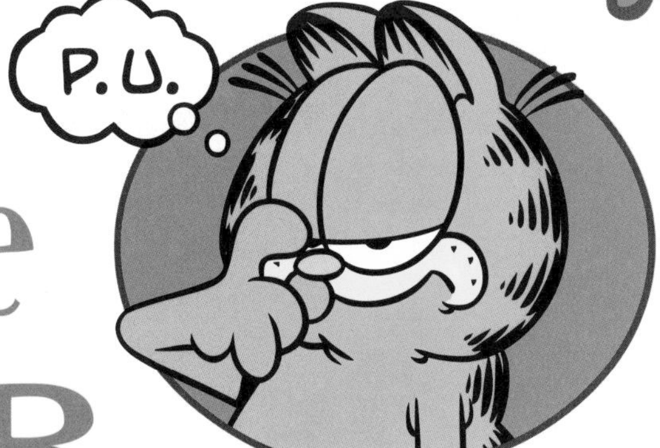
P.U.

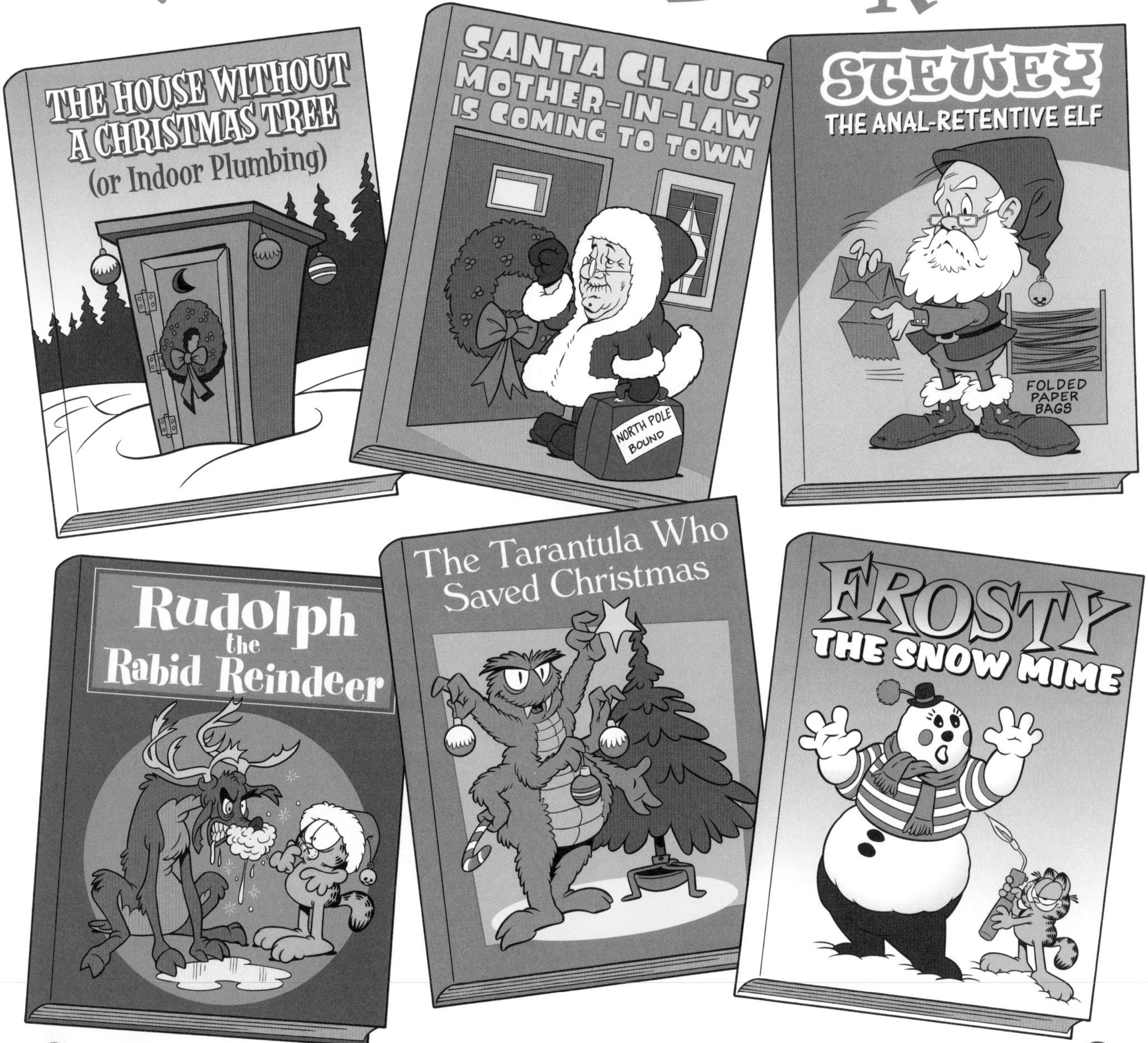
THE HOUSE WITHOUT A CHRISTMAS TREE
(or Indoor Plumbing)
SANTA CLAUS' MOTHER-IN-LAW IS COMING TO TOWN
NORTH POLE BOUND
STEWEY
THE ANAL-RETENTIVE ELF
FOLDED PAPER BAGS
Rudolph the Rabid Reindeer
The Tarantula Who Saved Christmas
FROSTY
THE SNOW MIME

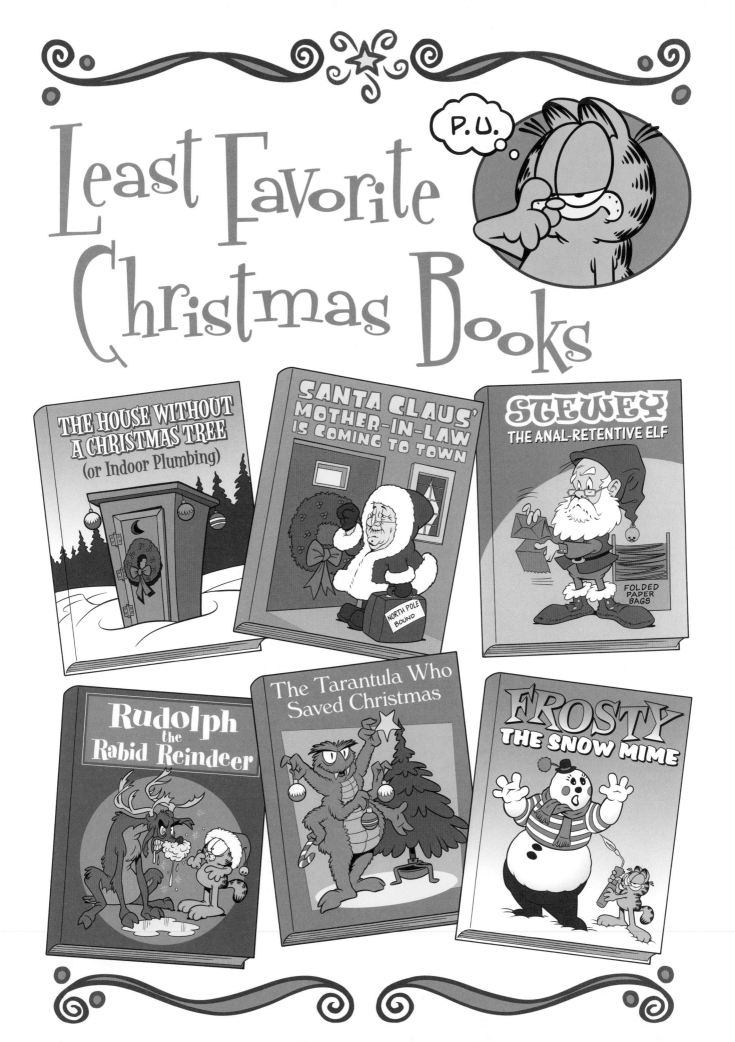

MORE BIG FAT MERRY HOLIDAY TIPS

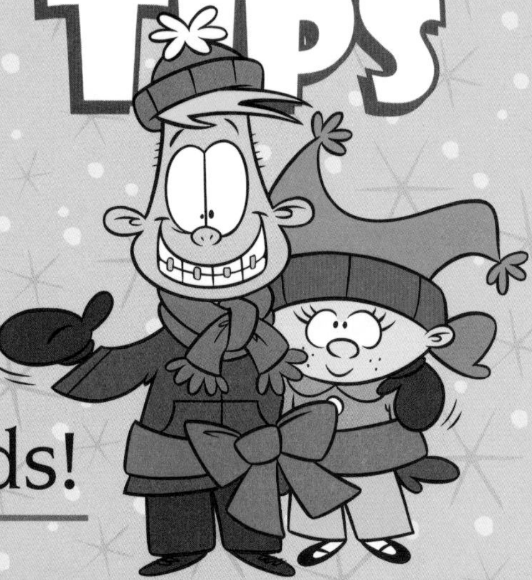

Don't send pictures of your kids. Send your kids!

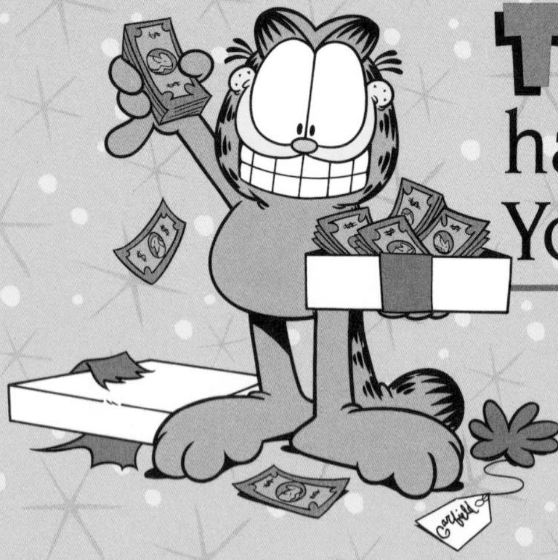

Tell people they don't have to buy you a gift. You accept cash!

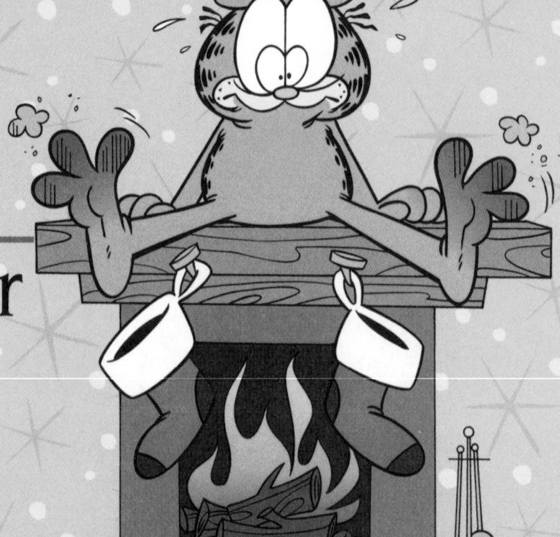

Before hanging your stockings by the fireplace...take your feet out of them!

Christmas shopping:
Only the strong survive!

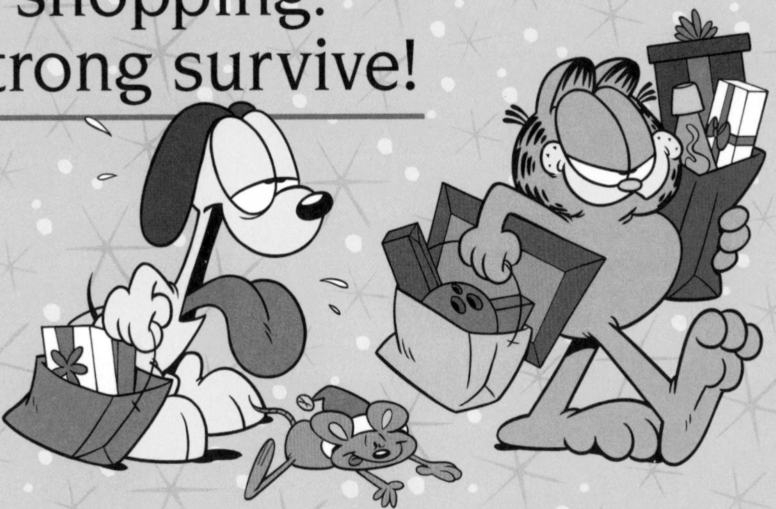

Those loud neckties
make great tree trimmers!

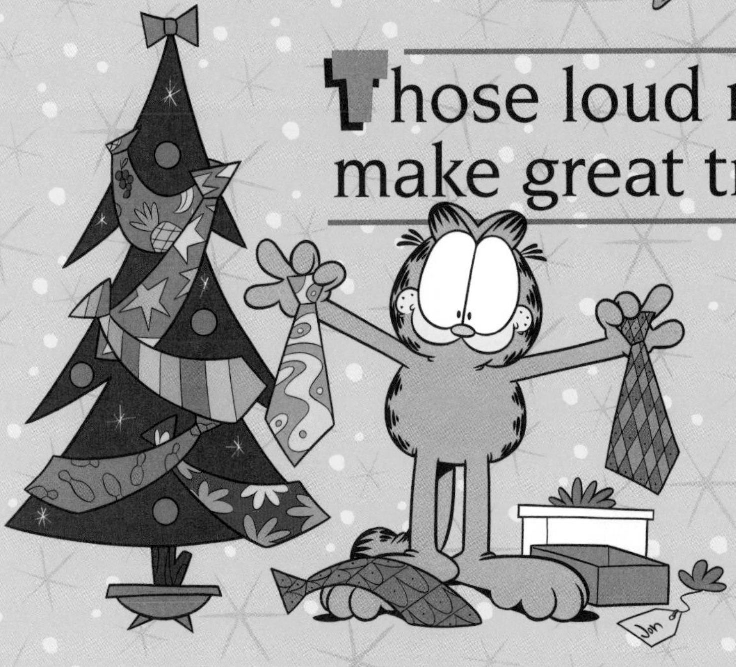

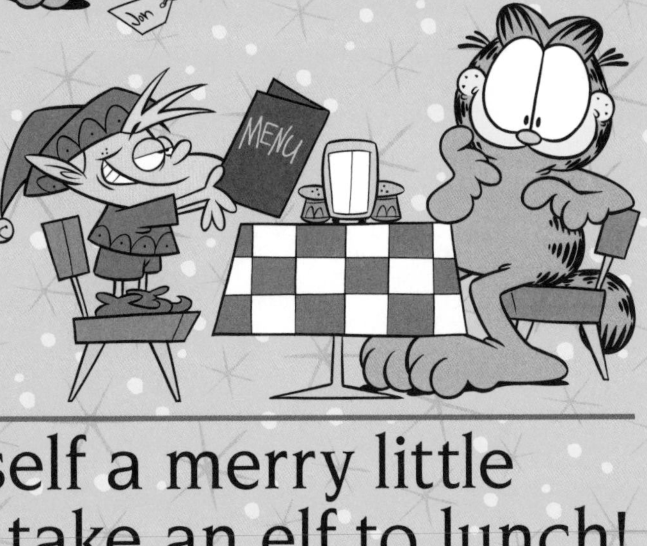
MENU

Have yourself a merry little
Christmas...take an elf to lunch!

CHRISTMAS TRIVIA QUIZ

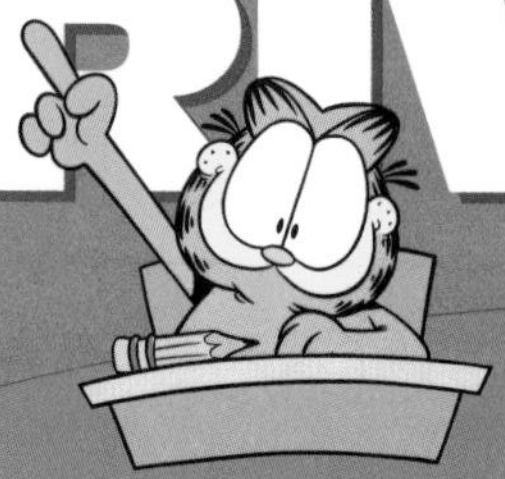

HO! HO! HO! TEST YOUR HOLIDAY KNOWLEDGE WITH THIS QUIRKY QUIZ!

1 Where does Santa live?

A. The North Pole
B. His mother's basement
C. A trailer park in Iceland
D. A time share condo with the Tooth Fairy and the Easter Bunny

2 Who helps Santa make toys?

A. Dwarves
B. Elves
C. Hobbits
D. Undocumented workers

3 In the Garfield Christmas TV special, what story does Jon's dad read every year?

A. *'Twas the Night Before Christmas*
B. *A Charlie Brown Christmas*
C. *Binky, the Clown Who Saved Christmas*
D. *Moby Dick*

4 What are the names of Santa's Reindeer?

A. Jackie, Tito, Jermaine, Marlon, Randy, Janet, La Toya, Michael
B. Legolas, Aragorn, Boromir, Gimli, Frodo, Samwise, Merry, Pippin
C. Cyclops, Colossus, Gambit, Rogue, Nightcrawler, Storm, Jubilee, Wolverine
D. Dasher, Dancer, Prancer, Vixen, Comet, Cupid, Donder, Blitzen

5 In the Garfield Christmas TV special, what dish does Grandma spice up with chili powder?

A. Plum pudding
B. Pork Dijonnaise
C. Sausage gravy
D. Reindeer stew

6 In *A Christmas Carol*, who visits Ebenezer Scrooge?

A. The Ghost of Christmas Past
B. The Ghost of Mr. Chicken
C. His in-laws
D. An Amway salesman

7 On Christmas Eve, what do you hang by the fireplace?

A. Garlic
B. Christmas stockings
C. Christmas pantyhose
D. Sausage links

8 In what type of vehicle does Santa travel?

A. Flying sleigh
B. Greyhound bus
C. '73 Monte Carlo
D. Zamboni

ANSWERS: 1. A, 2. B, 3. C, 4. D, 5. C, 6. A, 7. B, 8. A

TOP TEN LEAST-REQUESTED GARFIELD CHRISTMAS PRODUCTS

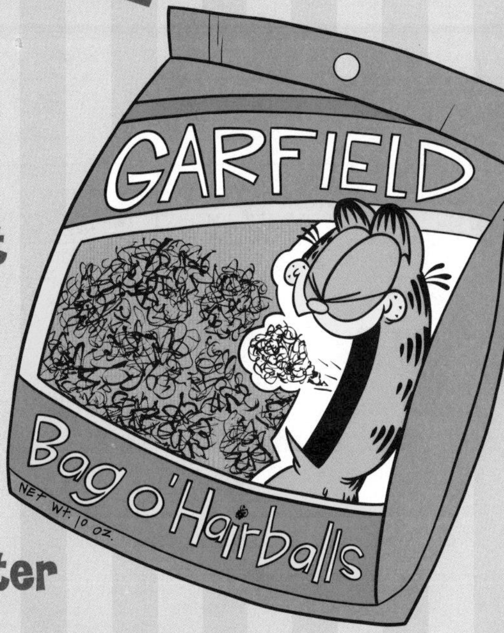
GARFIELD
Bag o' Hairballs
NET WT. 10 OZ.

10 Garfield "Bag o' Hairballs"

9 Garfield Home Colostomy Kit

8 Garfield Eczema Scraper

7 Garfield Bird Zapper

6 Garfield Exploding Kitty Litter

5 "Garfield Gets a Cold Sore" video game

4 Garfield "Baby Toxic Waste"

3 Garfield "Fruit and Fur" cake

2 "Garfield's Caterwauling Christmas" CD

1 Garfield "Puke on You"

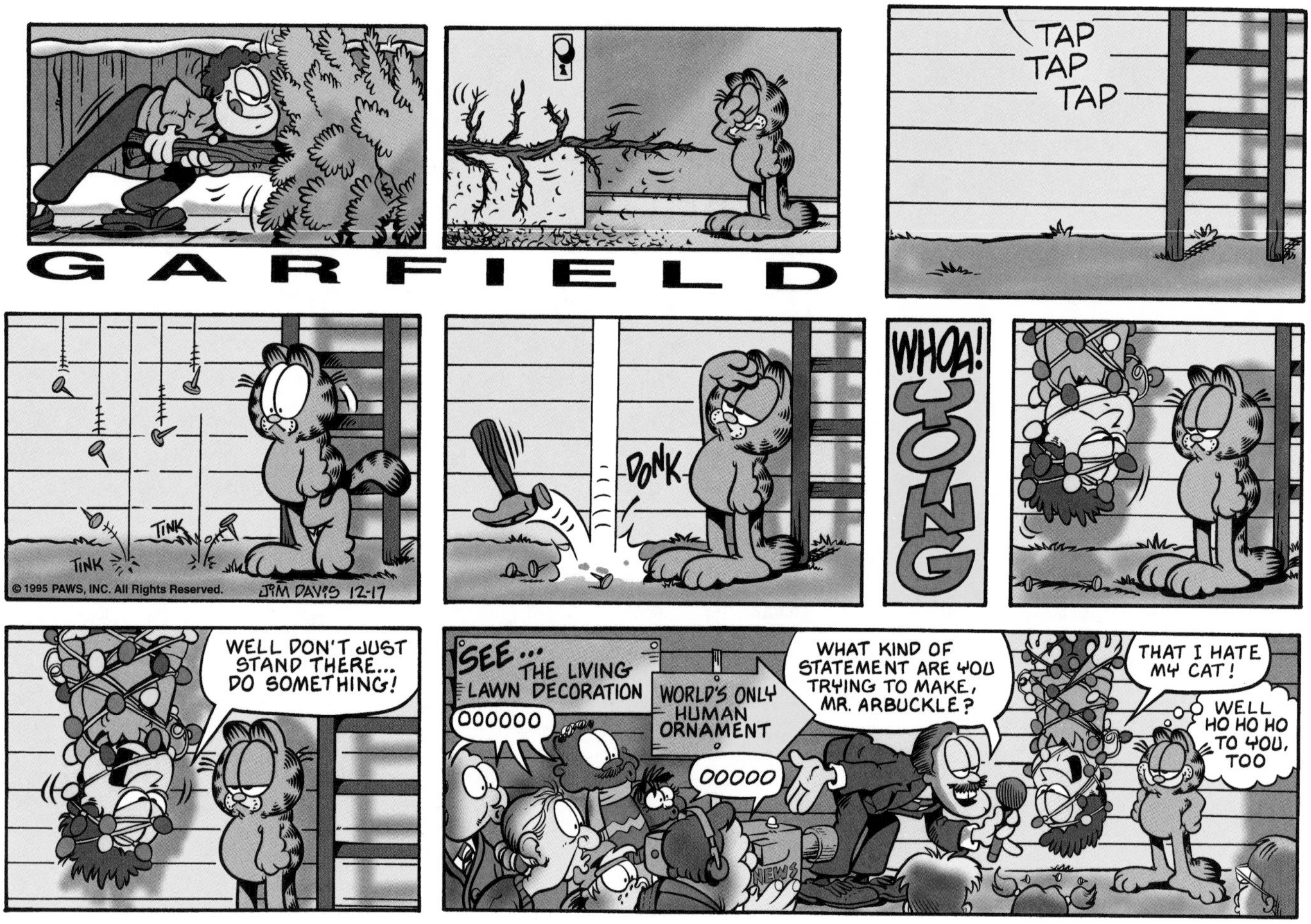
GARFIELD
TAP
TAP
TAP
TINK
TINK
© 1995 PAWS, INC. All Rights Reserved.
JIM DAVIS 12-17
DONK
WHOA!
YOING
WELL DON'T JUST STAND THERE... DO SOMETHING!
SEE... THE LIVING LAWN DECORATION
WORLD'S ONLY HUMAN ORNAMENT
OOOOOO
OOOOO
WHAT KIND OF STATEMENT ARE YOU TRYING TO MAKE, MR. ARBUCKLE?
THAT I HATE MY CAT!
WELL HO HO HO TO YOU, TOO
NEWS

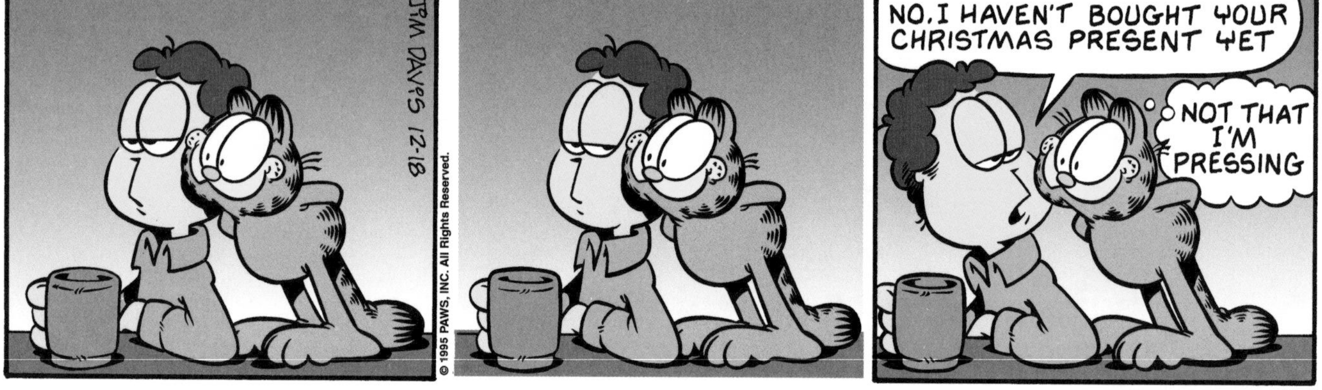
JIM DAVIS 12-18
© 1995 PAWS, INC. All Rights Reserved.
NO, I HAVEN'T BOUGHT YOUR CHRISTMAS PRESENT YET
NOT THAT I'M PRESSING

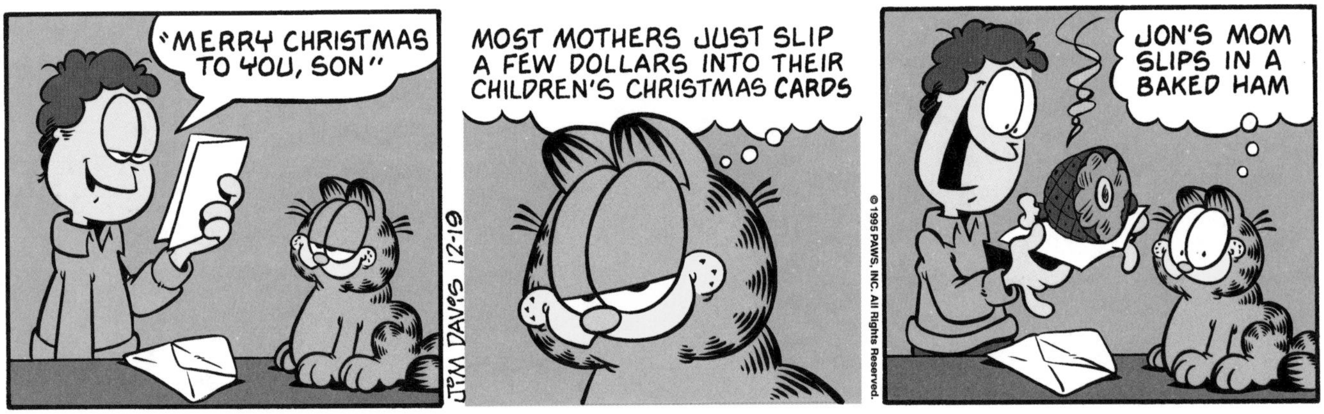
"MERRY CHRISTMAS TO YOU, SON"
MOST MOTHERS JUST SLIP A FEW DOLLARS INTO THEIR CHILDREN'S CHRISTMAS CARDS
JIM DAVIS 12-19
JON'S MOM SLIPS IN A BAKED HAM
© 1995 PAWS, INC. All Rights Reserved.

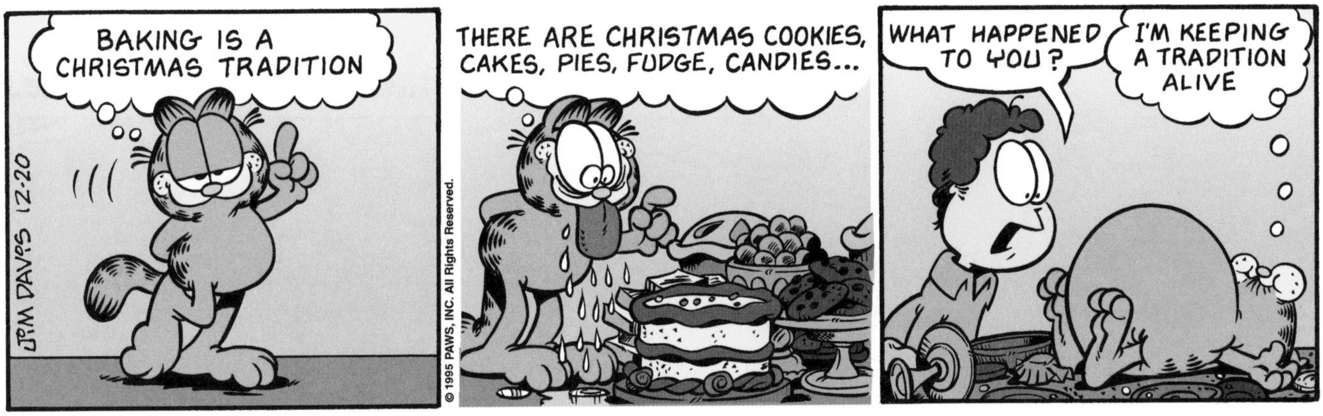
BAKING IS A CHRISTMAS TRADITION
JIM DAVIS 12-20
THERE ARE CHRISTMAS COOKIES, CAKES, PIES, FUDGE, CANDIES...
© 1995 PAWS, INC. All Rights Reserved.
WHAT HAPPENED TO YOU?
I'M KEEPING A TRADITION ALIVE

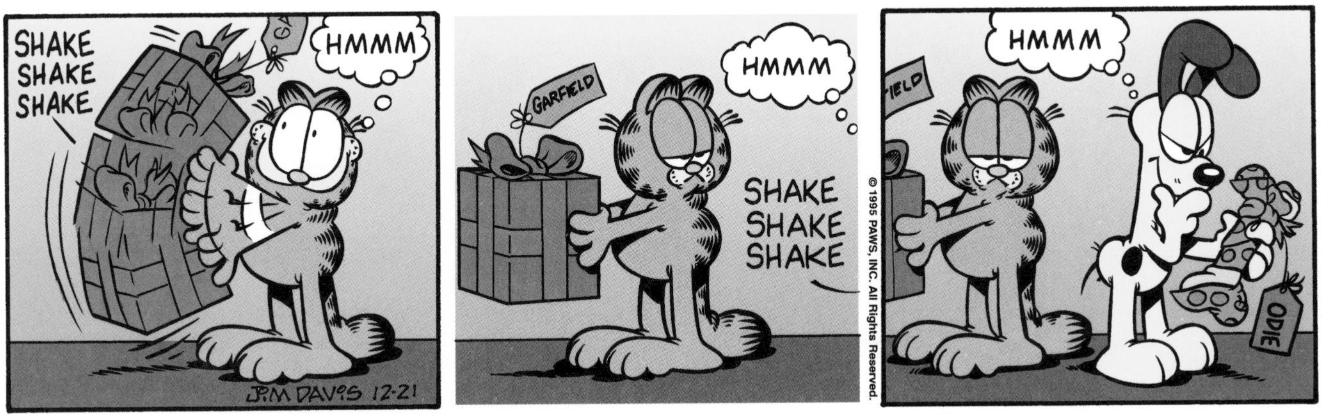
SHAKE SHAKE SHAKE
HMMM
JIM DAVIS 12-21
GARFIELD
HMMM
SHAKE SHAKE SHAKE
HMMM
ODIE
© 1995 PAWS, INC. All Rights Reserved.

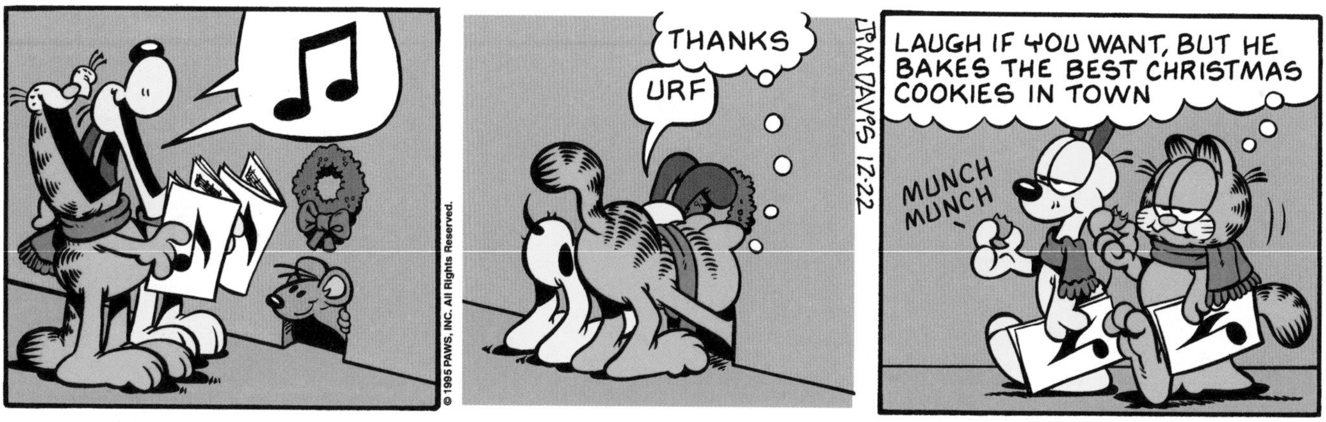
© 1995 PAWS, INC. All Rights Reserved.
THANKS
URF
JIM DAVIS 12-22
LAUGH IF YOU WANT, BUT HE BAKES THE BEST CHRISTMAS COOKIES IN TOWN
MUNCH MUNCH

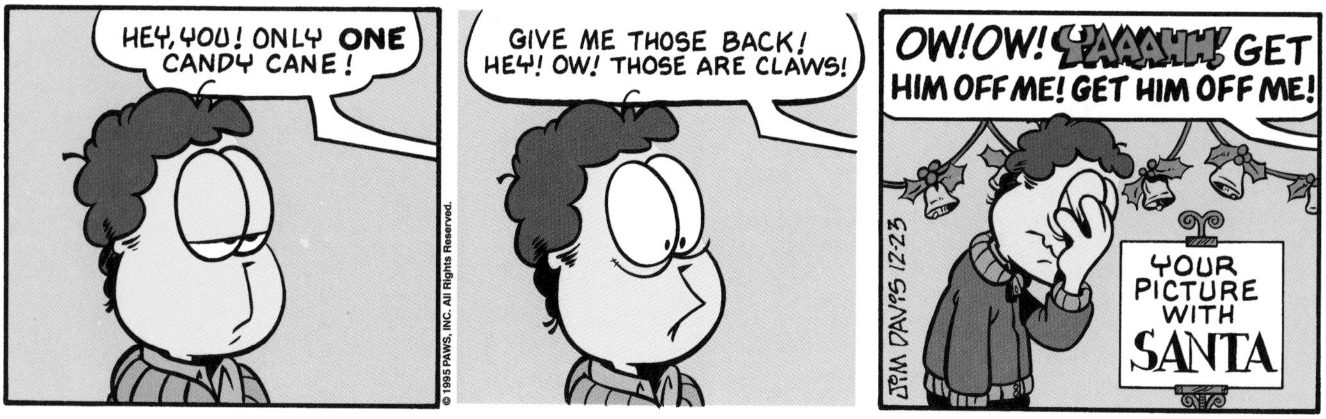
HEY, YOU! ONLY ONE CANDY CANE!
© 1995 PAWS, INC. All Rights Reserved.
GIVE ME THOSE BACK! HEY! OW! THOSE ARE CLAWS!
OW! OW! YAAAHH! GET HIM OFF ME! GET HIM OFF ME!
YOUR PICTURE WITH SANTA
JIM DAVIS 12-23

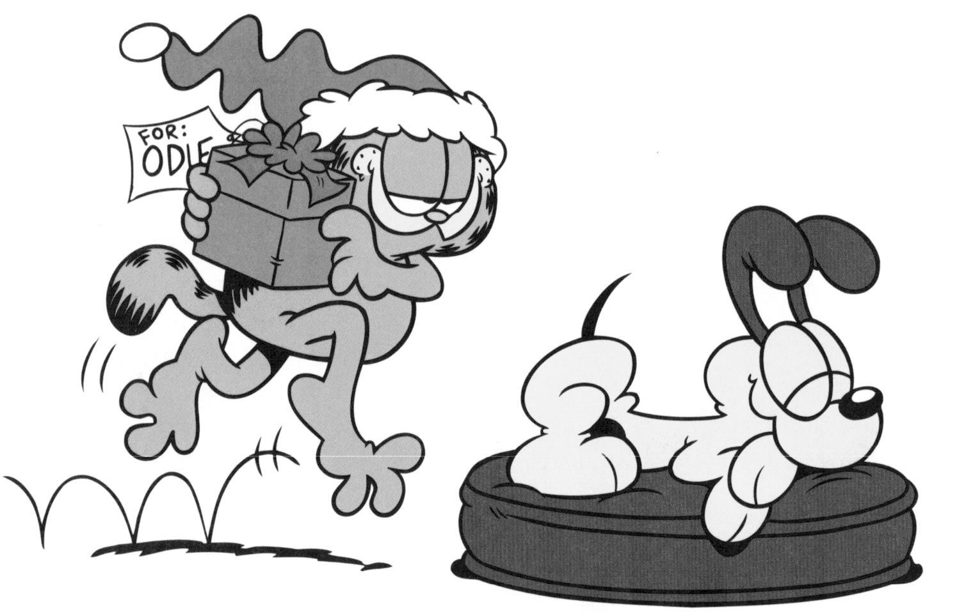
FOR: ODIE

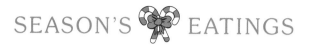

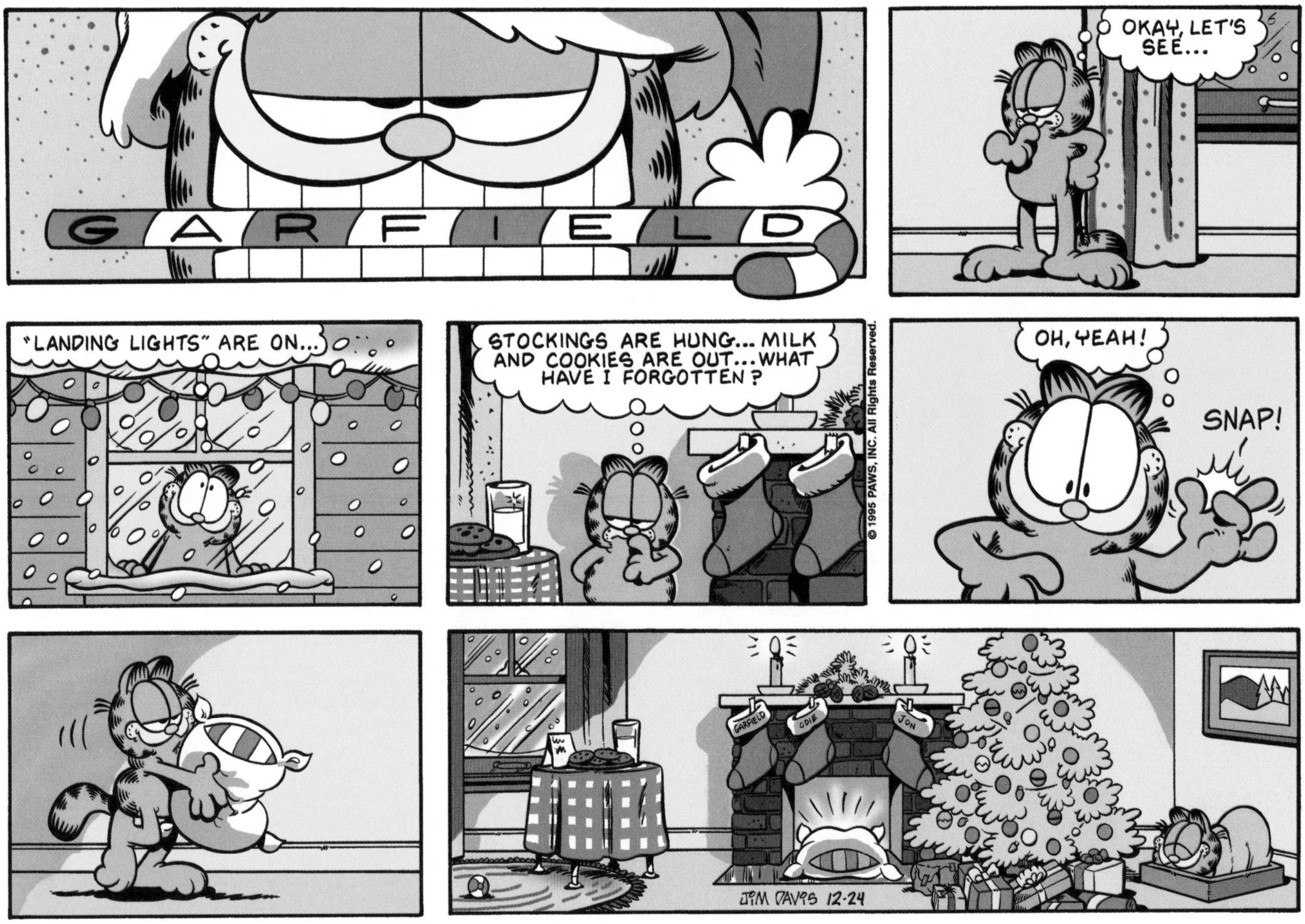
GARFIELD
OKAY, LET'S SEE...
"LANDING LIGHTS" ARE ON...
STOCKINGS ARE HUNG... MILK AND COOKIES ARE OUT... WHAT HAVE I FORGOTTEN?
© 1995 PAWS, INC. All Rights Reserved.
OH, YEAH!
SNAP!
GARFIELD
ODIE
JON
JIM DAVIS 12-24

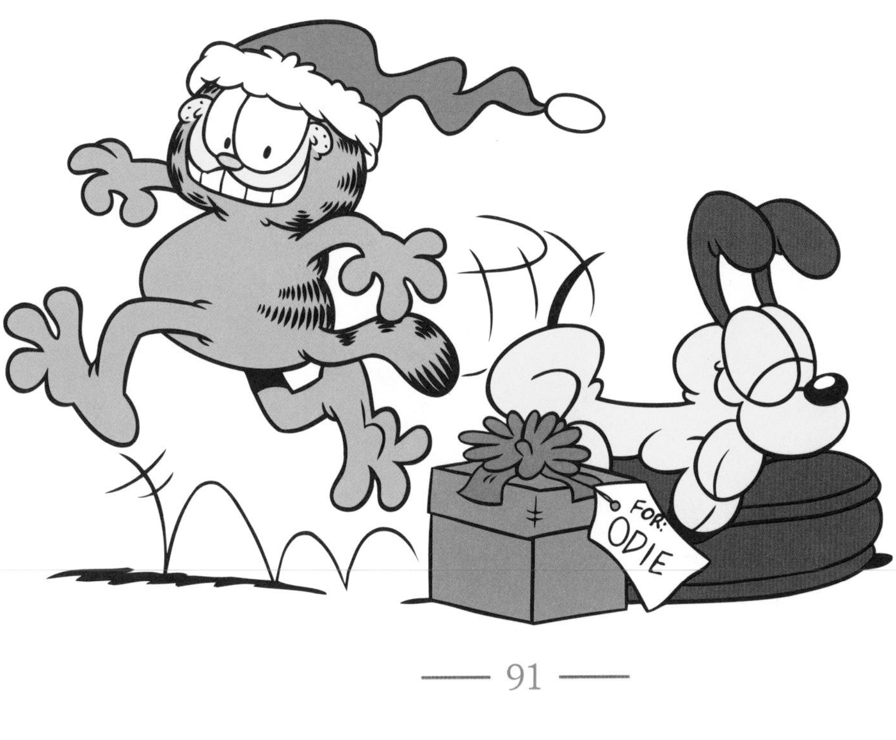
FOR: ODIE

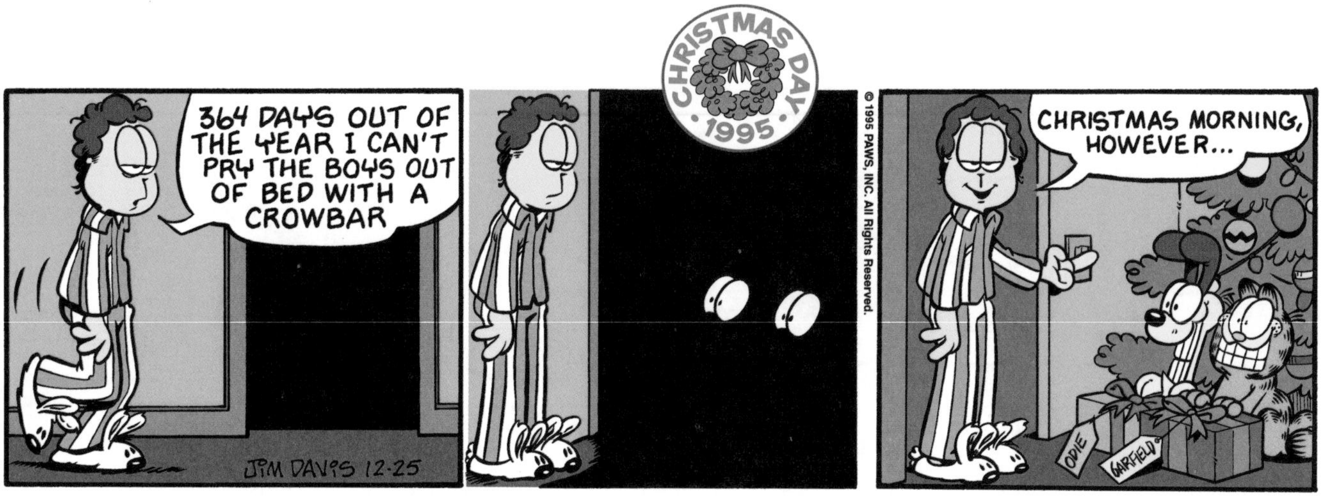
CHRISTMAS DAY 1995
364 DAYS OUT OF THE YEAR I CAN'T PRY THE BOYS OUT OF BED WITH A CROWBAR
JIM DAVIS 12-25
© 1995 PAWS, INC. All Rights Reserved.
CHRISTMAS MORNING, HOWEVER...
ODIE
GARFIELD

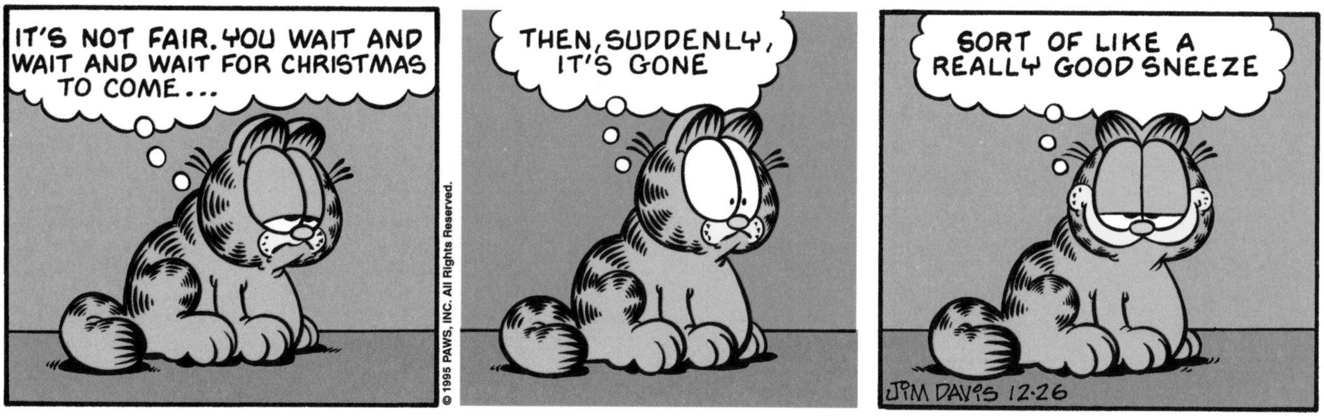
IT'S NOT FAIR. YOU WAIT AND WAIT AND WAIT FOR CHRISTMAS TO COME...
© 1995 PAWS, INC. All Rights Reserved.
THEN, SUDDENLY, IT'S GONE
SORT OF LIKE A REALLY GOOD SNEEZE
JIM DAVIS 12-26

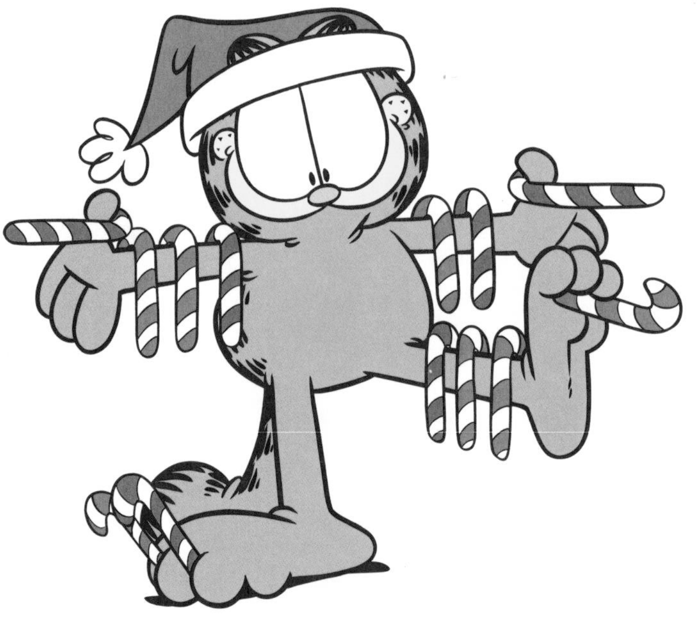

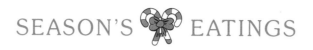

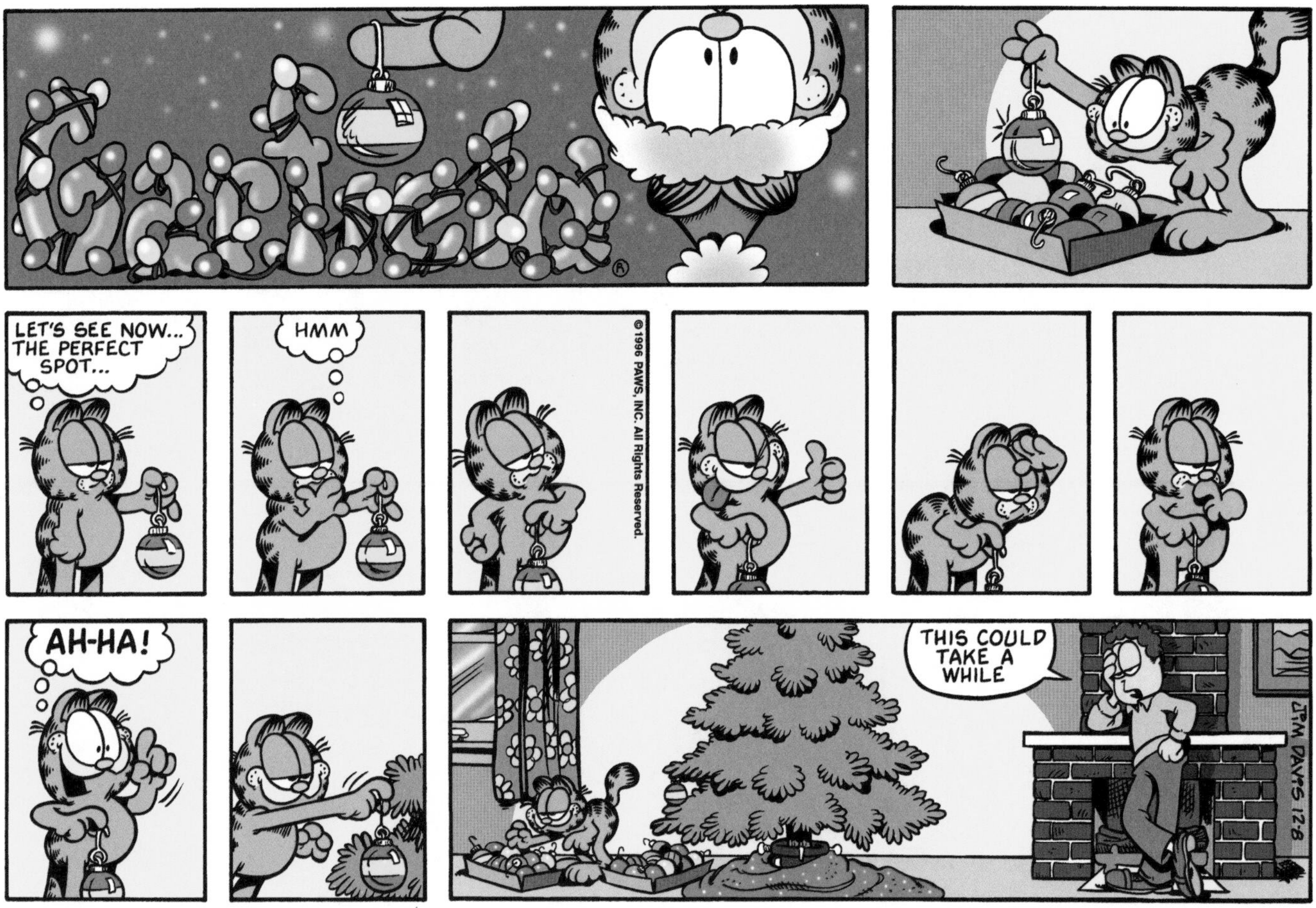
LET'S SEE NOW... THE PERFECT SPOT...
HMM
© 1996 PAWS, INC. All Rights Reserved.
AH-HA!
THIS COULD TAKE A WHILE
JIM DAVIS 12-8

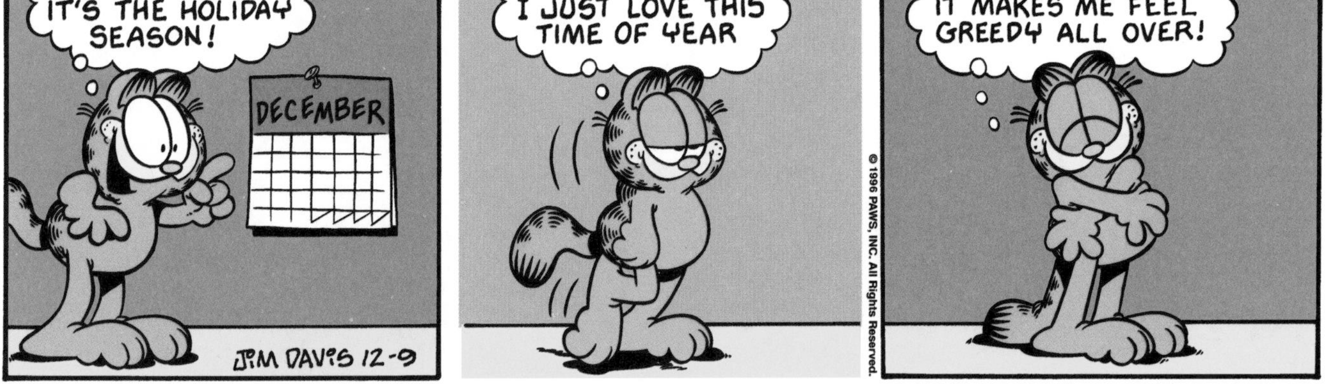
IT'S THE HOLIDAY SEASON!
DECEMBER
JIM DAVIS 12-9
I JUST LOVE THIS TIME OF YEAR
© 1996 PAWS, INC. All Rights Reserved.
IT MAKES ME FEEL GREEDY ALL OVER!

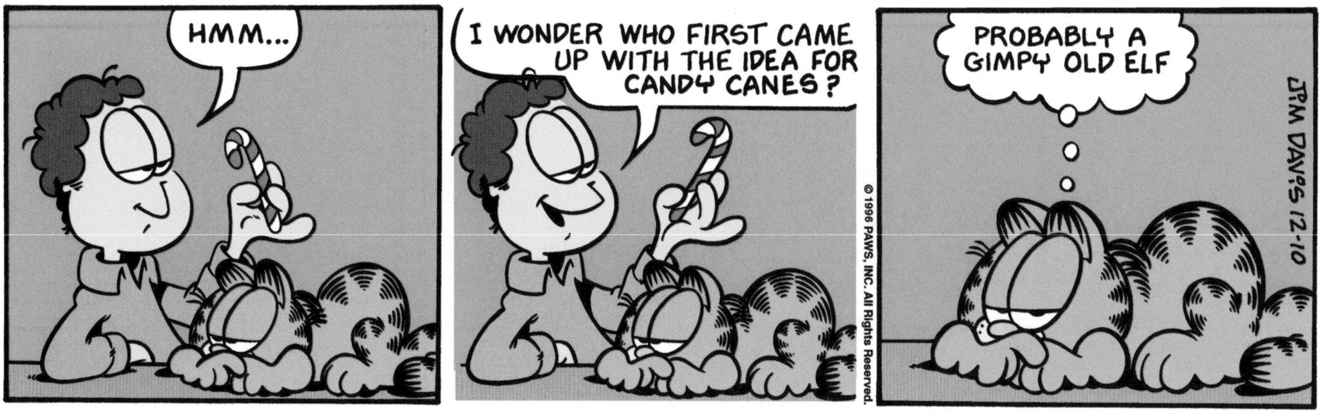
HMM...
I WONDER WHO FIRST CAME UP WITH THE IDEA FOR CANDY CANES?
PROBABLY A GIMPY OLD ELF
JIM DAVIS 12-10
© 1996 PAWS, INC. All Rights Reserved.

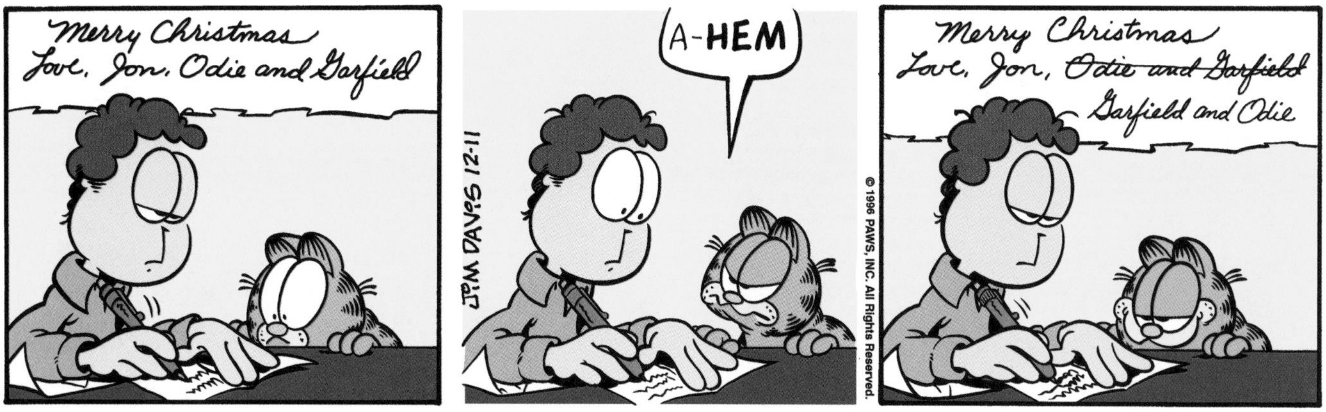
Merry Christmas
Love, Jon, Odie and Garfield
JIM DAVIS 12-11
A-HEM
Merry Christmas
Love, Jon, Odie and Garfield
Garfield and Odie
© 1996 PAWS, INC. All Rights Reserved.

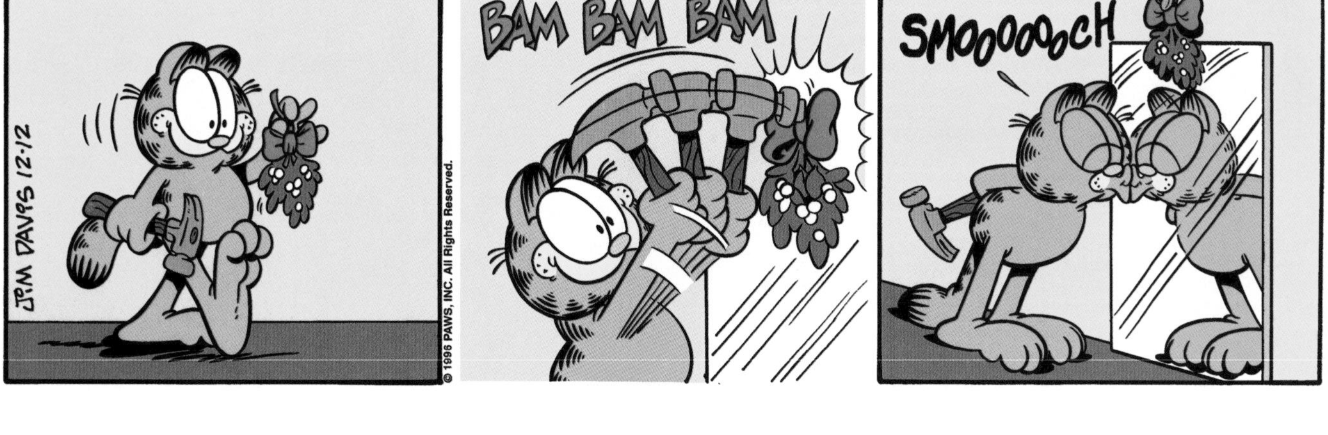
JIM DAVIS 12-12
© 1996 PAWS, INC. All Rights Reserved.
BAM BAM BAM
SMOOOOOOCH

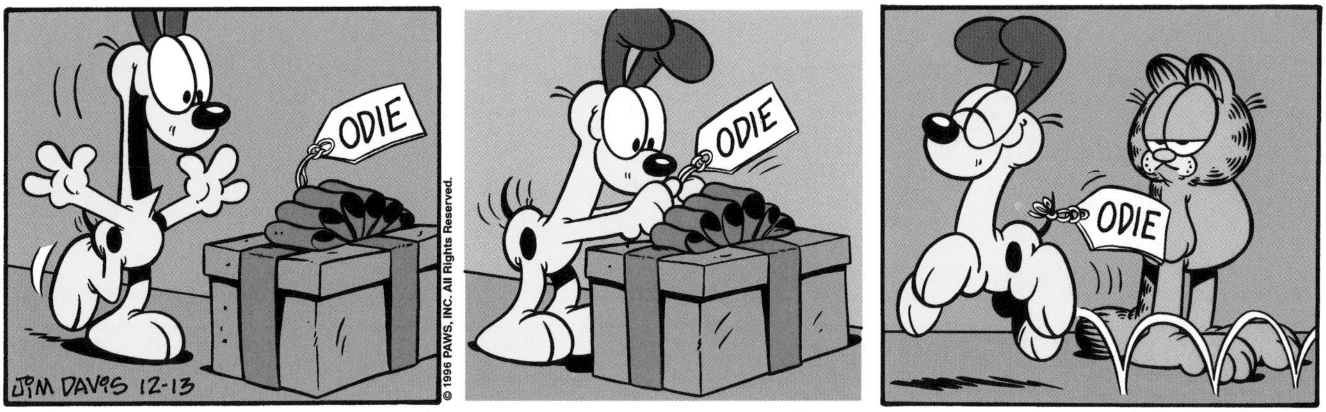
ODIE
ODIE
ODIE
JIM DAVIS 12-13
© 1996 PAWS, INC. All Rights Reserved.

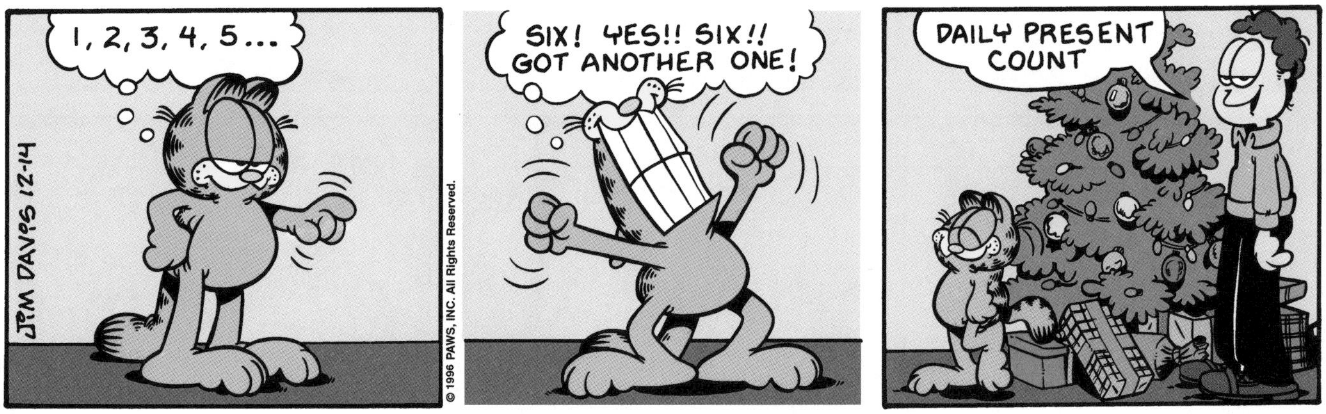
1, 2, 3, 4, 5...
SIX! YES!! SIX!! GOT ANOTHER ONE!
DAILY PRESENT COUNT
JIM DAVIS 12-14
© 1996 PAWS, INC. All Rights Reserved.

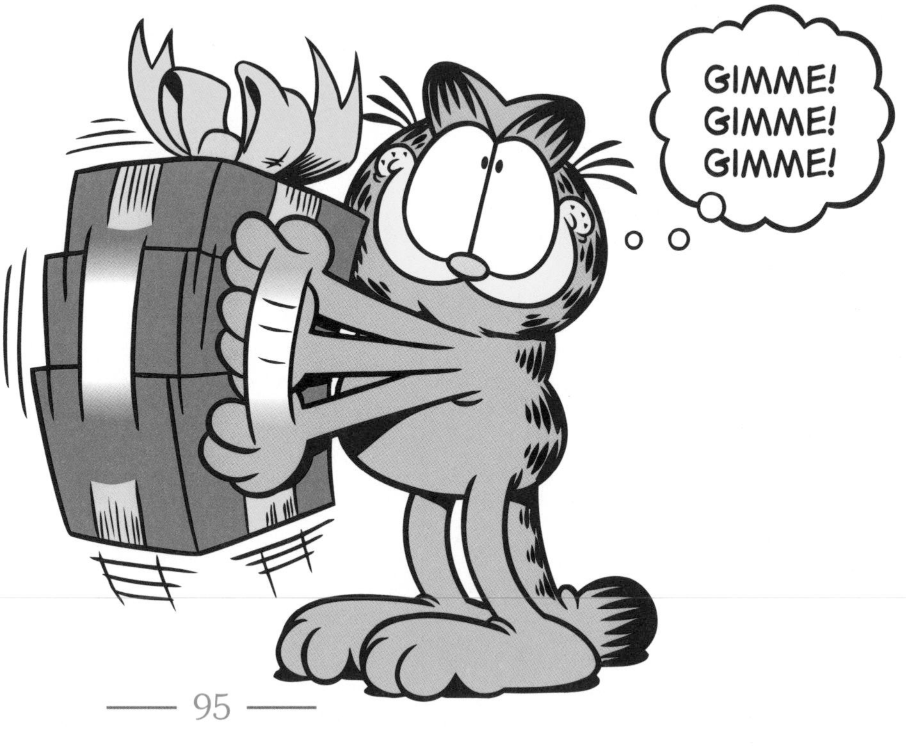
GIMME!
GIMME!
GIMME!

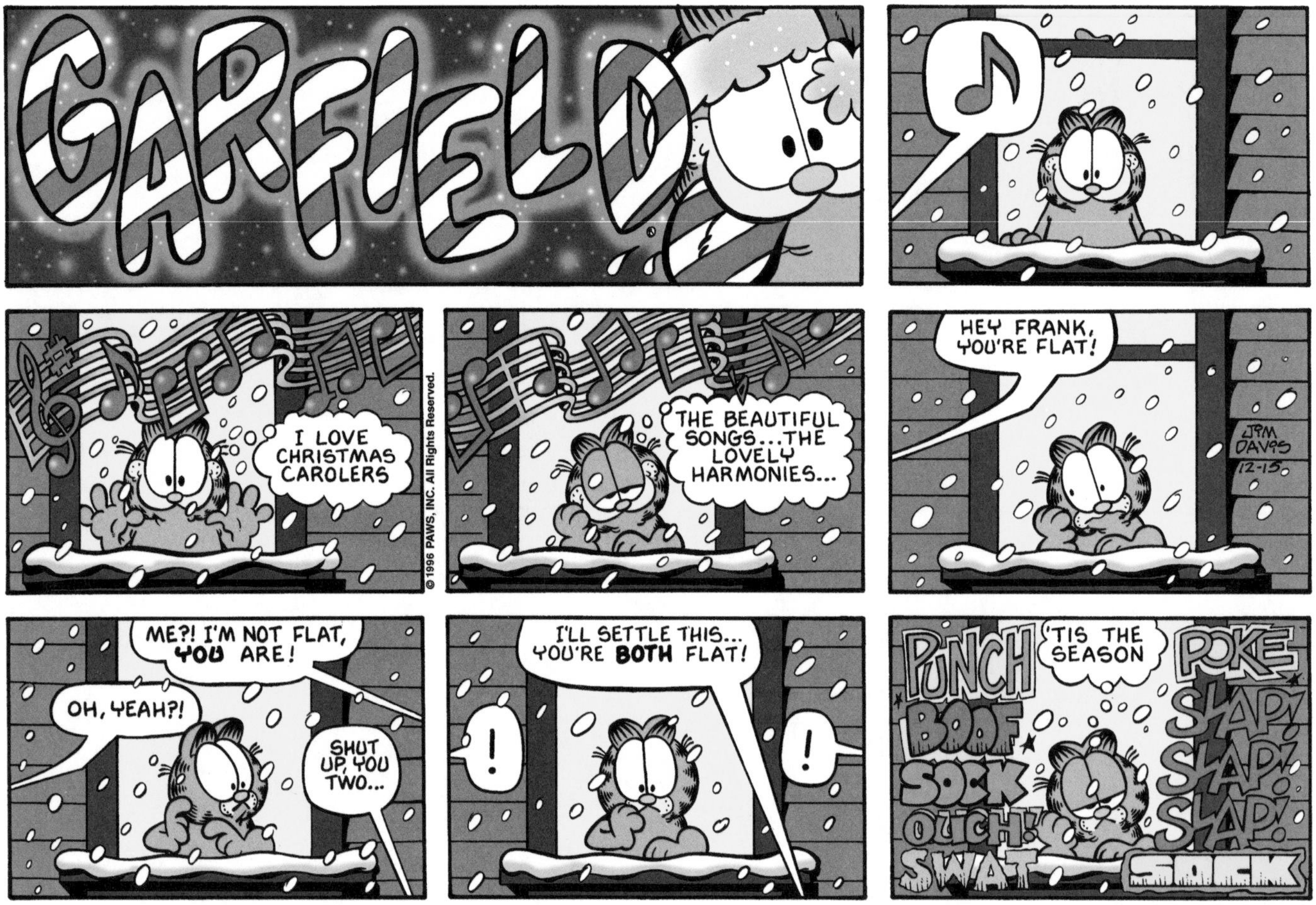
GARFIELD
I LOVE CHRISTMAS CAROLERS
THE BEAUTIFUL SONGS...THE LOVELY HARMONIES...
HEY FRANK, YOU'RE FLAT!
JIM DAVIS 12-15
ME?! I'M NOT FLAT, YOU ARE!
OH, YEAH?!
SHUT UP, YOU TWO...
I'LL SETTLE THIS... YOU'RE BOTH FLAT!
!
!
PUNCH
'TIS THE SEASON
POKE
BOOF
SOCK
SLAP!
SLAP!
SLAP!
OUCH!
SWAT
SOCK
© 1996 PAWS, INC. All Rights Reserved.

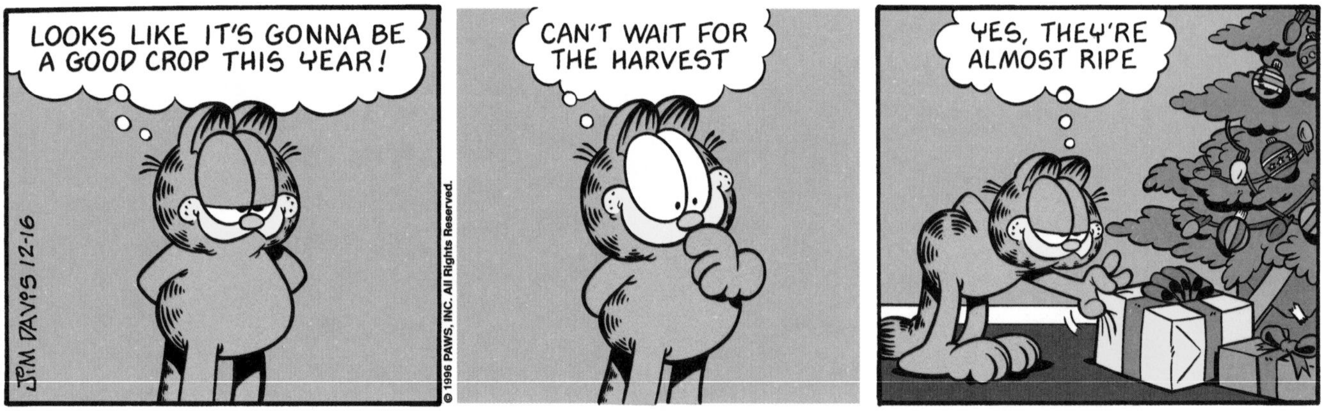
LOOKS LIKE IT'S GONNA BE A GOOD CROP THIS YEAR!
JIM DAVIS 12-16
CAN'T WAIT FOR THE HARVEST
YES, THEY'RE ALMOST RIPE
© 1996 PAWS, INC. All Rights Reserved.

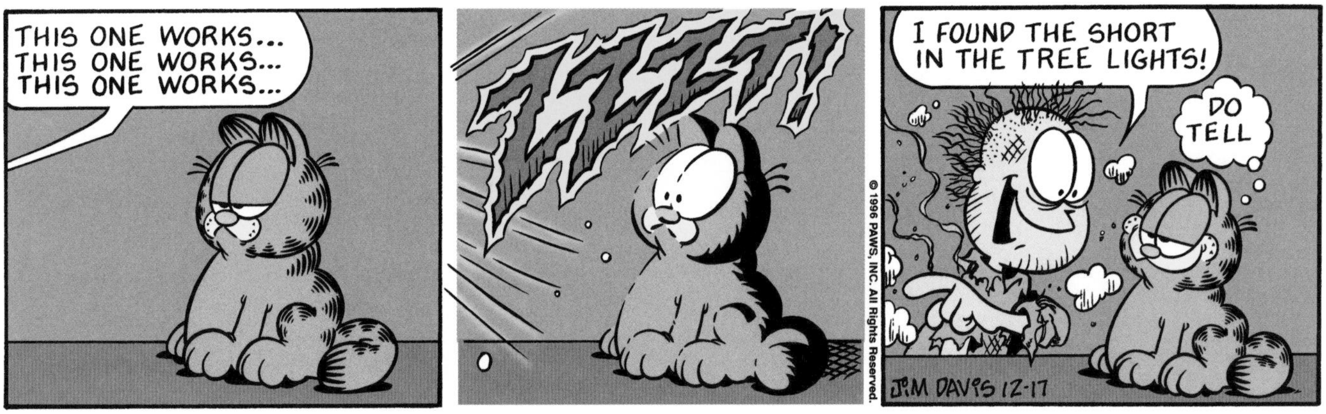
THIS ONE WORKS...
THIS ONE WORKS...
THIS ONE WORKS...
ZZZZT!
I FOUND THE SHORT IN THE TREE LIGHTS!
DO TELL
© 1996 PAWS, INC. All Rights Reserved.
JIM DAVIS 12-17

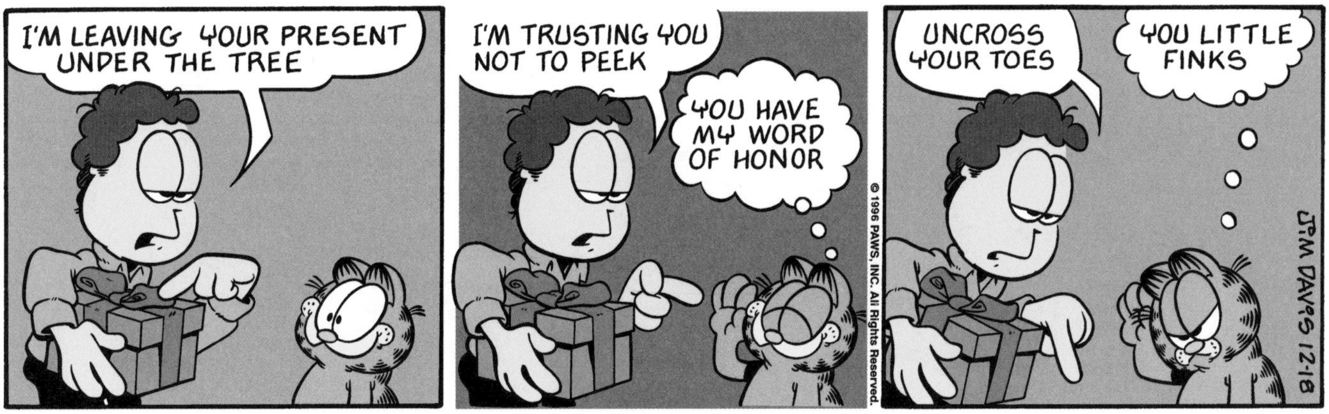
I'M LEAVING YOUR PRESENT UNDER THE TREE
I'M TRUSTING YOU NOT TO PEEK
YOU HAVE MY WORD OF HONOR
© 1996 PAWS, INC. All Rights Reserved.
UNCROSS YOUR TOES
YOU LITTLE FINKS
JIM DAVIS 12-18

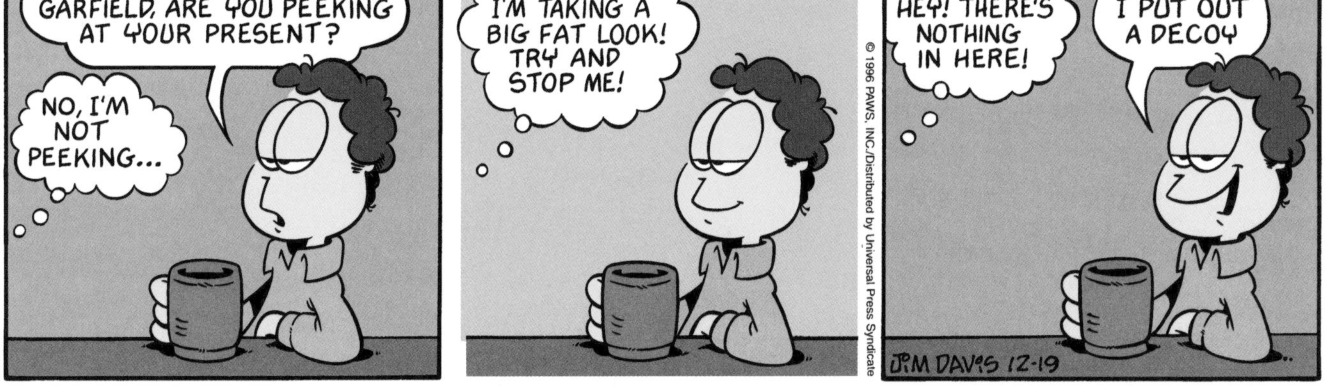
GARFIELD, ARE YOU PEEKING AT YOUR PRESENT?
NO, I'M NOT PEEKING...
I'M TAKING A BIG FAT LOOK! TRY AND STOP ME!
© 1996 PAWS, INC./Distributed by Universal Press Syndicate
HEY! THERE'S NOTHING IN HERE!
I PUT OUT A DECOY
JIM DAVIS 12-19

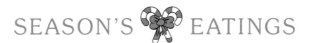

YOU TRICKED ME! THERE'S NOTHING IN THIS PRESENT!
YOU PROMISED ME YOU WOULDN'T PEEK
THAT'S WHAT YOU GET FOR PEEKING
© 1996 PAWS, INC. All Rights Reserved.
WELL THANKS FOR NOTHING!
JIM DAVIS 12-20

GARFIELD
JIM DAVIS 12-21
© 1996 PAWS, INC. All Rights Reserved.
ODIE
PRESENT ENVY

LET'S TALK PRESENTS!
CANDY
PASTA
CATNIP
COFFEE

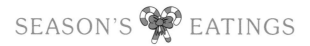

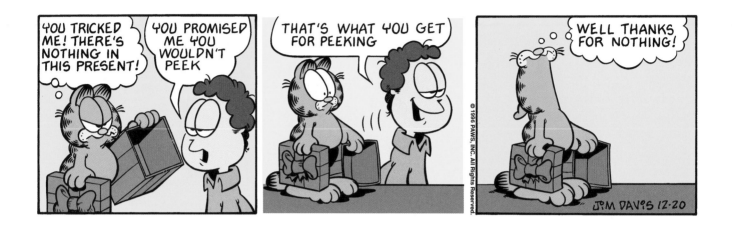

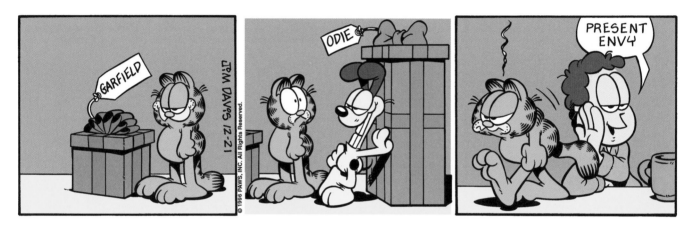

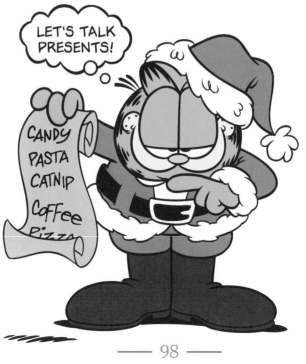

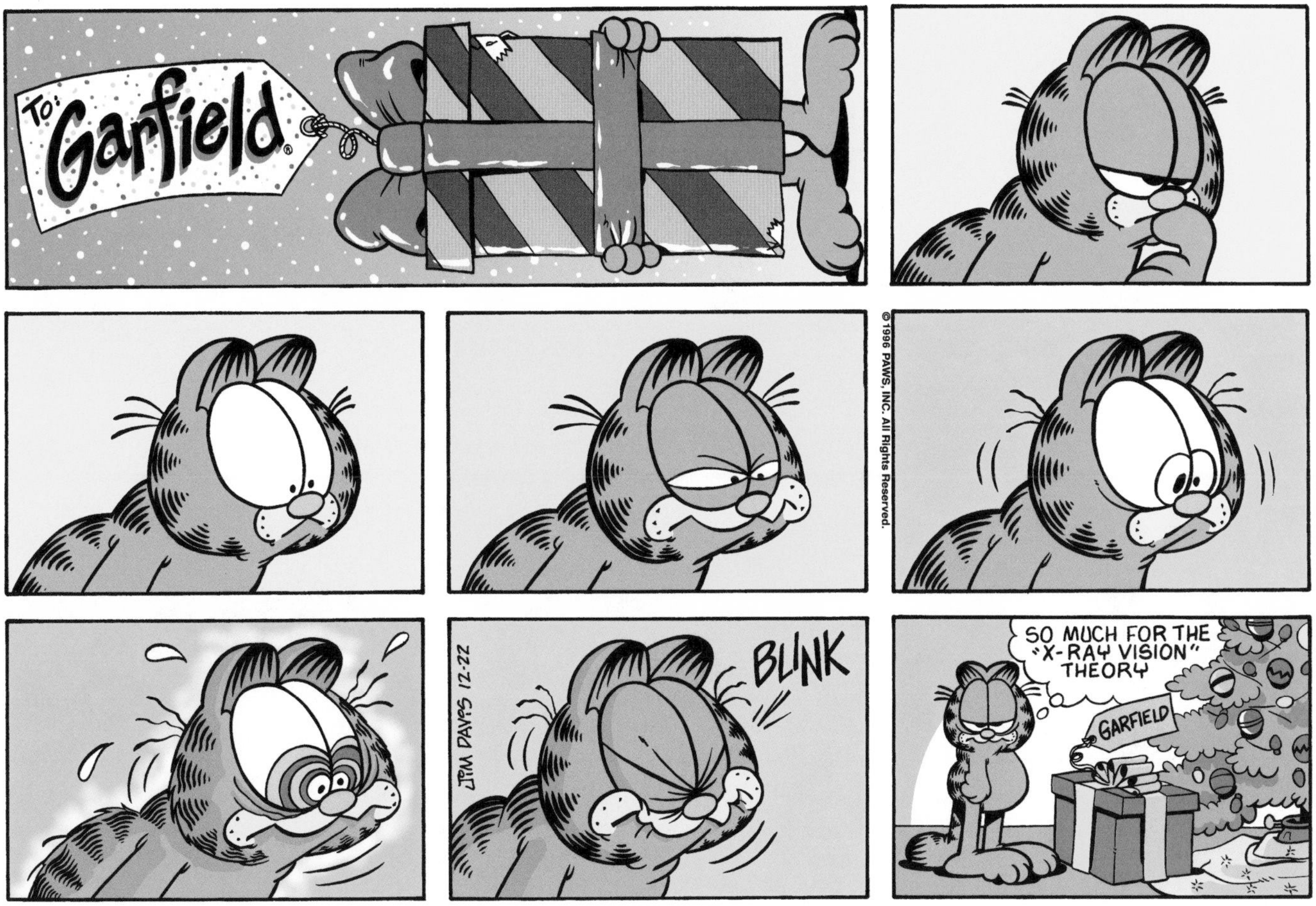
To: Garfield
© 1996 PAWS, INC. All Rights Reserved.
JIM DAVIS 12-22
BLINK
SO MUCH FOR THE "X-RAY VISION" THEORY
GARFIELD

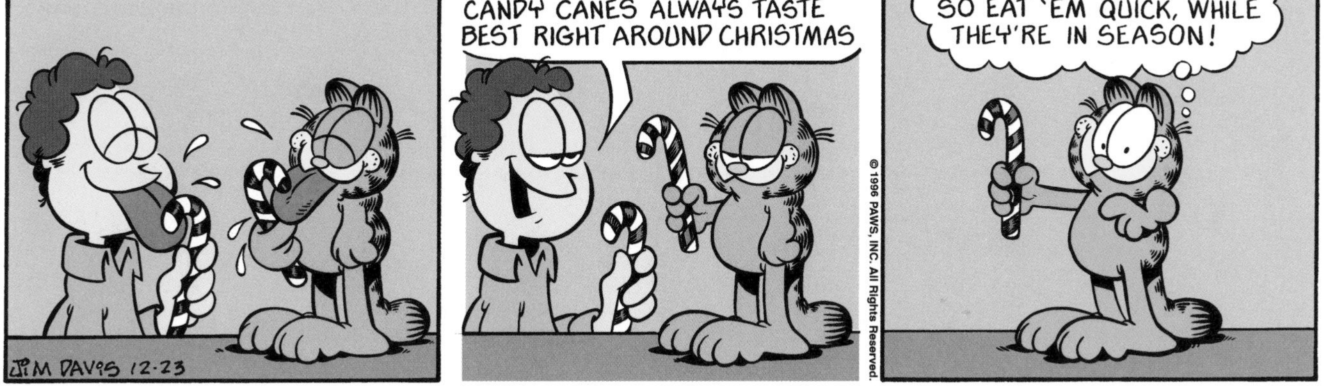
JIM DAVIS 12-23
CANDY CANES ALWAYS TASTE BEST RIGHT AROUND CHRISTMAS
© 1996 PAWS, INC. All Rights Reserved.
SO EAT 'EM QUICK, WHILE THEY'RE IN SEASON!

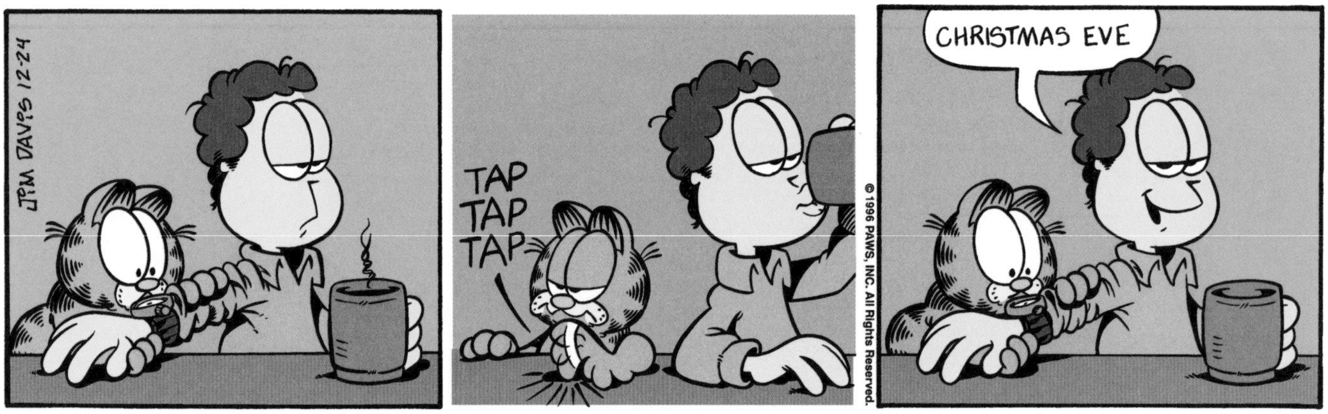
JIM DAVIS 12-24
TAP
TAP
TAP
© 1996 PAWS, INC. All Rights Reserved.
CHRISTMAS EVE

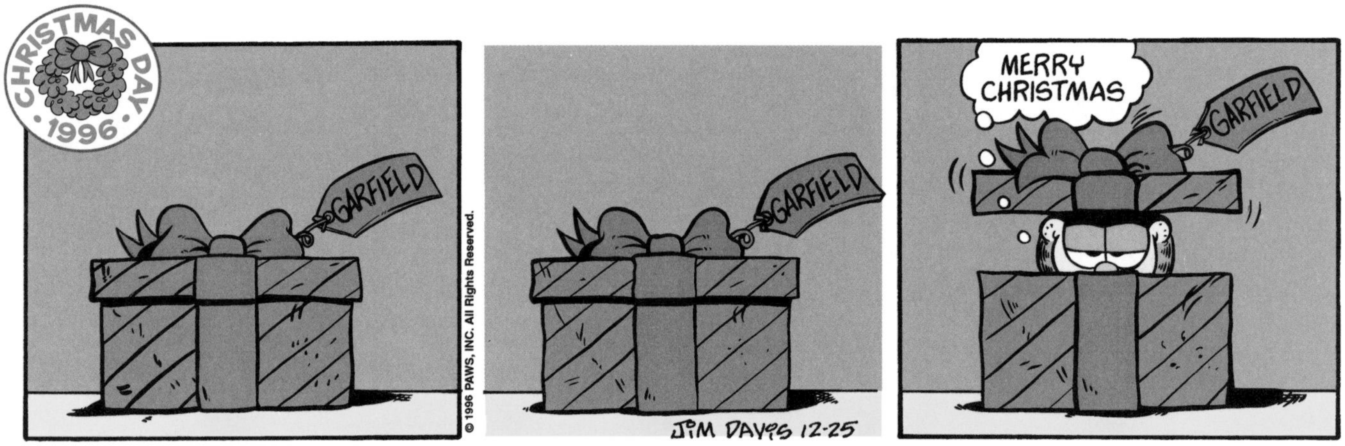
CHRISTMAS DAY 1996
GARFIELD
© 1996 PAWS, INC. All Rights Reserved.
GARFIELD
JIM DAVIS 12-25
MERRY CHRISTMAS
GARFIELD

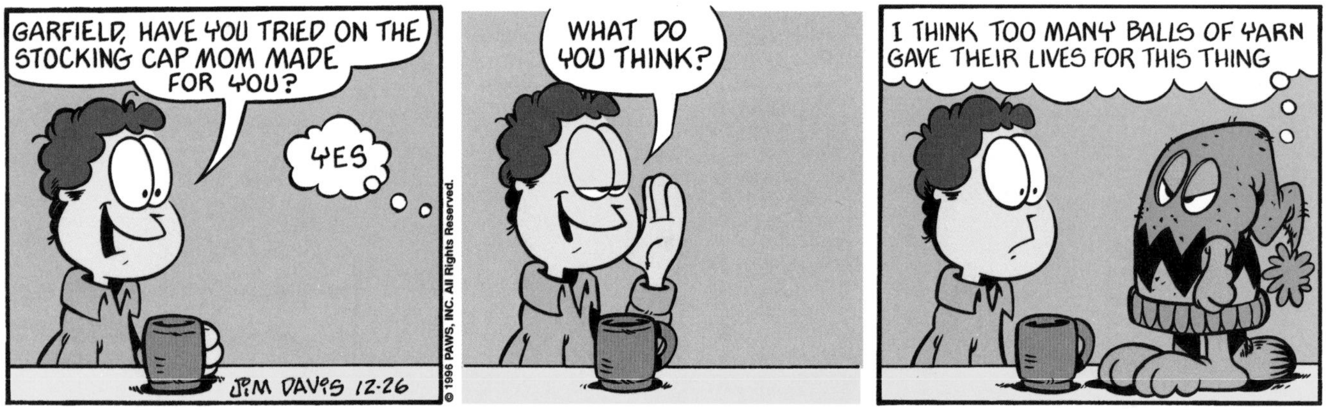
GARFIELD, HAVE YOU TRIED ON THE STOCKING CAP MOM MADE FOR YOU?
YES
JIM DAVIS 12-26
© 1996 PAWS, INC. All Rights Reserved.
WHAT DO YOU THINK?
I THINK TOO MANY BALLS OF YARN GAVE THEIR LIVES FOR THIS THING

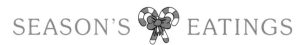

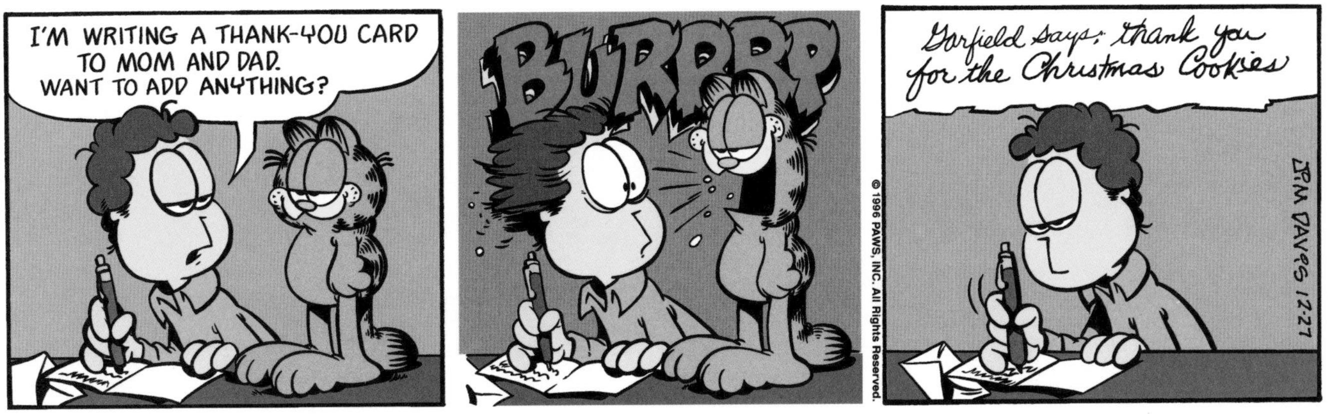
I'M WRITING A THANK-YOU CARD TO MOM AND DAD. WANT TO ADD ANYTHING?
BURPRP
Garfield says: thank you for the Christmas Cookies
© 1996 PAWS, INC. All Rights Reserved.

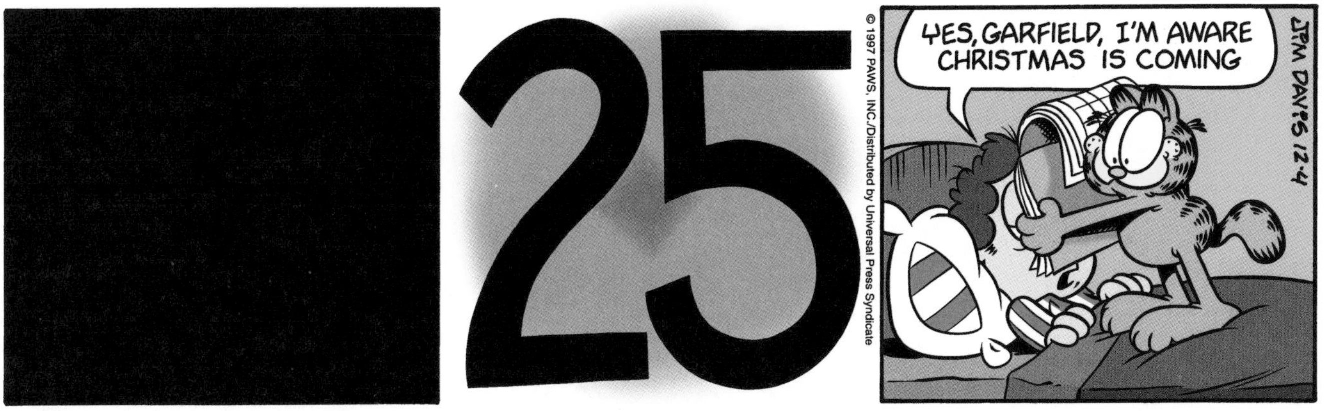
25
© 1997 PAWS, INC./Distributed by Universal Press Syndicate
YES, GARFIELD, I'M AWARE CHRISTMAS IS COMING

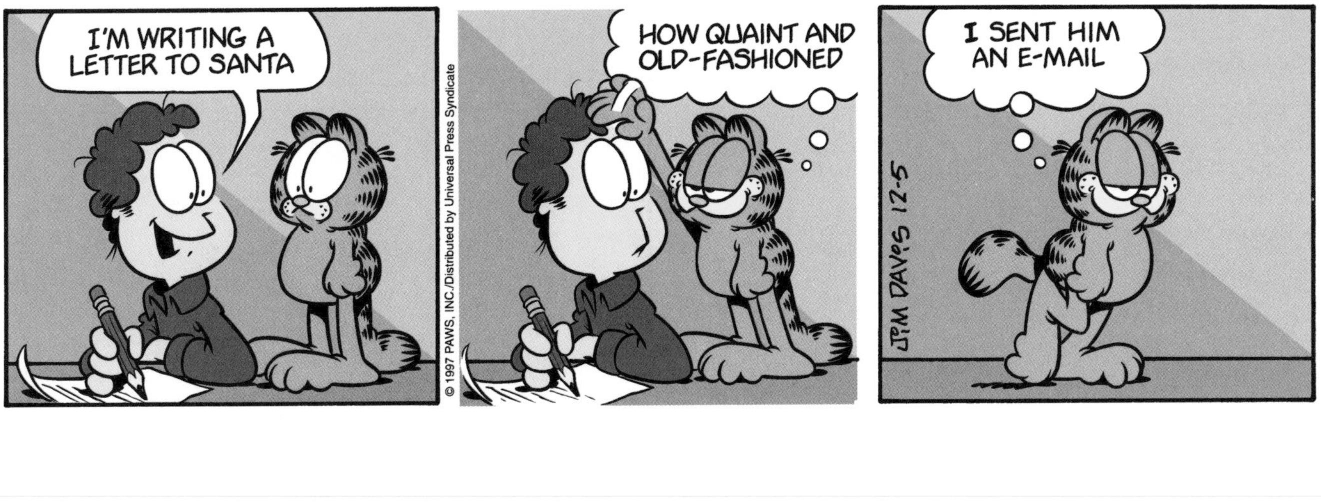
I'M WRITING A LETTER TO SANTA
© 1997 PAWS, INC./Distributed by Universal Press Syndicate
HOW QUAINT AND OLD-FASHIONED
I SENT HIM AN E-MAIL

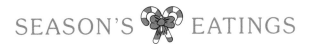

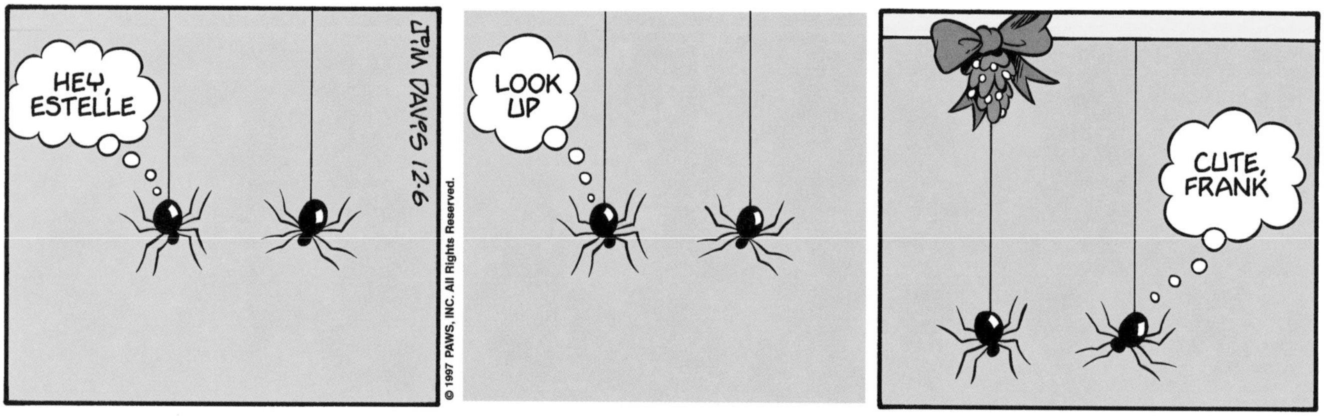
HEY, ESTELLE
JIM DAVIS 12-6
© 1997 PAWS, INC. All Rights Reserved.
LOOK UP
CUTE, FRANK

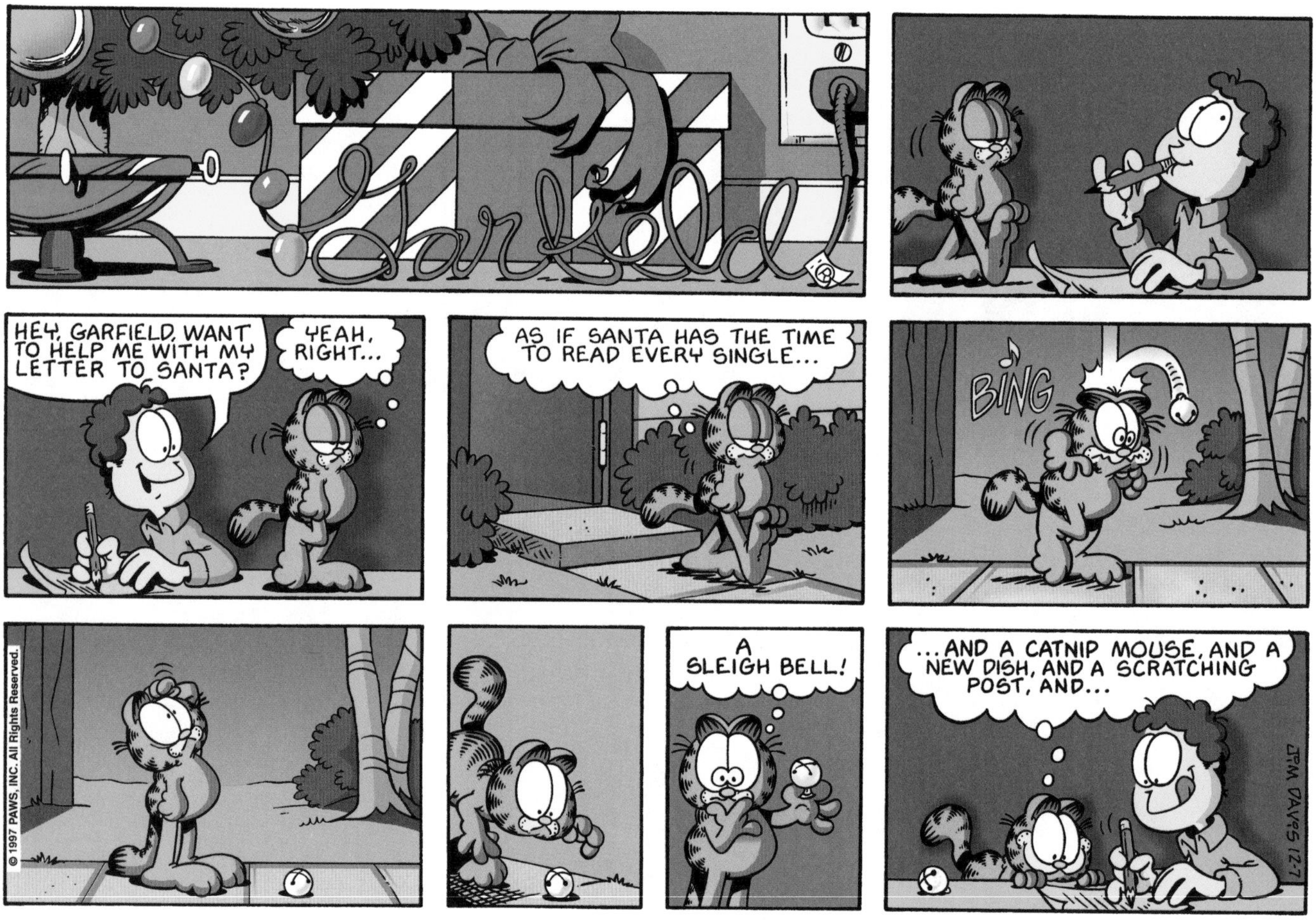
Garfield
HEY, GARFIELD, WANT TO HELP ME WITH MY LETTER TO SANTA?
YEAH, RIGHT...
AS IF SANTA HAS THE TIME TO READ EVERY SINGLE...
BING
© 1997 PAWS, INC. All Rights Reserved.
A SLEIGH BELL!
...AND A CATNIP MOUSE, AND A NEW DISH, AND A SCRATCHING POST, AND...
JIM DAVIS 12-7

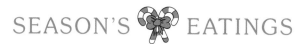

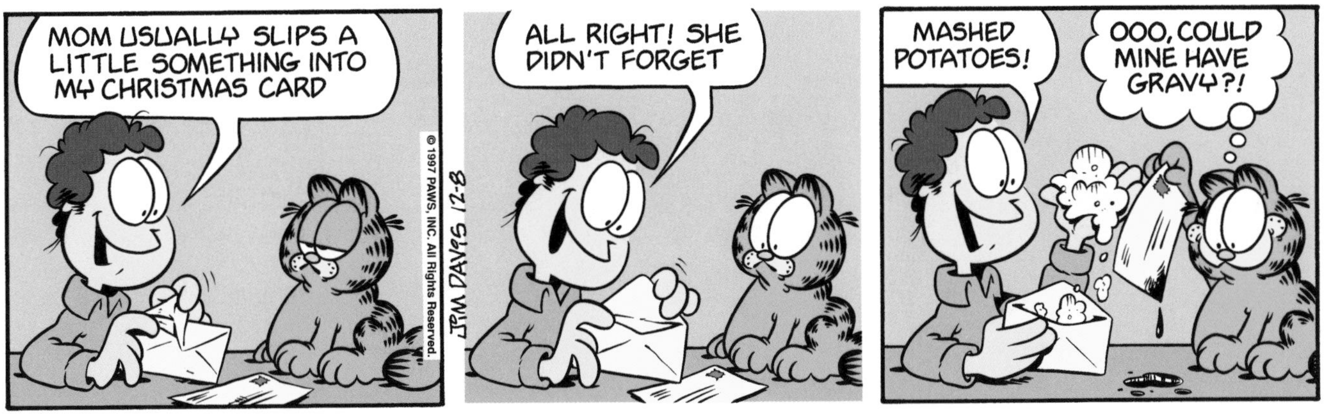
MOM USUALLY SLIPS A LITTLE SOMETHING INTO MY CHRISTMAS CARD
© 1997 PAWS, INC. All Rights Reserved.
JIM DAVIS 12-8
ALL RIGHT! SHE DIDN'T FORGET
MASHED POTATOES!
OOO, COULD MINE HAVE GRAVY?!

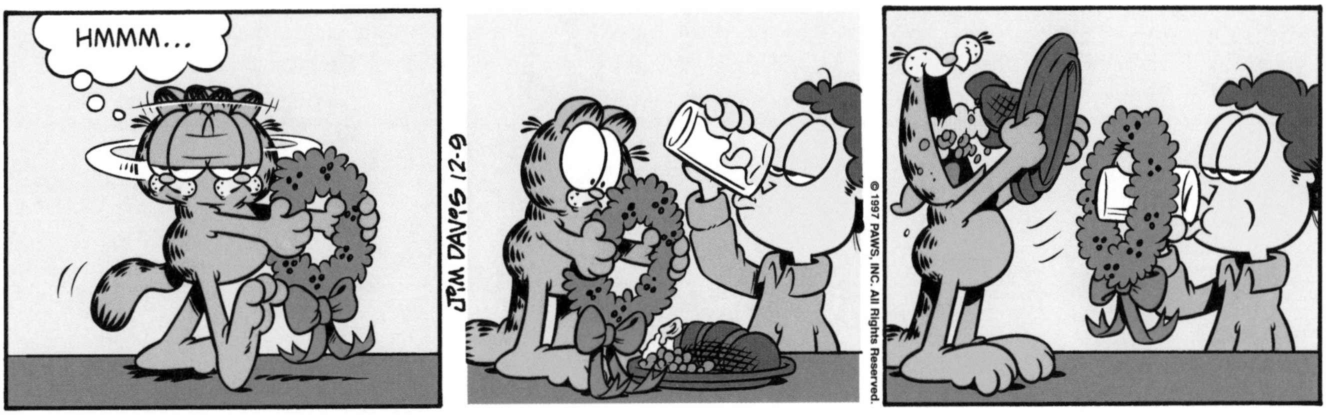
HMMM...
JIM DAVIS 12-9
© 1997 PAWS, INC. All Rights Reserved.

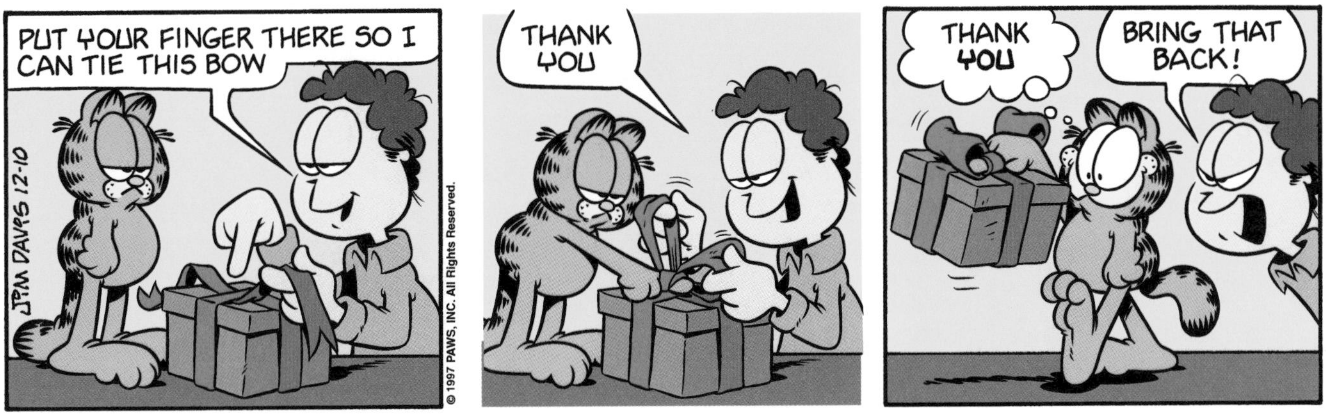
PUT YOUR FINGER THERE SO I CAN TIE THIS BOW
JIM DAVIS 12-10
© 1997 PAWS, INC. All Rights Reserved.
THANK YOU
THANK **YOU**
BRING THAT BACK!

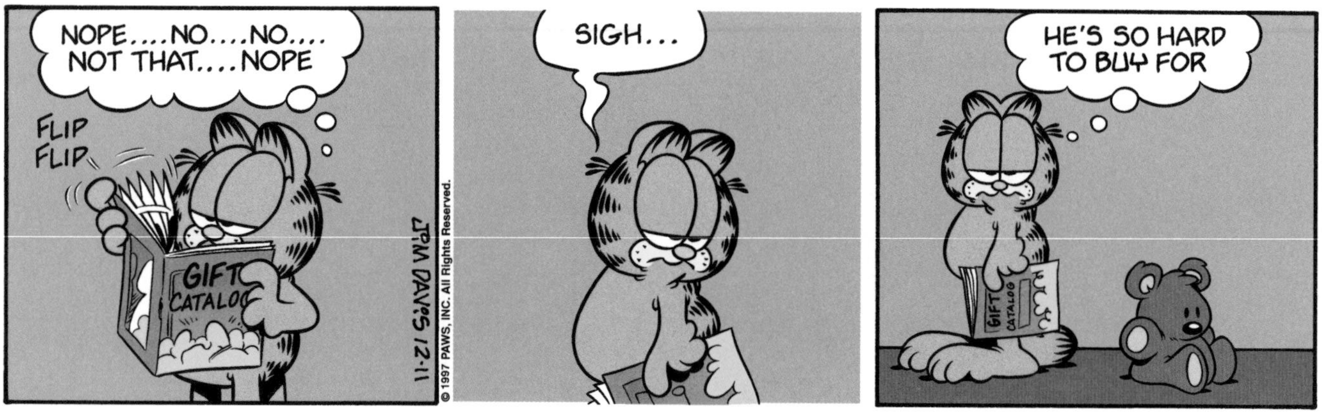
NOPE....NO....NO.... NOT THAT....NOPE
FLIP FLIP
GIFT CATALOG
JIM DAVIS 12-11
© 1997 PAWS, INC. All Rights Reserved.
SIGH...
HE'S SO HARD TO BUY FOR
GIFT CATALOG

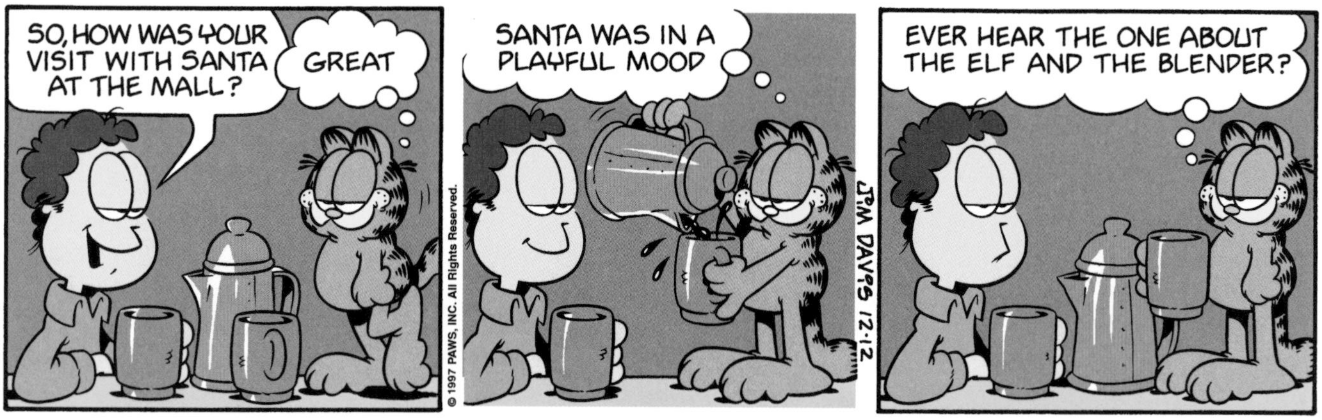
SO, HOW WAS YOUR VISIT WITH SANTA AT THE MALL?
GREAT
© 1997 PAWS, INC. All Rights Reserved.
SANTA WAS IN A PLAYFUL MOOD
JIM DAVIS 12-12
EVER HEAR THE ONE ABOUT THE ELF AND THE BLENDER?

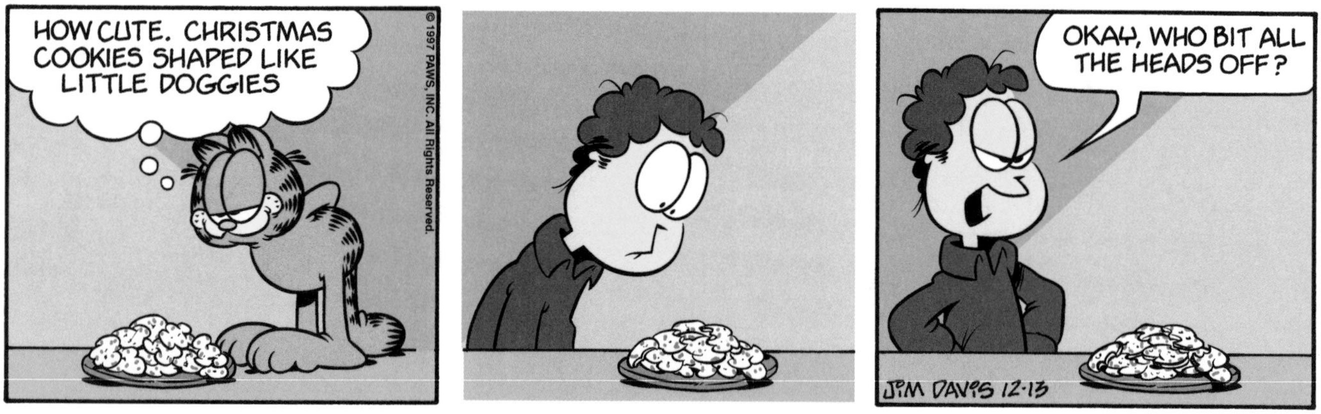
HOW CUTE. CHRISTMAS COOKIES SHAPED LIKE LITTLE DOGGIES
© 1997 PAWS, INC. All Rights Reserved.
OKAY, WHO BIT ALL THE HEADS OFF?
JIM DAVIS 12-13

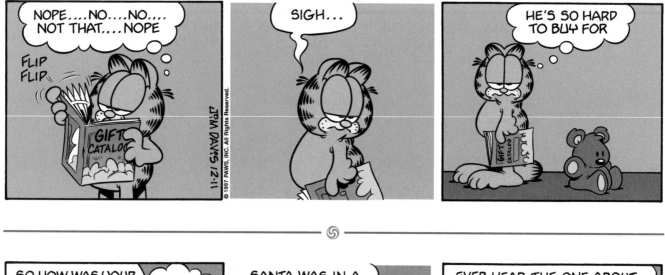

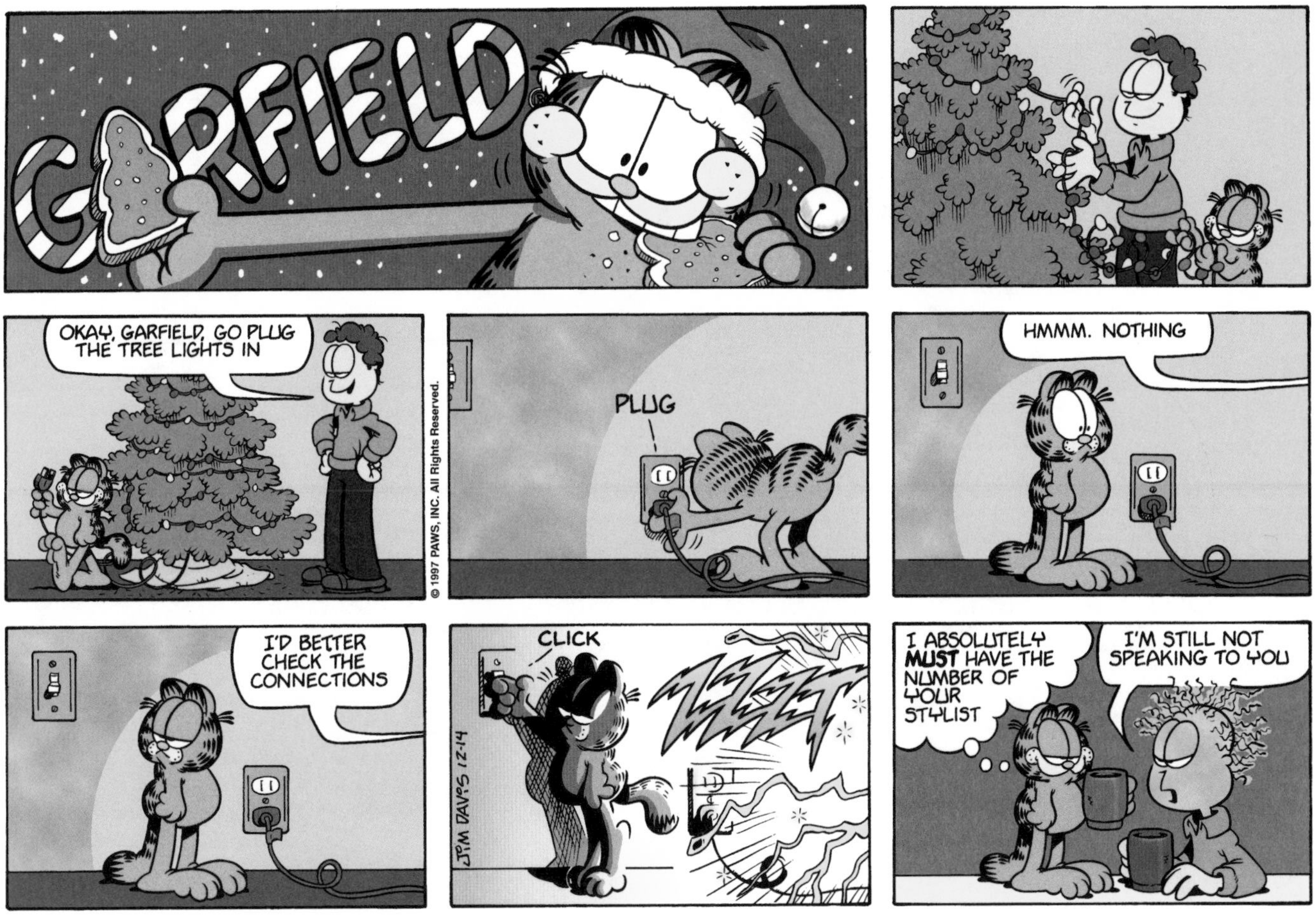
GARFIELD
OKAY, GARFIELD, GO PLUG THE TREE LIGHTS IN
© 1997 PAWS, INC. All Rights Reserved.
PLUG
HMMM. NOTHING
I'D BETTER CHECK THE CONNECTIONS
CLICK
JIM DAVIS 12-14
I ABSOLUTELY MUST HAVE THE NUMBER OF YOUR STYLIST
I'M STILL NOT SPEAKING TO YOU

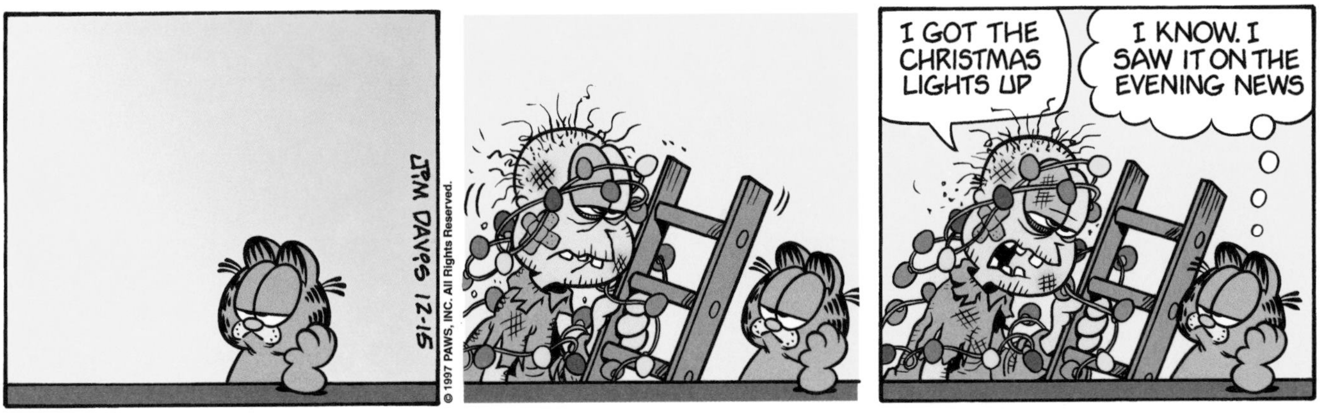
JIM DAVIS 12-15
© 1997 PAWS, INC. All Rights Reserved.
I GOT THE CHRISTMAS LIGHTS UP
I KNOW. I SAW IT ON THE EVENING NEWS

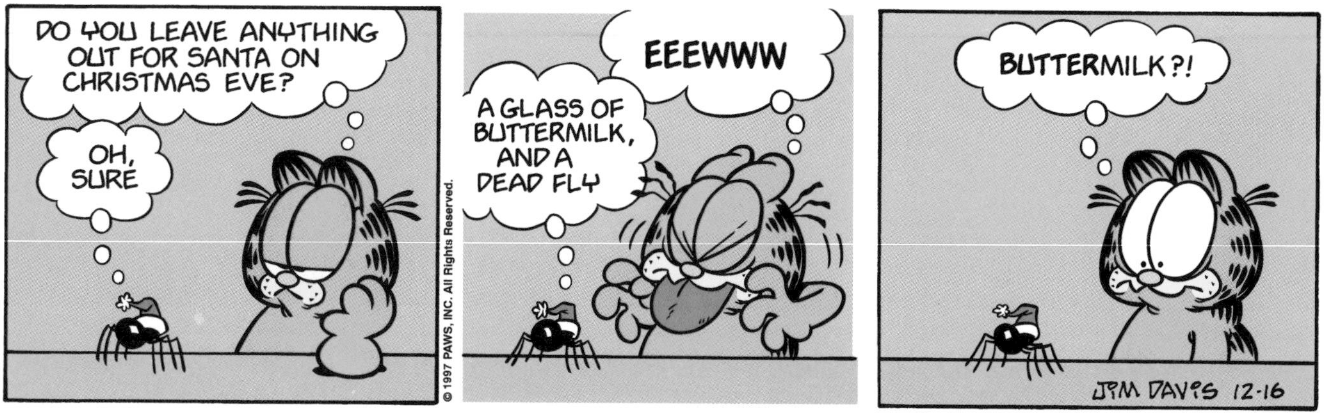
DO YOU LEAVE ANYTHING OUT FOR SANTA ON CHRISTMAS EVE?
OH, SURE
A GLASS OF BUTTERMILK, AND A DEAD FLY
EEEWWW
BUTTERMILK?!
© 1997 PAWS, INC. All Rights Reserved.
JIM DAVIS 12-16

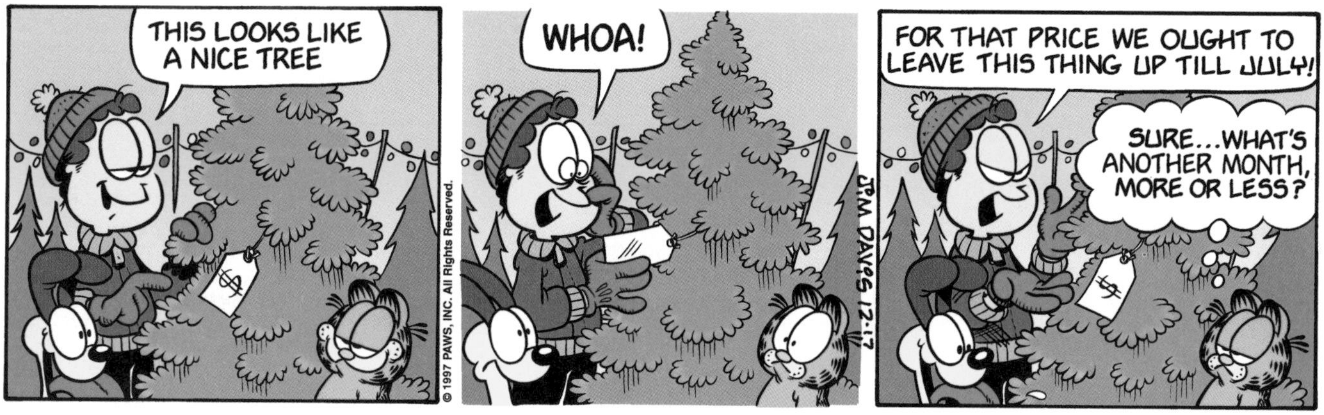
THIS LOOKS LIKE A NICE TREE
WHOA!
FOR THAT PRICE WE OUGHT TO LEAVE THIS THING UP TILL JULY!
SURE...WHAT'S ANOTHER MONTH, MORE OR LESS?
© 1997 PAWS, INC. All Rights Reserved.
JIM DAVIS 12-17

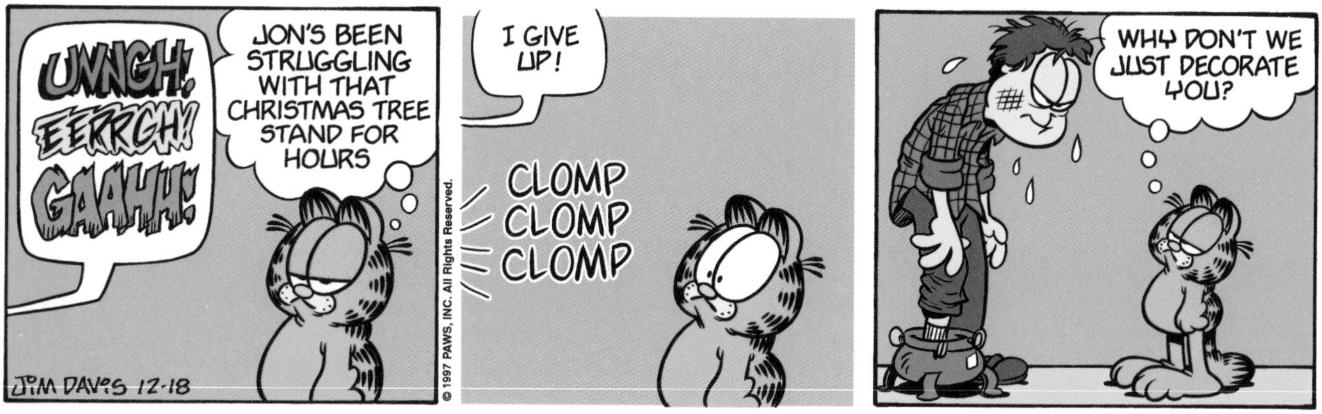
UNNGH! EERRGH! GAAHH!
JON'S BEEN STRUGGLING WITH THAT CHRISTMAS TREE STAND FOR HOURS
I GIVE UP!
CLOMP
CLOMP
CLOMP
WHY DON'T WE JUST DECORATE YOU?
© 1997 PAWS, INC. All Rights Reserved.
JIM DAVIS 12-18

I'LL LEAVE YOUR PRESENT UNDER THE TREE IF YOU PROMISE NOT TO PEEK
YOU HAVE MY WORD
HA! HA! HA!
HA! HA! HA!
I'LL HIDE IT
I'LL FIND IT
JIM DAVIS 12-19
© 1997 PAWS, INC. All Rights Reserved.

JIM DAVIS 12-20
© 1997 PAWS, INC. All Rights Reserved.

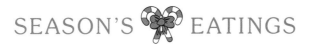

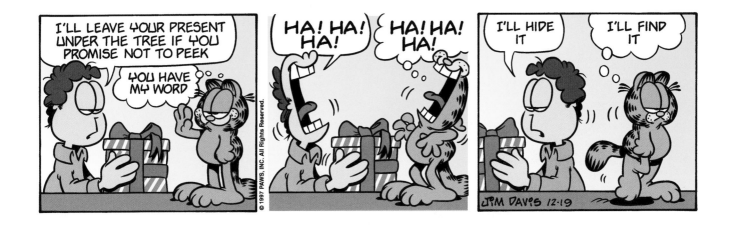

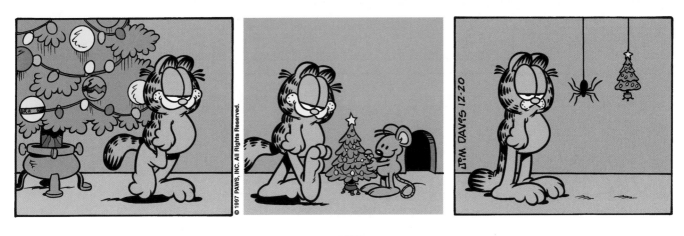

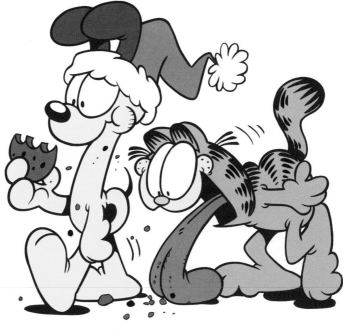

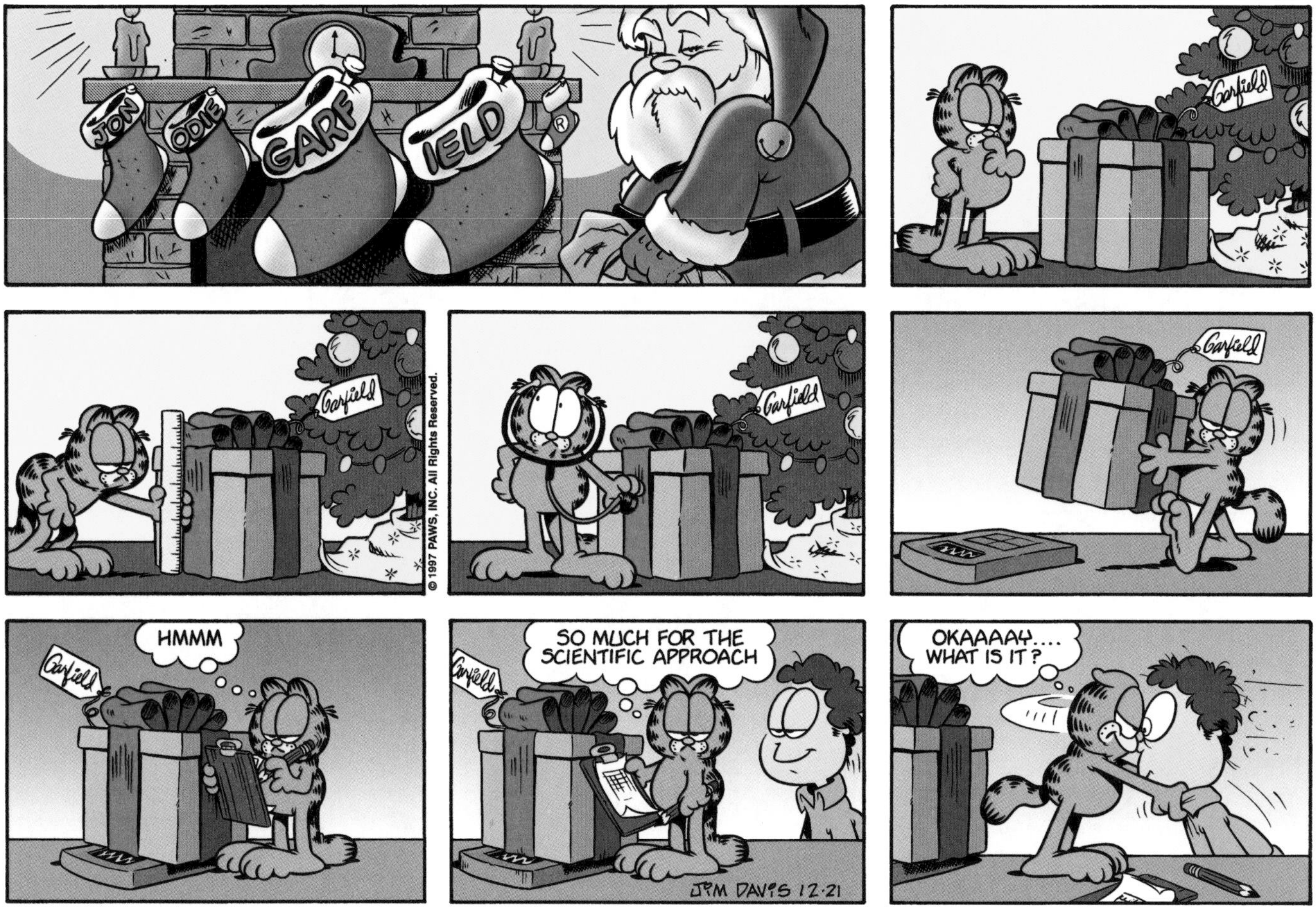
JON
ODIE
GARF
IELD
Garfield
HMMM
SO MUCH FOR THE SCIENTIFIC APPROACH
OKAAAAY.... WHAT IS IT?
JIM DAVIS 12-21
© 1997 PAWS, INC. All Rights Reserved.

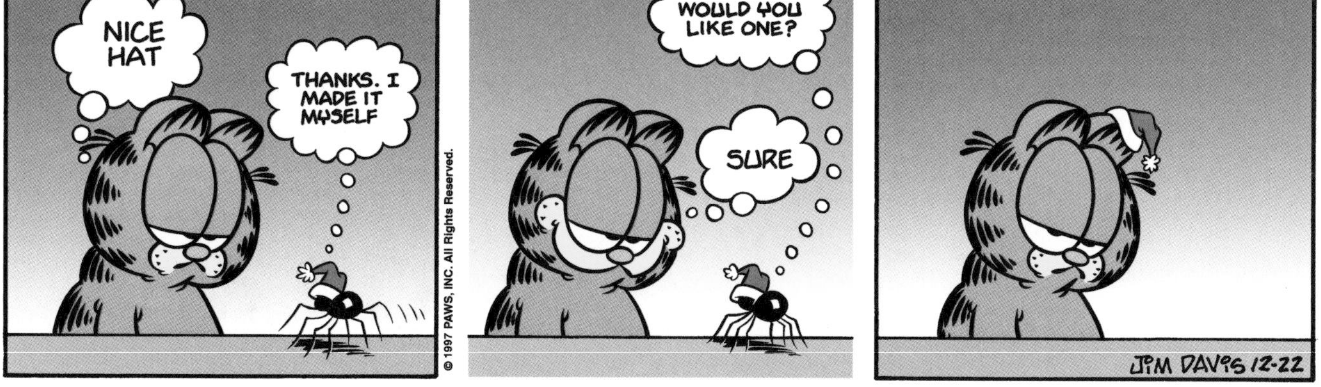
NICE HAT
THANKS. I MADE IT MYSELF
WOULD YOU LIKE ONE?
SURE
JIM DAVIS 12-22
© 1997 PAWS, INC. All Rights Reserved.

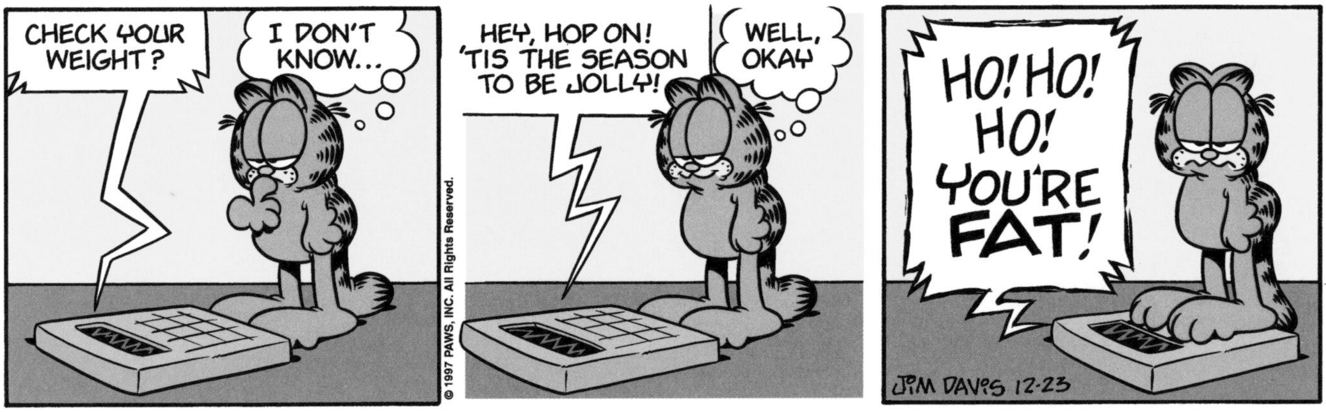
CHECK YOUR WEIGHT?
I DON'T KNOW...
HEY, HOP ON! 'TIS THE SEASON TO BE JOLLY!
WELL, OKAY
HO! HO! HO! YOU'RE FAT!
© 1997 PAWS, INC. All Rights Reserved.
JIM DAVIS 12-23

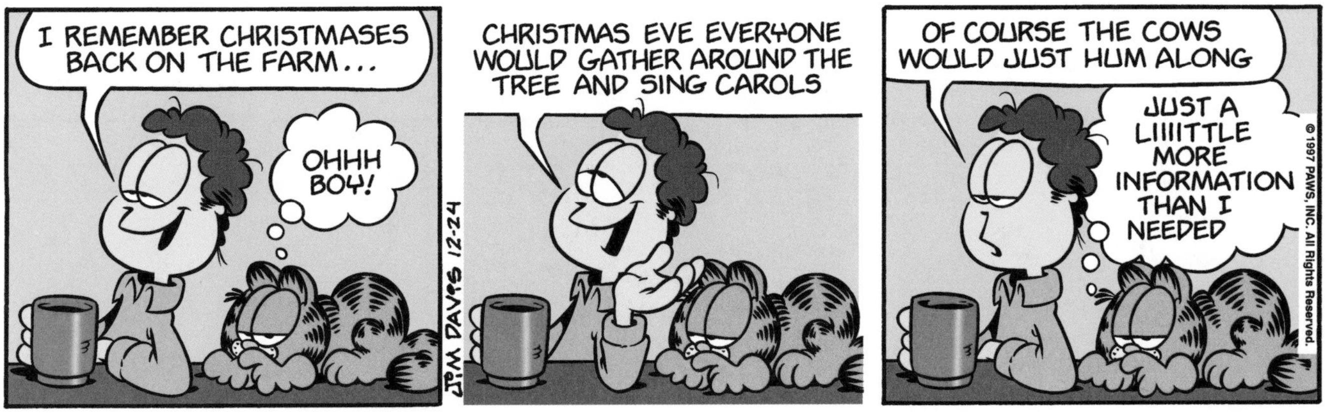
I REMEMBER CHRISTMASES BACK ON THE FARM...
OHHH BOY!
CHRISTMAS EVE EVERYONE WOULD GATHER AROUND THE TREE AND SING CAROLS
OF COURSE THE COWS WOULD JUST HUM ALONG
JUST A LIIIITTLE MORE INFORMATION THAN I NEEDED
© 1997 PAWS, INC. All Rights Reserved.
JIM DAVIS 12-24

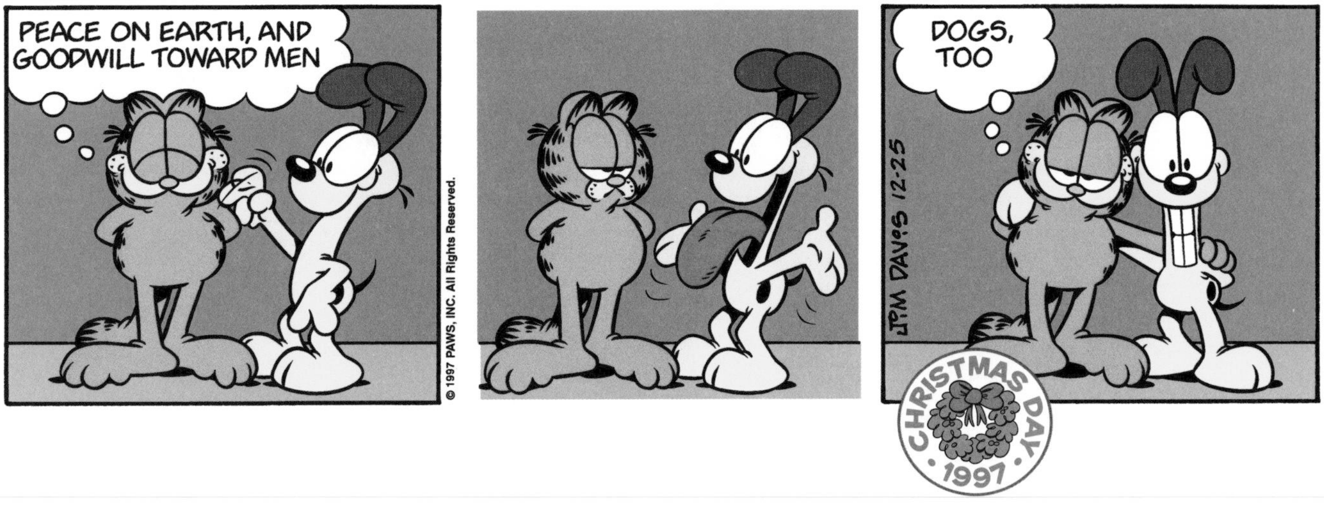
PEACE ON EARTH, AND GOODWILL TOWARD MEN
DOGS, TOO
© 1997 PAWS, INC. All Rights Reserved.
JIM DAVIS 12-25
CHRISTMAS DAY 1997

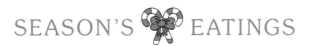

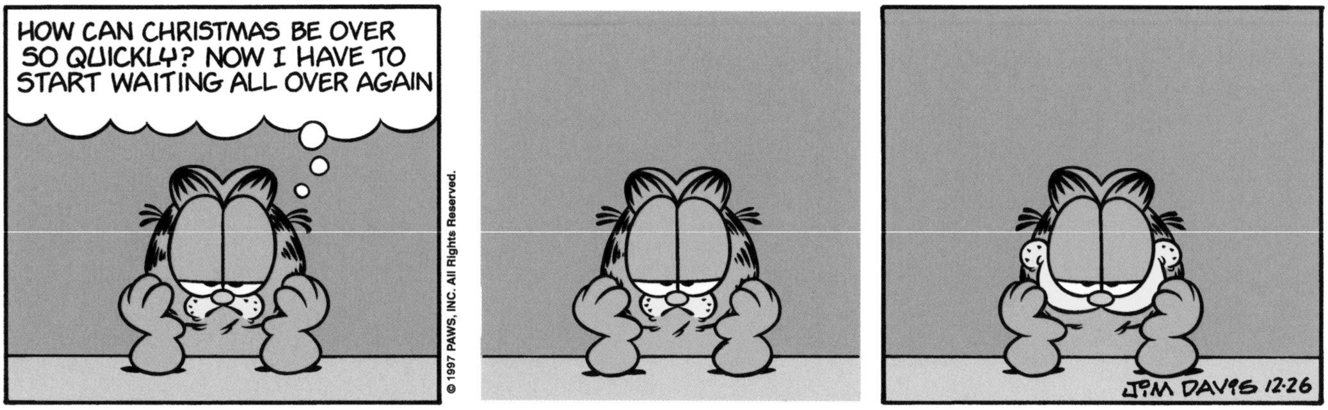
HOW CAN CHRISTMAS BE OVER SO QUICKLY? NOW I HAVE TO START WAITING ALL OVER AGAIN
© 1997 PAWS, INC. All Rights Reserved.
JIM DAVIS 12-26

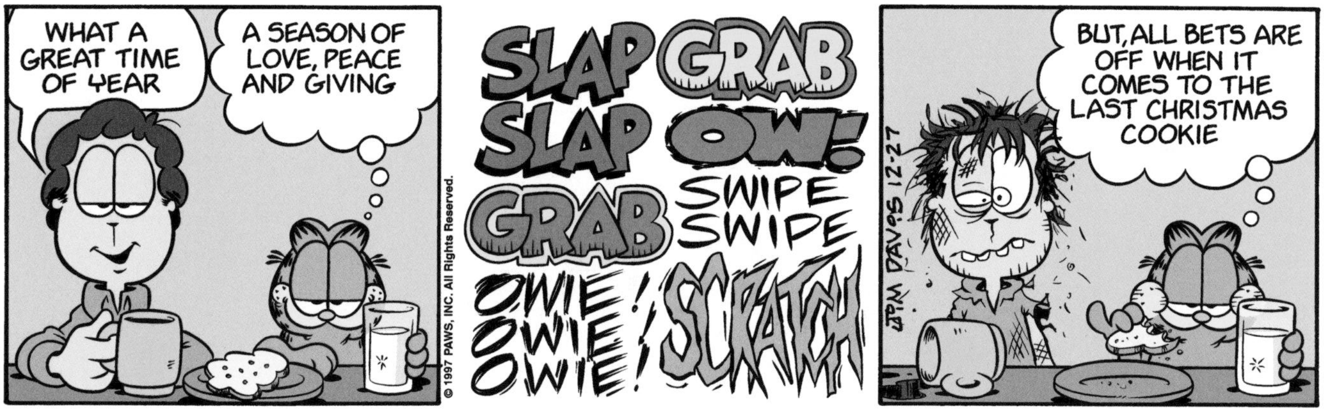
WHAT A GREAT TIME OF YEAR
A SEASON OF LOVE, PEACE AND GIVING
© 1997 PAWS, INC. All Rights Reserved.
SLAP GRAB
SLAP OW!
GRAB SWIPE SWIPE
OWIE! OWIE! OWIE!
SCRATCH
JIM DAVIS 12-27
BUT, ALL BETS ARE OFF WHEN IT COMES TO THE LAST CHRISTMAS COOKIE

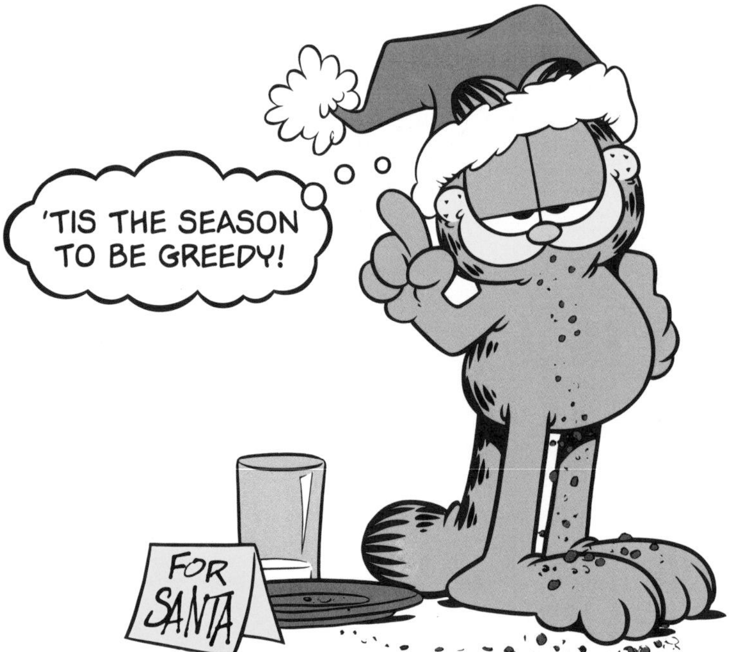
'TIS THE SEASON TO BE GREEDY!
FOR SANTA

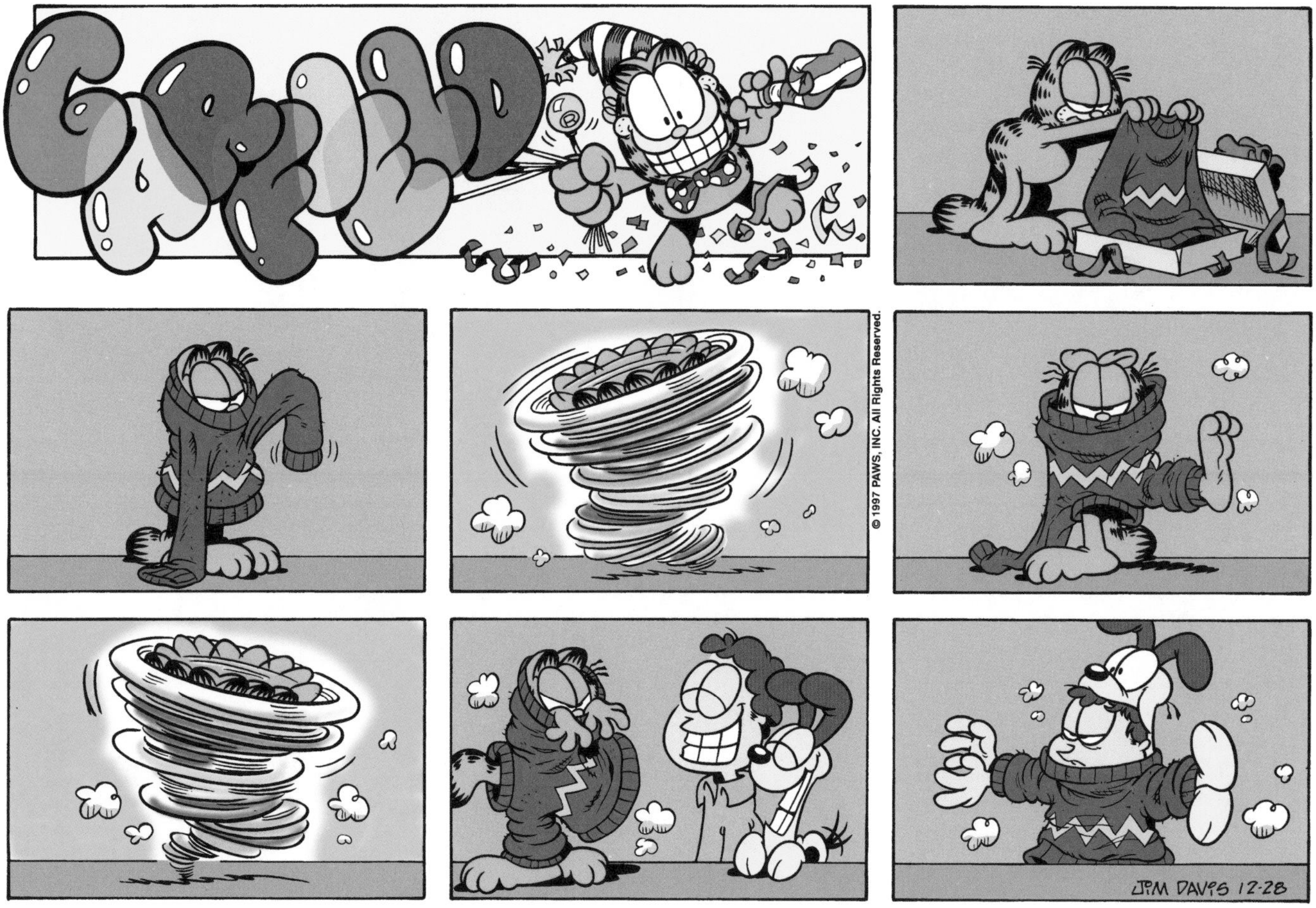
GARFIELD
© 1997 PAWS, INC. All Rights Reserved.
JIM DAVIS 12-28

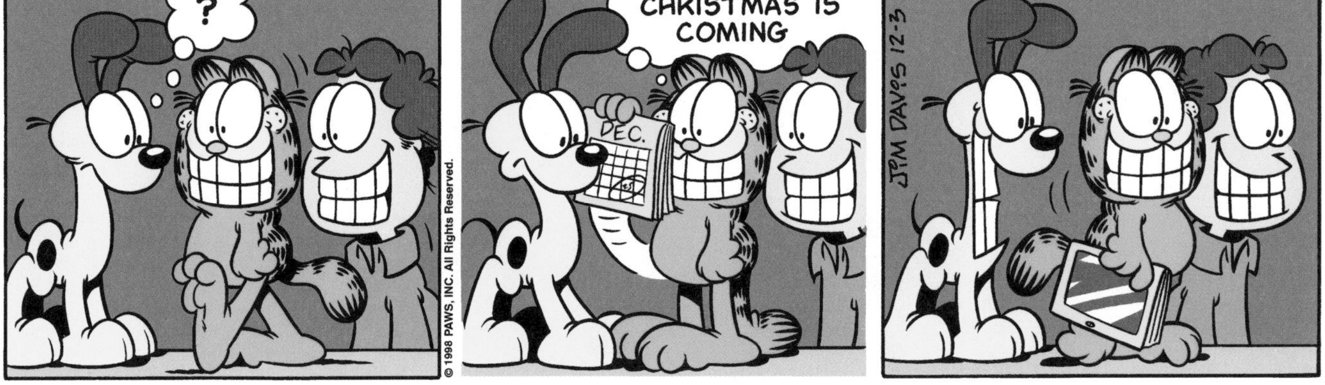
?
© 1998 PAWS, INC. All Rights Reserved.
CHRISTMAS IS COMING
DEC.
JIM DAVIS 12-3

Dear Santa,
I am writing this for my cat.
JIM DAVIS 12-4
© 1998 PAWS, INC. All Rights Reserved.
He would like you to bring him ten thousand pizzas.
ANYTHING ELSE?
AND AN ANTACID TABLET

© 1998 PAWS, INC. All Rights Reserved.
YOU ATE THE ENTIRE BOWL OF HARD CANDY?!
JIM DAVIS 12-5
RATTLE
RATTLE
RATTLE

CHRISTMAS CANDIES

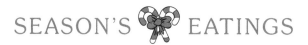

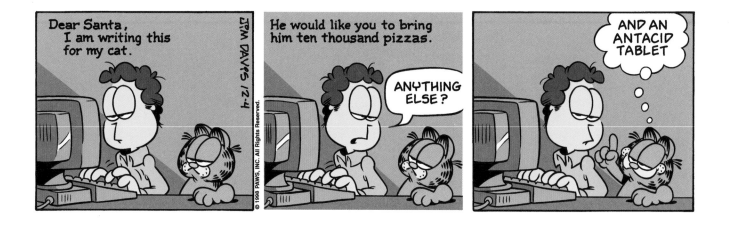

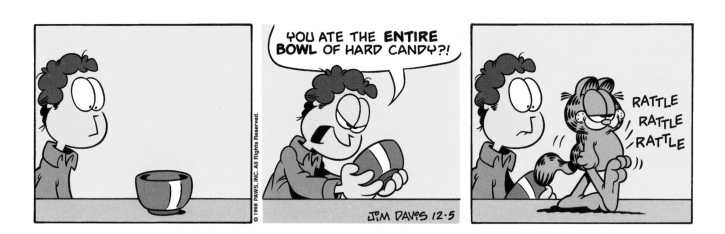

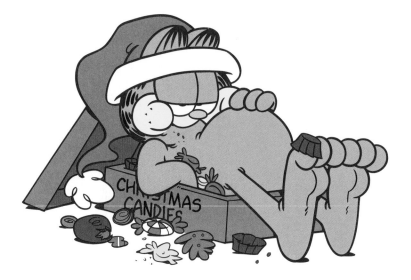

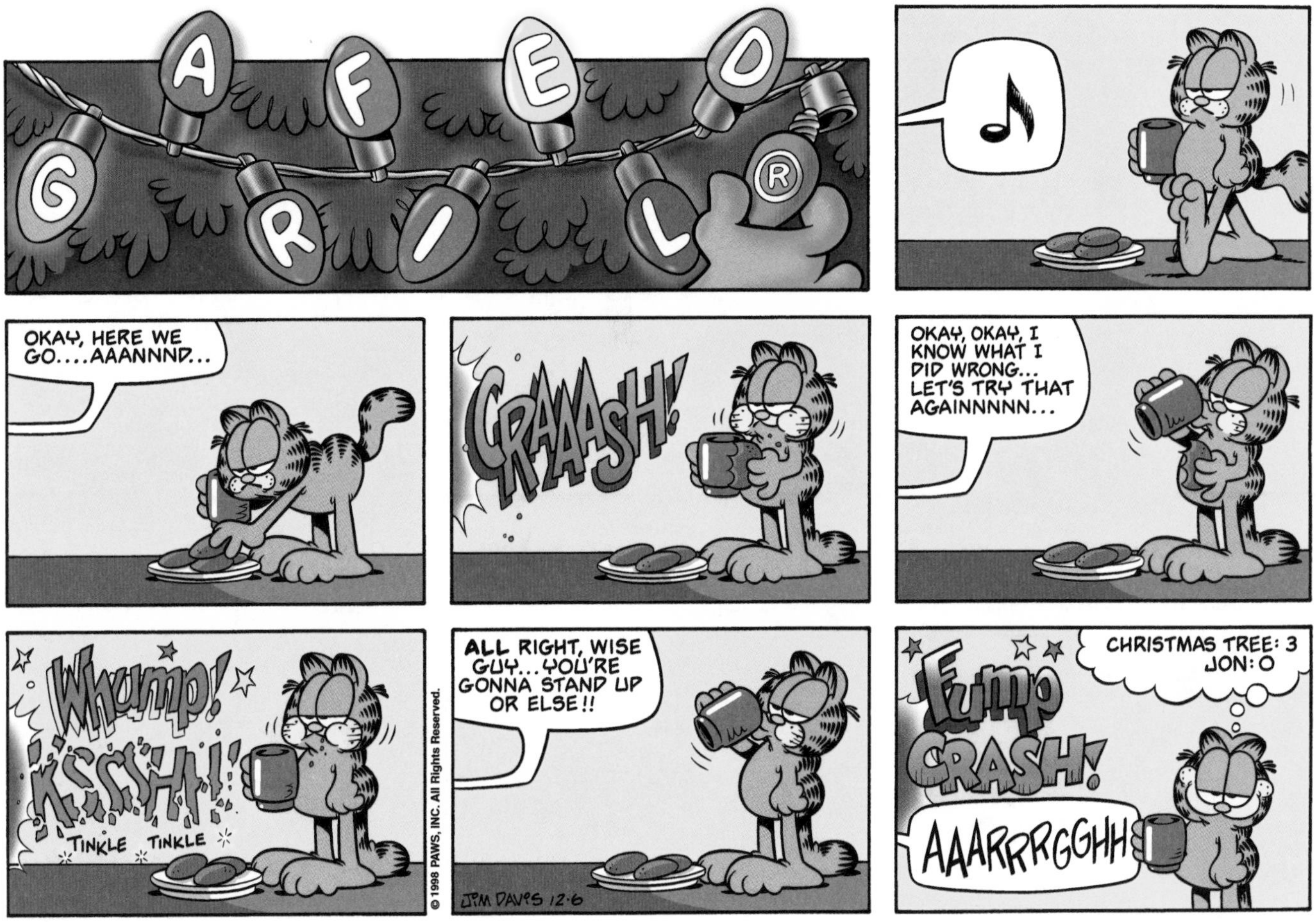
GARFIELD®
OKAY, HERE WE GO....AAANNND...
CRAAASH!
OKAY, OKAY, I KNOW WHAT I DID WRONG... LET'S TRY THAT AGAINNNNN...
Whump!
KSSSH!
TINKLE TINKLE
© 1998 PAWS, INC. All Rights Reserved.
ALL RIGHT, WISE GUY... YOU'RE GONNA STAND UP OR ELSE!!
JIM DAVIS 12-6
Fump
CRASH!
AAARRRGGHH
CHRISTMAS TREE: 3
JON: 0

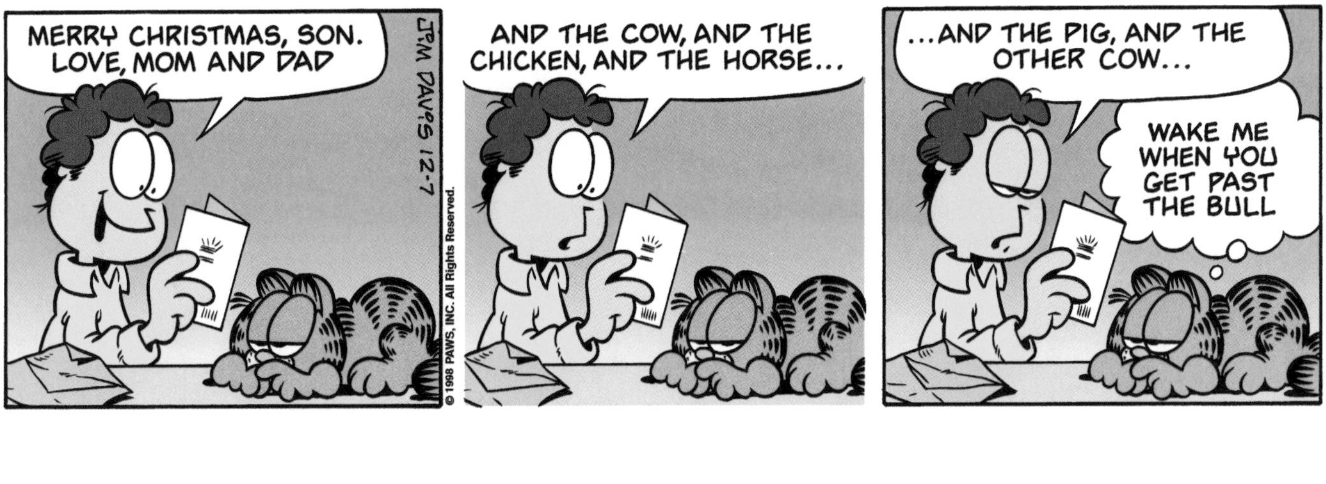
MERRY CHRISTMAS, SON. LOVE, MOM AND DAD
JIM DAVIS 12-7
© 1998 PAWS, INC. All Rights Reserved.
AND THE COW, AND THE CHICKEN, AND THE HORSE...
...AND THE PIG, AND THE OTHER COW...
WAKE ME WHEN YOU GET PAST THE BULL

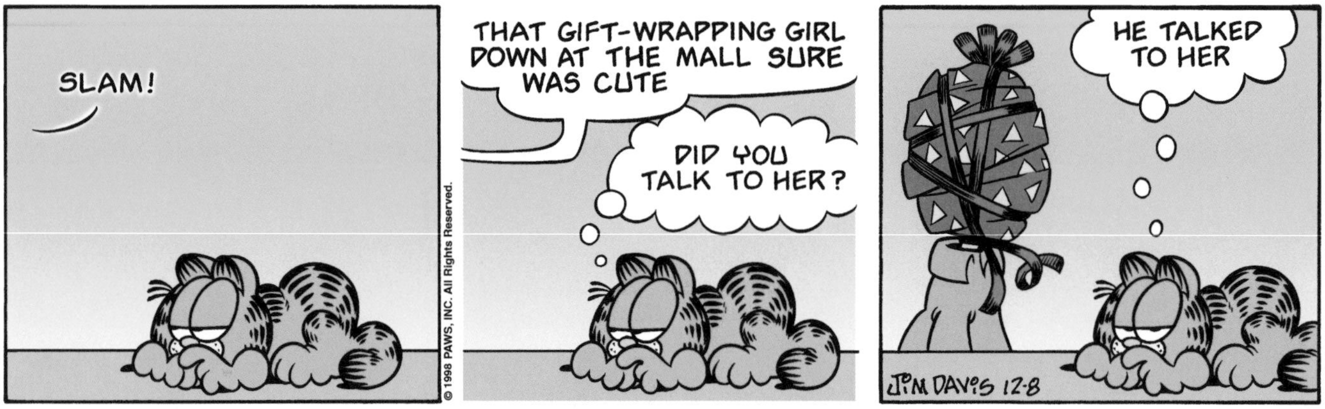
SLAM!
THAT GIFT-WRAPPING GIRL DOWN AT THE MALL SURE WAS CUTE
DID YOU TALK TO HER?
HE TALKED TO HER
© 1998 PAWS, INC. All Rights Reserved.
JIM DAVIS 12-8

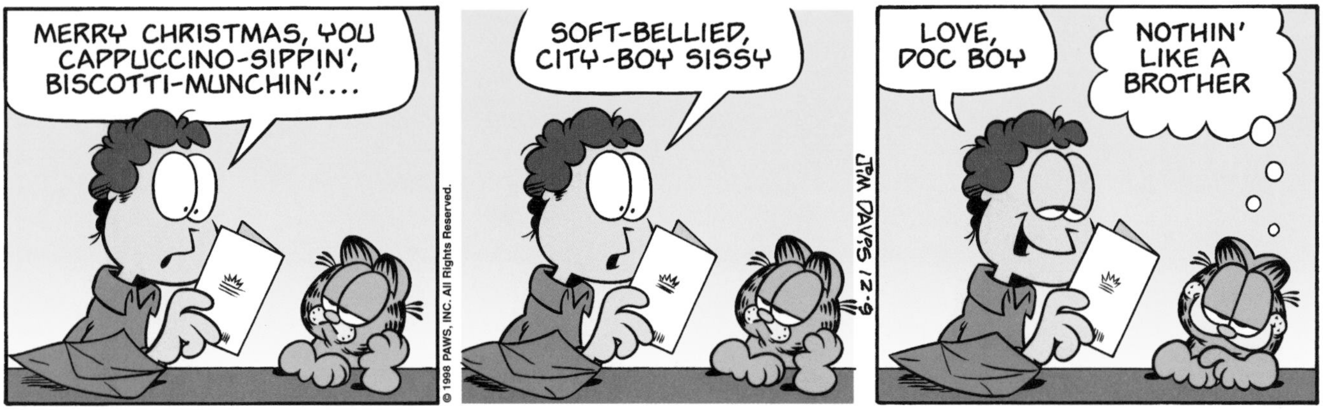
MERRY CHRISTMAS, YOU CAPPUCCINO-SIPPIN', BISCOTTI-MUNCHIN'....
SOFT-BELLIED, CITY-BOY SISSY
LOVE, DOC BOY
NOTHIN' LIKE A BROTHER
© 1998 PAWS, INC. All Rights Reserved.
JIM DAVIS 12-9

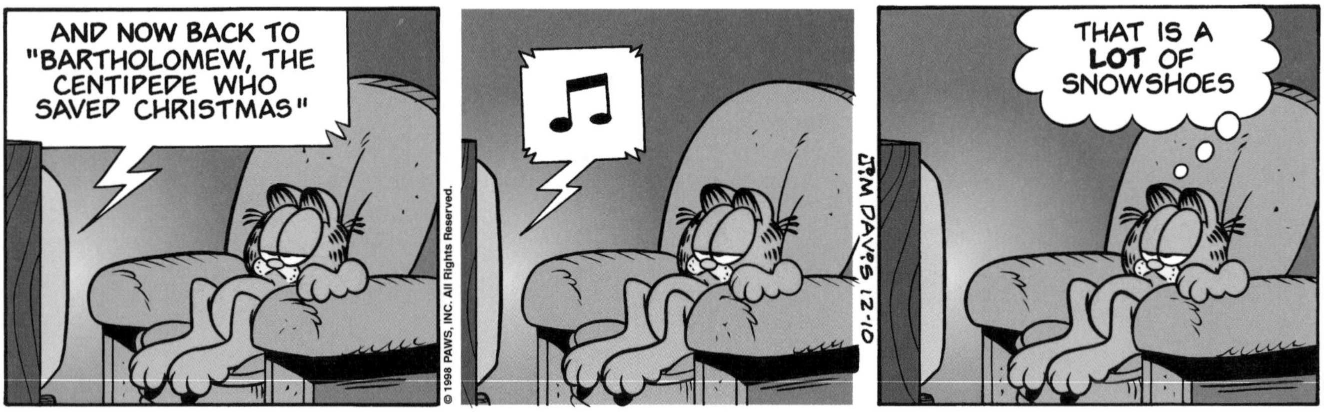
AND NOW BACK TO "BARTHOLOMEW, THE CENTIPEDE WHO SAVED CHRISTMAS"
THAT IS A **LOT** OF SNOWSHOES
© 1998 PAWS, INC. All Rights Reserved.
JIM DAVIS 12-10

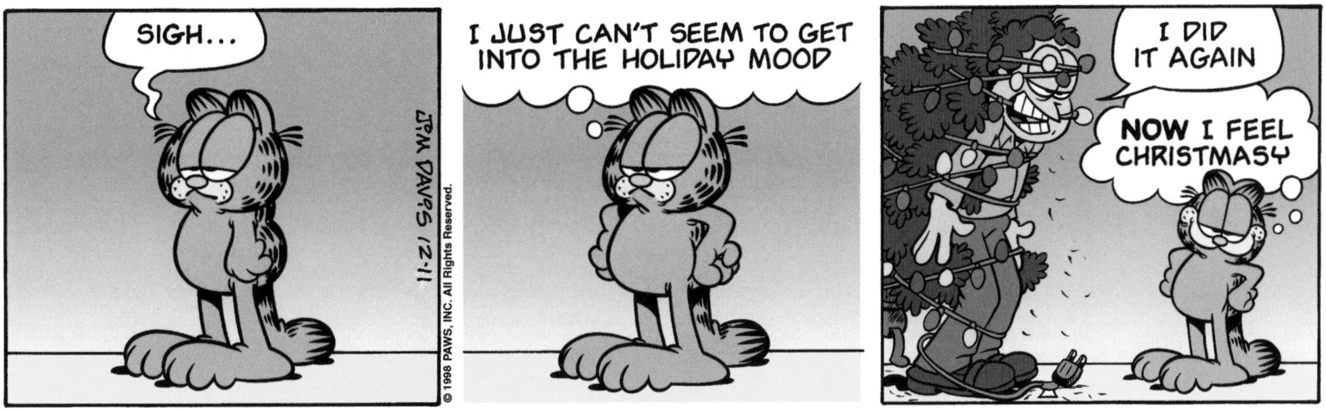
SIGH...
JIM DAVIS 12-11
© 1998 PAWS, INC. All Rights Reserved.
I JUST CAN'T SEEM TO GET INTO THE HOLIDAY MOOD
I DID IT AGAIN
NOW I FEEL CHRISTMASY

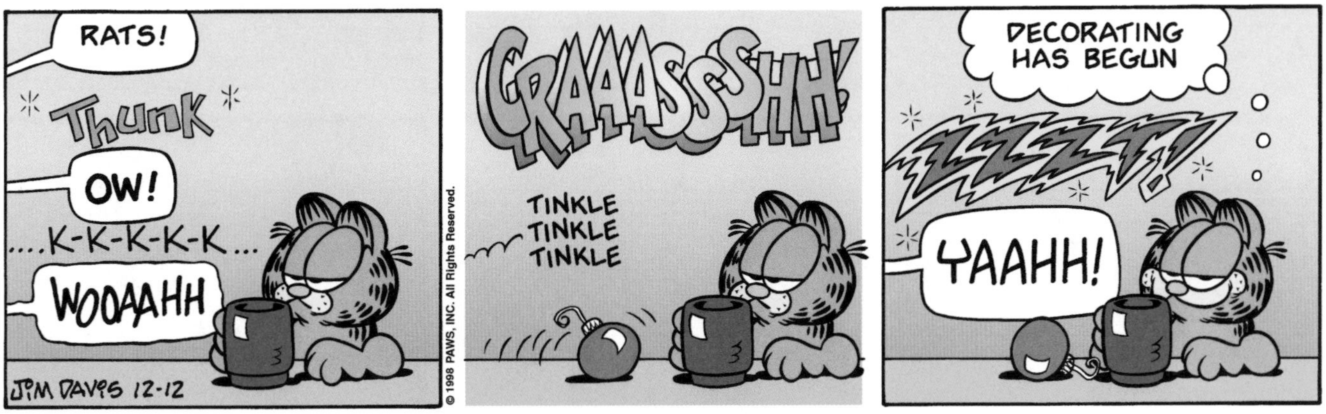
RATS!
Thunk
OW!
....K-K-K-K-K....
WOOAAHH
JIM DAVIS 12-12
© 1998 PAWS, INC. All Rights Reserved.
CRAAAASSSHH!
TINKLE
TINKLE
TINKLE
DECORATING HAS BEGUN
ZZZZT!
YAAHH!

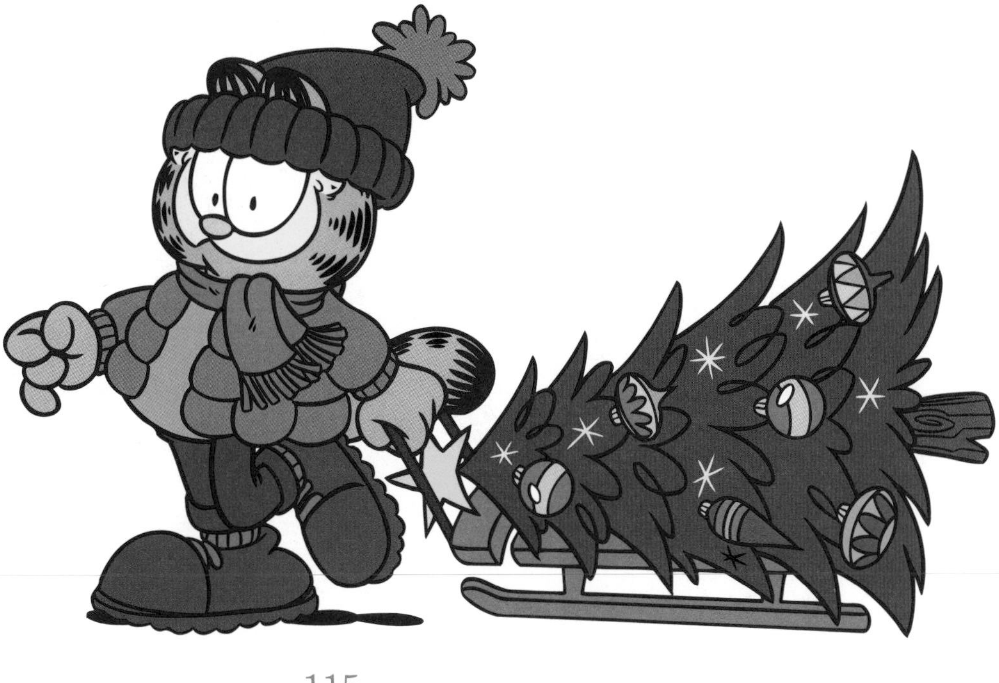

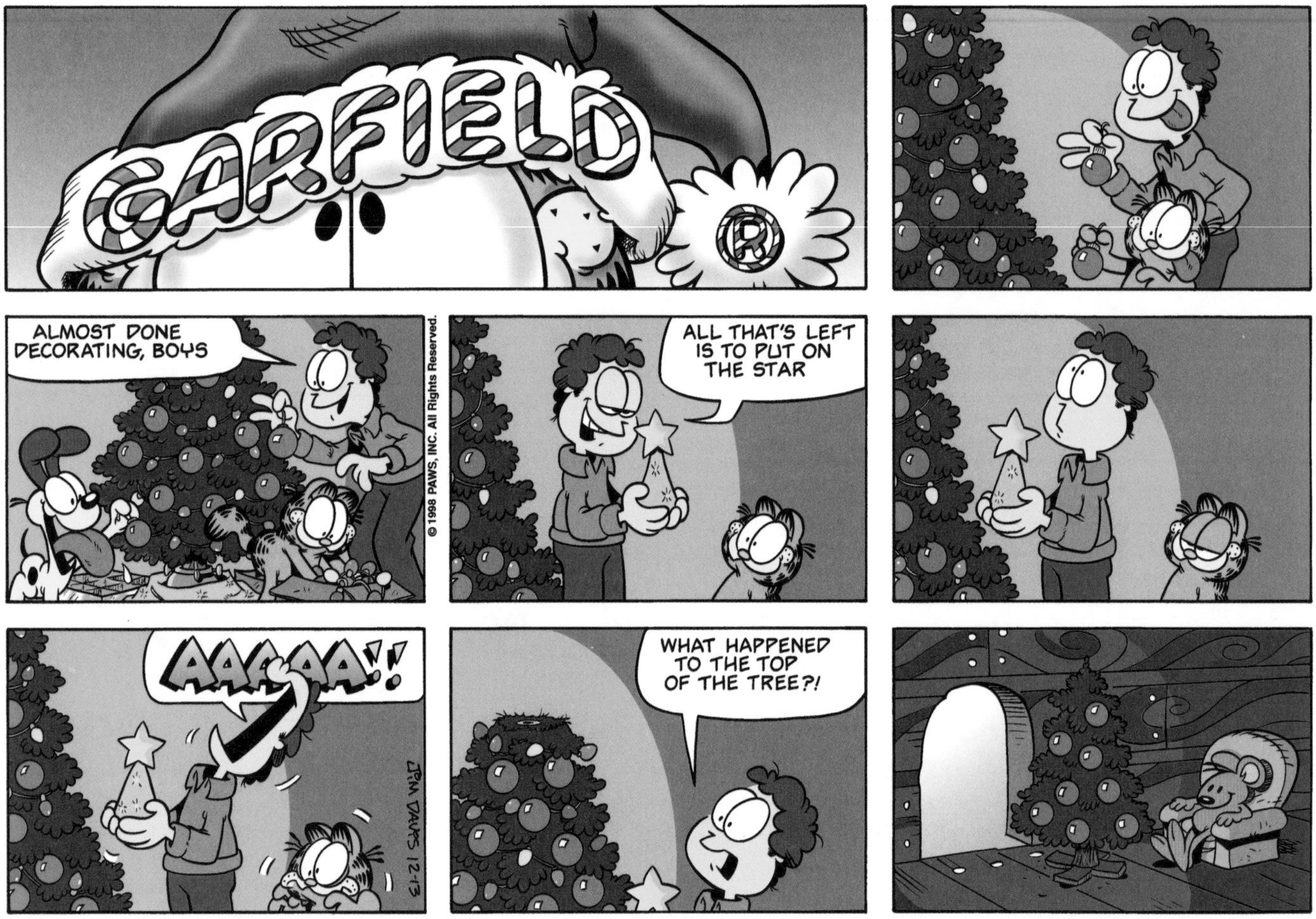
GARFIELD
ALMOST DONE DECORATING, BOYS
© 1998 PAWS, INC. All Rights Reserved.
ALL THAT'S LEFT IS TO PUT ON THE STAR
AAAAA!!
JIM DAVIS 12-13
WHAT HAPPENED TO THE TOP OF THE TREE?!

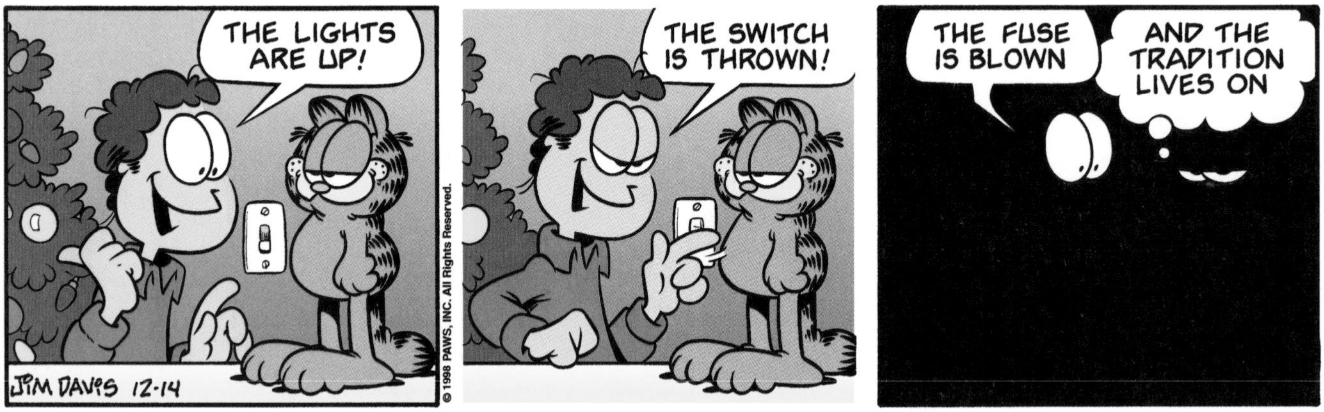
THE LIGHTS ARE UP!
JIM DAVIS 12-14
© 1998 PAWS, INC. All Rights Reserved.
THE SWITCH IS THROWN!
THE FUSE IS BLOWN
AND THE TRADITION LIVES ON

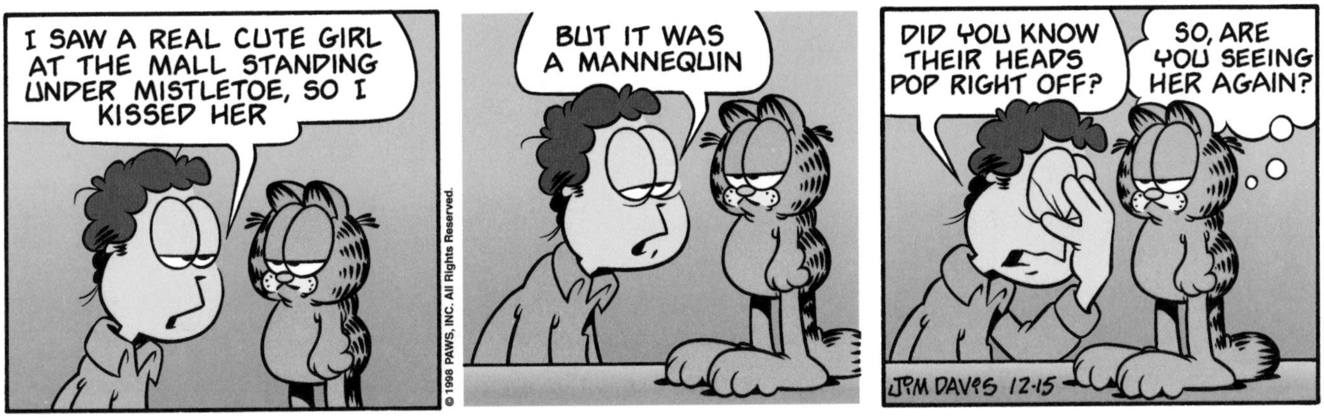
I SAW A REAL CUTE GIRL AT THE MALL STANDING UNDER MISTLETOE, SO I KISSED HER
© 1998 PAWS, INC. All Rights Reserved.
BUT IT WAS A MANNEQUIN
DID YOU KNOW THEIR HEADS POP RIGHT OFF?
SO, ARE YOU SEEING HER AGAIN?
JIM DAVIS 12-15

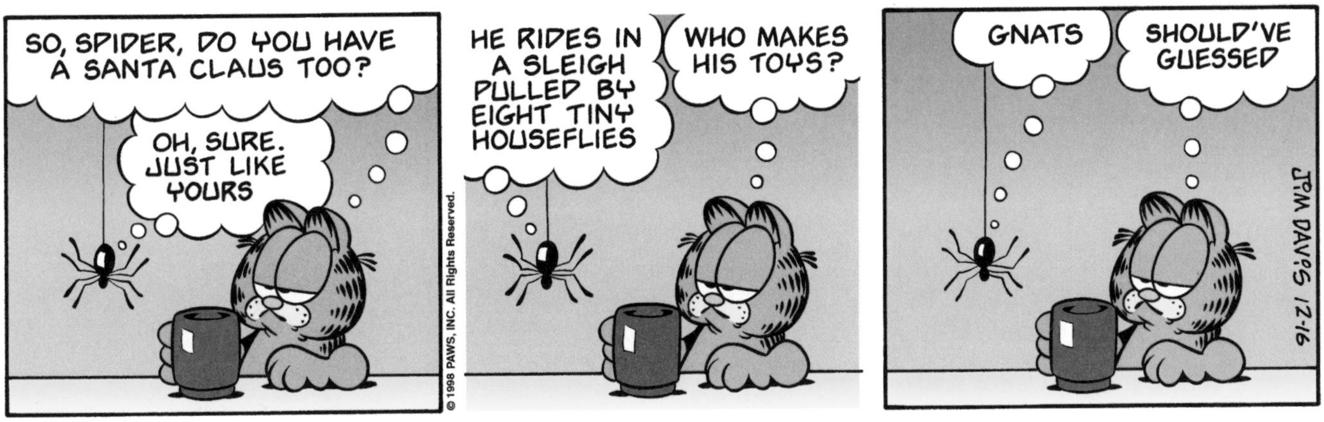
SO, SPIDER, DO YOU HAVE A SANTA CLAUS TOO?
OH, SURE. JUST LIKE YOURS
© 1998 PAWS, INC. All Rights Reserved.
HE RIDES IN A SLEIGH PULLED BY EIGHT TINY HOUSEFLIES
WHO MAKES HIS TOYS?
GNATS
SHOULD'VE GUESSED
JIM DAVIS 12-16

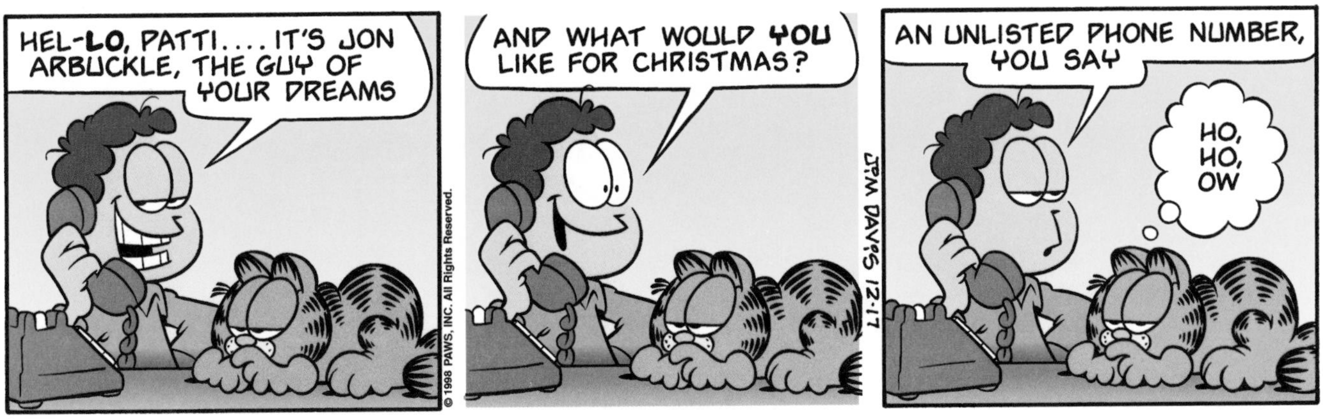
HEL-**LO**, PATTI.... IT'S JON ARBUCKLE, THE GUY OF YOUR DREAMS
© 1998 PAWS, INC. All Rights Reserved.
AND WHAT WOULD **YOU** LIKE FOR CHRISTMAS?
JIM DAVIS 12-17
AN UNLISTED PHONE NUMBER, YOU SAY
HO, HO, OW

WHAT IS IT ABOUT CHRISTMAS THAT FILLS MY HEART SO?
IS IT THE LIGHTS, THE PRESENTS, THE SMILES ON THE FACES OF LITTLE CHILDREN, THE FEELING OF GOOD WILL THAT FILLS THE AIR?...
YEAH...DEFINITELY THE PRESENTS
JIM DAVIS 12-18
© 1998 PAWS, INC. All Rights Reserved.

♪JINGLE BELLS, JINGLE BELLS...
JIM DAVIS 12-19
© 1998 PAWS, INC. All Rights Reserved.
YOU'RE FLAT
NO, I'M NOT
YES, YOU ARE

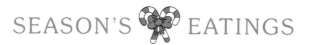

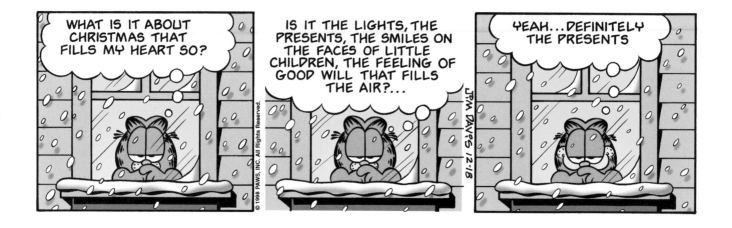

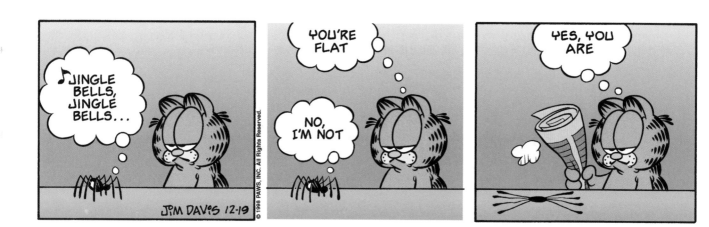

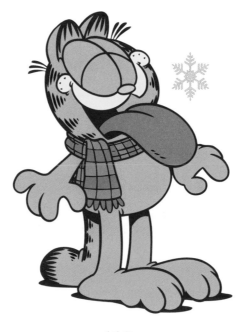

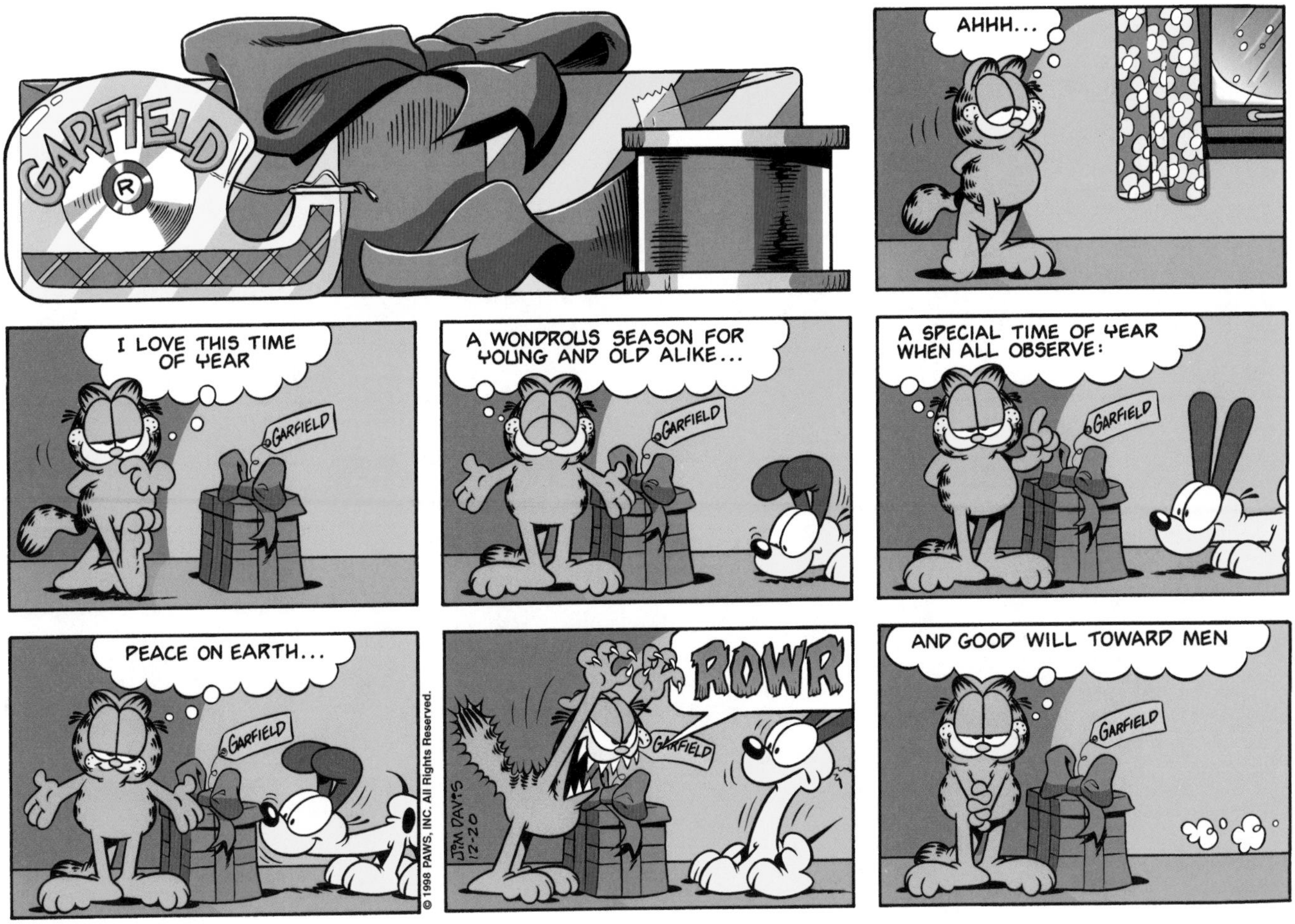
GARFIELD
AHHH...
I LOVE THIS TIME OF YEAR
A WONDROUS SEASON FOR YOUNG AND OLD ALIKE...
A SPECIAL TIME OF YEAR WHEN ALL OBSERVE:
PEACE ON EARTH...
ROWR
AND GOOD WILL TOWARD MEN
© 1998 PAWS, INC. All Rights Reserved.
JIM DAVIS 12-20

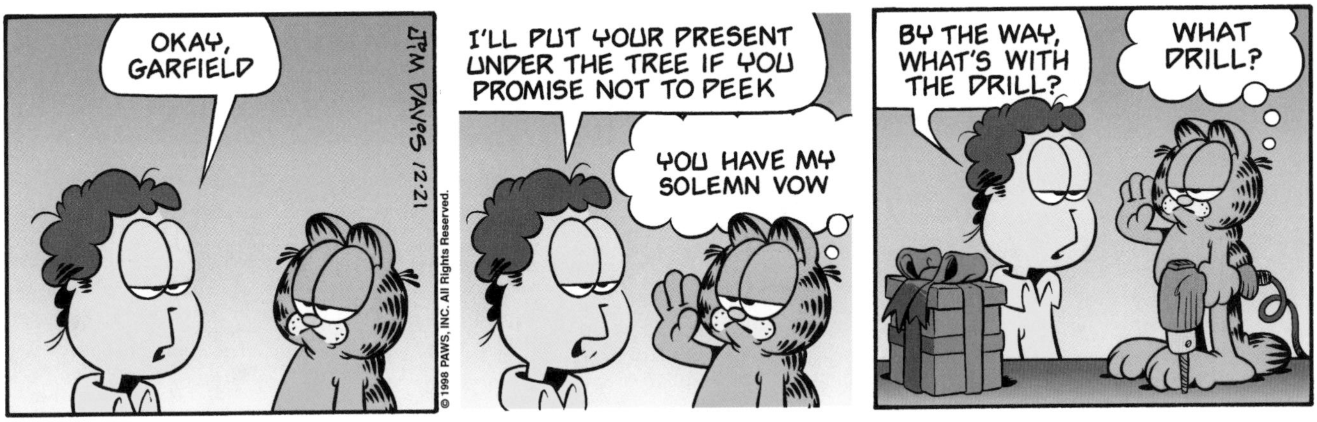
OKAY, GARFIELD
JIM DAVIS 12-21
© 1998 PAWS, INC. All Rights Reserved.
I'LL PUT YOUR PRESENT UNDER THE TREE IF YOU PROMISE NOT TO PEEK
YOU HAVE MY SOLEMN VOW
BY THE WAY, WHAT'S WITH THE DRILL?
WHAT DRILL?

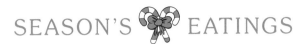

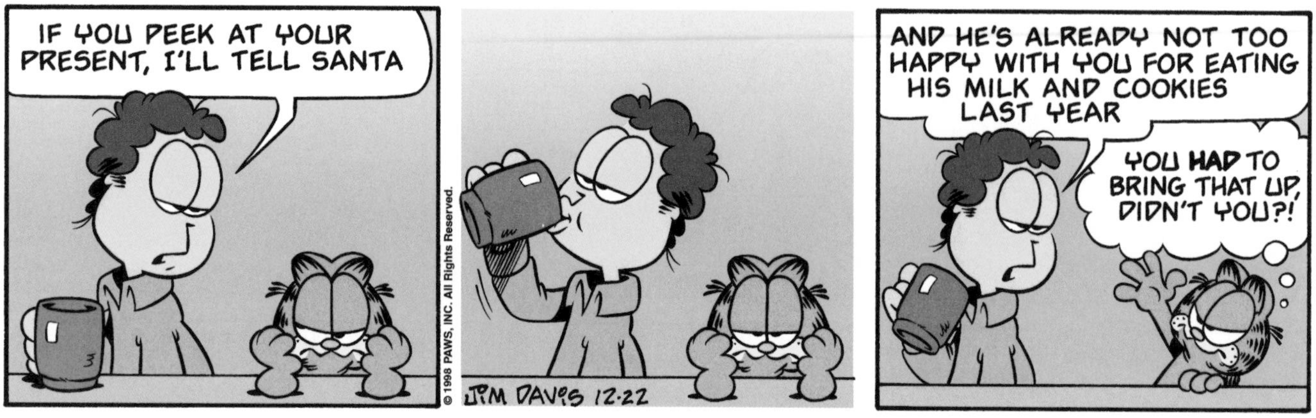
IF YOU PEEK AT YOUR PRESENT, I'LL TELL SANTA
© 1998 PAWS, INC. All Rights Reserved.
JIM DAVIS 12-22
AND HE'S ALREADY NOT TOO HAPPY WITH YOU FOR EATING HIS MILK AND COOKIES LAST YEAR
YOU **HAD** TO BRING THAT UP, DIDN'T YOU?!

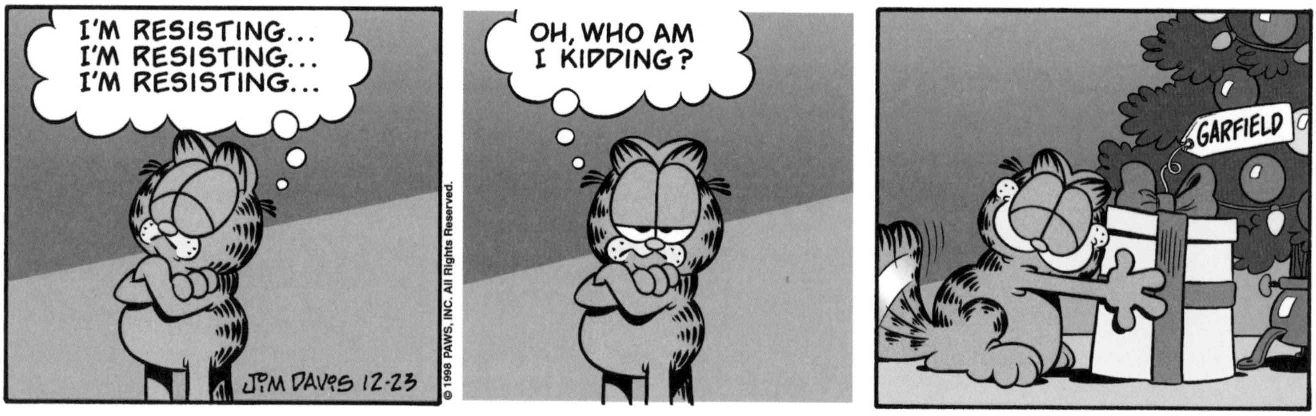
I'M RESISTING... I'M RESISTING... I'M RESISTING...
JIM DAVIS 12-23
© 1998 PAWS, INC. All Rights Reserved.
OH, WHO AM I KIDDING?
GARFIELD

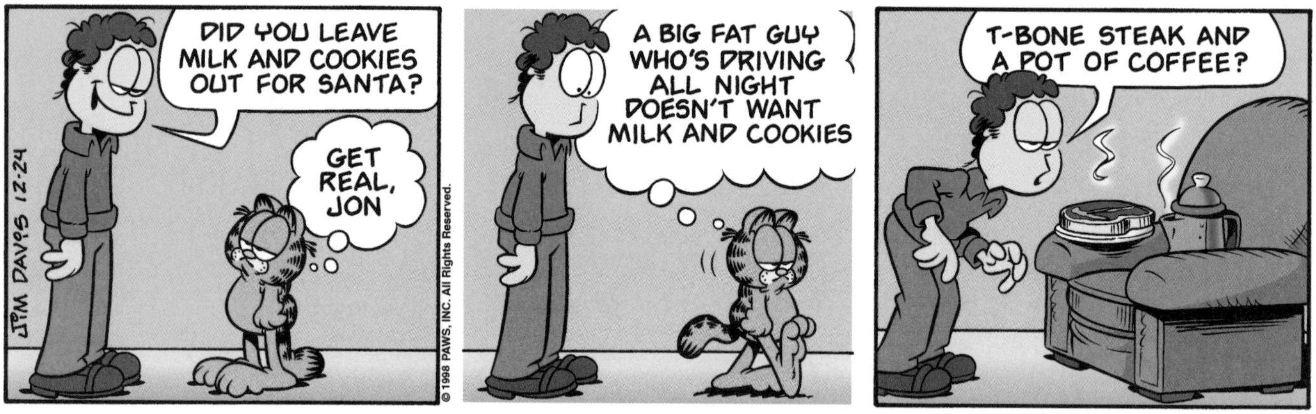
DID YOU LEAVE MILK AND COOKIES OUT FOR SANTA?
GET REAL, JON
JIM DAVIS 12-24
© 1998 PAWS, INC. All Rights Reserved.
A BIG FAT GUY WHO'S DRIVING ALL NIGHT DOESN'T WANT MILK AND COOKIES
T-BONE STEAK AND A POT OF COFFEE?

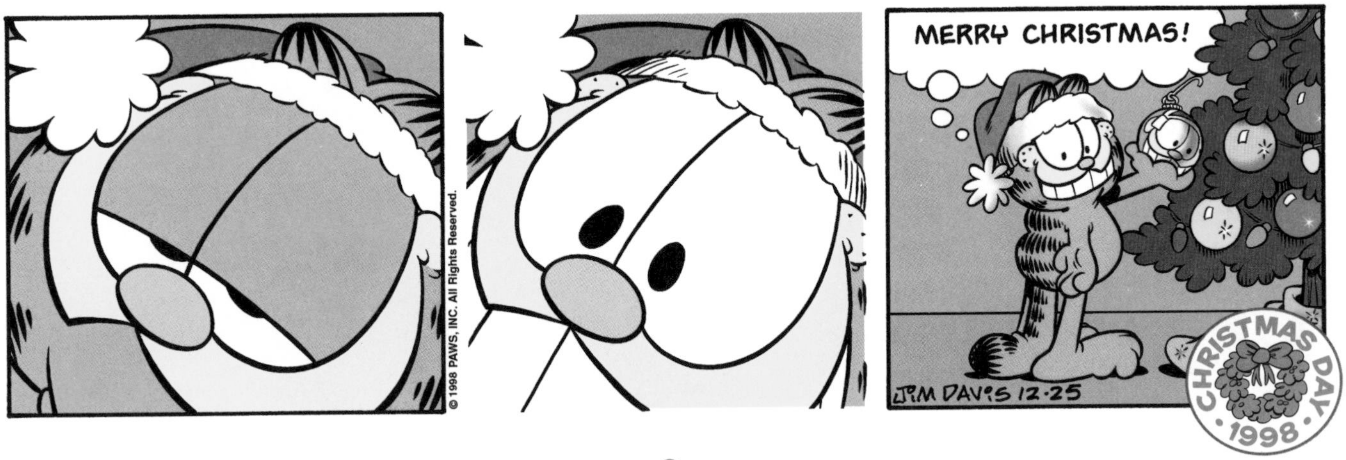
© 1998 PAWS, INC. All Rights Reserved.
MERRY CHRISTMAS!
JIM DAVIS 12-25
CHRISTMAS DAY 1998

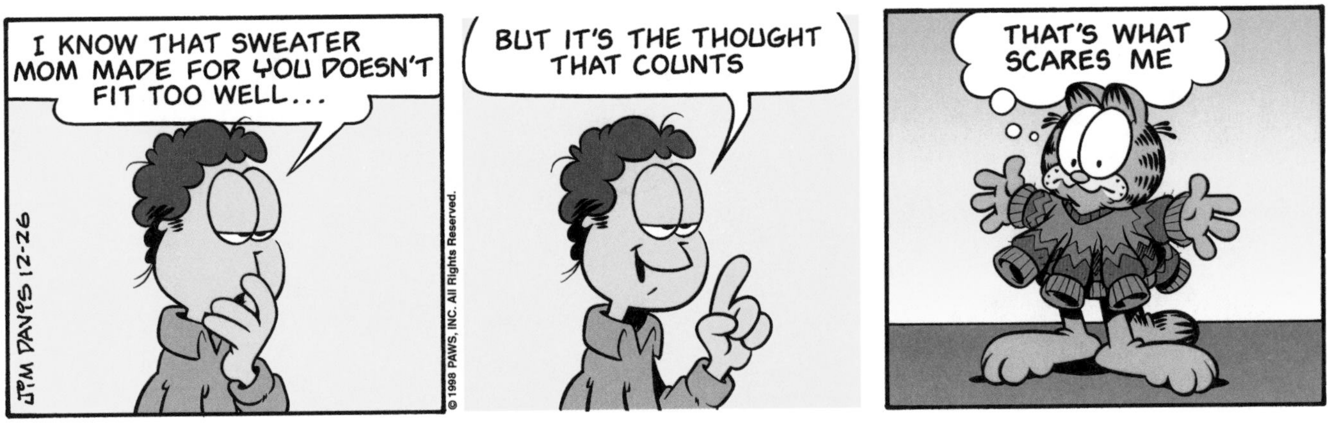
I KNOW THAT SWEATER MOM MADE FOR YOU DOESN'T FIT TOO WELL...
JIM DAVIS 12-26
BUT IT'S THE THOUGHT THAT COUNTS
© 1998 PAWS, INC. All Rights Reserved.
THAT'S WHAT SCARES ME

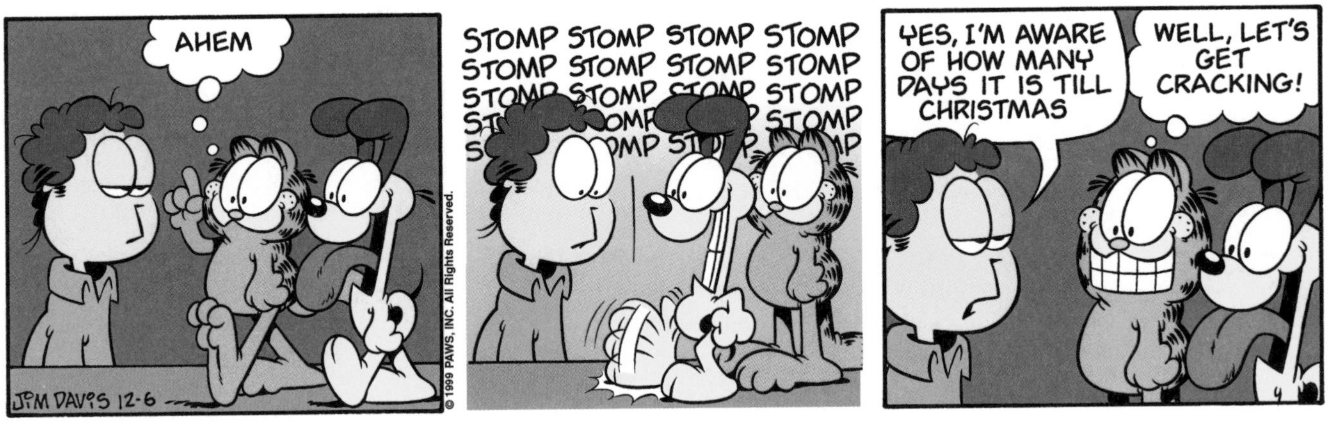
AHEM
JIM DAVIS 12-6
© 1999 PAWS, INC. All Rights Reserved.
STOMP STOMP STOMP STOMP
STOMP STOMP STOMP STOMP
STOMP STOMP STOMP STOMP
YES, I'M AWARE OF HOW MANY DAYS IT IS TILL CHRISTMAS
WELL, LET'S GET CRACKING!

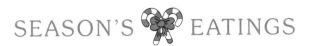

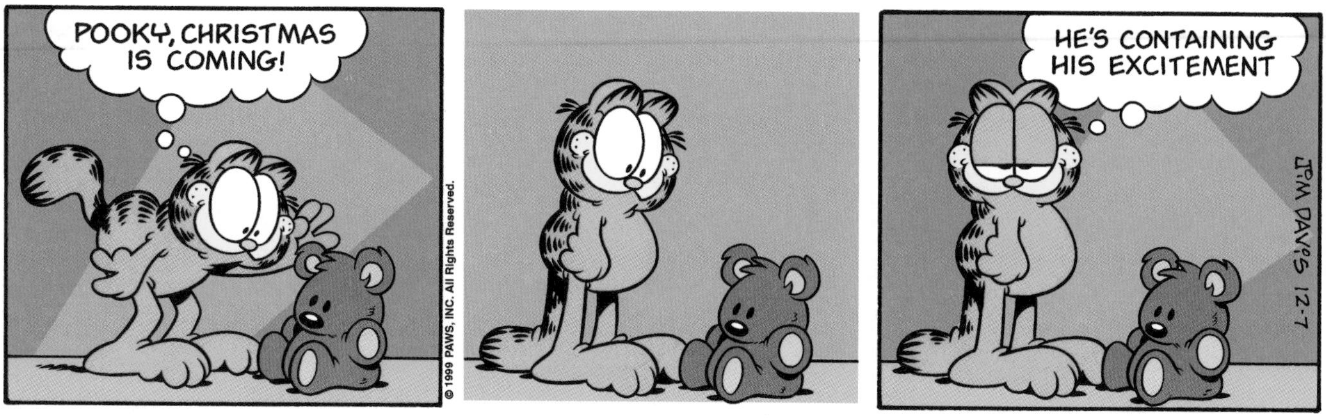
POOKY, CHRISTMAS IS COMING!
© 1999 PAWS, INC. All Rights Reserved.
HE'S CONTAINING HIS EXCITEMENT
JIM DAVIS 12-7

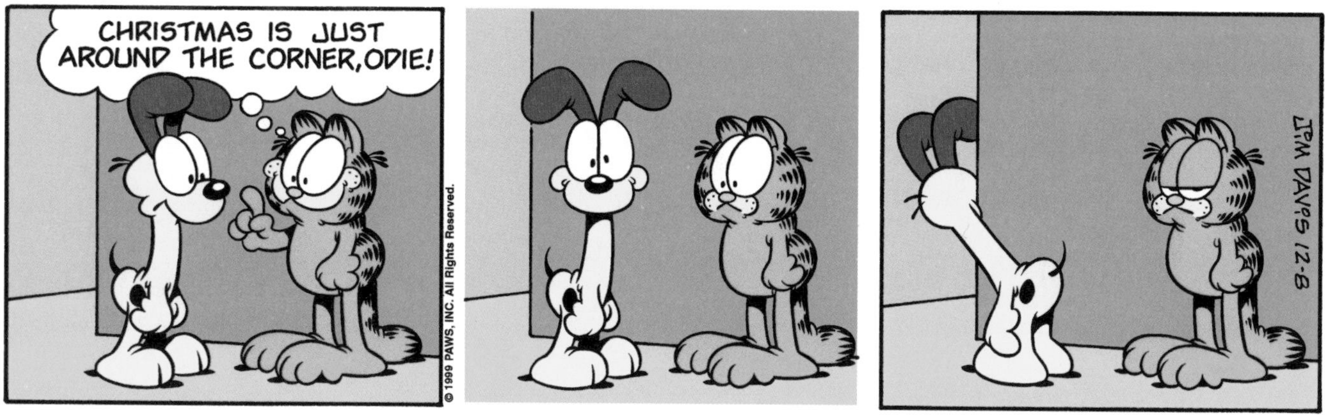
CHRISTMAS IS JUST AROUND THE CORNER, ODIE!
© 1999 PAWS, INC. All Rights Reserved.
JIM DAVIS 12-8

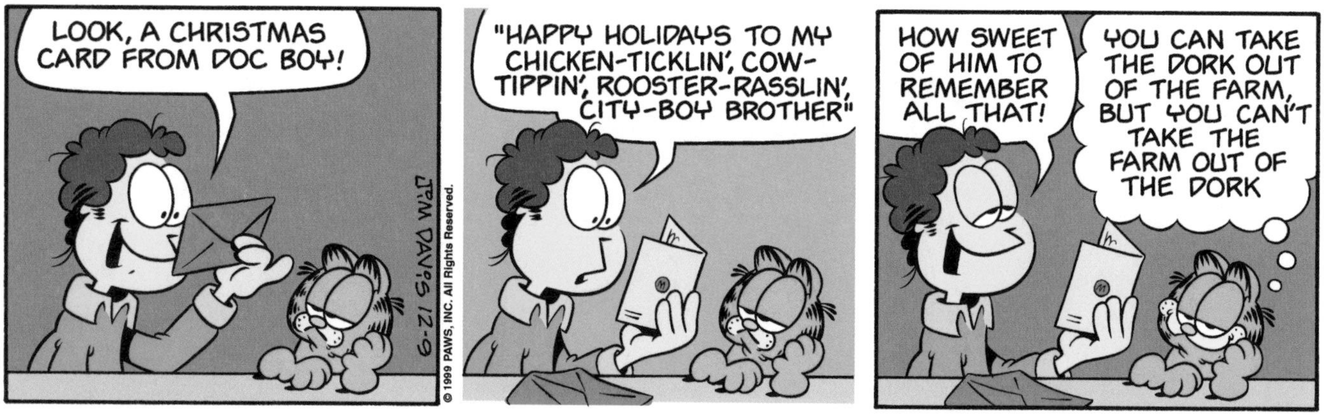
LOOK, A CHRISTMAS CARD FROM DOC BOY!
JIM DAVIS 12-9
© 1999 PAWS, INC. All Rights Reserved.
"HAPPY HOLIDAYS TO MY CHICKEN-TICKLIN', COW-TIPPIN', ROOSTER-RASSLIN', CITY-BOY BROTHER"
HOW SWEET OF HIM TO REMEMBER ALL THAT!
YOU CAN TAKE THE DORK OUT OF THE FARM, BUT YOU CAN'T TAKE THE FARM OUT OF THE DORK

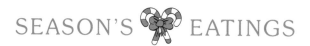

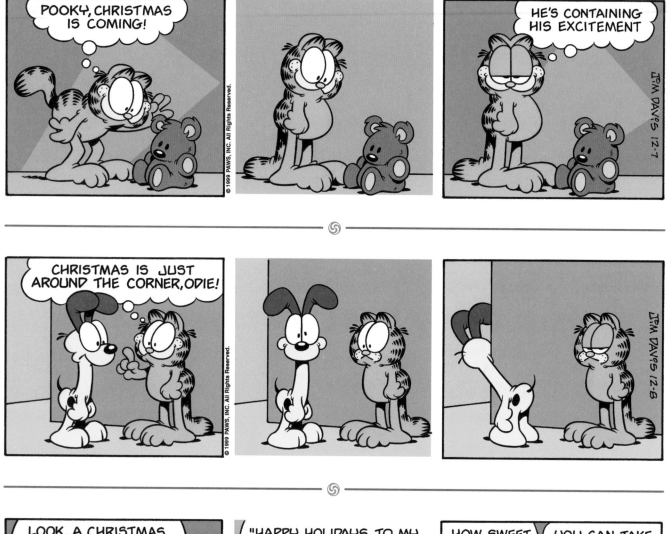

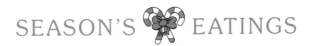

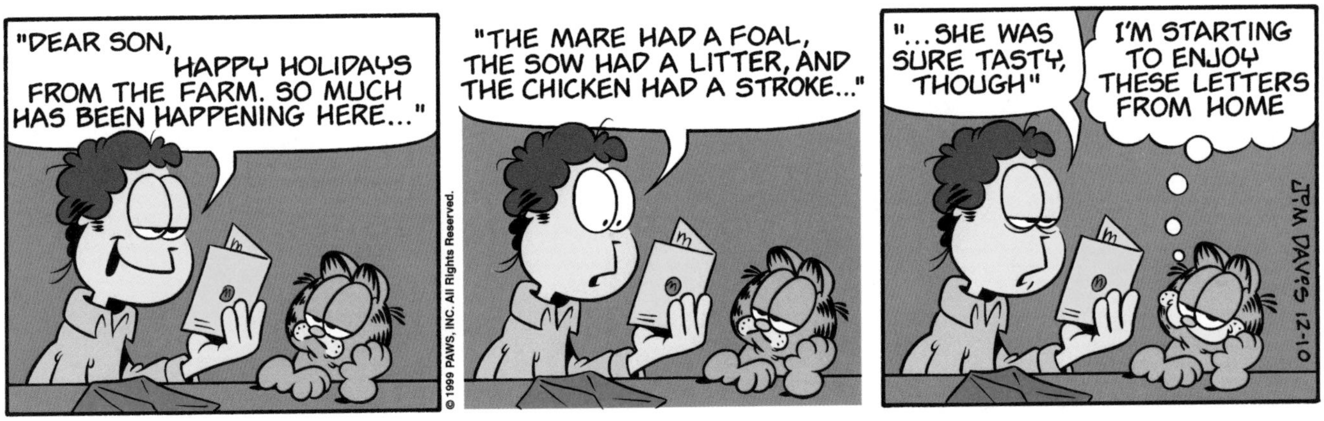
"DEAR SON,
HAPPY HOLIDAYS FROM THE FARM. SO MUCH HAS BEEN HAPPENING HERE..."
"THE MARE HAD A FOAL, THE SOW HAD A LITTER, AND THE CHICKEN HAD A STROKE..."
"...SHE WAS SURE TASTY, THOUGH"
I'M STARTING TO ENJOY THESE LETTERS FROM HOME
JIM DAVIS 12-10
© 1999 PAWS, INC. All Rights Reserved.

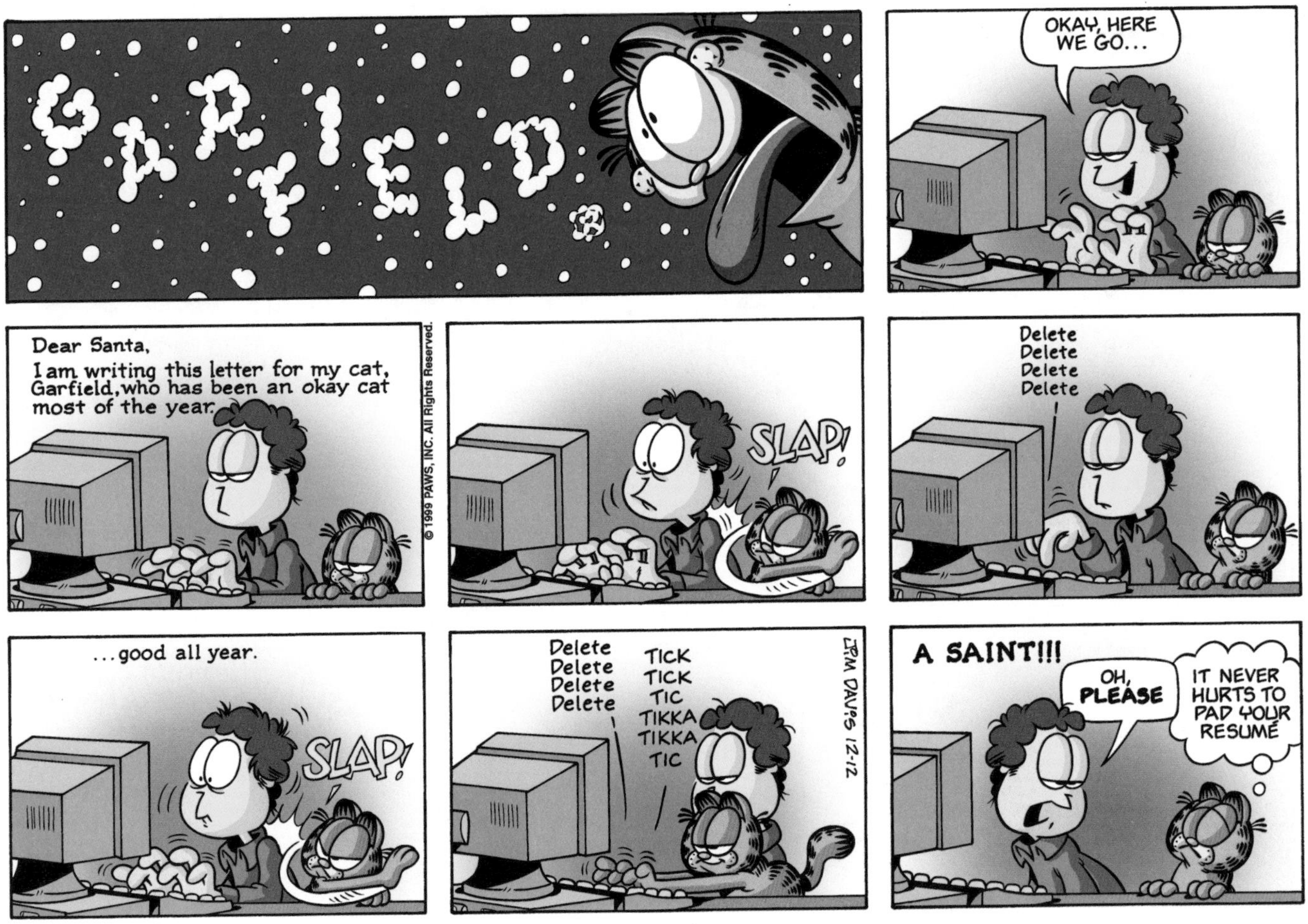
GARFIELD
OKAY, HERE WE GO...
Dear Santa,
I am writing this letter for my cat, Garfield, who has been an okay cat most of the year.
© 1999 PAWS, INC. All Rights Reserved.
SLAP!
Delete
Delete
Delete
Delete
...good all year.
SLAP!
Delete
Delete
Delete
Delete
TICK
TICK
TIC
TIKKA
TIKKA
TIC
JIM DAVIS 12-12
A SAINT!!!
OH, PLEASE
IT NEVER HURTS TO PAD YOUR RESUMÉ

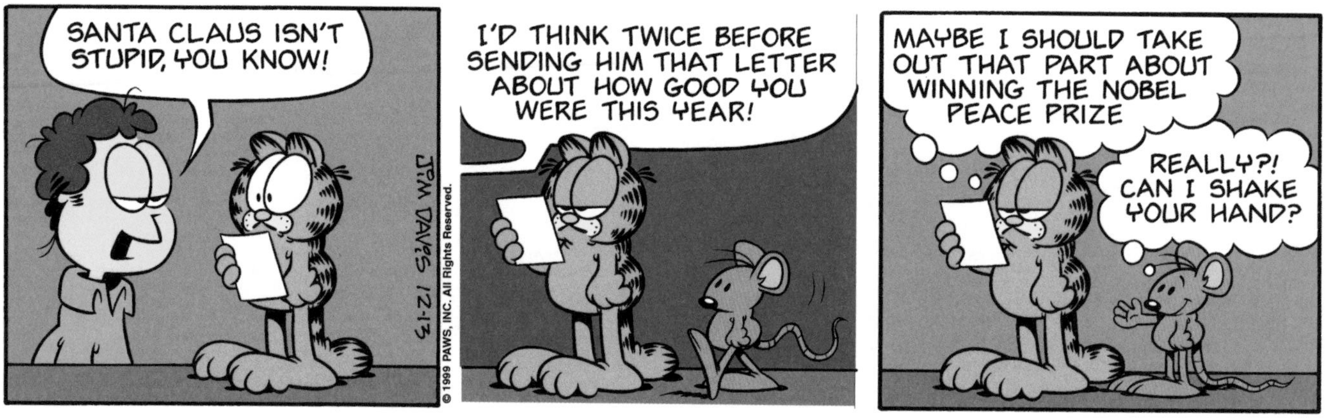
SANTA CLAUS ISN'T STUPID, YOU KNOW!
JIM DAVIS 12-13
© 1999 PAWS, INC. All Rights Reserved.
I'D THINK TWICE BEFORE SENDING HIM THAT LETTER ABOUT HOW GOOD YOU WERE THIS YEAR!
MAYBE I SHOULD TAKE OUT THAT PART ABOUT WINNING THE NOBEL PEACE PRIZE
REALLY?! CAN I SHAKE YOUR HAND?

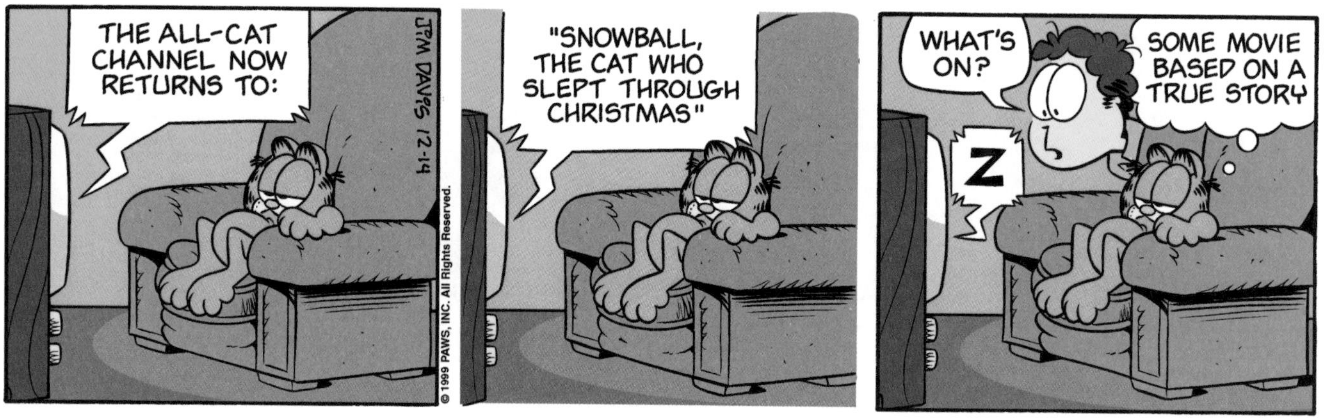
THE ALL-CAT CHANNEL NOW RETURNS TO:
JIM DAVIS 12-14
© 1999 PAWS, INC. All Rights Reserved.
"SNOWBALL, THE CAT WHO SLEPT THROUGH CHRISTMAS"
WHAT'S ON?
Z
SOME MOVIE BASED ON A TRUE STORY

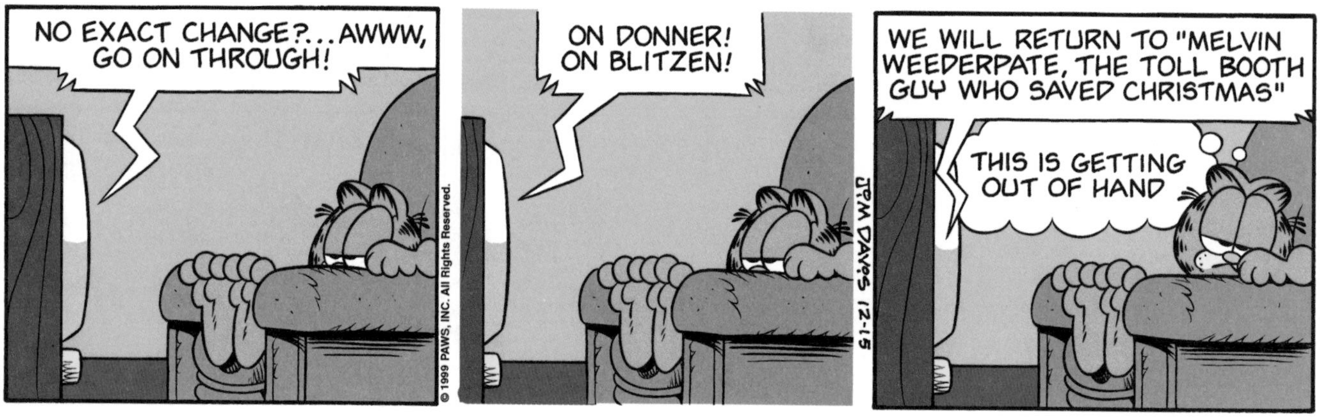
NO EXACT CHANGE?... AWWW, GO ON THROUGH!
© 1999 PAWS, INC. All Rights Reserved.
ON DONNER! ON BLITZEN!
JIM DAVIS 12-15
WE WILL RETURN TO "MELVIN WEEDERPATE, THE TOLL BOOTH GUY WHO SAVED CHRISTMAS"
THIS IS GETTING OUT OF HAND

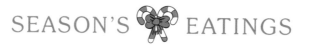

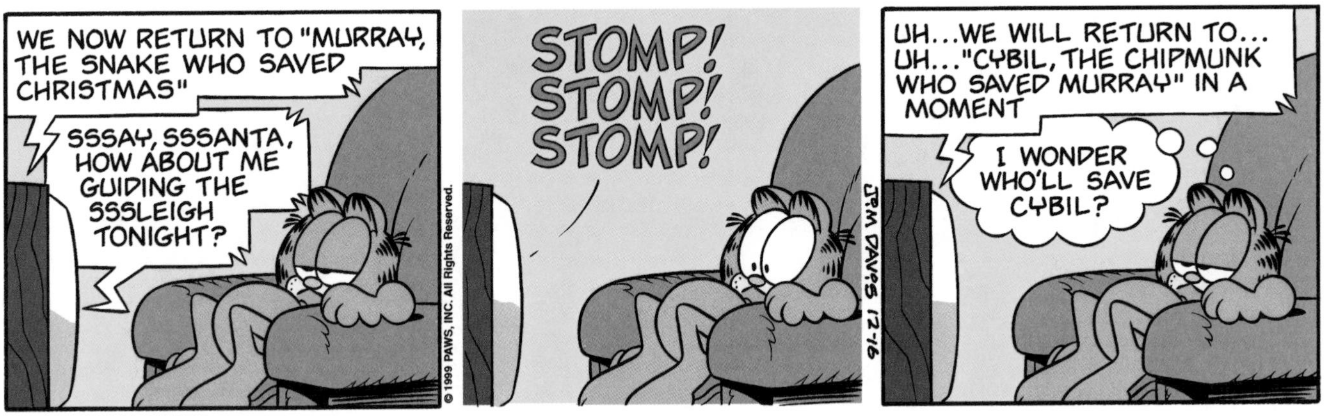
WE NOW RETURN TO "MURRAY, THE SNAKE WHO SAVED CHRISTMAS"
SSSAY, SSSANTA, HOW ABOUT ME GUIDING THE SSSLEIGH TONIGHT?
© 1999 PAWS, INC. All Rights Reserved.
STOMP! STOMP! STOMP!
JIM DAVIS 12-16
UH...WE WILL RETURN TO... UH..."CYBIL, THE CHIPMUNK WHO SAVED MURRAY" IN A MOMENT
I WONDER WHO'LL SAVE CYBIL?

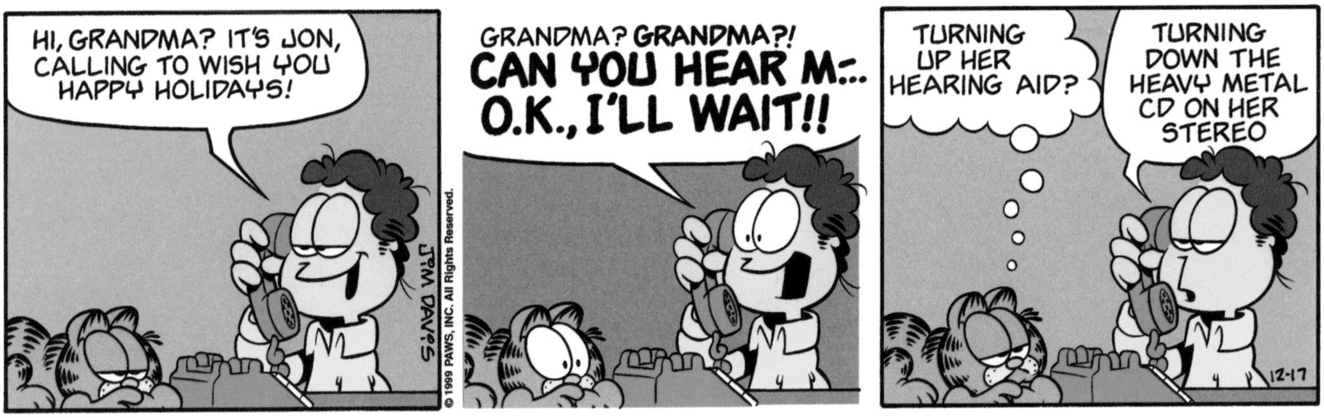
HI, GRANDMA? IT'S JON, CALLING TO WISH YOU HAPPY HOLIDAYS!
JIM DAVIS
© 1999 PAWS, INC. All Rights Reserved.
GRANDMA? GRANDMA?! CAN YOU HEAR M... O.K., I'LL WAIT!!
TURNING UP HER HEARING AID?
TURNING DOWN THE HEAVY METAL CD ON HER STEREO
12-17

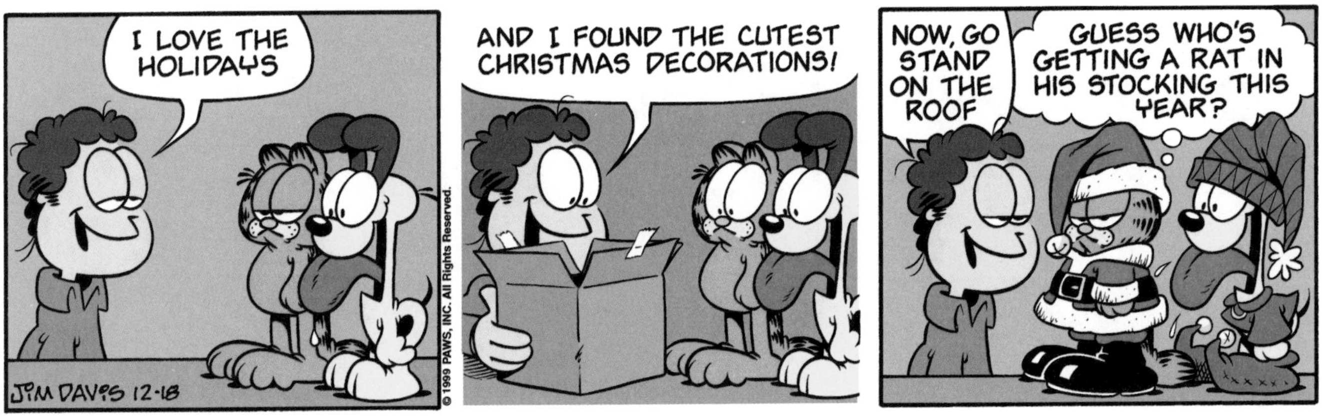
I LOVE THE HOLIDAYS
JIM DAVIS 12-18
© 1999 PAWS, INC. All Rights Reserved.
AND I FOUND THE CUTEST CHRISTMAS DECORATIONS!
NOW, GO STAND ON THE ROOF
GUESS WHO'S GETTING A RAT IN HIS STOCKING THIS YEAR?

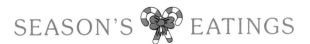

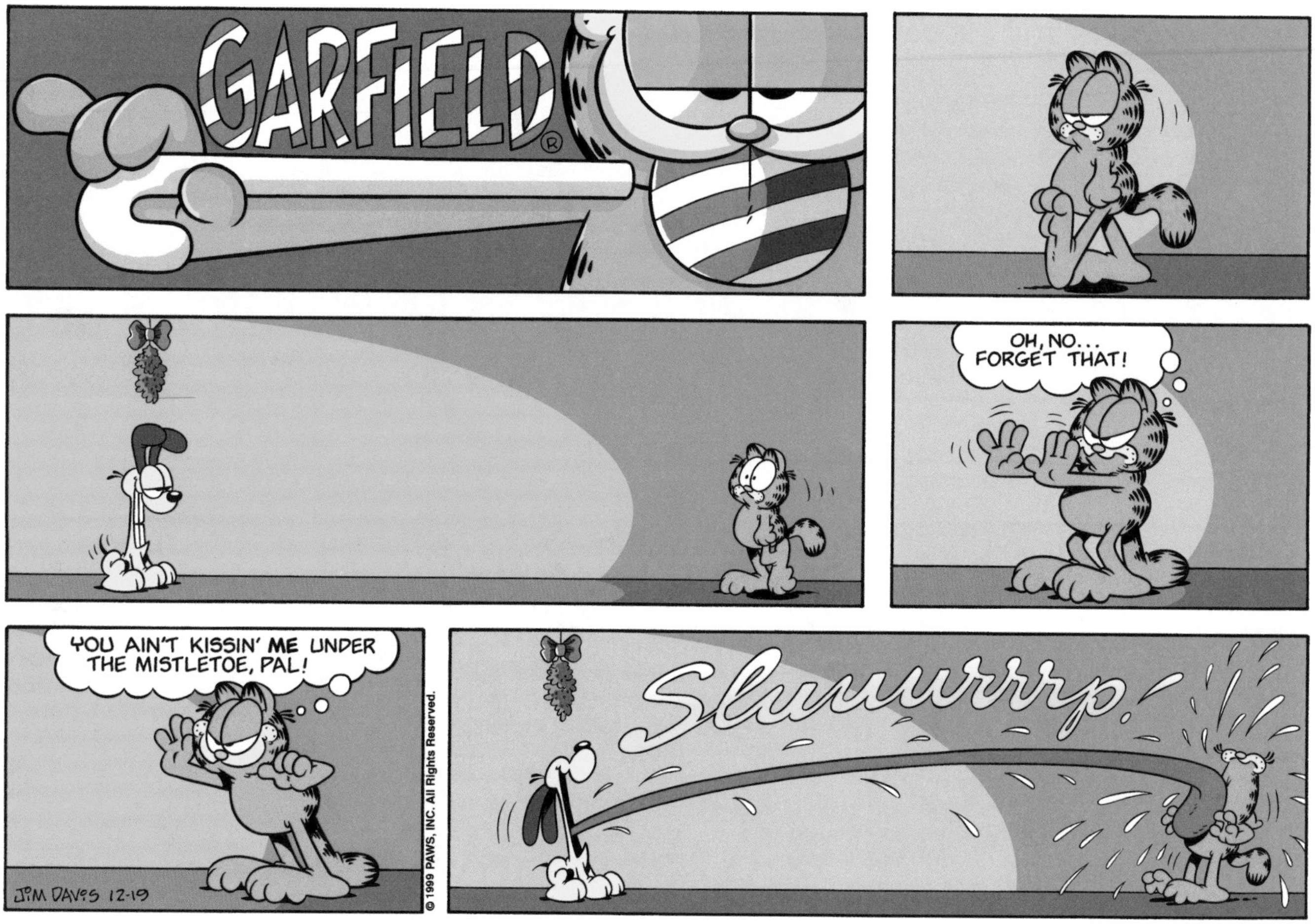
GARFIELD®
OH, NO... FORGET THAT!
YOU AIN'T KISSIN' ME UNDER THE MISTLETOE, PAL!
JIM DAVIS 12-19
© 1999 PAWS, INC. All Rights Reserved.
Sluuurrrp!

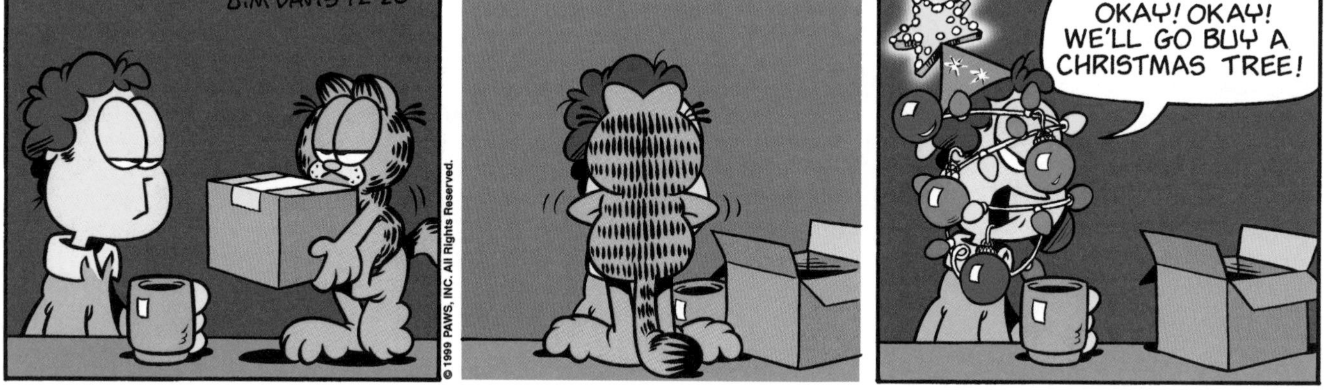
JIM DAVIS 12-20
© 1999 PAWS, INC. All Rights Reserved.
OKAY! OKAY! WE'LL GO BUY A CHRISTMAS TREE!

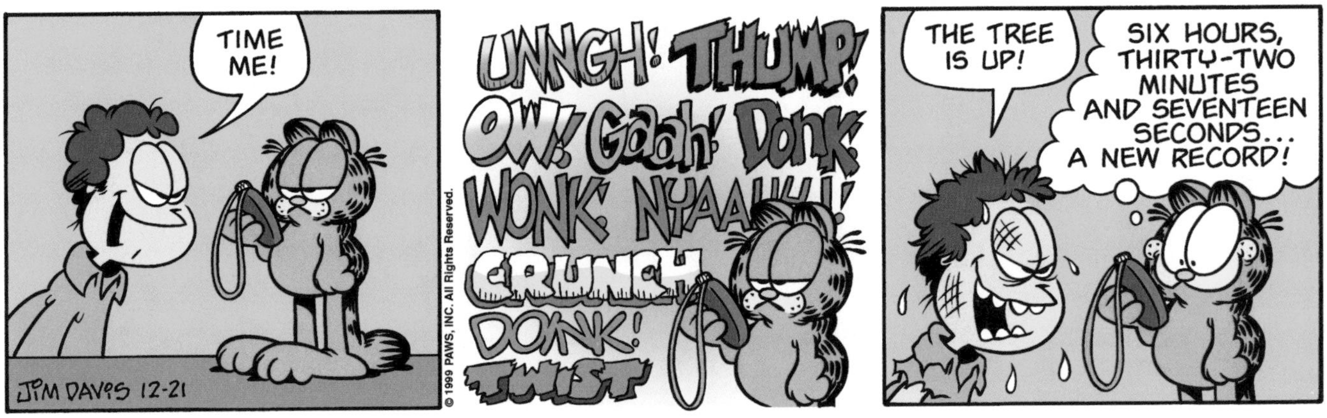
TIME ME!
JIM DAVIS 12-21
UNNGH! THUMP!
OW! Gaah! Donk
WONK NYAAHH!!
CRUNCH
DONK!
TWIST
© 1999 PAWS, INC. All Rights Reserved.
THE TREE IS UP!
SIX HOURS, THIRTY-TWO MINUTES AND SEVENTEEN SECONDS... A NEW RECORD!

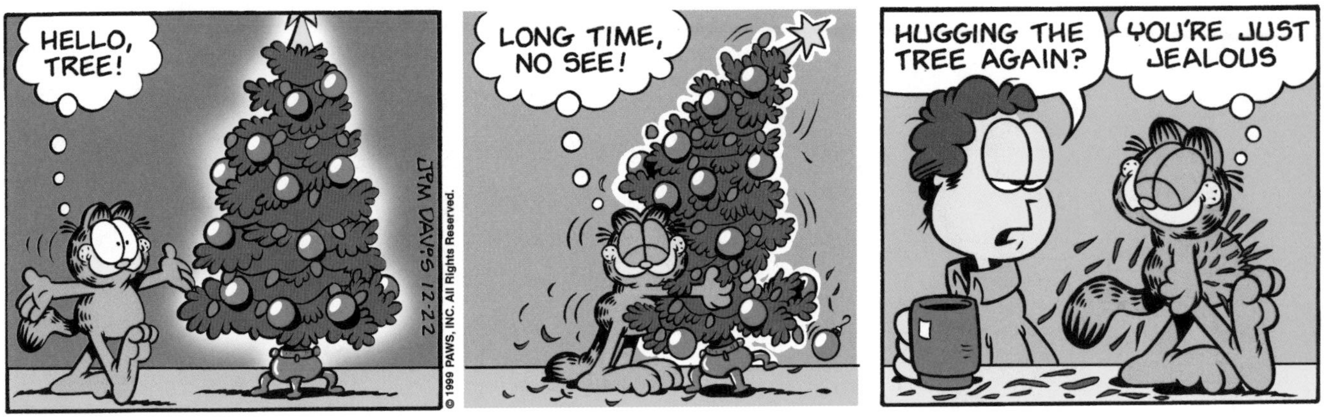
HELLO, TREE!
JIM DAVIS 12-22
© 1999 PAWS, INC. All Rights Reserved.
LONG TIME, NO SEE!
HUGGING THE TREE AGAIN?
YOU'RE JUST JEALOUS

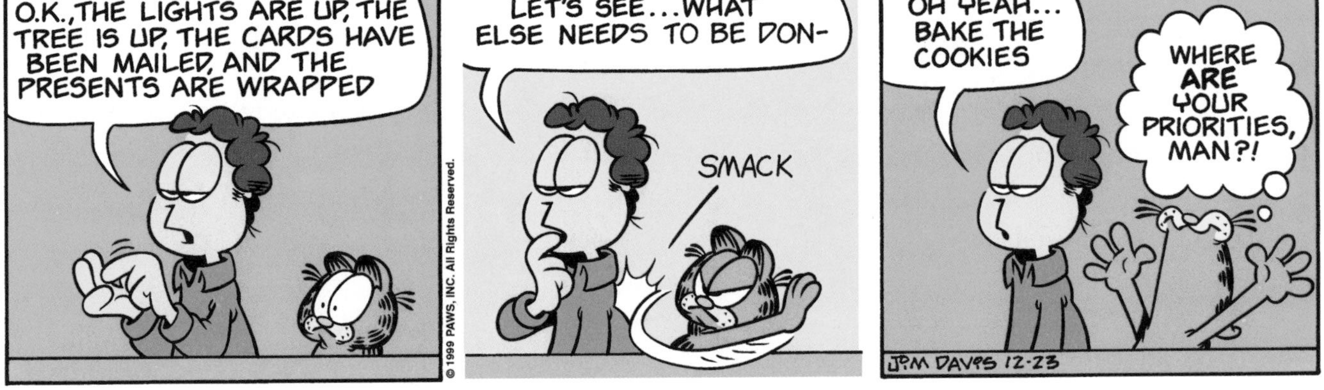
O.K., THE LIGHTS ARE UP, THE TREE IS UP, THE CARDS HAVE BEEN MAILED, AND THE PRESENTS ARE WRAPPED
© 1999 PAWS, INC. All Rights Reserved.
LET'S SEE...WHAT ELSE NEEDS TO BE DON-
SMACK
OH YEAH... BAKE THE COOKIES
WHERE ARE YOUR PRIORITIES, MAN?!
JIM DAVIS 12-23

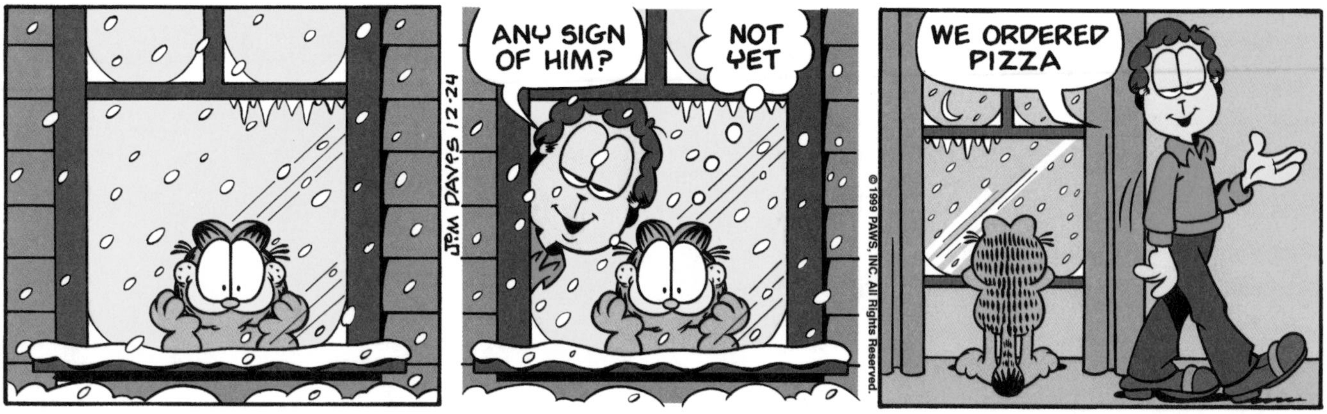
JIM DAVIS 12-24
ANY SIGN OF HIM?
NOT YET
© 1999 PAWS, INC. All Rights Reserved.
WE ORDERED PIZZA

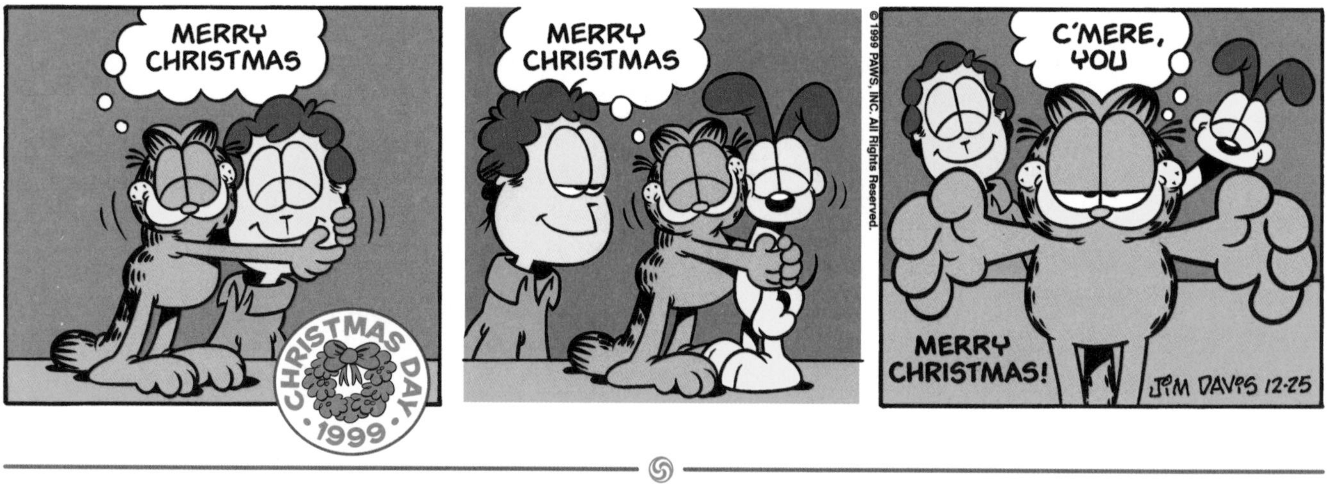
MERRY CHRISTMAS
CHRISTMAS DAY 1999
MERRY CHRISTMAS
© 1999 PAWS, INC. All Rights Reserved.
C'MERE, YOU
MERRY CHRISTMAS!
JIM DAVIS 12-25

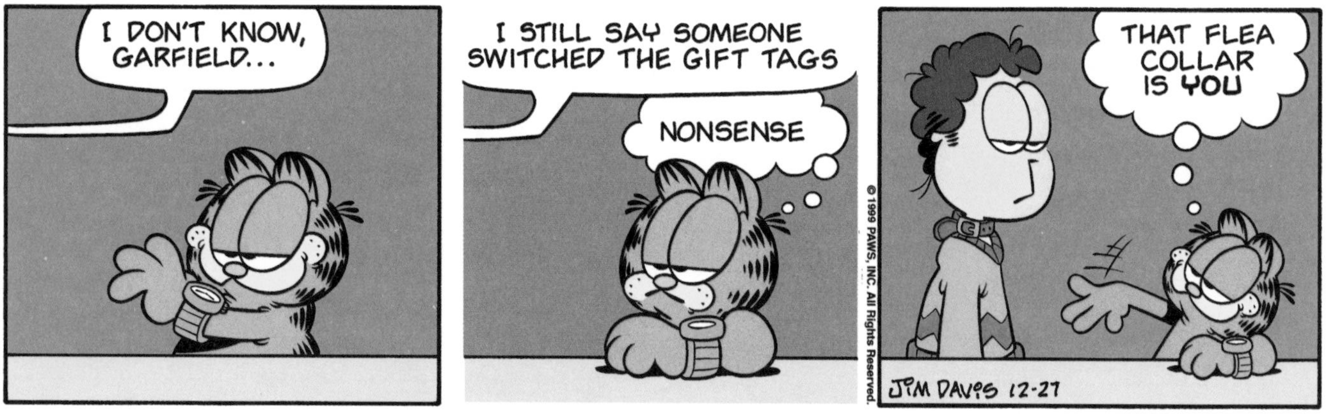
I DON'T KNOW, GARFIELD...
I STILL SAY SOMEONE SWITCHED THE GIFT TAGS
NONSENSE
© 1999 PAWS, INC. All Rights Reserved.
THAT FLEA COLLAR IS YOU
JIM DAVIS 12-27

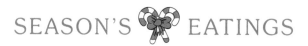

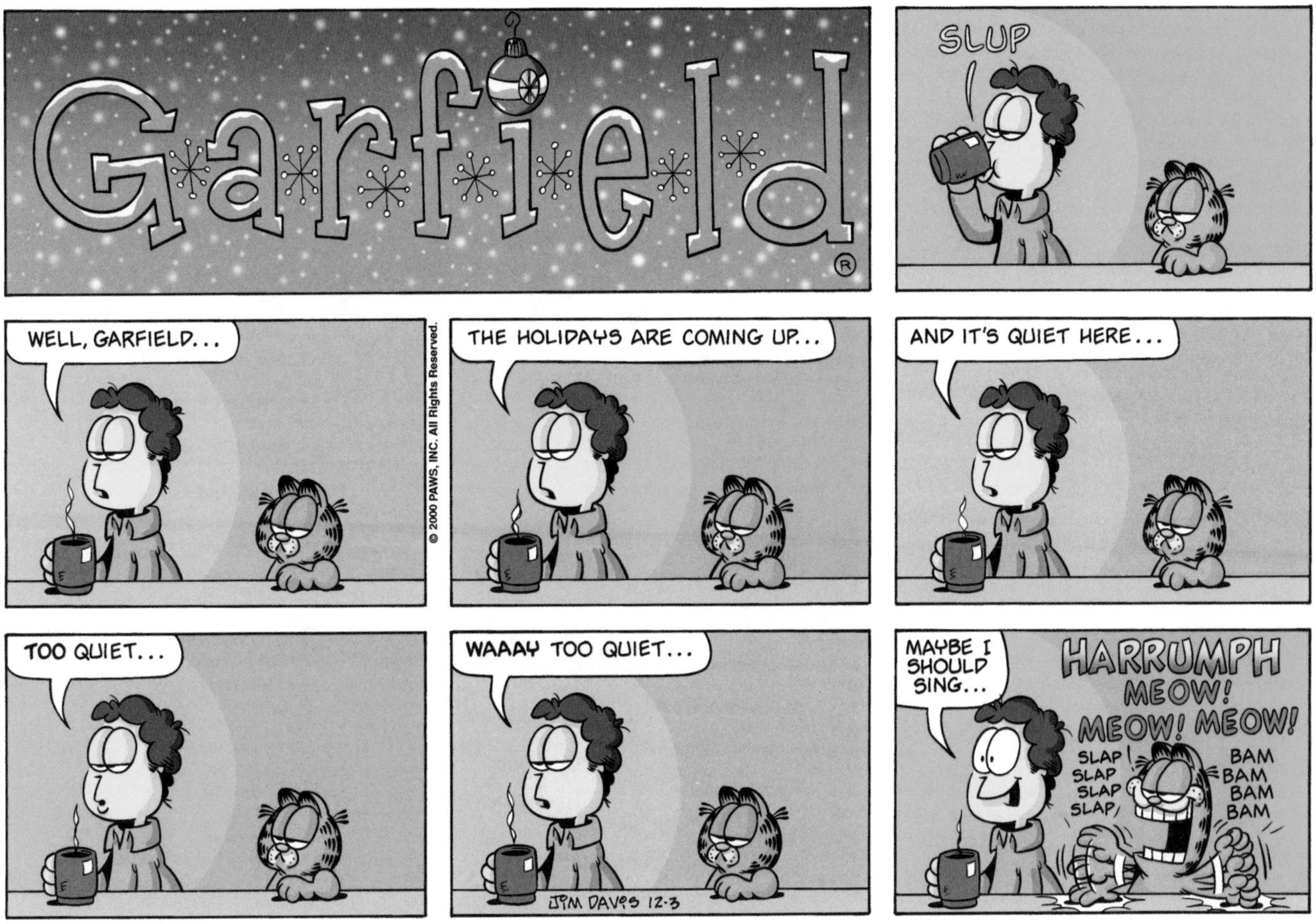
Garfield
SLUP
WELL, GARFIELD...
THE HOLIDAYS ARE COMING UP...
AND IT'S QUIET HERE...
TOO QUIET...
WAAAY TOO QUIET...
JIM DAVIS 12-3
MAYBE I SHOULD SING...
HARRUMPH
MEOW!
MEOW! MEOW!
SLAP! SLAP SLAP SLAP
BAM BAM BAM BAM
© 2000 PAWS, INC. All Rights Reserved.

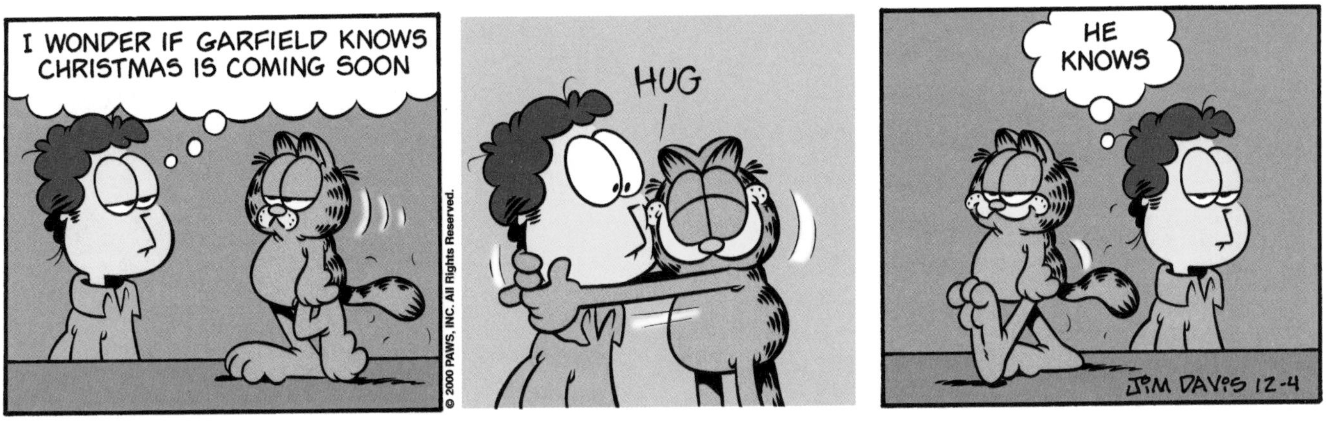
I WONDER IF GARFIELD KNOWS CHRISTMAS IS COMING SOON
HUG
HE KNOWS
JIM DAVIS 12-4
© 2000 PAWS, INC. All Rights Reserved.

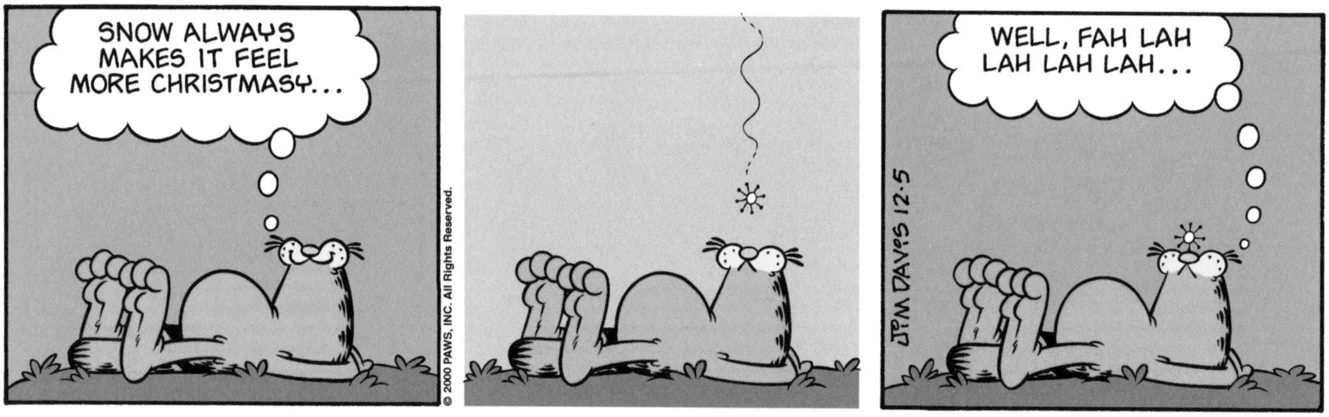
SNOW ALWAYS MAKES IT FEEL MORE CHRISTMASY...
© 2000 PAWS, INC. All Rights Reserved.
JIM DAVIS 12-5
WELL, FAH LAH LAH LAH LAH...

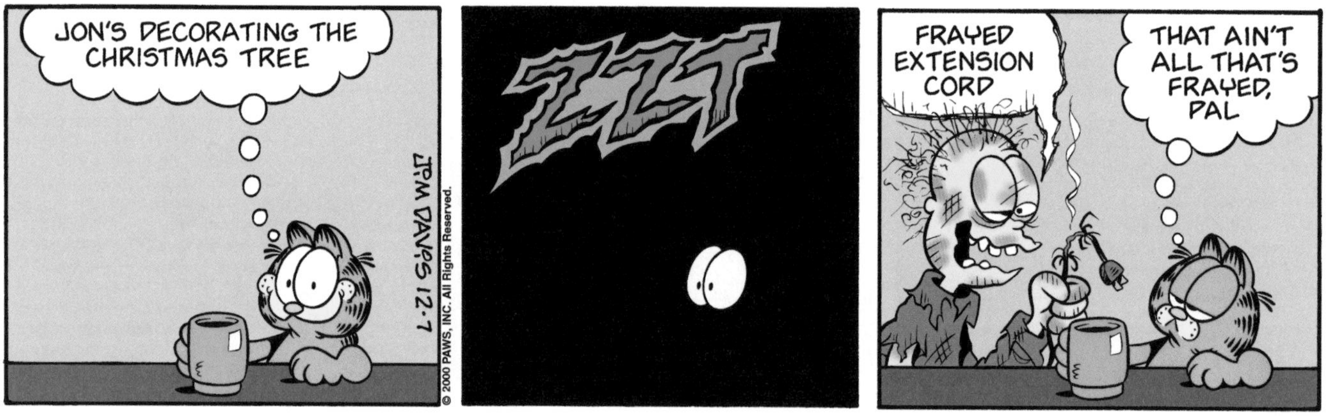
JON'S DECORATING THE CHRISTMAS TREE
JIM DAVIS 12-7
© 2000 PAWS, INC. All Rights Reserved.
ZZT
FRAYED EXTENSION CORD
THAT AIN'T ALL THAT'S FRAYED, PAL

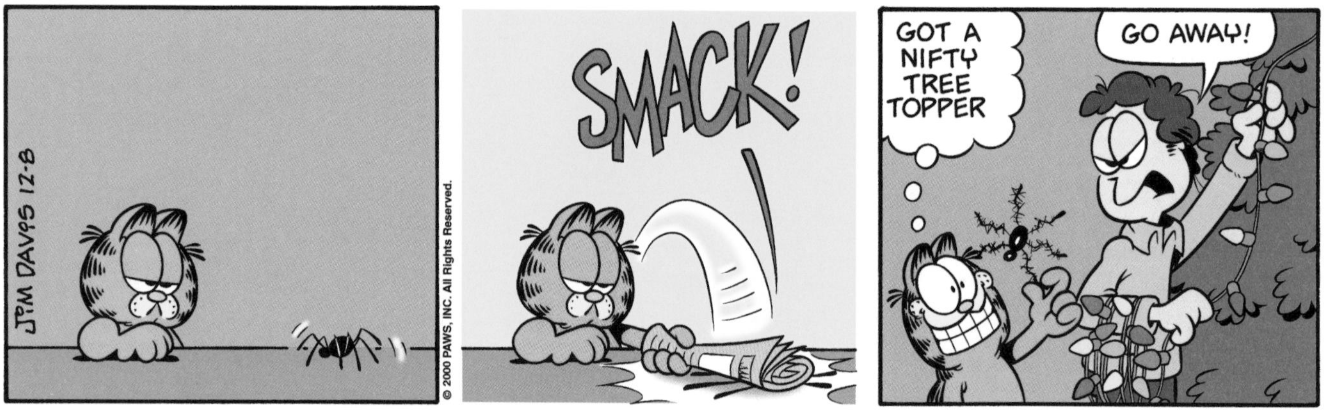
JIM DAVIS 12-8
© 2000 PAWS, INC. All Rights Reserved.
SMACK!
GOT A NIFTY TREE TOPPER
GO AWAY!

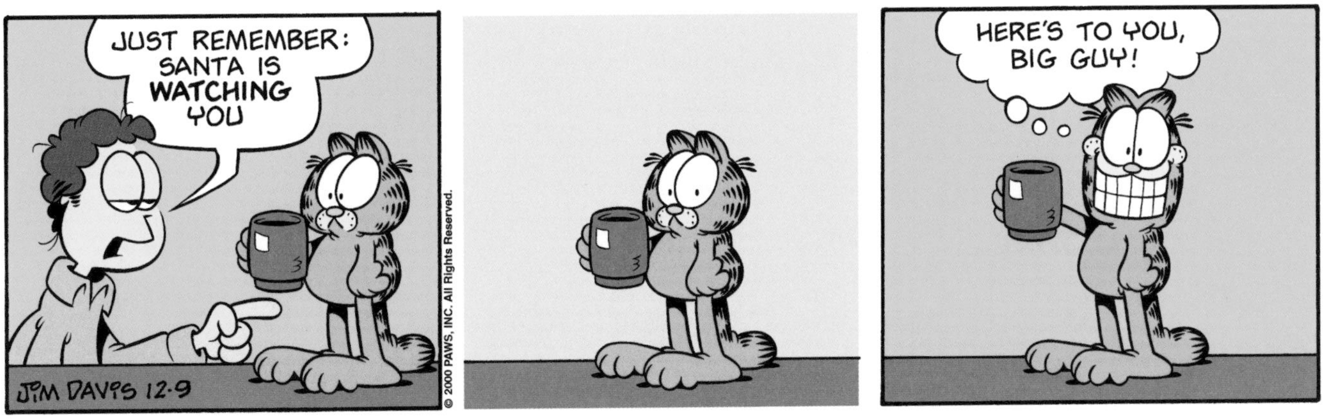
JUST REMEMBER: SANTA IS WATCHING YOU
JIM DAVIS 12-9
© 2000 PAWS, INC. All Rights Reserved.
HERE'S TO YOU, BIG GUY!

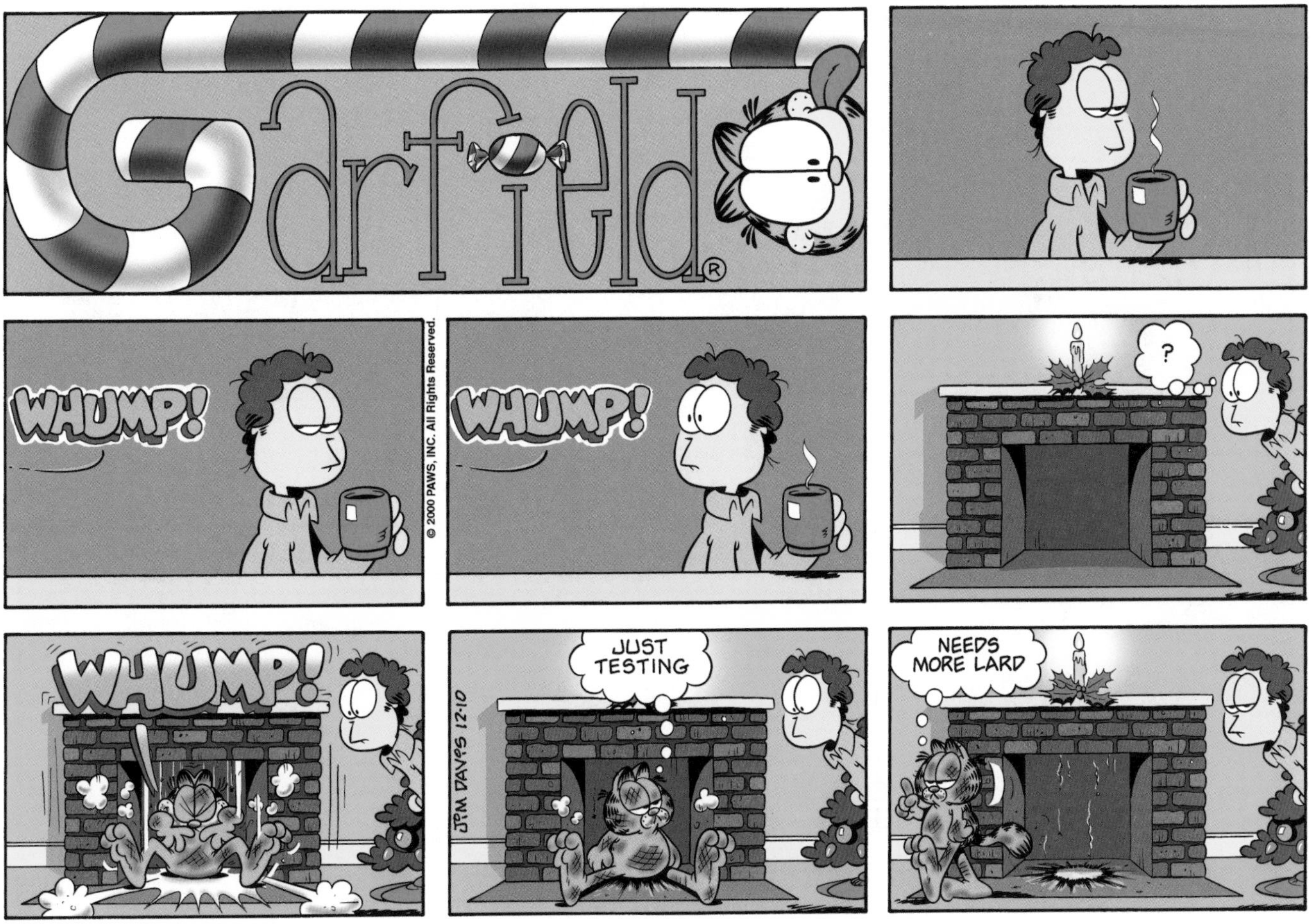
Garfield®
WHUMP!
© 2000 PAWS, INC. All Rights Reserved.
WHUMP!
?
WHUMP!
JUST TESTING
JIM DAVIS 12-10
NEEDS MORE LARD

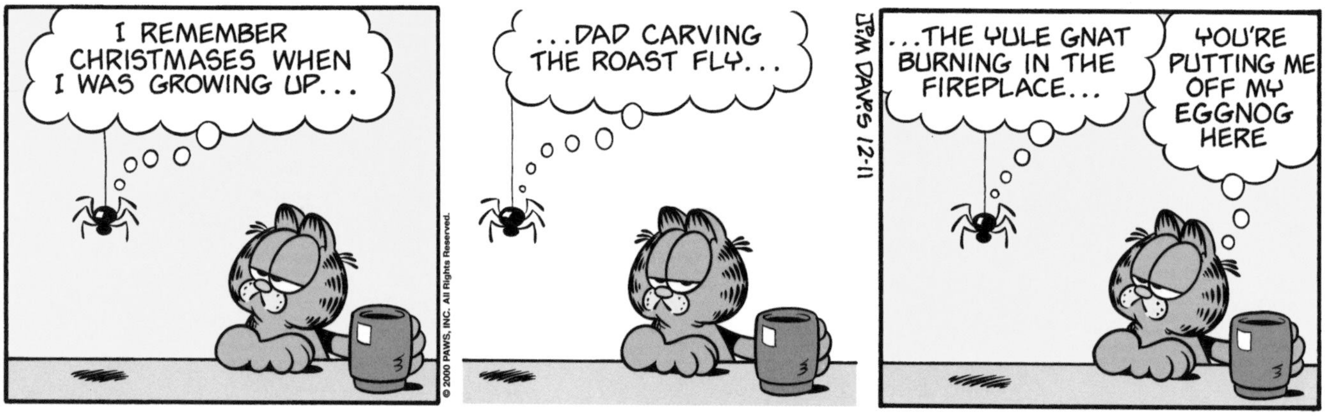
I REMEMBER CHRISTMASES WHEN I WAS GROWING UP...
...DAD CARVING THE ROAST FLY...
...THE YULE GNAT BURNING IN THE FIREPLACE...
YOU'RE PUTTING ME OFF MY EGGNOG HERE
© 2000 PAWS, INC. All Rights Reserved.
JIM DAVIS 12-11

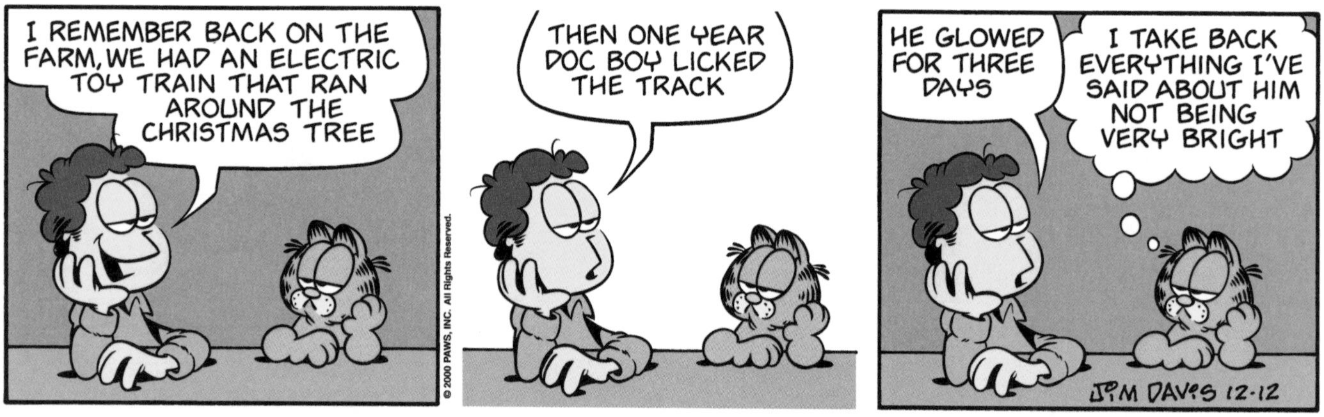
I REMEMBER BACK ON THE FARM, WE HAD AN ELECTRIC TOY TRAIN THAT RAN AROUND THE CHRISTMAS TREE
THEN ONE YEAR DOC BOY LICKED THE TRACK
HE GLOWED FOR THREE DAYS
I TAKE BACK EVERYTHING I'VE SAID ABOUT HIM NOT BEING VERY BRIGHT
© 2000 PAWS, INC. All Rights Reserved.
JIM DAVIS 12-12

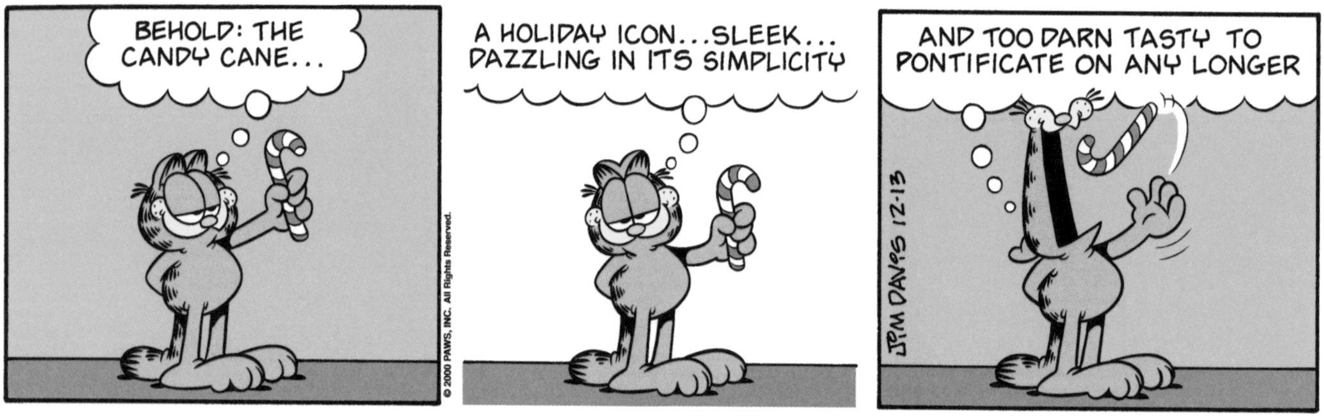
BEHOLD: THE CANDY CANE...
A HOLIDAY ICON...SLEEK... DAZZLING IN ITS SIMPLICITY
AND TOO DARN TASTY TO PONTIFICATE ON ANY LONGER
© 2000 PAWS, INC. All Rights Reserved.
JIM DAVIS 12-13

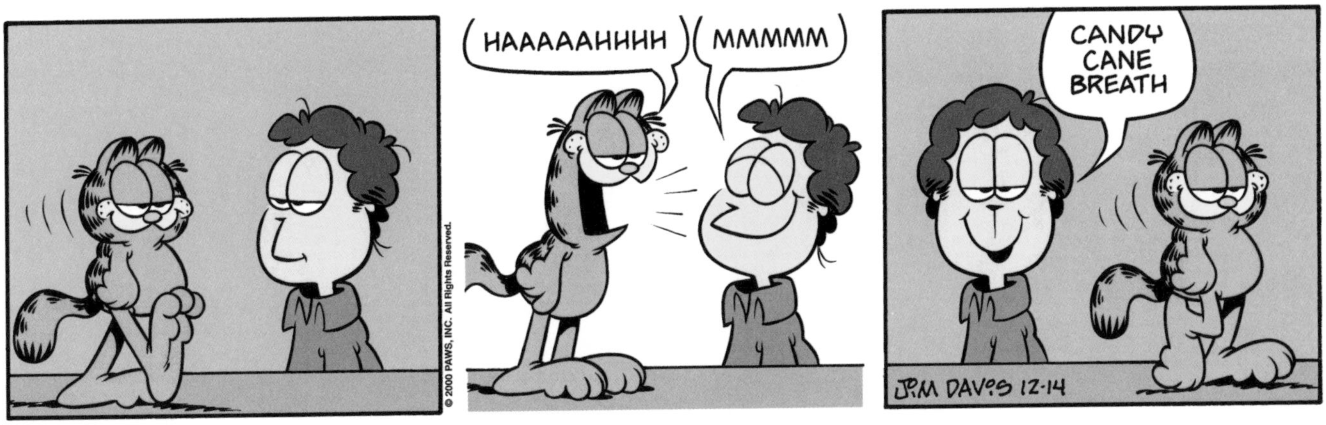
HAAAAAHHHH
MMMMM
CANDY CANE BREATH
JIM DAVIS 12-14
© 2000 PAWS, INC. All Rights Reserved.

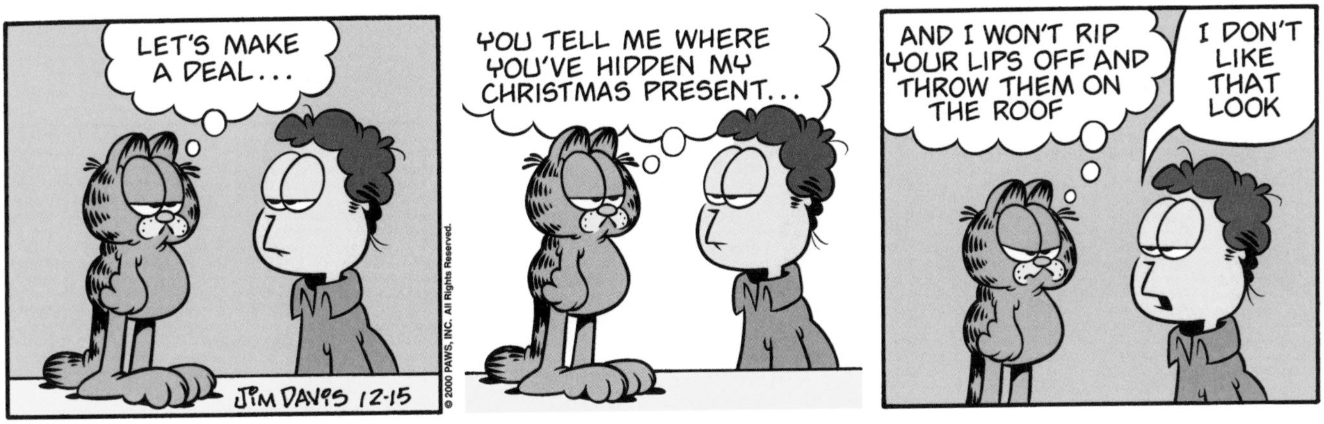
LET'S MAKE A DEAL...
YOU TELL ME WHERE YOU'VE HIDDEN MY CHRISTMAS PRESENT...
AND I WON'T RIP YOUR LIPS OFF AND THROW THEM ON THE ROOF
I DON'T LIKE THAT LOOK
JIM DAVIS 12-15
© 2000 PAWS, INC. All Rights Reserved.

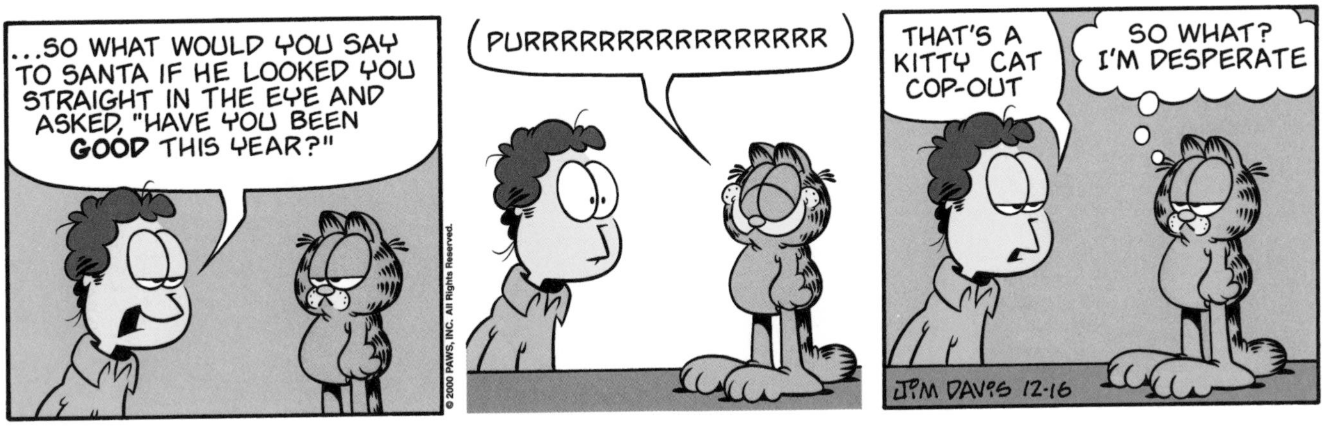
...SO WHAT WOULD YOU SAY TO SANTA IF HE LOOKED YOU STRAIGHT IN THE EYE AND ASKED, "HAVE YOU BEEN GOOD THIS YEAR?"
PURRRRRRRRRRRRRRRR
THAT'S A KITTY CAT COP-OUT
SO WHAT? I'M DESPERATE
JIM DAVIS 12-16
© 2000 PAWS, INC. All Rights Reserved.

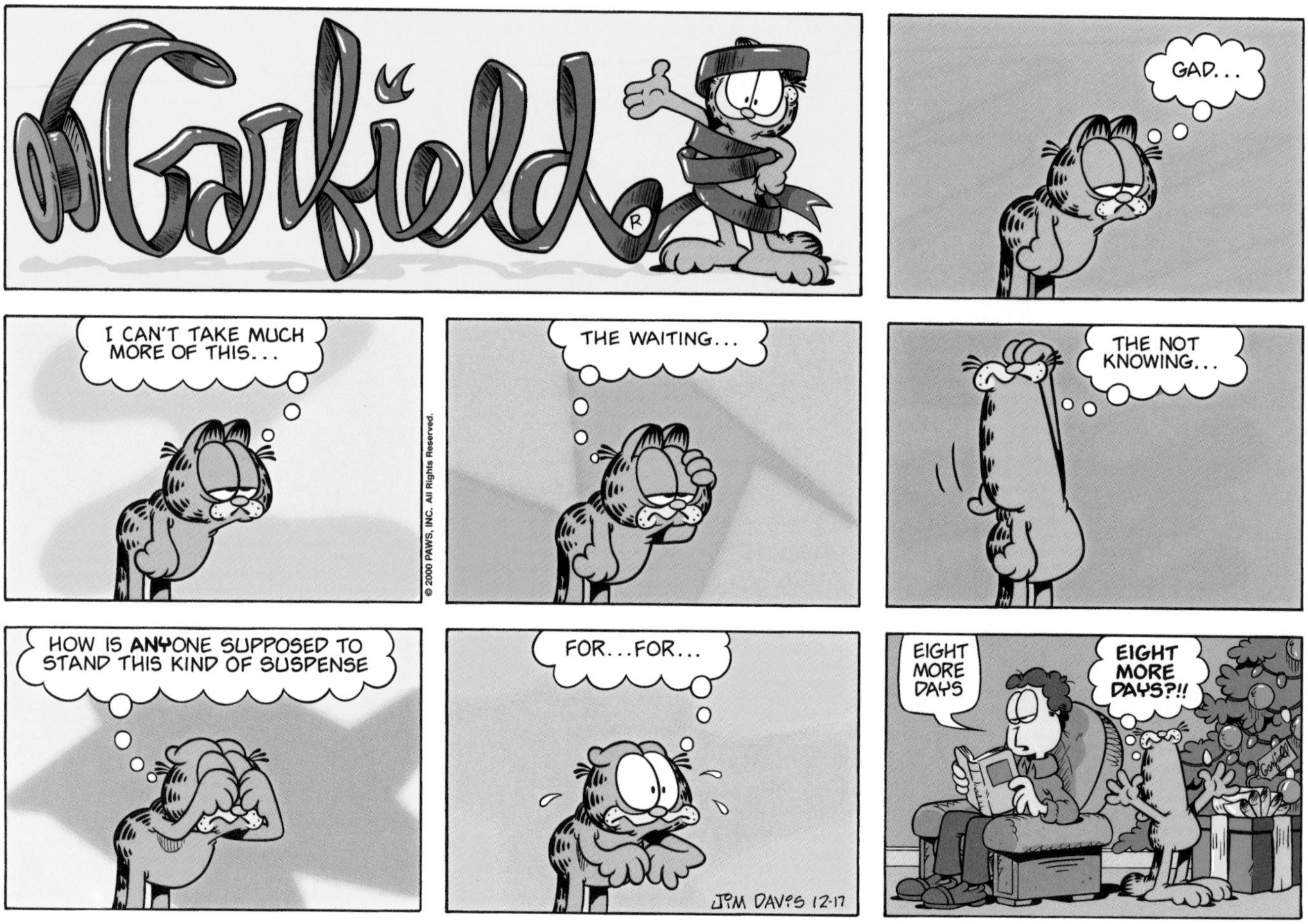
Garfield
GAD...
I CAN'T TAKE MUCH MORE OF THIS...
THE WAITING...
THE NOT KNOWING...
HOW IS ANYONE SUPPOSED TO STAND THIS KIND OF SUSPENSE
FOR...FOR...
EIGHT MORE DAYS
EIGHT MORE DAYS?!!
JIM DAVIS 12-17
© 2000 PAWS, INC. All Rights Reserved.

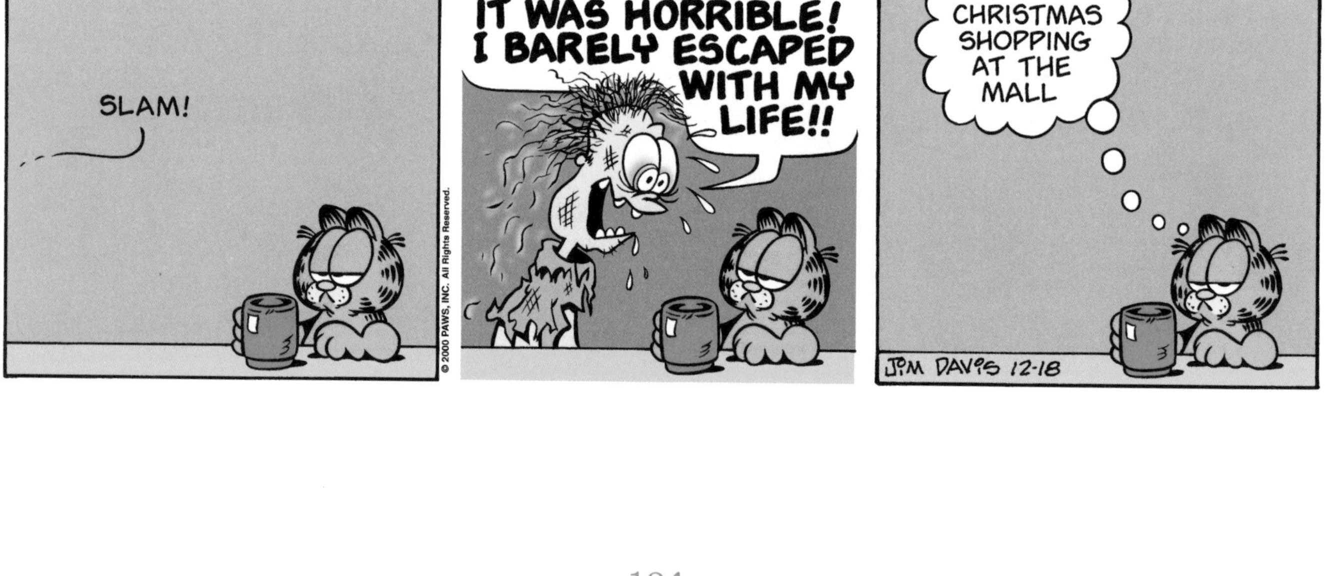
SLAM!
IT WAS HORRIBLE! I BARELY ESCAPED WITH MY LIFE!!
CHRISTMAS SHOPPING AT THE MALL
JIM DAVIS 12-18
© 2000 PAWS, INC. All Rights Reserved.

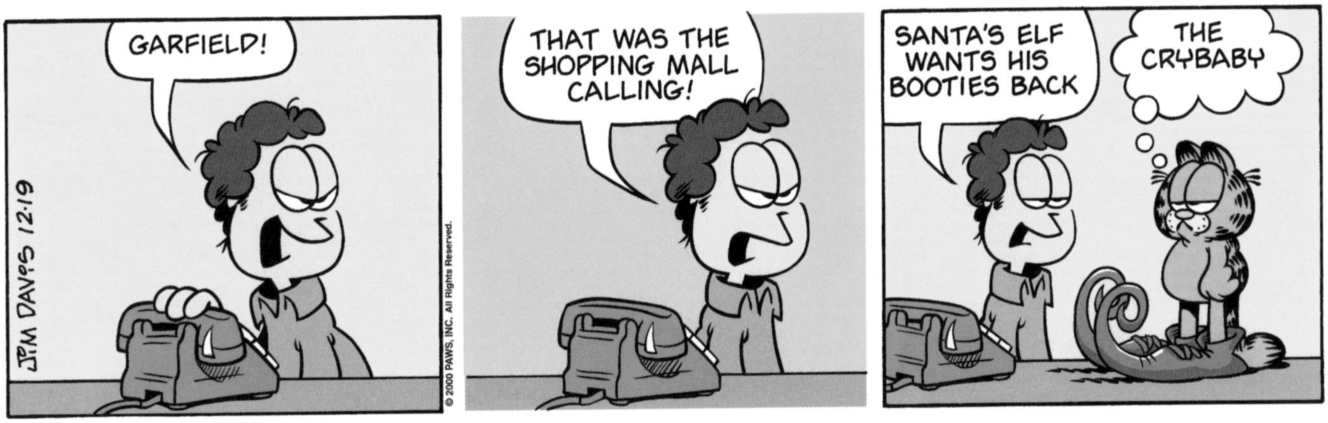
GARFIELD!
JIM DAVIS 12-19
THAT WAS THE SHOPPING MALL CALLING!
© 2000 PAWS, INC. All Rights Reserved.
SANTA'S ELF WANTS HIS BOOTIES BACK
THE CRYBABY

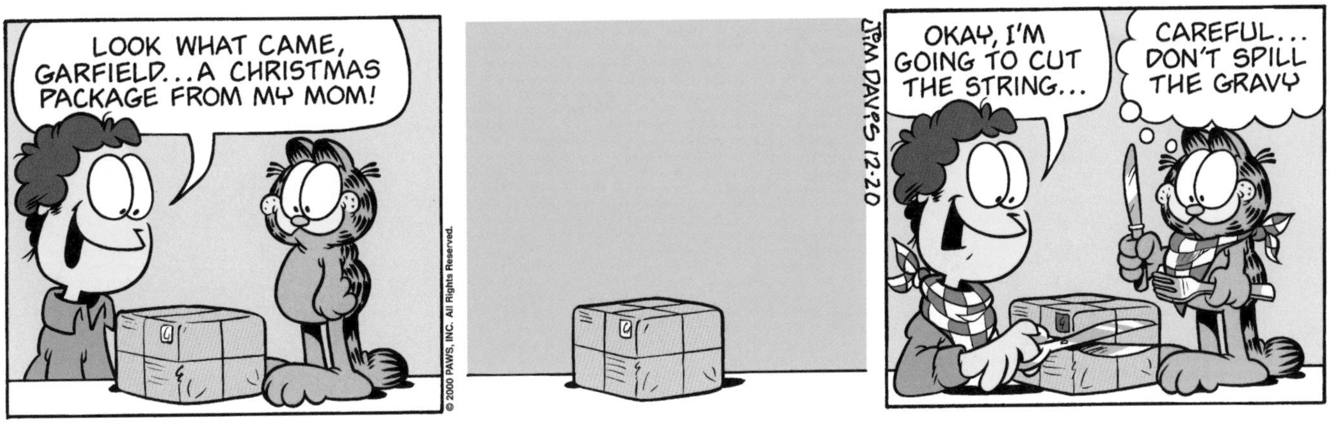
LOOK WHAT CAME, GARFIELD...A CHRISTMAS PACKAGE FROM MY MOM!
© 2000 PAWS, INC. All Rights Reserved.
JIM DAVIS 12-20
OKAY, I'M GOING TO CUT THE STRING...
CAREFUL... DON'T SPILL THE GRAVY

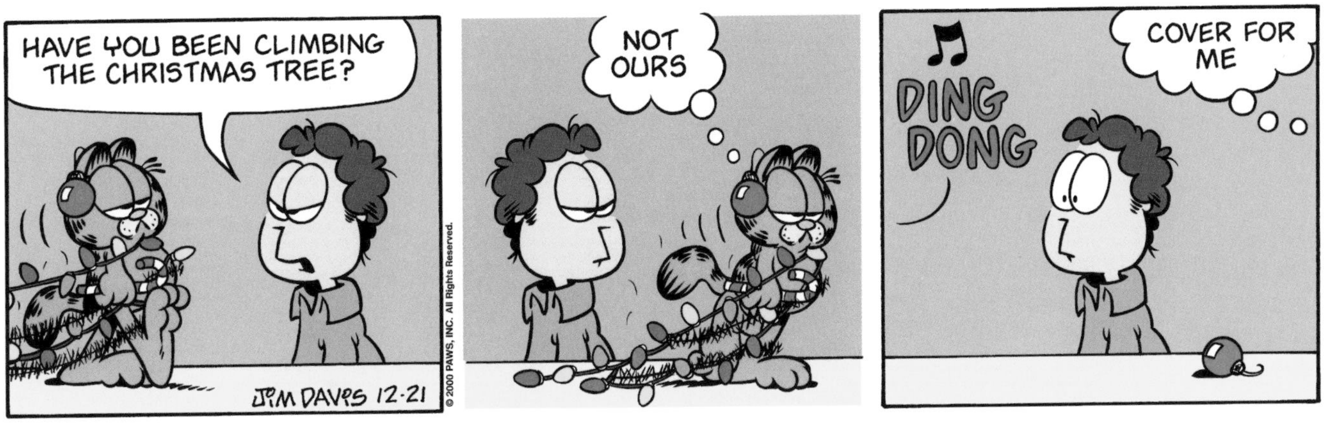
HAVE YOU BEEN CLIMBING THE CHRISTMAS TREE?
JIM DAVIS 12-21
© 2000 PAWS, INC. All Rights Reserved.
NOT OURS
DING DONG
COVER FOR ME

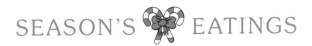

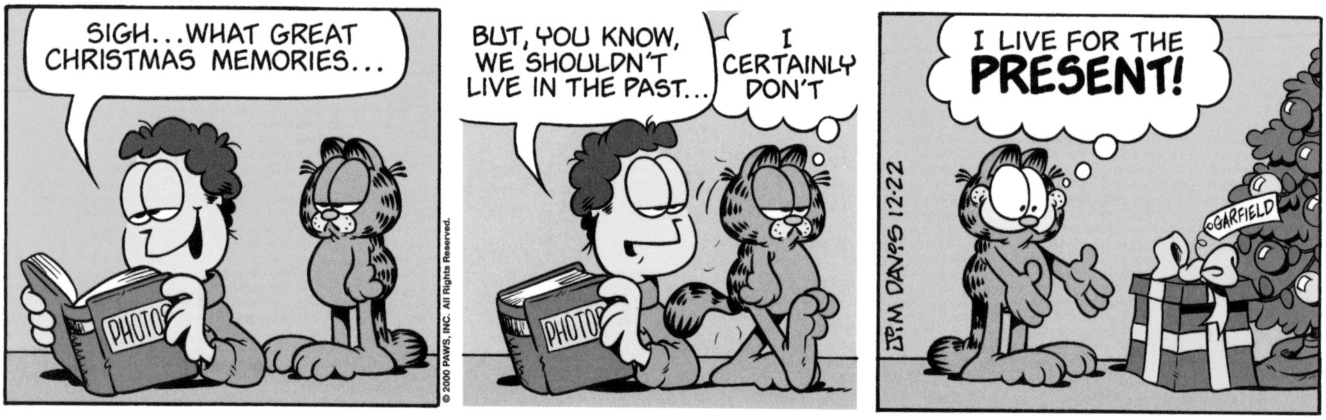
SIGH...WHAT GREAT CHRISTMAS MEMORIES...
PHOTOS
© 2000 PAWS, INC. All Rights Reserved.
BUT, YOU KNOW, WE SHOULDN'T LIVE IN THE PAST...
I CERTAINLY DON'T
JIM DAVIS 12·22
I LIVE FOR THE PRESENT!
GARFIELD

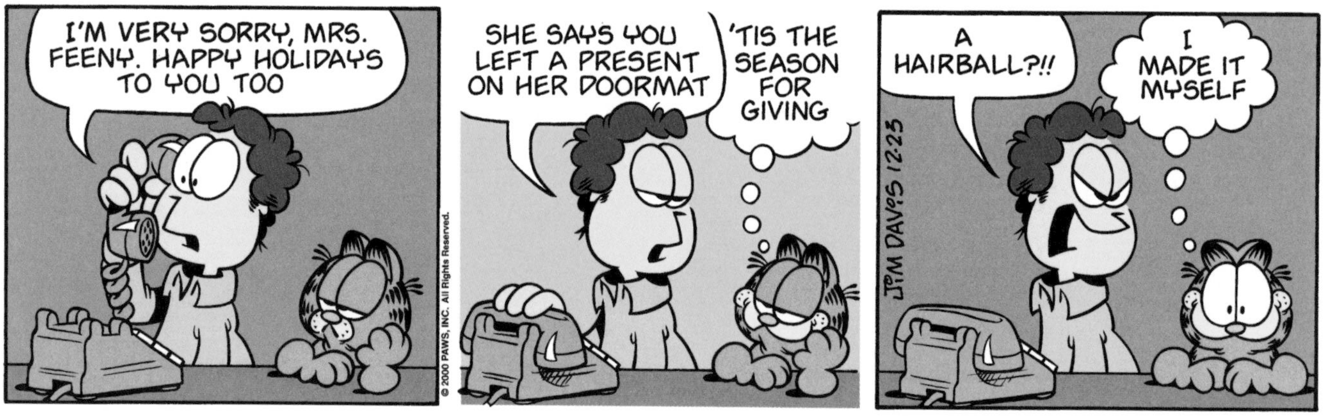
I'M VERY SORRY, MRS. FEENY. HAPPY HOLIDAYS TO YOU TOO
© 2000 PAWS, INC. All Rights Reserved.
SHE SAYS YOU LEFT A PRESENT ON HER DOORMAT
'TIS THE SEASON FOR GIVING
JIM DAVIS 12·23
A HAIRBALL?!!
I MADE IT MYSELF

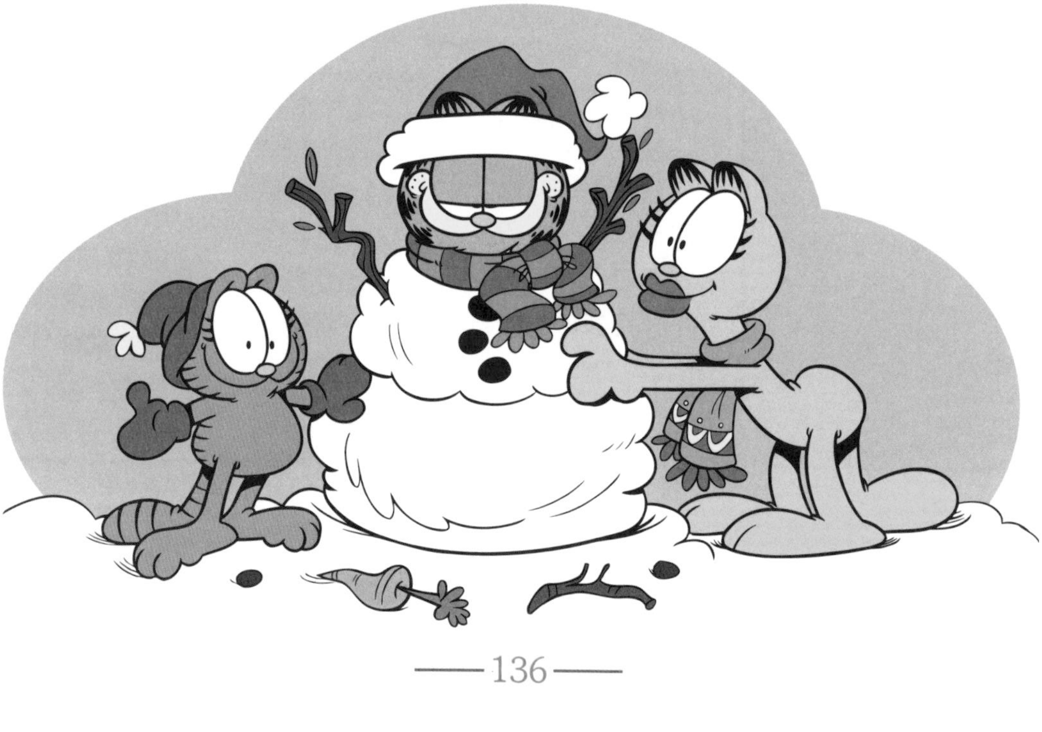

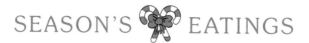

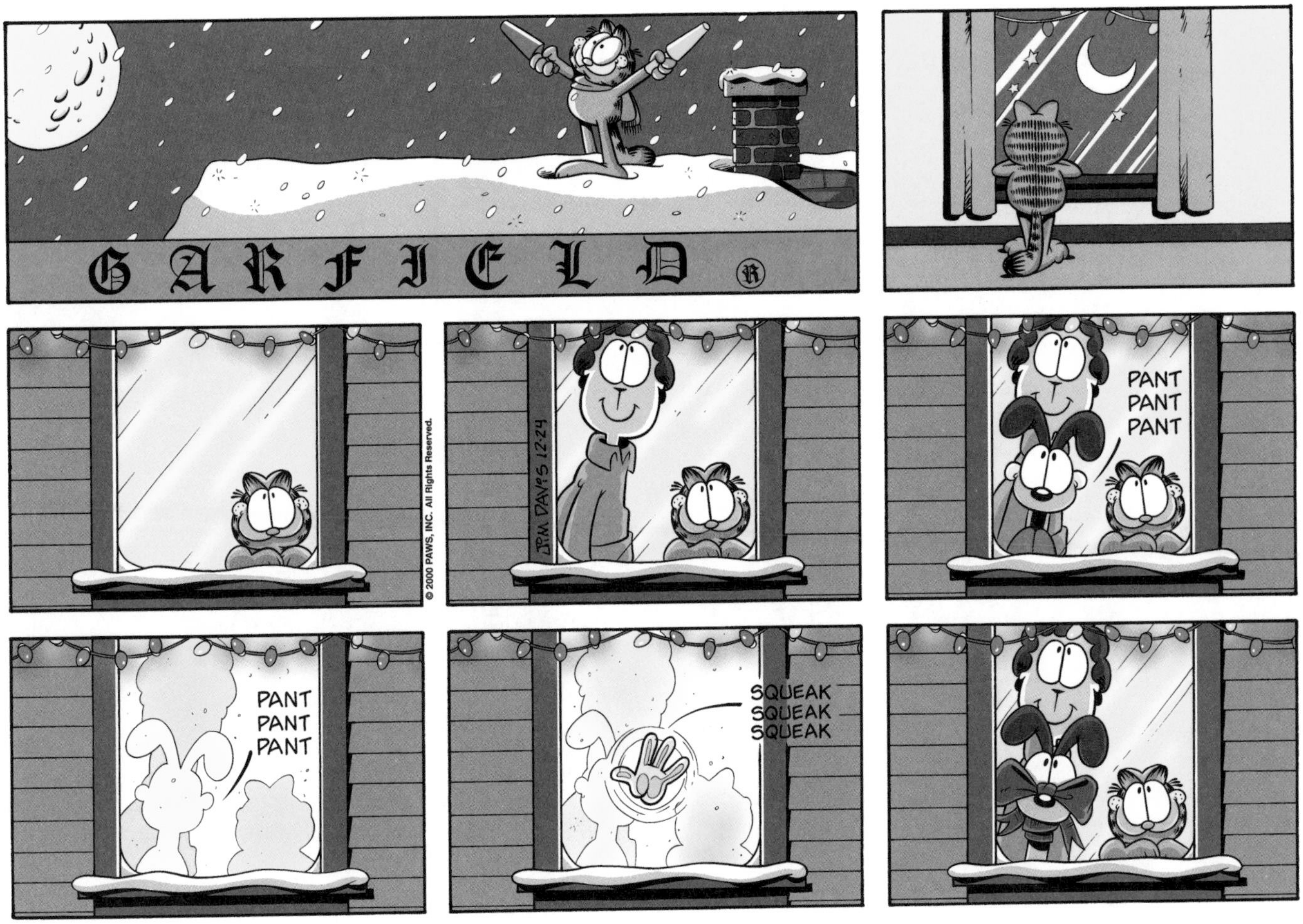
GARFIELD
© 2000 PAWS, INC. All Rights Reserved.
JPM DAVIS 12-24
PANT PANT PANT
PANT PANT PANT
SQUEAK SQUEAK SQUEAK

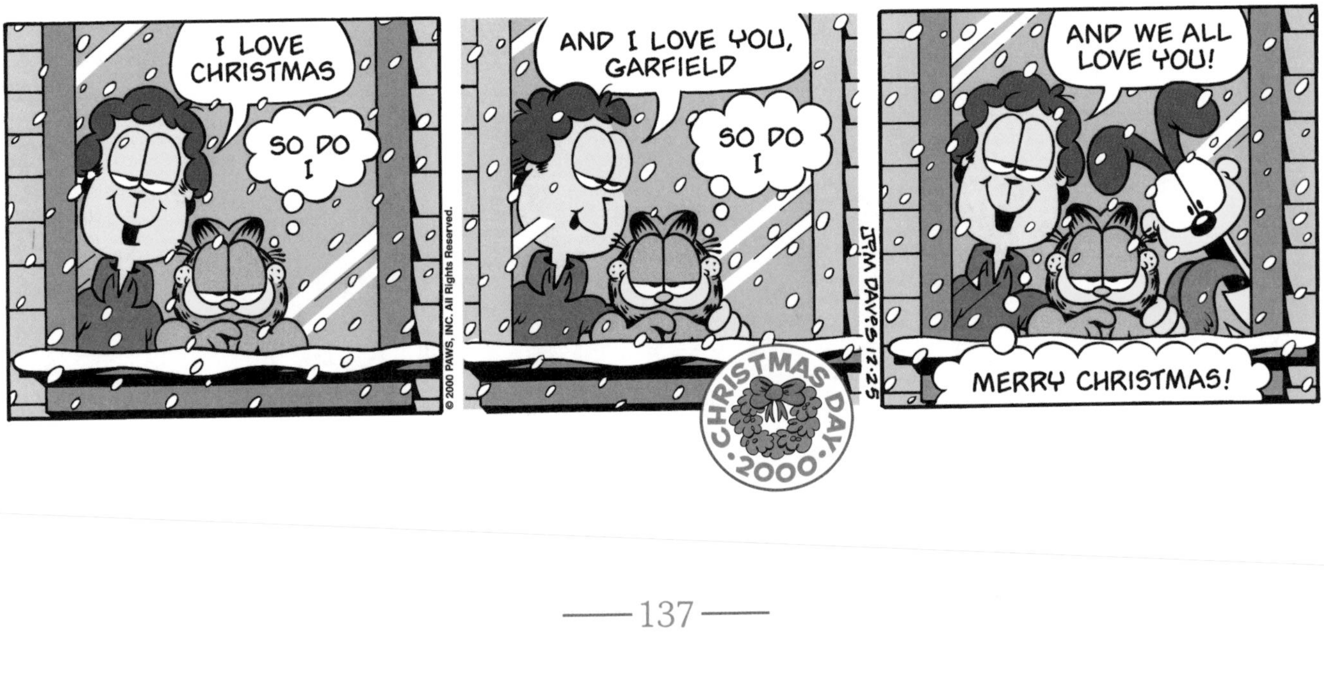
I LOVE CHRISTMAS
SO DO I
© 2000 PAWS, INC. All Rights Reserved.
AND I LOVE YOU, GARFIELD
SO DO I
JPM DAVIS 12-25
CHRISTMAS DAY 2000
AND WE ALL LOVE YOU!
MERRY CHRISTMAS!

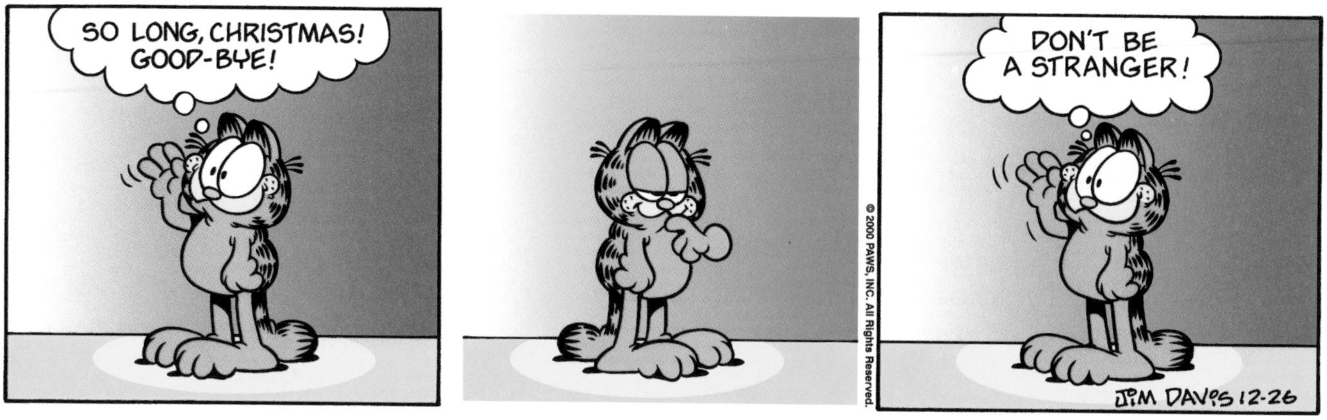
SO LONG, CHRISTMAS! GOOD-BYE!
DON'T BE A STRANGER!
© 2000 PAWS, INC. All Rights Reserved.
JIM DAVIS 12-26

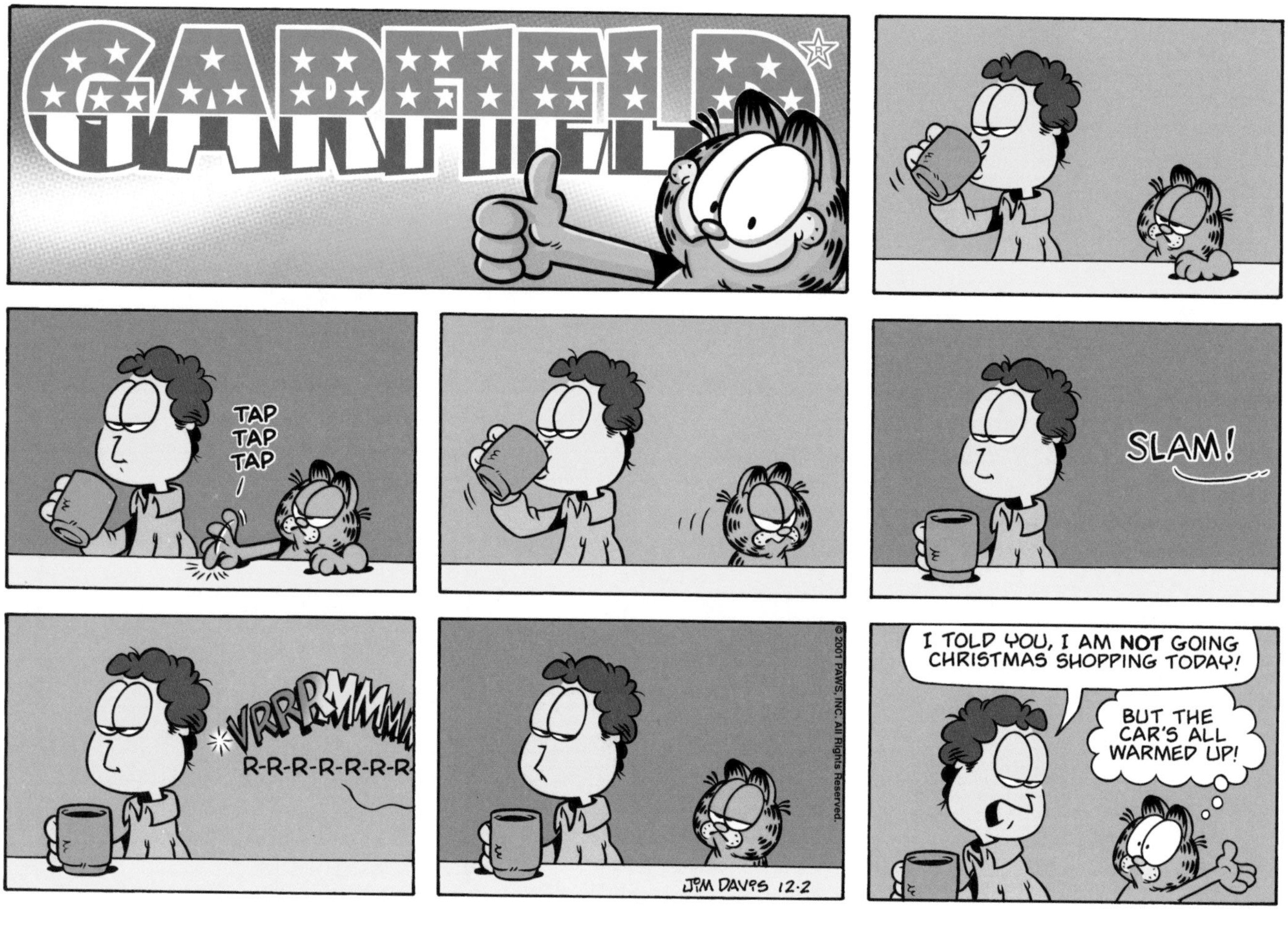
GARFIELD
TAP TAP TAP
SLAM!
VRRRMMMM
R-R-R-R-R-R-R-
© 2001 PAWS, INC. All Rights Reserved.
JIM DAVIS 12-2
I TOLD YOU, I AM **NOT** GOING CHRISTMAS SHOPPING TODAY!
BUT THE CAR'S ALL WARMED UP!

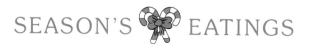

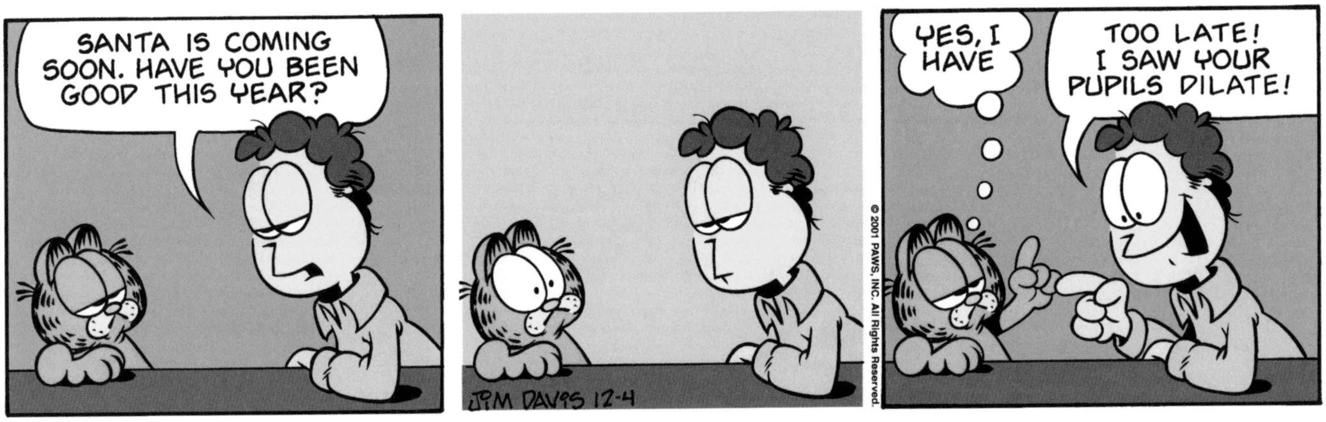
SANTA IS COMING SOON. HAVE YOU BEEN GOOD THIS YEAR?
YES, I HAVE
TOO LATE! I SAW YOUR PUPILS DILATE!
JIM DAVIS 12-4
© 2001 PAWS, INC. All Rights Reserved.

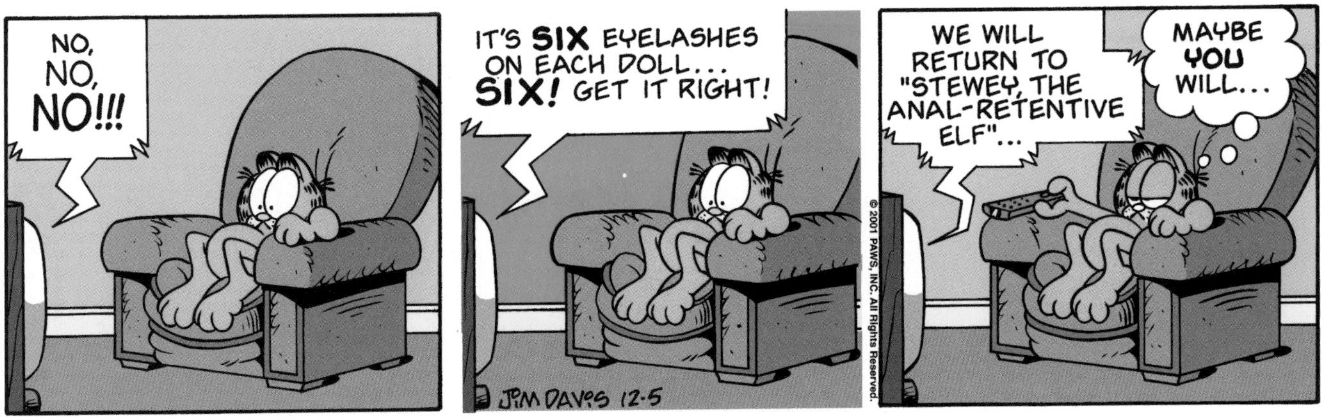
NO, NO, NO!!!
IT'S SIX EYELASHES ON EACH DOLL... SIX! GET IT RIGHT!
WE WILL RETURN TO "STEWEY, THE ANAL-RETENTIVE ELF"...
MAYBE YOU WILL...
JIM DAVIS 12-5
© 2001 PAWS, INC. All Rights Reserved.

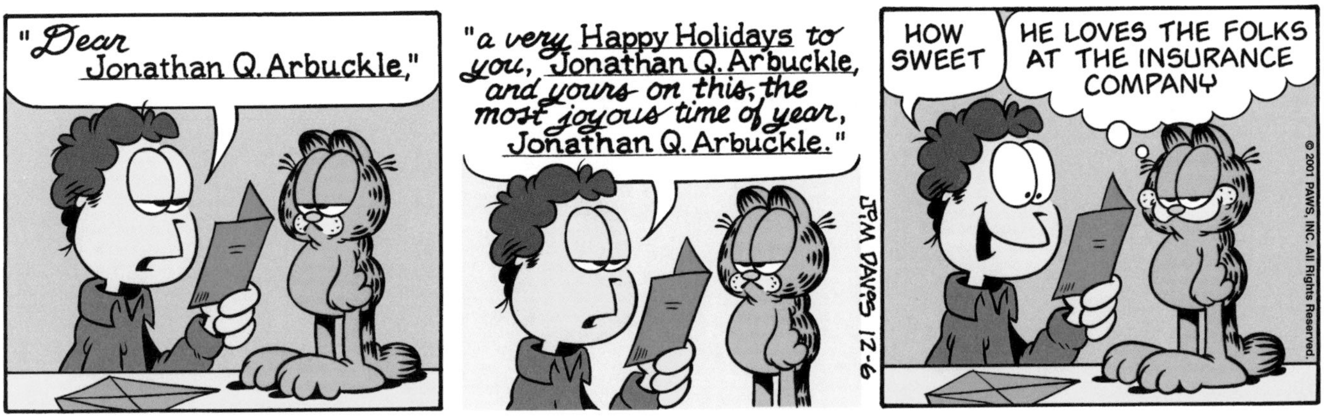
"Dear Jonathan Q. Arbuckle,"
"a very Happy Holidays to you, Jonathan Q. Arbuckle, and yours on this, the most joyous time of year, Jonathan Q. Arbuckle."
HOW SWEET
HE LOVES THE FOLKS AT THE INSURANCE COMPANY
JIM DAVIS 12-6
© 2001 PAWS, INC. All Rights Reserved.

JIM DAVIS 12-7
HAVE YOU WRITTEN YOUR LETTER TO SANTA YET?
RIIINNG
HELLO?
THIS IS SANTA
© 2001 PAWS, INC. All Rights Reserved.
...YOU PAGED MY BEEPER?
HERE'S MY LIST

SLUURRP!
AAAGGHH
© 2001 PAWS, INC. All Rights Reserved.
JIM DAVIS 12-8
EWW...WHAT IS HE DOING?
WRINGING OUT HIS BEARD
VISIT SANTA

"IF YOU'VE BEEN NAUGHTY, PRESS 1. IF YOU'VE BEEN NICE, PRESS 2."
1-(800) KRI-NGLE

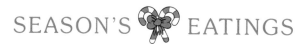

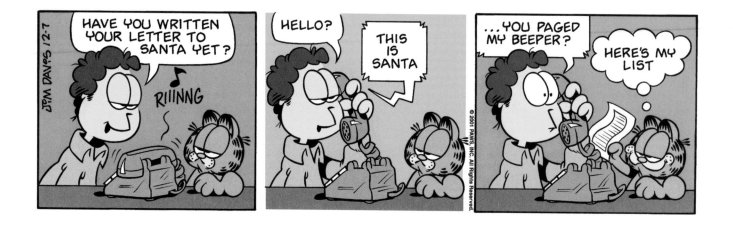

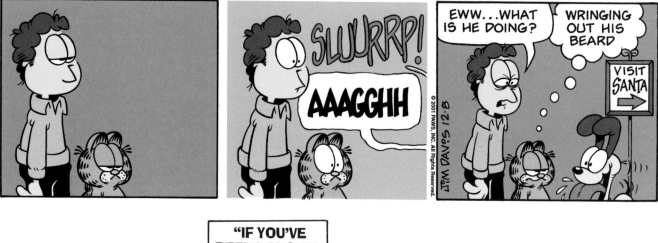

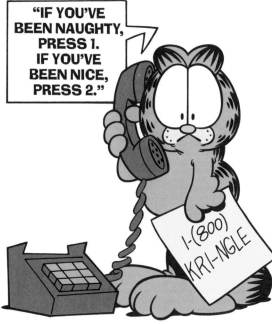

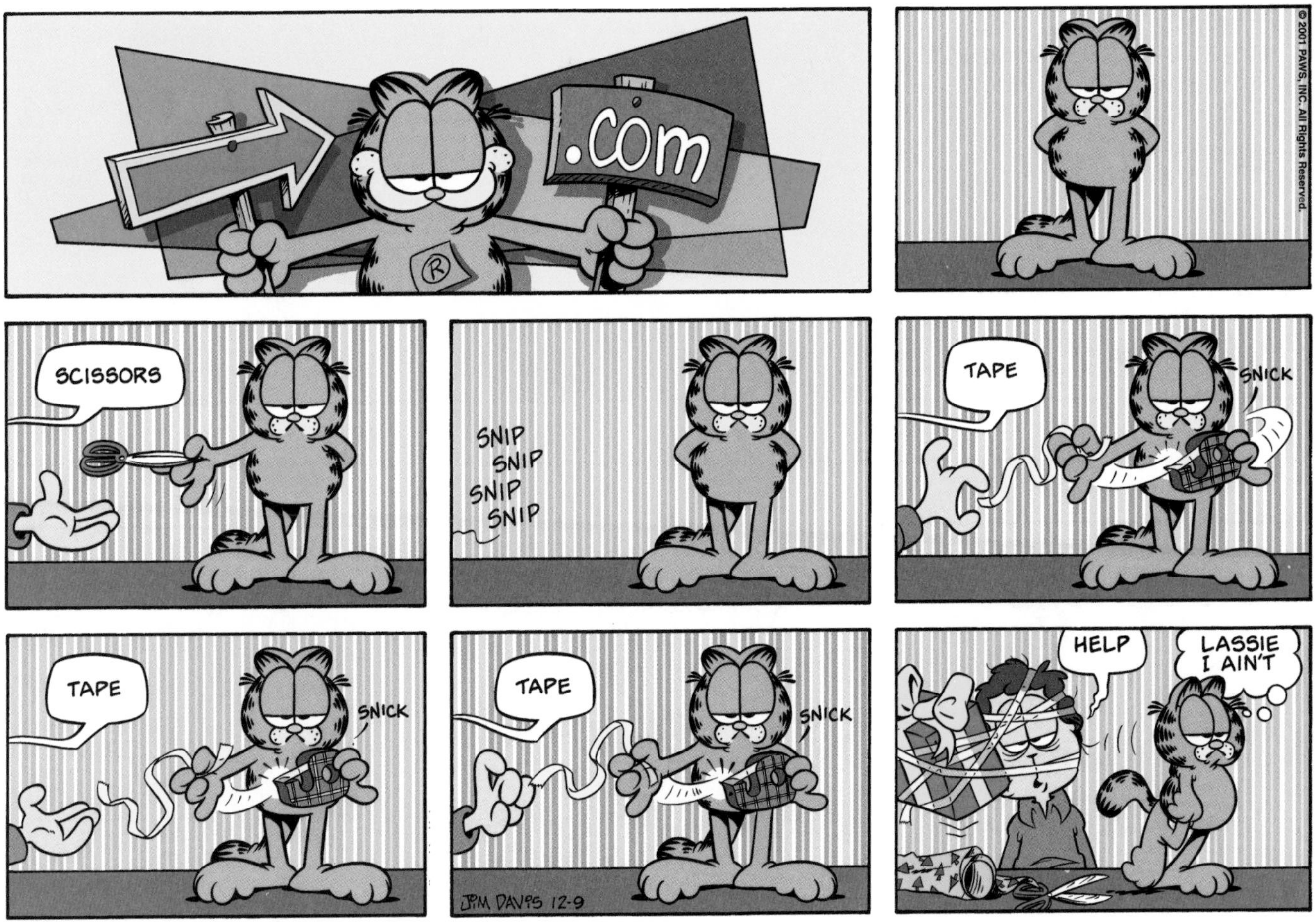
.com
© 2001 PAWS, INC. All Rights Reserved.
SCISSORS
SNIP
SNIP
SNIP
SNIP
TAPE
SNICK
TAPE
SNICK
TAPE
SNICK
JIM DAVIS 12-9
HELP
LASSIE I AIN'T

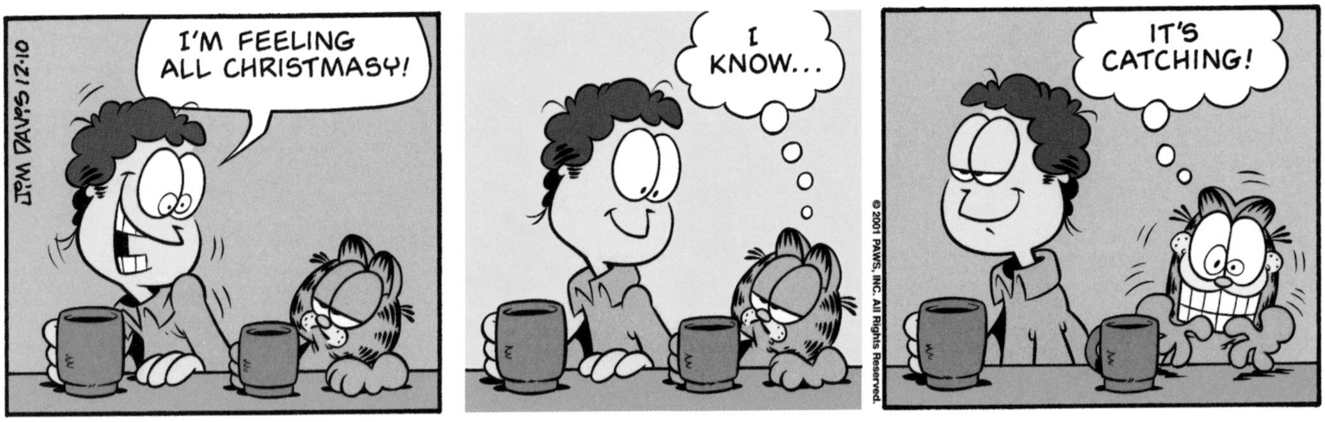
JIM DAVIS 12-10
I'M FEELING ALL CHRISTMASY!
I KNOW...
© 2001 PAWS, INC. All Rights Reserved.
IT'S CATCHING!

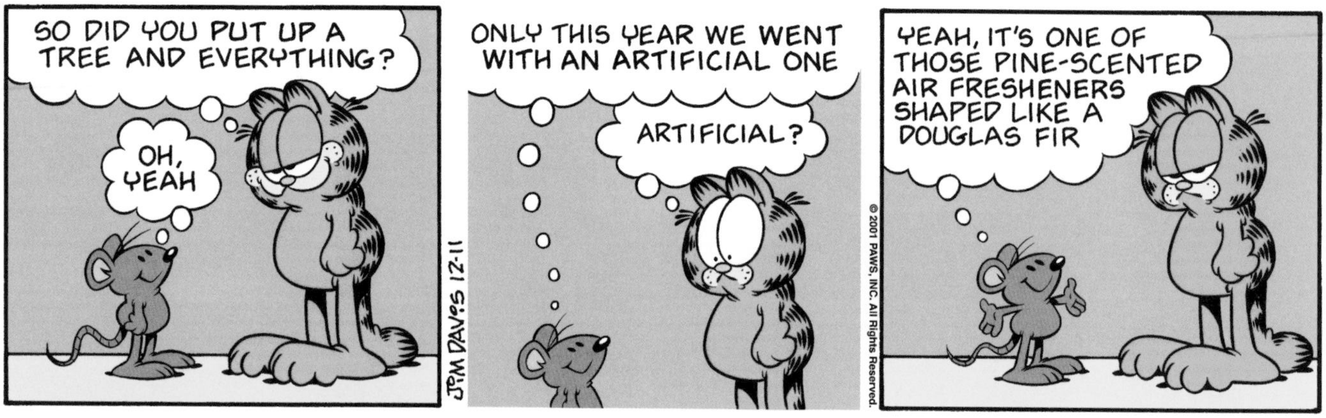
SO DID YOU PUT UP A TREE AND EVERYTHING?
OH, YEAH
ONLY THIS YEAR WE WENT WITH AN ARTIFICIAL ONE
ARTIFICIAL?
YEAH, IT'S ONE OF THOSE PINE-SCENTED AIR FRESHENERS SHAPED LIKE A DOUGLAS FIR
JIM DAVIS 12-11
© 2001 PAWS, INC. All Rights Reserved.

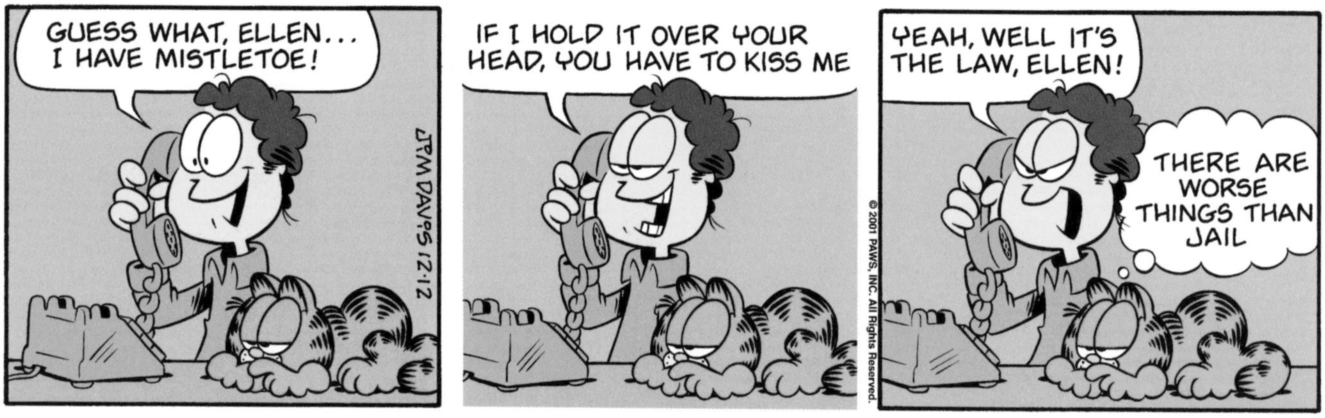
GUESS WHAT, ELLEN... I HAVE MISTLETOE!
JIM DAVIS 12-12
IF I HOLD IT OVER YOUR HEAD, YOU HAVE TO KISS ME
YEAH, WELL IT'S THE LAW, ELLEN!
THERE ARE WORSE THINGS THAN JAIL
© 2001 PAWS, INC. All Rights Reserved.

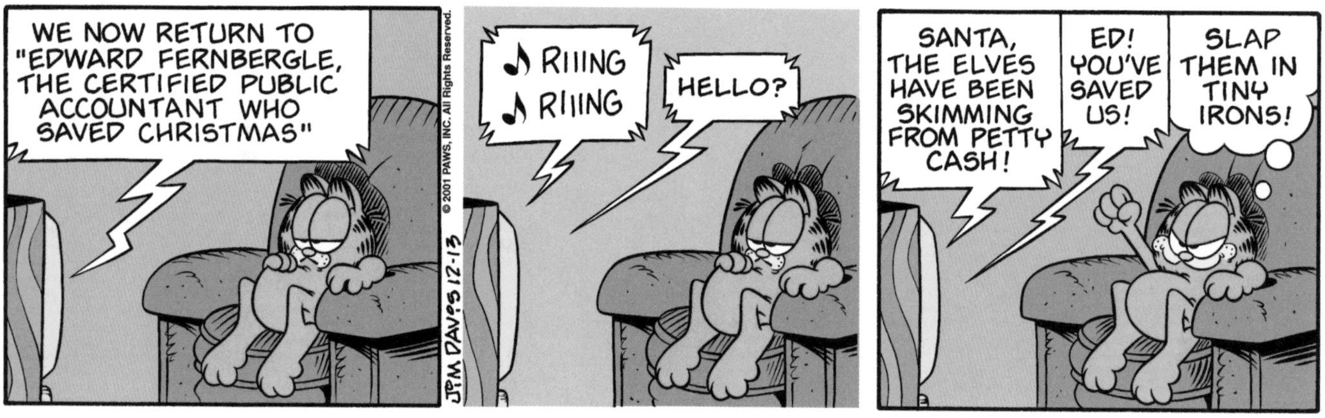
WE NOW RETURN TO "EDWARD FERNBERGLE, THE CERTIFIED PUBLIC ACCOUNTANT WHO SAVED CHRISTMAS"
© 2001 PAWS, INC. All Rights Reserved.
JIM DAVIS 12-13
♪ RIIING
♪ RIIING
HELLO?
SANTA, THE ELVES HAVE BEEN SKIMMING FROM PETTY CASH!
ED! YOU'VE SAVED US!
SLAP THEM IN TINY IRONS!

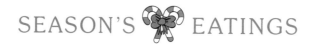

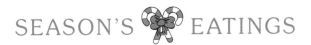

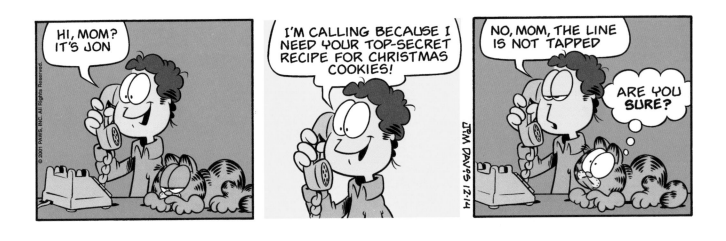

HI, MOM? IT'S JON
I'M CALLING BECAUSE I NEED YOUR TOP-SECRET RECIPE FOR CHRISTMAS COOKIES!
NO, MOM, THE LINE IS NOT TAPPED
ARE YOU SURE?
JIM DAVIS 12-14
© 2001 PAWS, INC. All Rights Reserved.

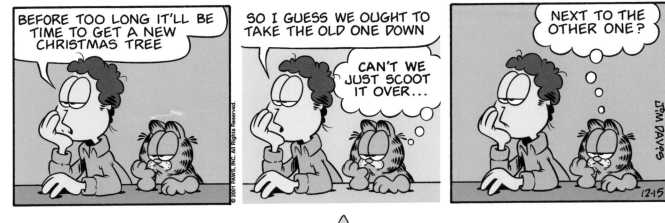

BEFORE TOO LONG IT'LL BE TIME TO GET A NEW CHRISTMAS TREE
SO I GUESS WE OUGHT TO TAKE THE OLD ONE DOWN
CAN'T WE JUST SCOOT IT OVER...
NEXT TO THE OTHER ONE?
JIM DAVIS 12-15
© 2001 PAWS, INC. All Rights Reserved.

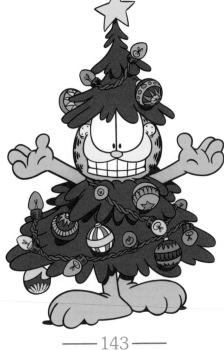

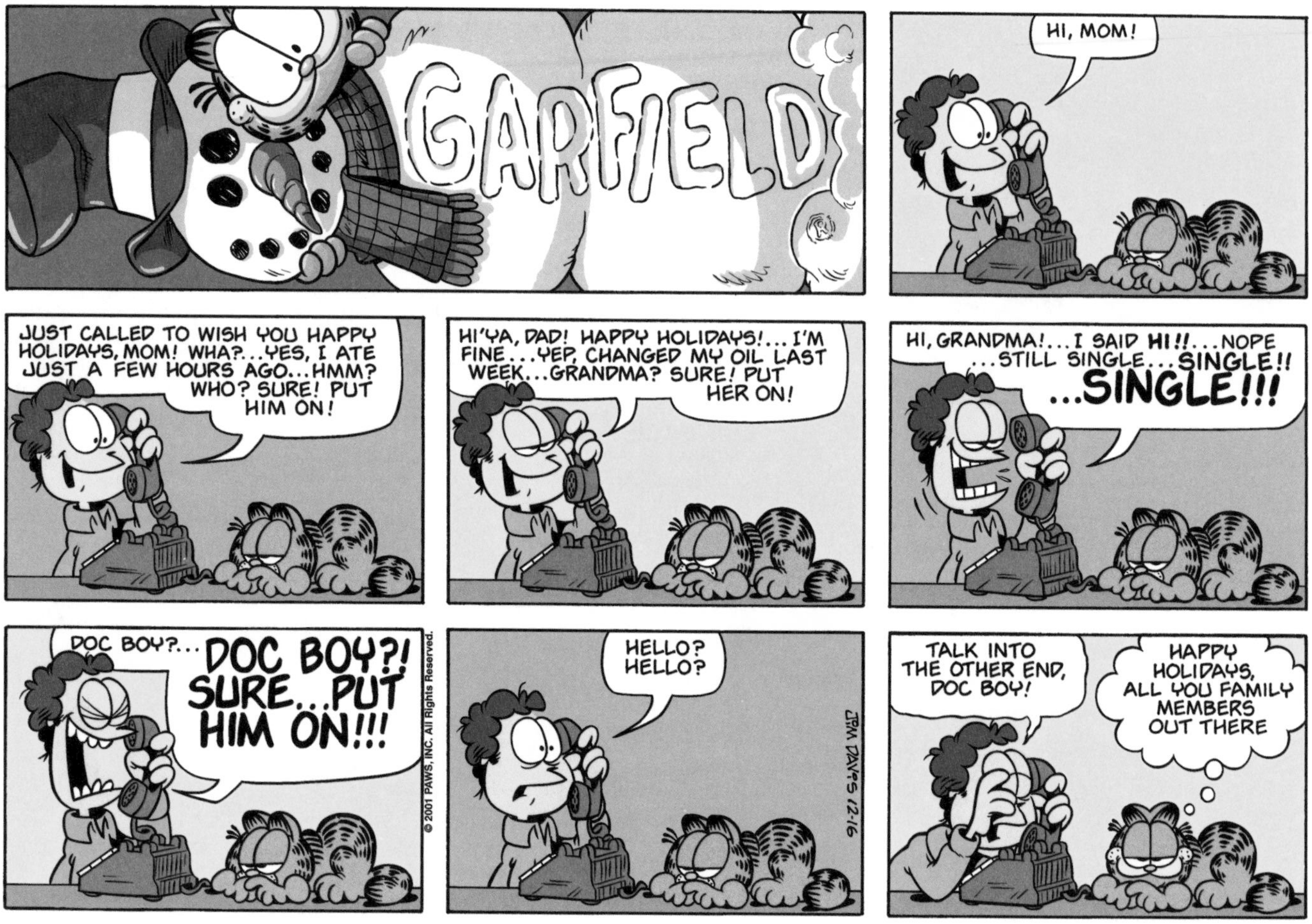
GARFIELD
HI, MOM!
JUST CALLED TO WISH YOU HAPPY HOLIDAYS, MOM! WHA?...YES, I ATE JUST A FEW HOURS AGO...HMM? WHO? SURE! PUT HIM ON!
HI'YA, DAD! HAPPY HOLIDAYS!...I'M FINE...YEP, CHANGED MY OIL LAST WEEK...GRANDMA? SURE! PUT HER ON!
HI, GRANDMA!...I SAID HI!!...NOPE ...STILL SINGLE...SINGLE!! ...SINGLE!!!
DOC BOY?...DOC BOY?! SURE...PUT HIM ON!!!
© 2001 PAWS, INC. All Rights Reserved.
JIM DAVIS 12-16
HELLO? HELLO?
TALK INTO THE OTHER END, DOC BOY!
HAPPY HOLIDAYS, ALL YOU FAMILY MEMBERS OUT THERE

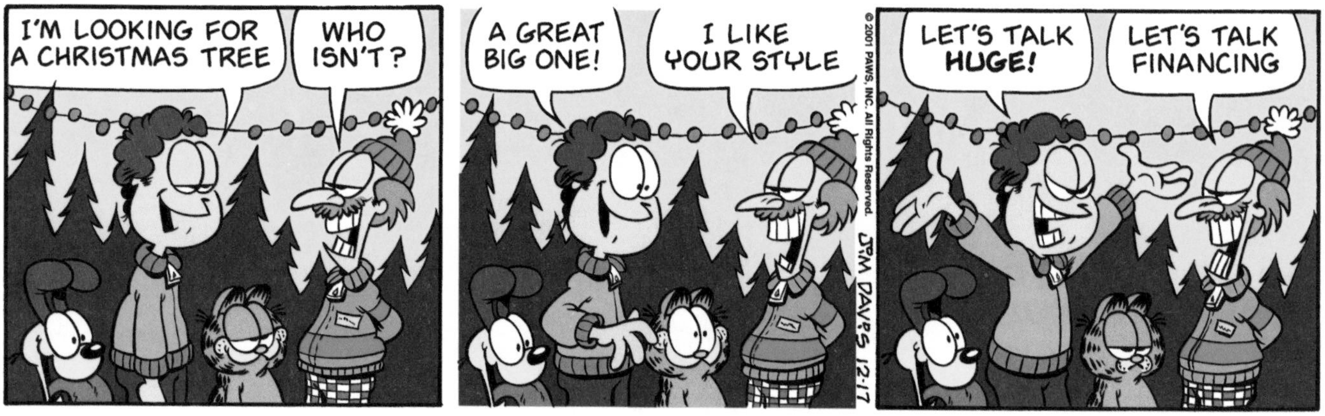
I'M LOOKING FOR A CHRISTMAS TREE
WHO ISN'T?
A GREAT BIG ONE!
I LIKE YOUR STYLE
© 2001 PAWS, INC. All Rights Reserved.
JIM DAVIS 12-17
LET'S TALK HUGE!
LET'S TALK FINANCING

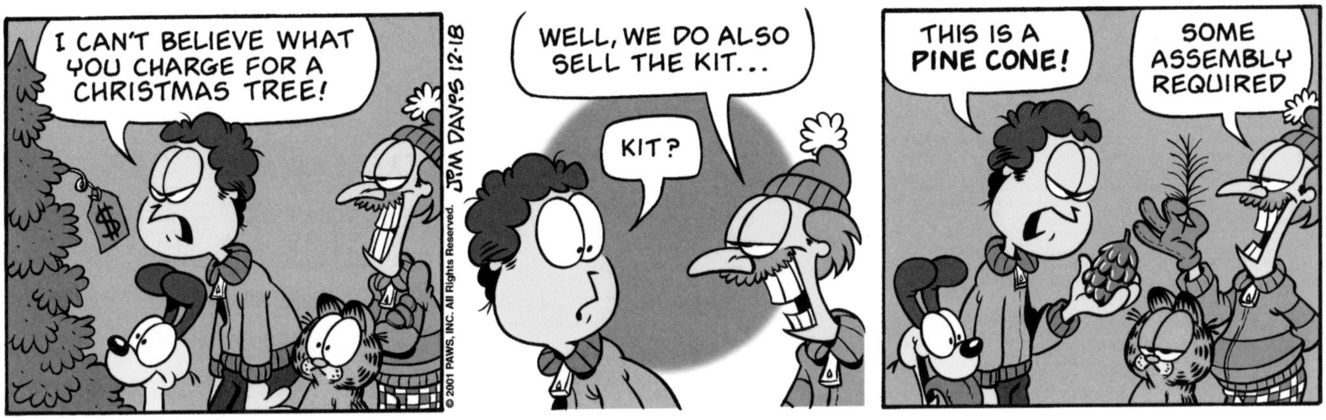
I CAN'T BELIEVE WHAT YOU CHARGE FOR A CHRISTMAS TREE!
$
JIM DAVIS 12-18
© 2001 PAWS, INC. All Rights Reserved.
WELL, WE DO ALSO SELL THE KIT...
KIT?
THIS IS A PINE CONE!
SOME ASSEMBLY REQUIRED

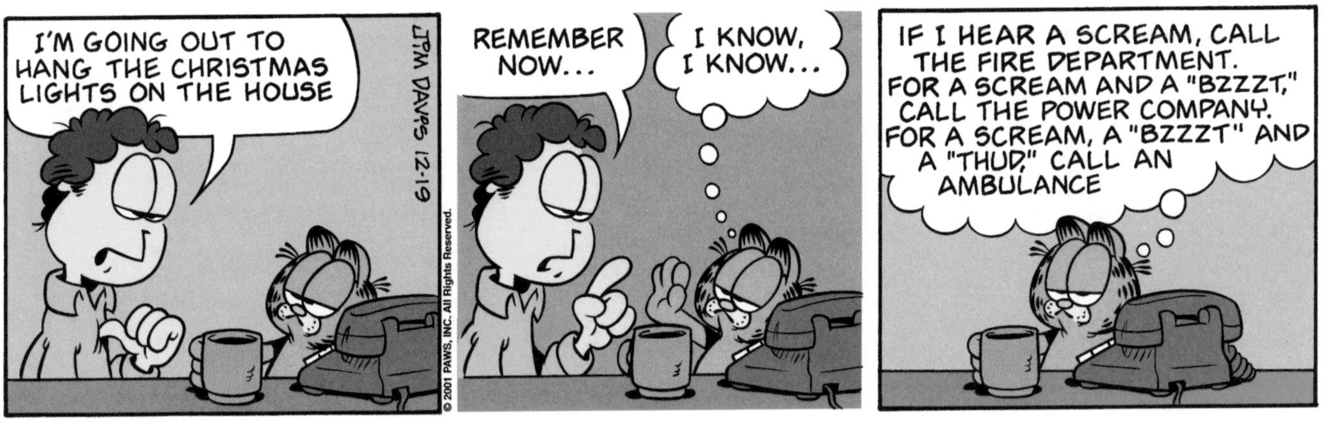
I'M GOING OUT TO HANG THE CHRISTMAS LIGHTS ON THE HOUSE
JIM DAVIS 12-19
© 2001 PAWS, INC. All Rights Reserved.
REMEMBER NOW...
I KNOW, I KNOW...
IF I HEAR A SCREAM, CALL THE FIRE DEPARTMENT. FOR A SCREAM AND A "BZZZT," CALL THE POWER COMPANY. FOR A SCREAM, A "BZZZT" AND A "THUD," CALL AN AMBULANCE

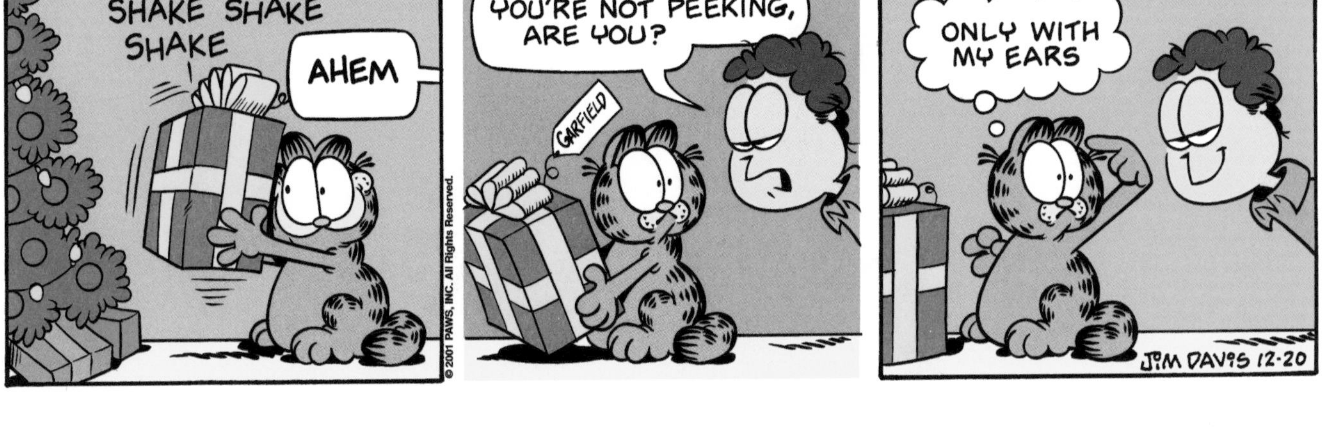
SHAKE SHAKE SHAKE
AHEM
© 2001 PAWS, INC. All Rights Reserved.
YOU'RE NOT PEEKING, ARE YOU?
GARFIELD
ONLY WITH MY EARS
JIM DAVIS 12-20

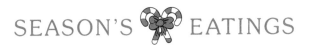

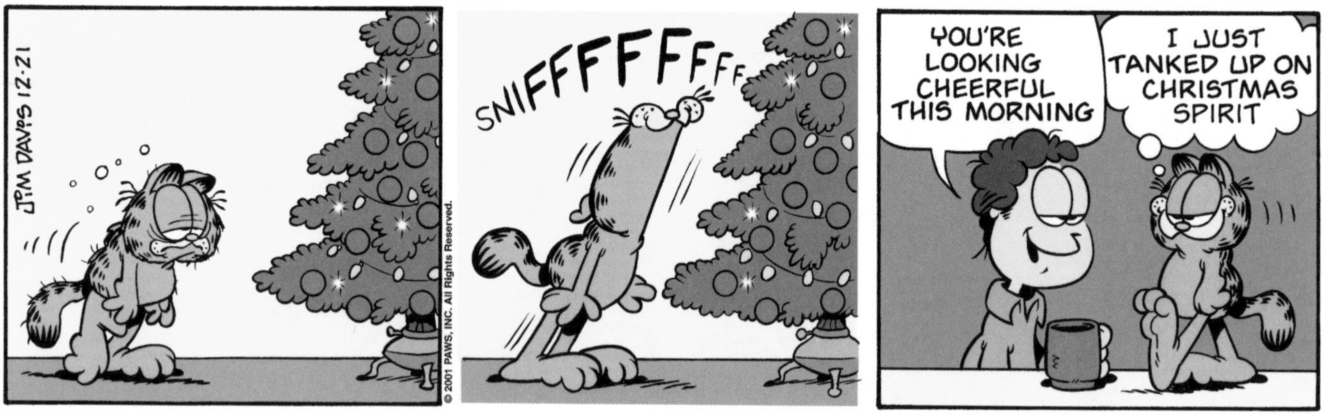
JIM DAVIS 12-21
SNIFFFFFFFFF
© 2001 PAWS, INC. All Rights Reserved.
YOU'RE LOOKING CHEERFUL THIS MORNING
I JUST TANKED UP ON CHRISTMAS SPIRIT

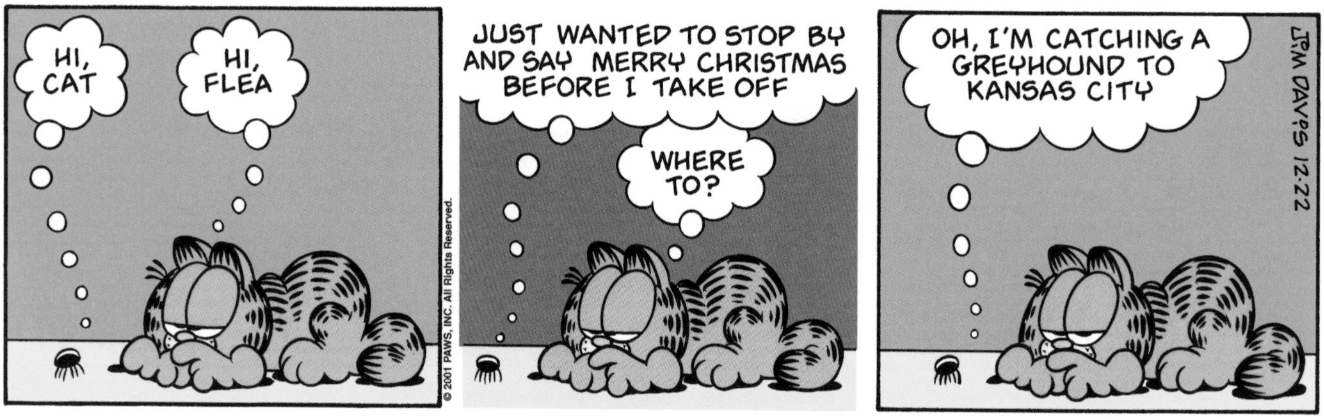
HI, CAT
HI, FLEA
© 2001 PAWS, INC. All Rights Reserved.
JUST WANTED TO STOP BY AND SAY MERRY CHRISTMAS BEFORE I TAKE OFF
WHERE TO?
OH, I'M CATCHING A GREYHOUND TO KANSAS CITY
JIM DAVIS 12-22

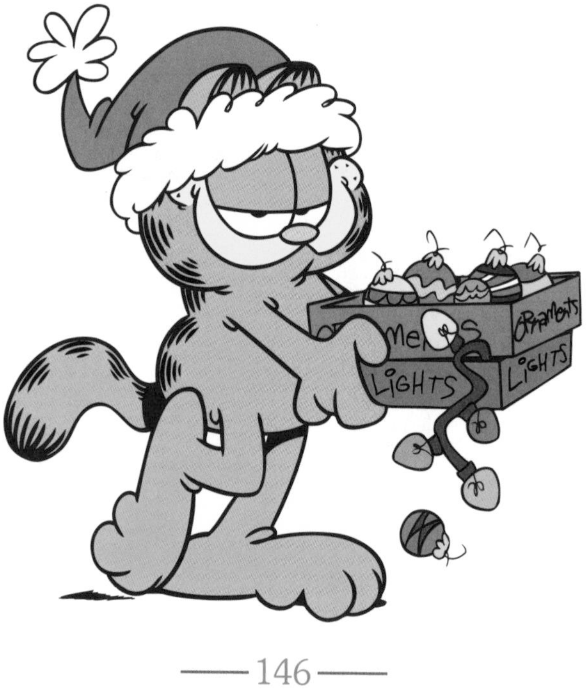
LIGHTS
LIGHTS

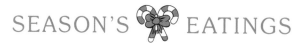

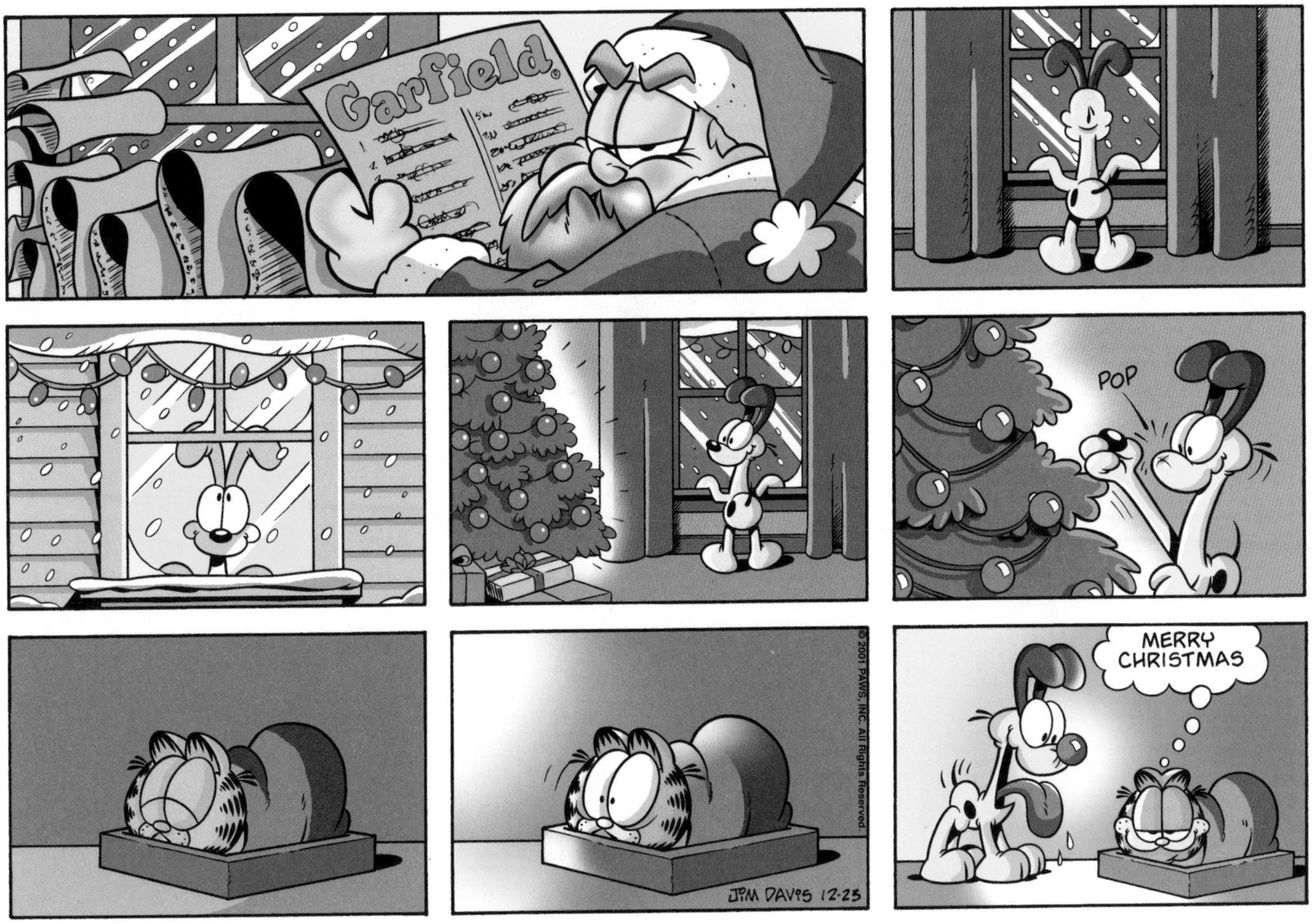
Garfield
POP
© 2001 PAWS, INC. All Rights Reserved.
MERRY CHRISTMAS
JIM DAVIS 12-23

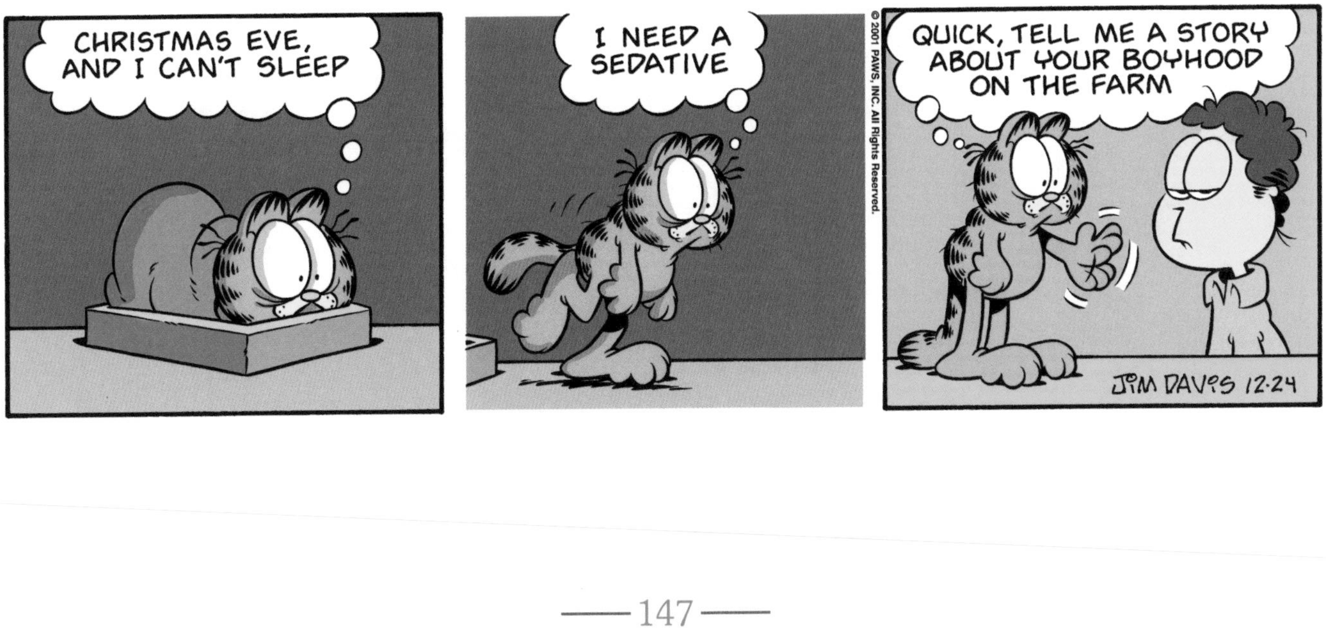
CHRISTMAS EVE, AND I CAN'T SLEEP
I NEED A SEDATIVE
© 2001 PAWS, INC. All Rights Reserved.
QUICK, TELL ME A STORY ABOUT YOUR BOYHOOD ON THE FARM
JIM DAVIS 12-24

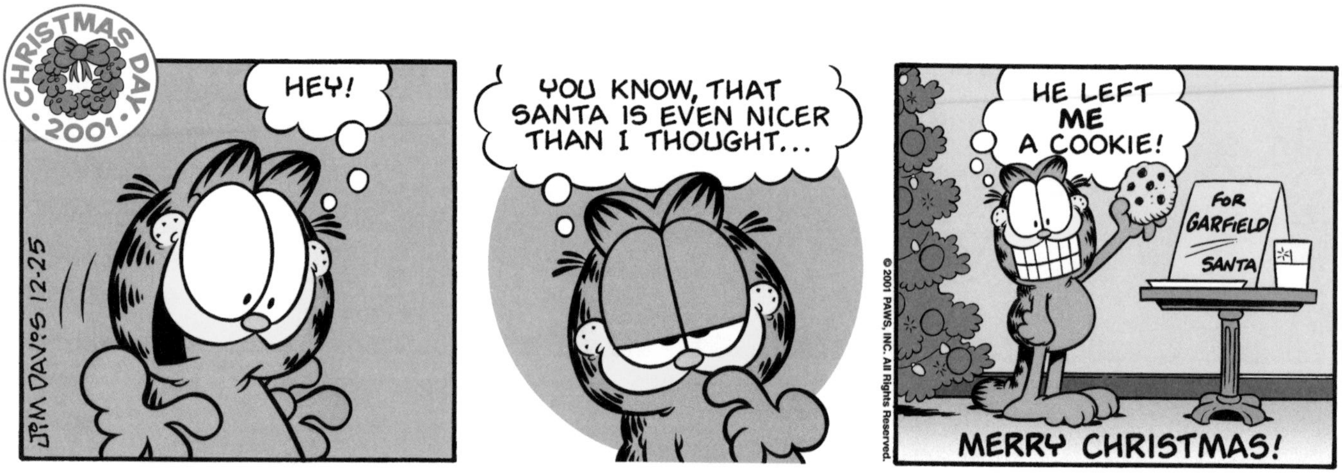
CHRISTMAS DAY 2001
JIM DAVIS 12-25
HEY!
YOU KNOW, THAT SANTA IS EVEN NICER THAN I THOUGHT...
HE LEFT ME A COOKIE!
FOR GARFIELD
SANTA
MERRY CHRISTMAS!
© 2001 PAWS, INC. All Rights Reserved.

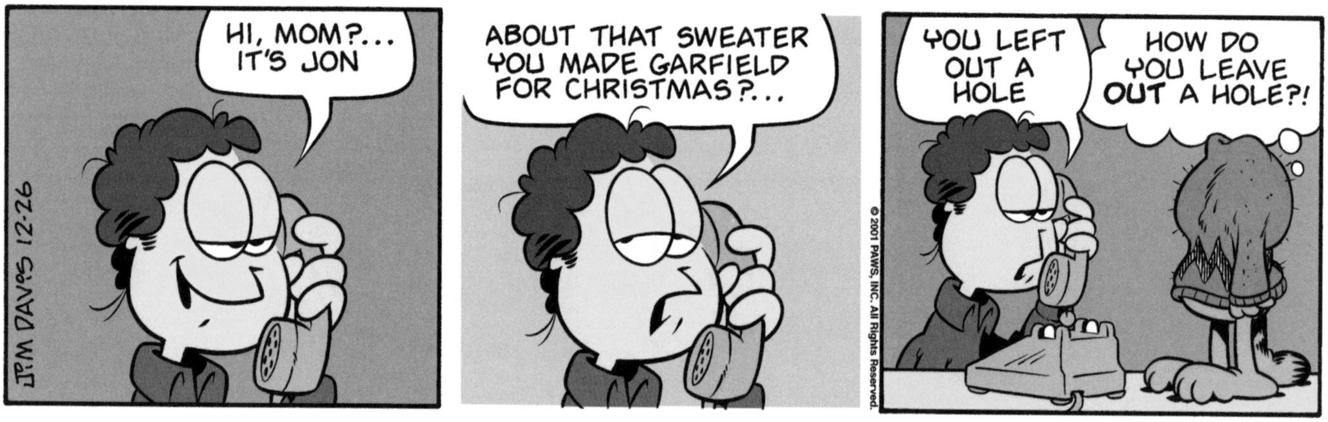
JIM DAVIS 12-26
HI, MOM?... IT'S JON
ABOUT THAT SWEATER YOU MADE GARFIELD FOR CHRISTMAS?...
YOU LEFT OUT A HOLE
HOW DO YOU LEAVE OUT A HOLE?!
© 2001 PAWS, INC. All Rights Reserved.

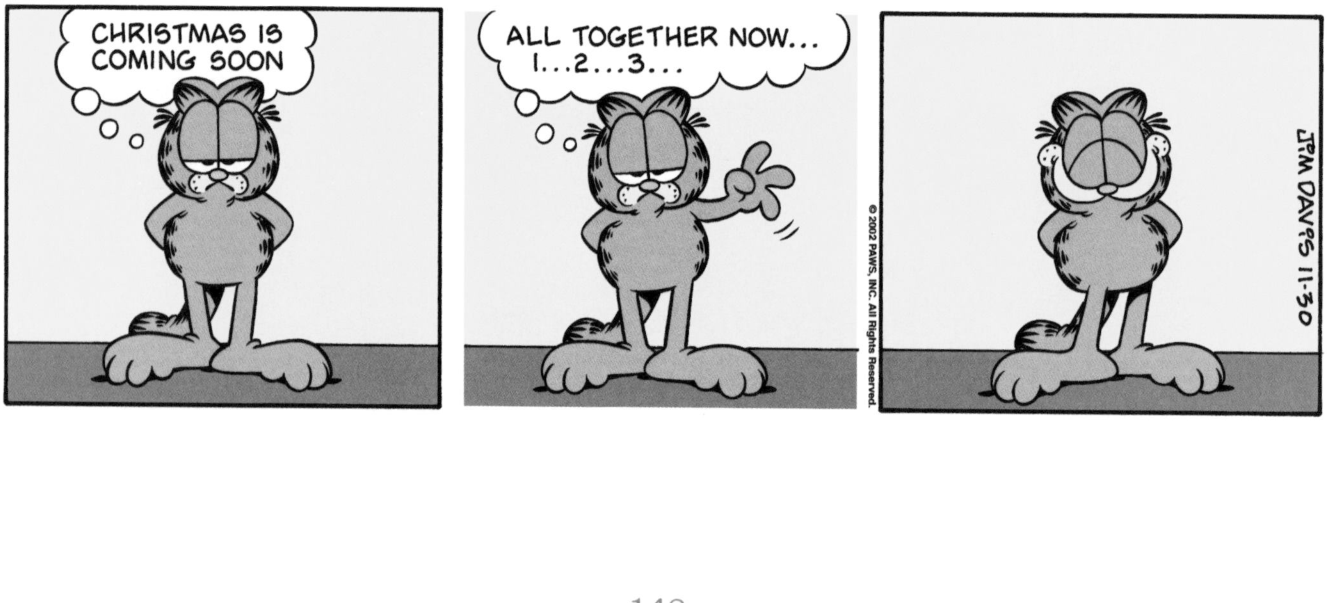
CHRISTMAS IS COMING SOON
ALL TOGETHER NOW... 1...2...3...
© 2002 PAWS, INC. All Rights Reserved.
JIM DAVIS 11-30

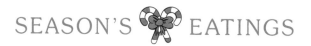

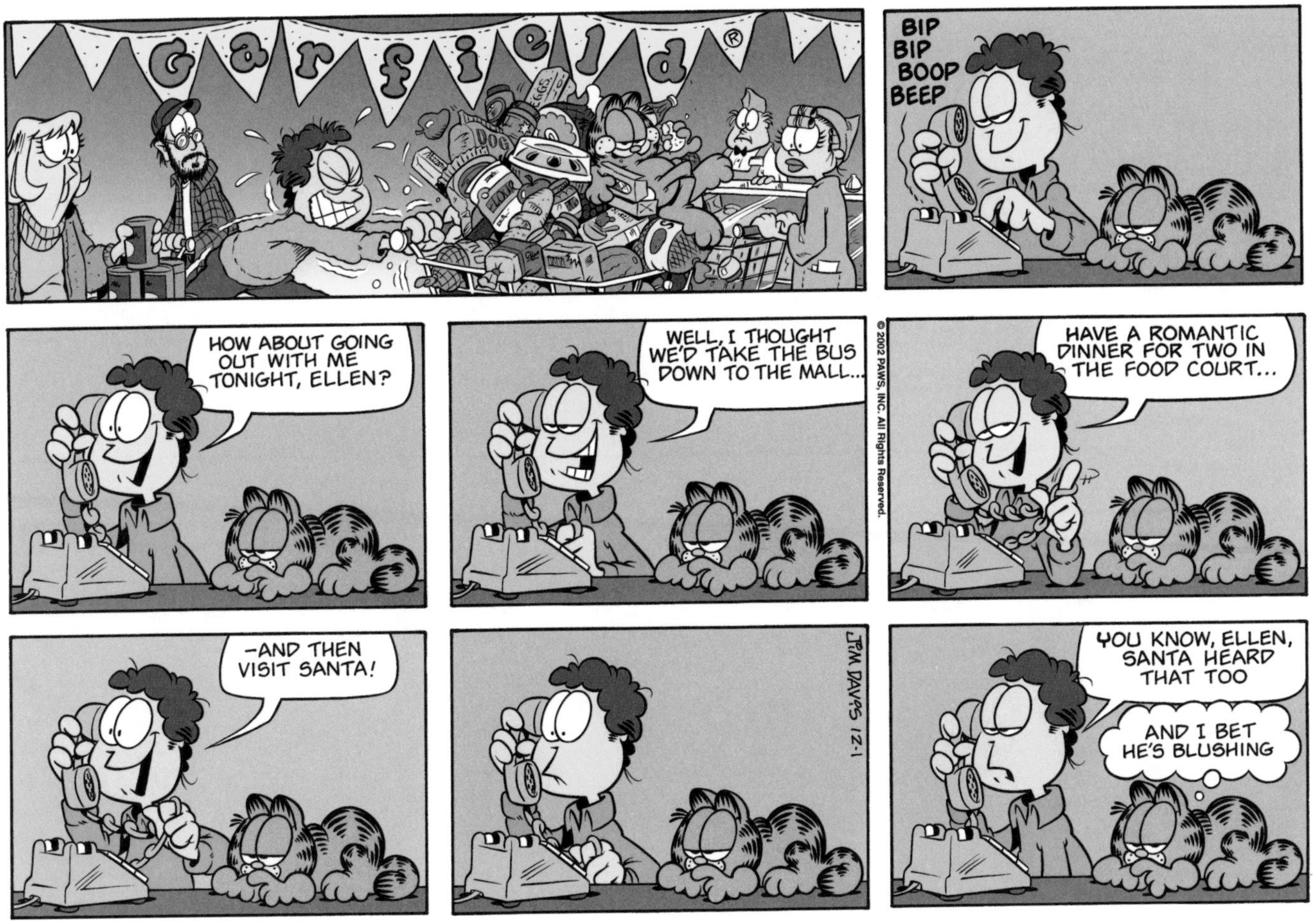
Garfield®
BIP BIP BOOP BEEP
HOW ABOUT GOING OUT WITH ME TONIGHT, ELLEN?
WELL, I THOUGHT WE'D TAKE THE BUS DOWN TO THE MALL...
© 2002 PAWS, INC. All Rights Reserved.
HAVE A ROMANTIC DINNER FOR TWO IN THE FOOD COURT...
–AND THEN VISIT SANTA!
JIM DAVIS 12-1
YOU KNOW, ELLEN, SANTA HEARD THAT TOO
AND I BET HE'S BLUSHING

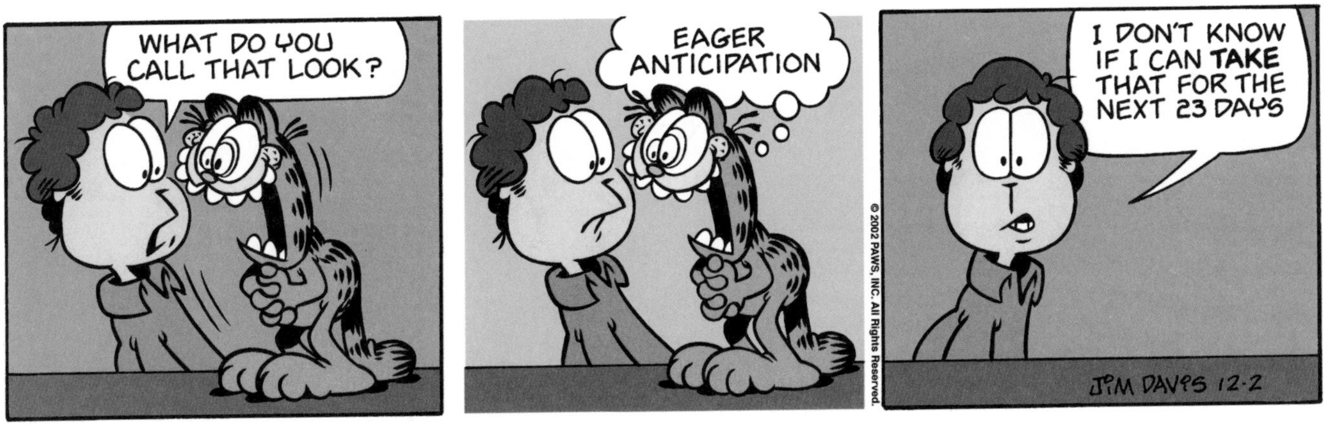
WHAT DO YOU CALL THAT LOOK?
EAGER ANTICIPATION
© 2002 PAWS, INC. All Rights Reserved.
I DON'T KNOW IF I CAN TAKE THAT FOR THE NEXT 23 DAYS
JIM DAVIS 12-2

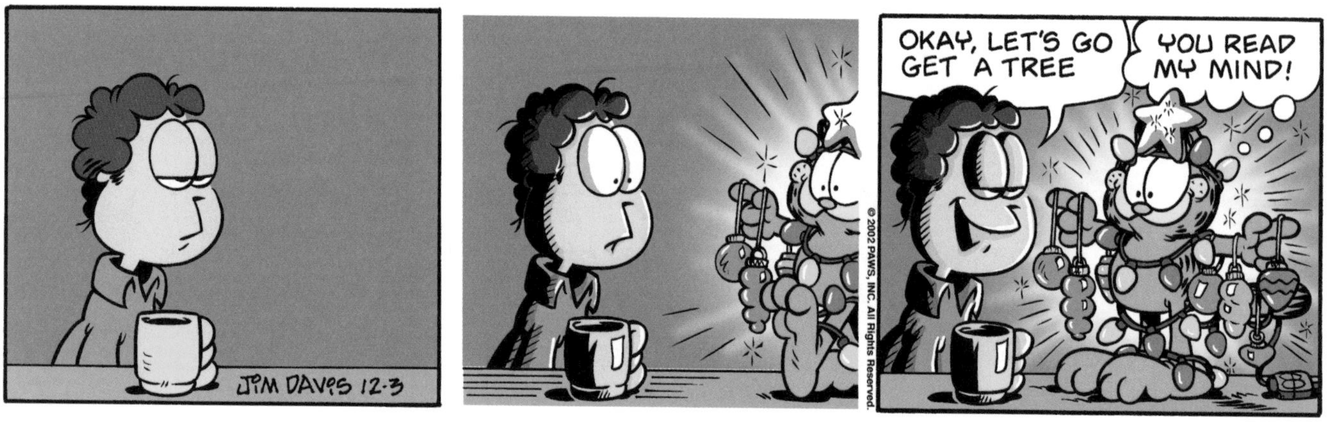
JIM DAVIS 12-3
© 2002 PAWS, INC. All Rights Reserved.
OKAY, LET'S GO GET A TREE
YOU READ MY MIND!

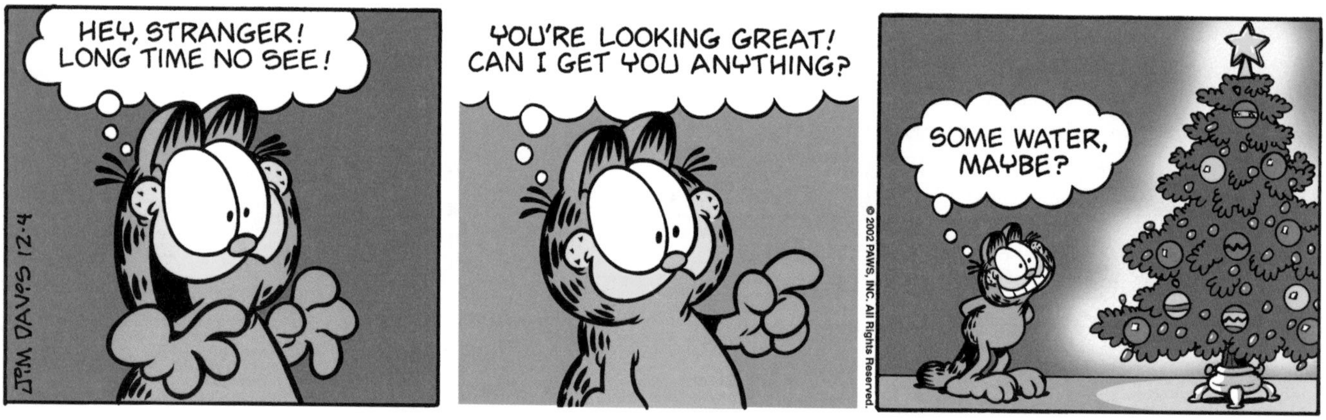
JIM DAVIS 12-4
HEY, STRANGER! LONG TIME NO SEE!
YOU'RE LOOKING GREAT! CAN I GET YOU ANYTHING?
© 2002 PAWS, INC. All Rights Reserved.
SOME WATER, MAYBE?

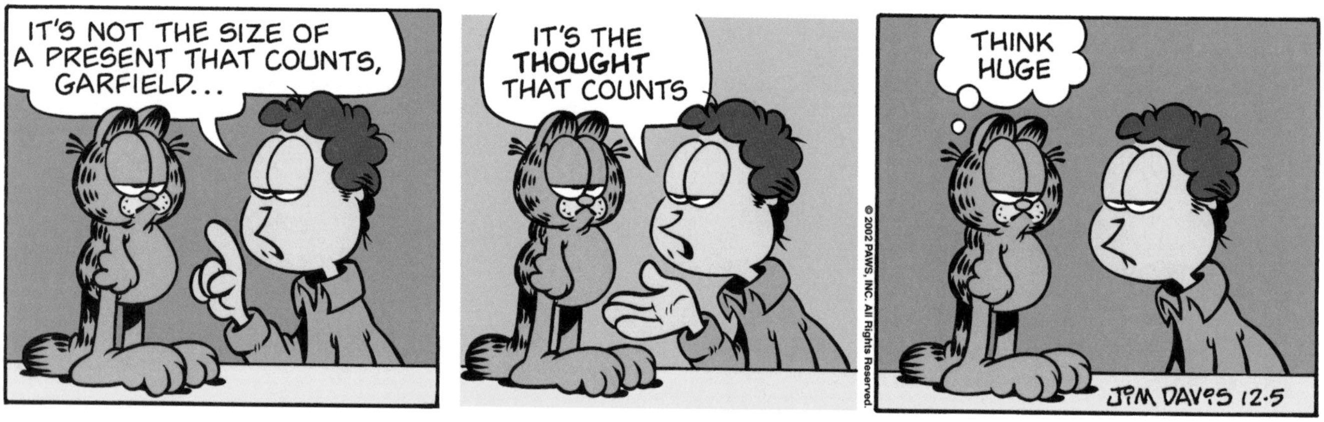
IT'S NOT THE SIZE OF A PRESENT THAT COUNTS, GARFIELD...
IT'S THE **THOUGHT** THAT COUNTS
© 2002 PAWS, INC. All Rights Reserved.
THINK HUGE
JIM DAVIS 12-5

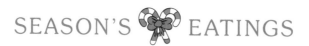

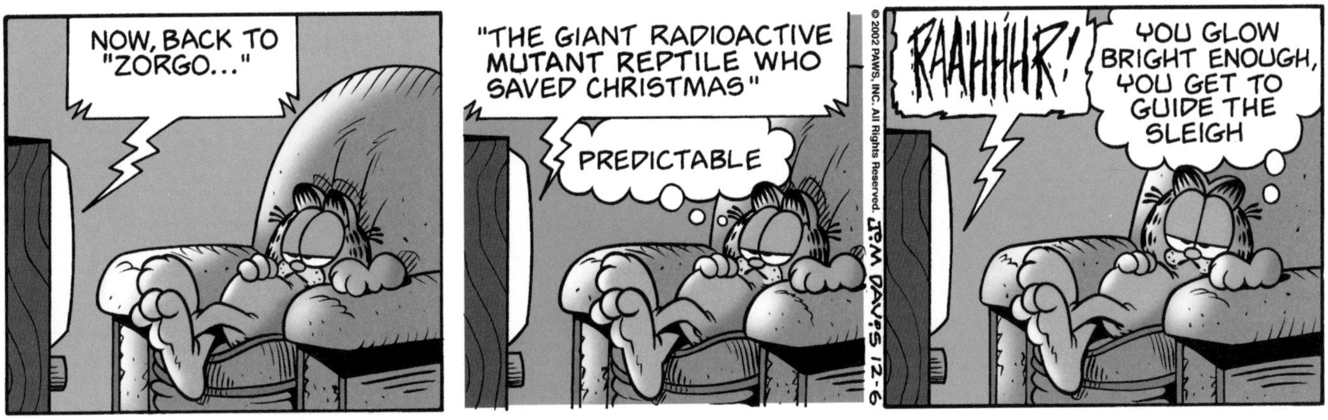
NOW, BACK TO "ZORGO..."
"THE GIANT RADIOACTIVE MUTANT REPTILE WHO SAVED CHRISTMAS"
PREDICTABLE
RAAHHHR!
YOU GLOW BRIGHT ENOUGH, YOU GET TO GUIDE THE SLEIGH
© 2002 PAWS, INC. All Rights Reserved.
JIM DAVIS 12-6

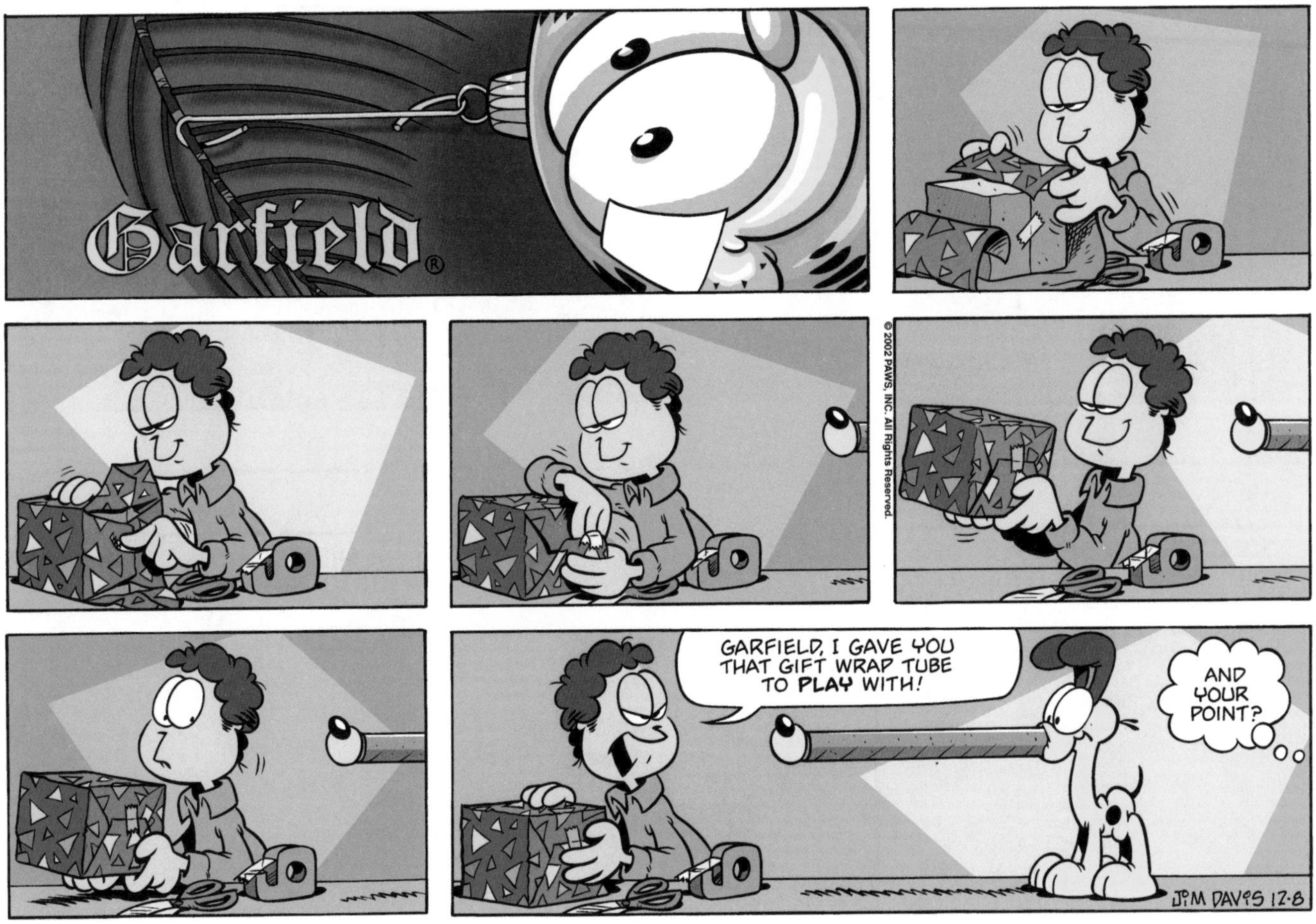
Garfield®
© 2002 PAWS, INC. All Rights Reserved.
GARFIELD, I GAVE YOU THAT GIFT WRAP TUBE TO PLAY WITH!
AND YOUR POINT?
JIM DAVIS 12-8

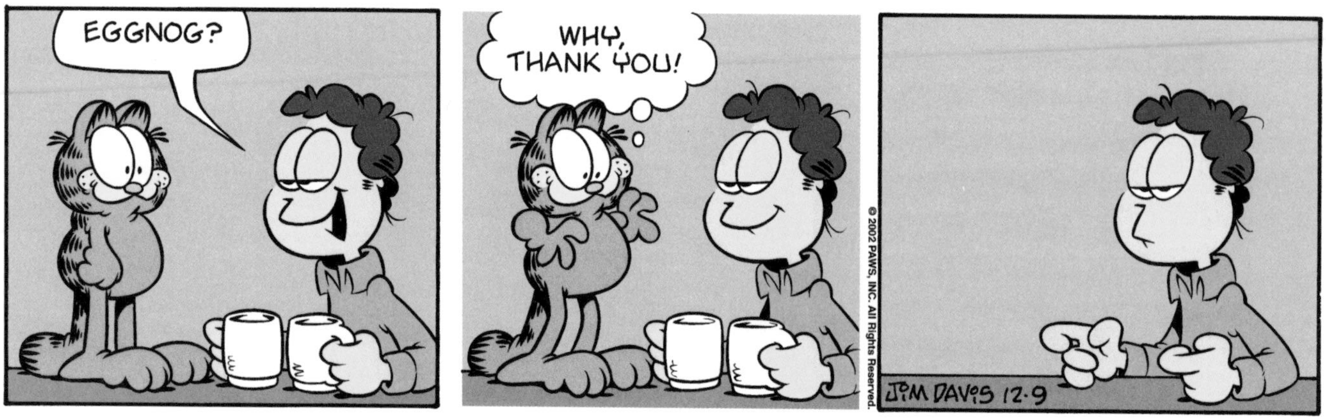
EGGNOG?
WHY, THANK YOU!
© 2002 PAWS, INC. All Rights Reserved.
JIM DAVIS 12-9

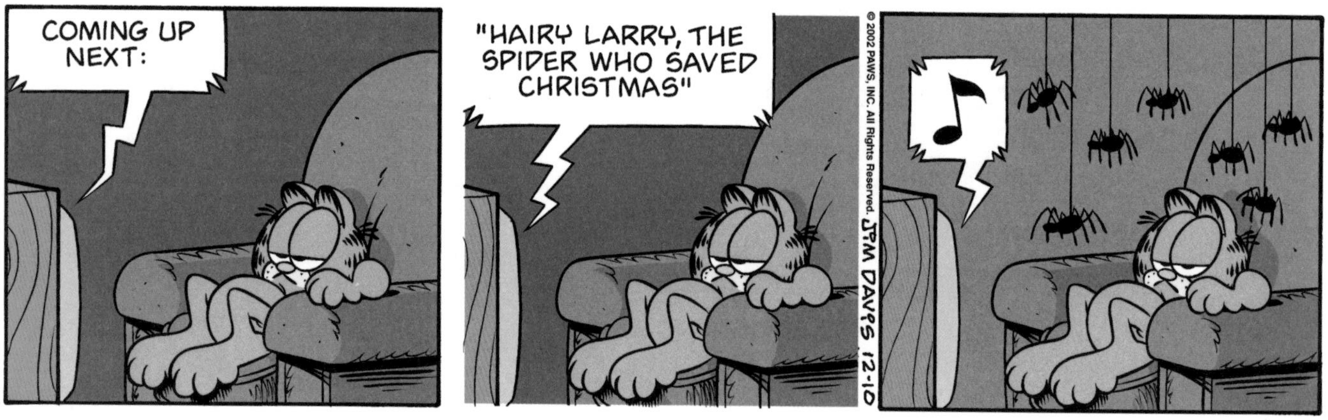
COMING UP NEXT:
"HAIRY LARRY, THE SPIDER WHO SAVED CHRISTMAS"
© 2002 PAWS, INC. All Rights Reserved.
JIM DAVIS 12-10

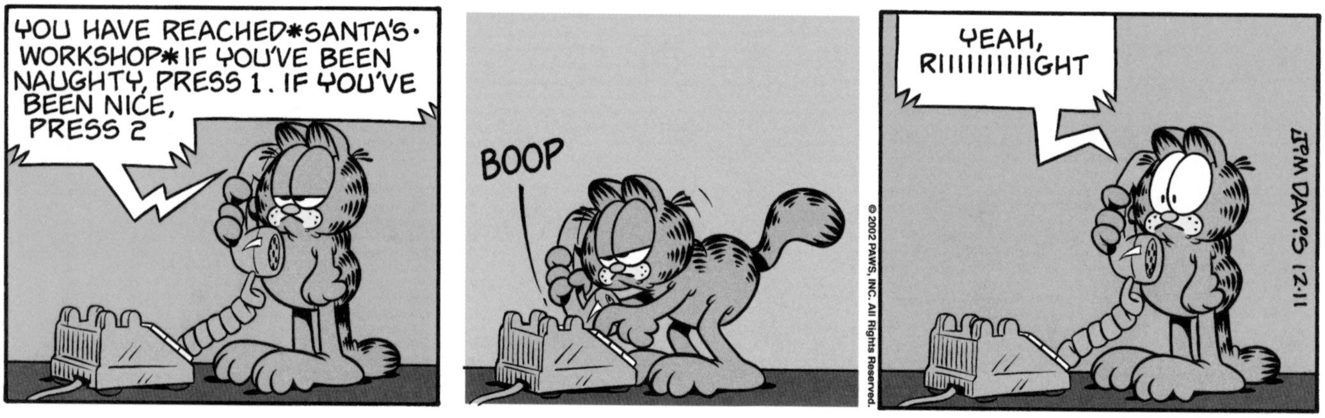
YOU HAVE REACHED*SANTA'S•WORKSHOP*IF YOU'VE BEEN NAUGHTY, PRESS 1. IF YOU'VE BEEN NICE, PRESS 2
BOOP
© 2002 PAWS, INC. All Rights Reserved.
YEAH, RIIIIIIIIIIGHT
JIM DAVIS 12-11

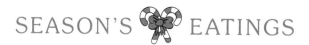

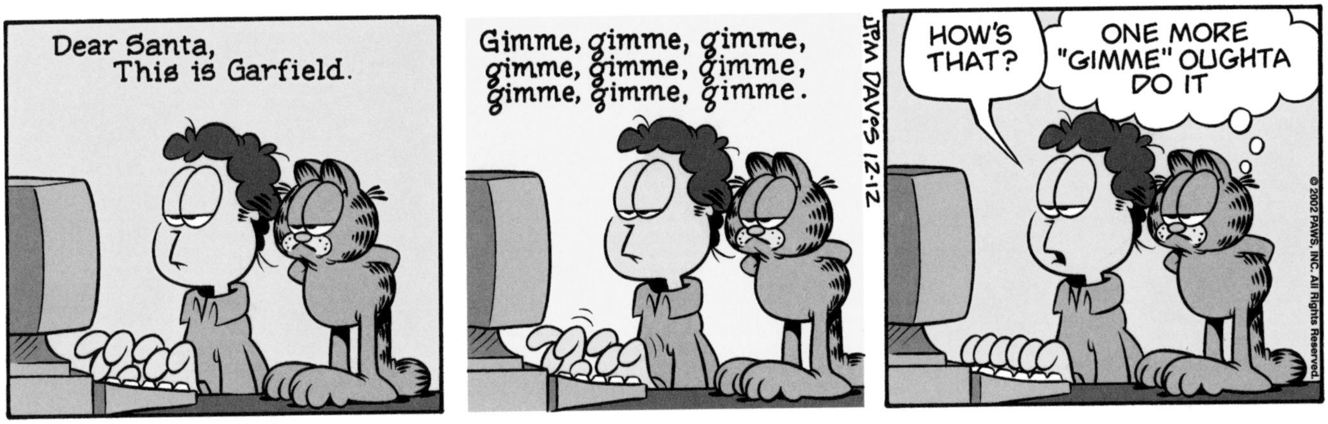
Dear Santa,
This is Garfield.
Gimme, gimme, gimme, gimme, gimme, gimme, gimme, gimme, gimme.
JPM DAVIS 12-12
HOW'S THAT?
ONE MORE "GIMME" OUGHTA DO IT
© 2002 PAWS, INC. All Rights Reserved.

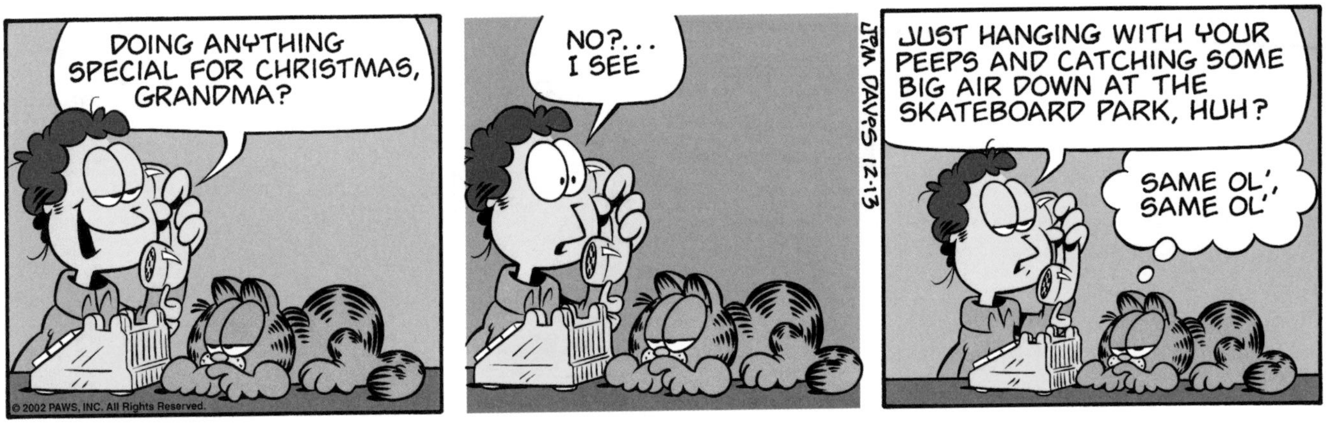
DOING ANYTHING SPECIAL FOR CHRISTMAS, GRANDMA?
© 2002 PAWS, INC. All Rights Reserved.
NO?... I SEE
JPM DAVIS 12-13
JUST HANGING WITH YOUR PEEPS AND CATCHING SOME BIG AIR DOWN AT THE SKATEBOARD PARK, HUH?
SAME OL', SAME OL'

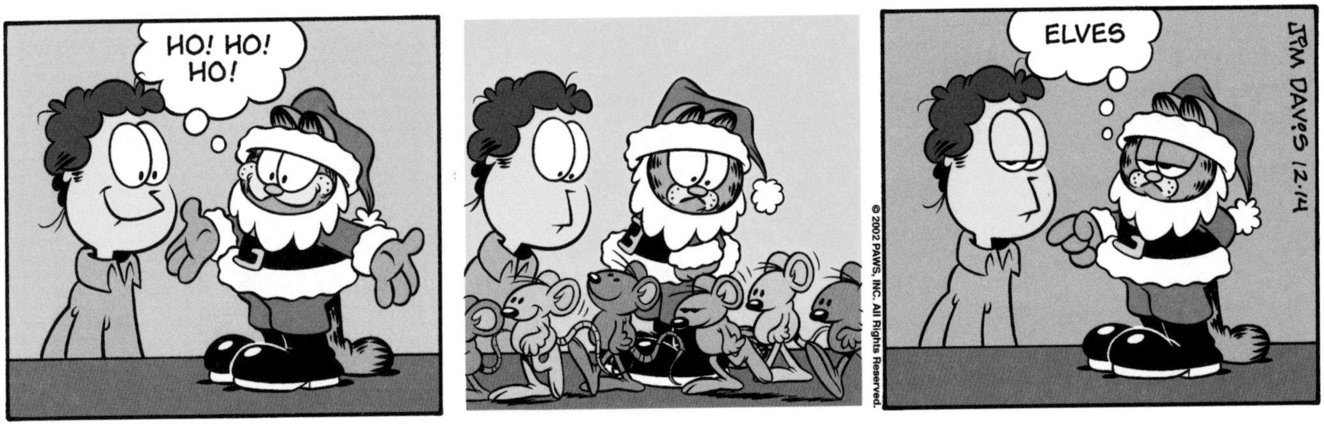
HO! HO! HO!
© 2002 PAWS, INC. All Rights Reserved.
ELVES
JPM DAVIS 12-14

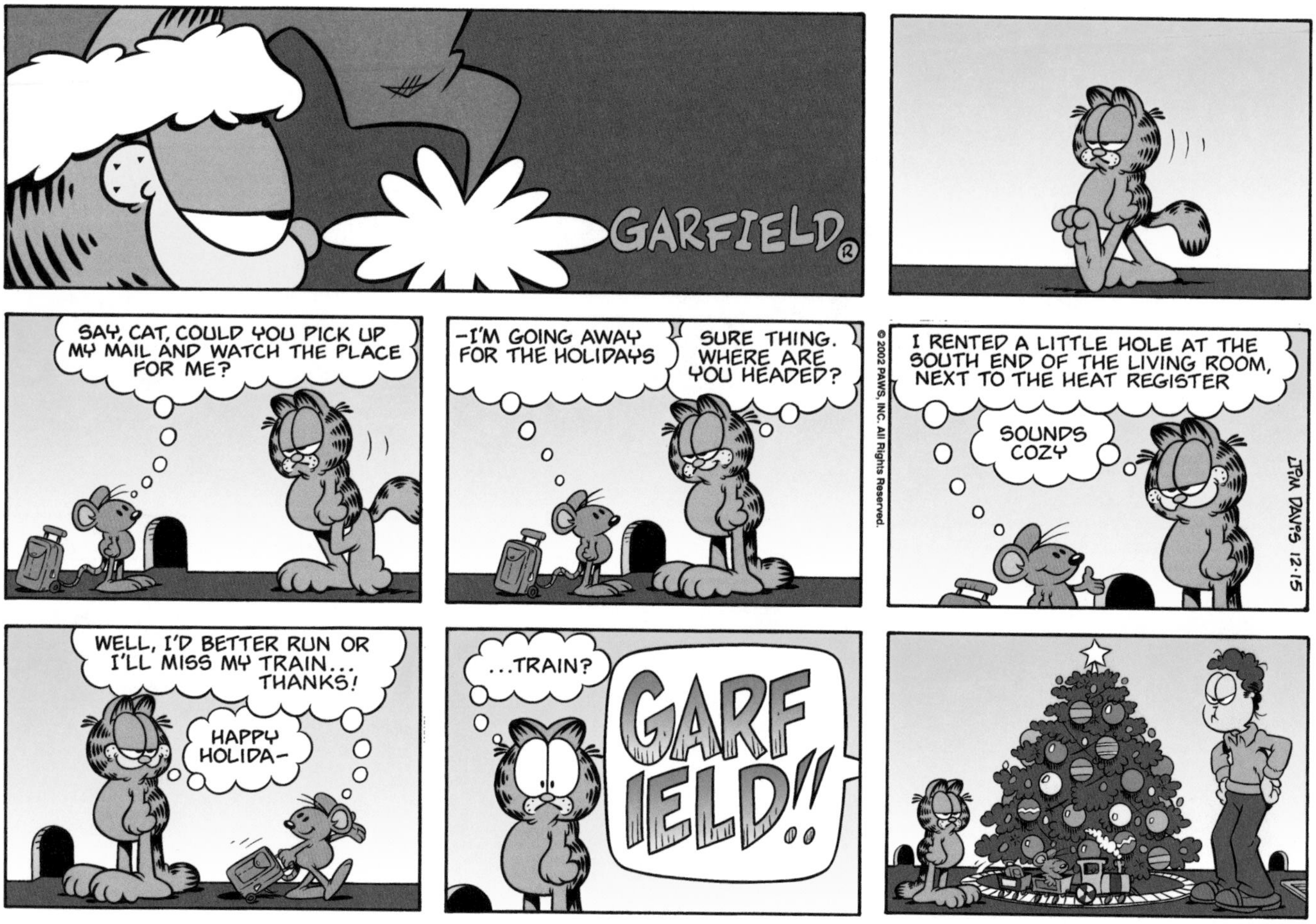
GARFIELD
SAY, CAT, COULD YOU PICK UP MY MAIL AND WATCH THE PLACE FOR ME?
-I'M GOING AWAY FOR THE HOLIDAYS
SURE THING. WHERE ARE YOU HEADED?
© 2002 PAWS, INC. All Rights Reserved.
I RENTED A LITTLE HOLE AT THE SOUTH END OF THE LIVING ROOM, NEXT TO THE HEAT REGISTER
SOUNDS COZY
JPM DAVPS 12-15
WELL, I'D BETTER RUN OR I'LL MISS MY TRAIN... THANKS!
HAPPY HOLIDA-
...TRAIN?
GARFIELD!!

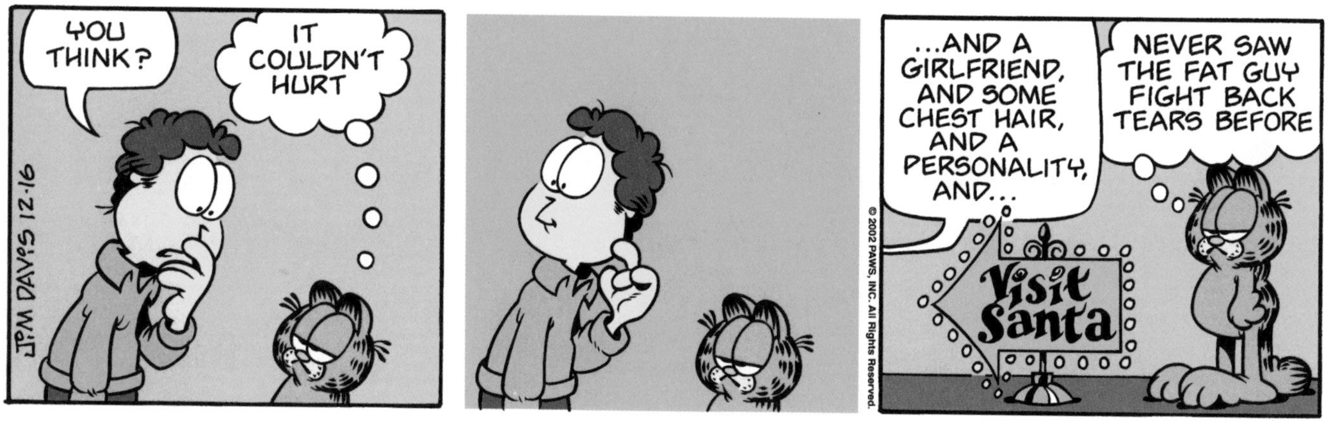
YOU THINK?
IT COULDN'T HURT
JPM DAVPS 12-16
© 2002 PAWS, INC. All Rights Reserved.
...AND A GIRLFRIEND, AND SOME CHEST HAIR, AND A PERSONALITY, AND...
NEVER SAW THE FAT GUY FIGHT BACK TEARS BEFORE
Visit Santa

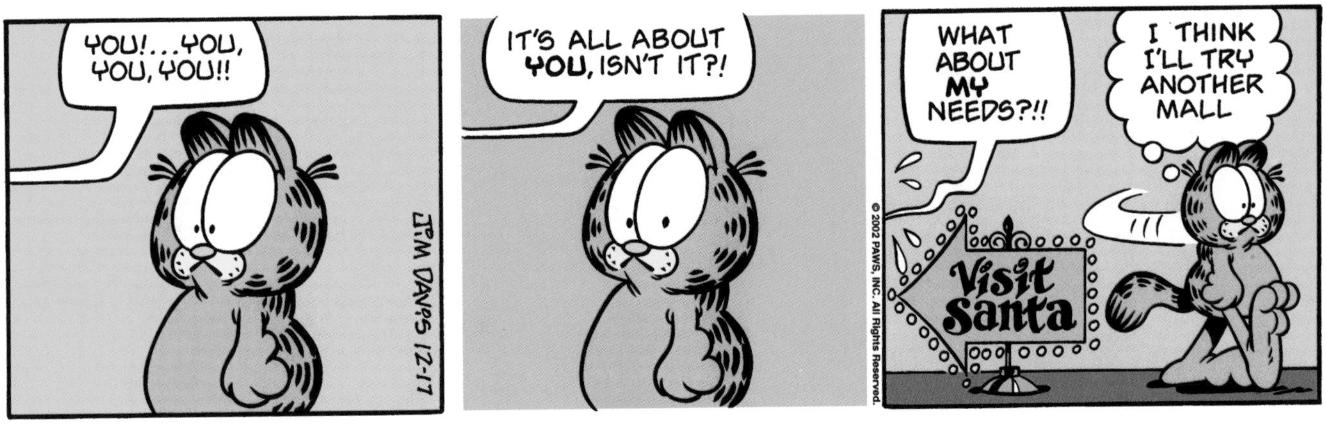
YOU!...YOU, YOU, YOU!!
JIM DAVIS 12-17
IT'S ALL ABOUT **YOU**, ISN'T IT?!
WHAT ABOUT **MY** NEEDS?!!
I THINK I'LL TRY ANOTHER MALL
Visit Santa
© 2002 PAWS, INC. All Rights Reserved.

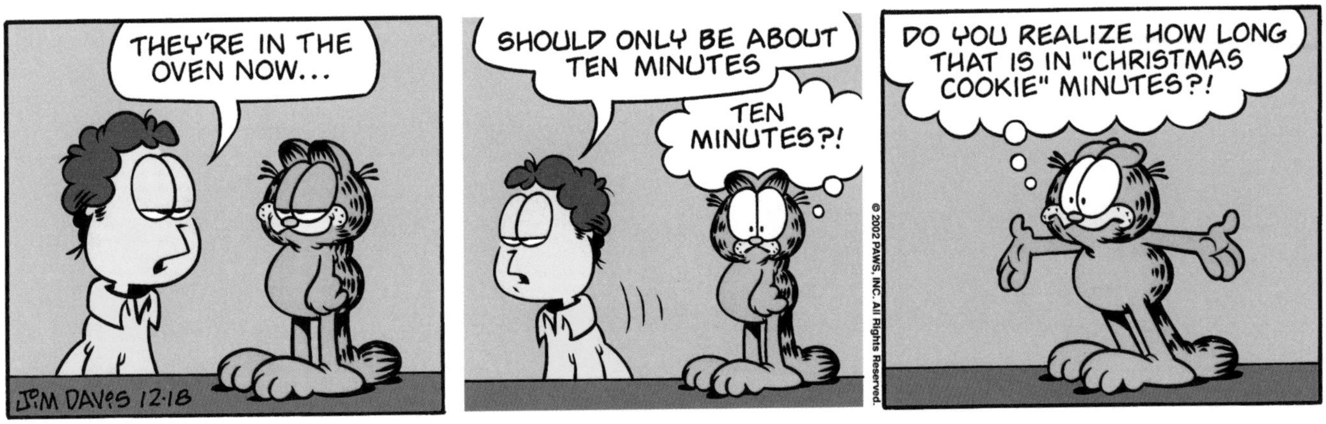
THEY'RE IN THE OVEN NOW...
JIM DAVIS 12-18
SHOULD ONLY BE ABOUT TEN MINUTES
TEN MINUTES?!
© 2002 PAWS, INC. All Rights Reserved.
DO YOU REALIZE HOW LONG THAT IS IN "CHRISTMAS COOKIE" MINUTES?!

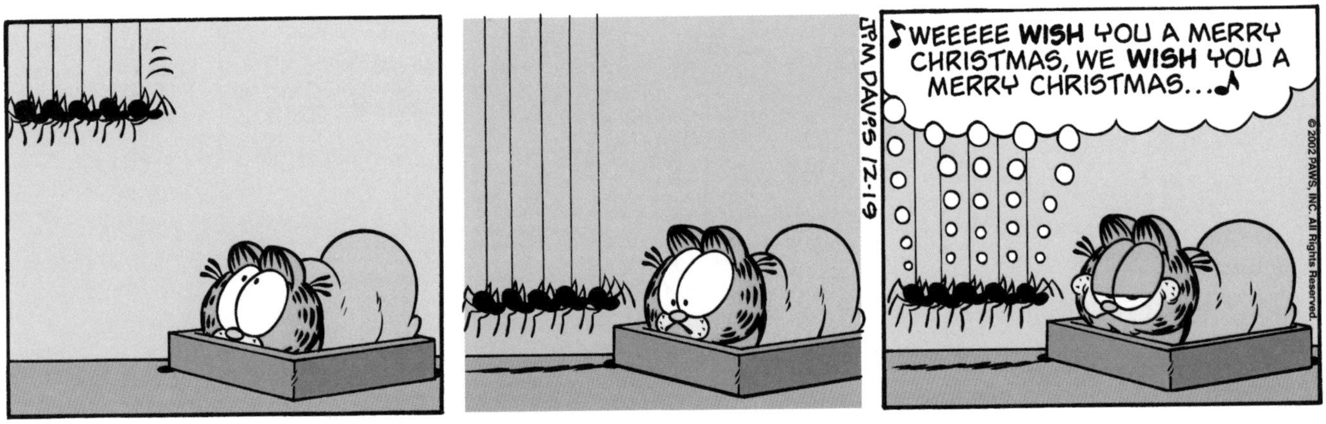
JIM DAVIS 12-19
♪WEEEEE **WISH** YOU A MERRY CHRISTMAS, WE **WISH** YOU A MERRY CHRISTMAS...♪
© 2002 PAWS, INC. All Rights Reserved.

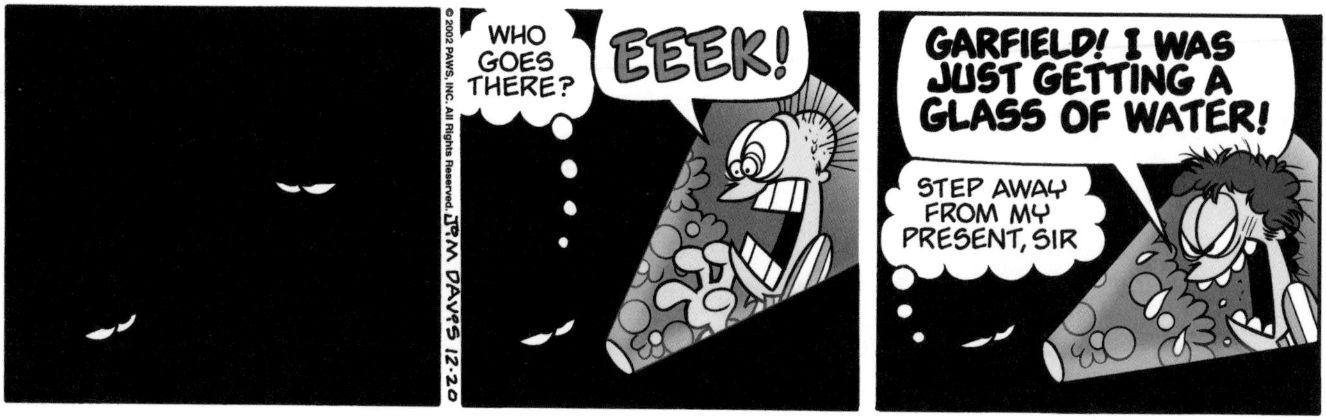
© 2002 PAWS, INC. All Rights Reserved.
JIM DAVIS 12-20
WHO GOES THERE?
EEEK!
GARFIELD! I WAS JUST GETTING A GLASS OF WATER!
STEP AWAY FROM MY PRESENT, SIR

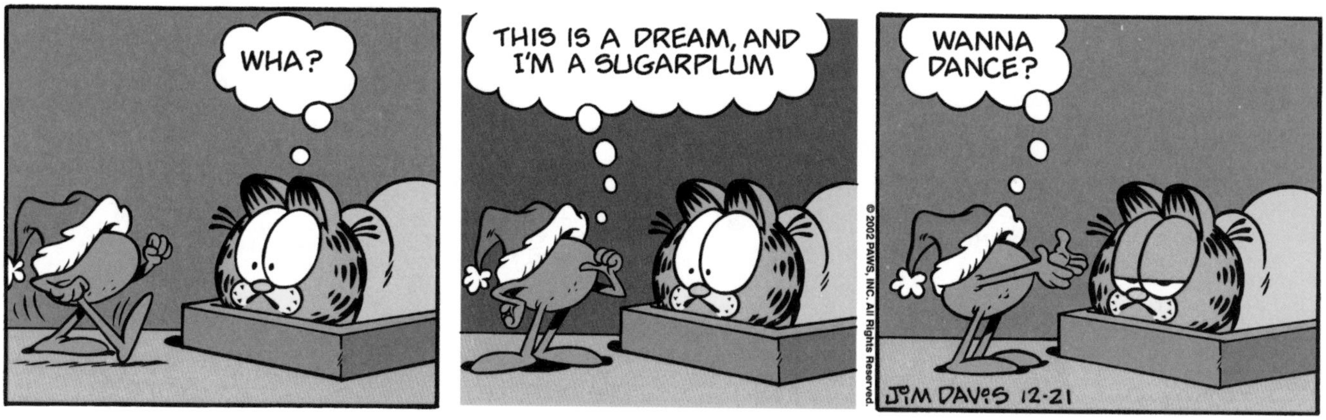
WHA?
THIS IS A DREAM, AND I'M A SUGARPLUM
WANNA DANCE?
© 2002 PAWS, INC. All Rights Reserved.
JIM DAVIS 12-21

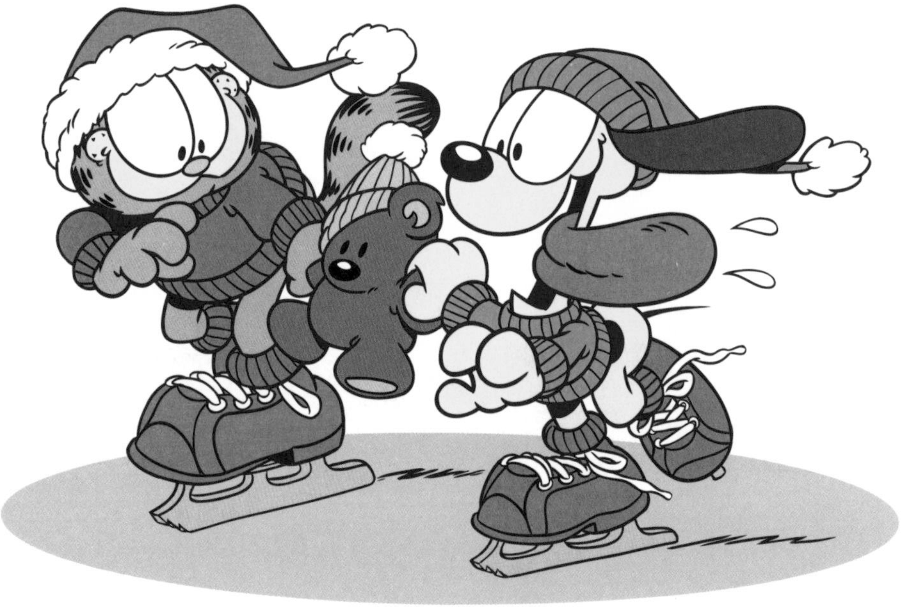

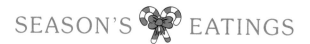

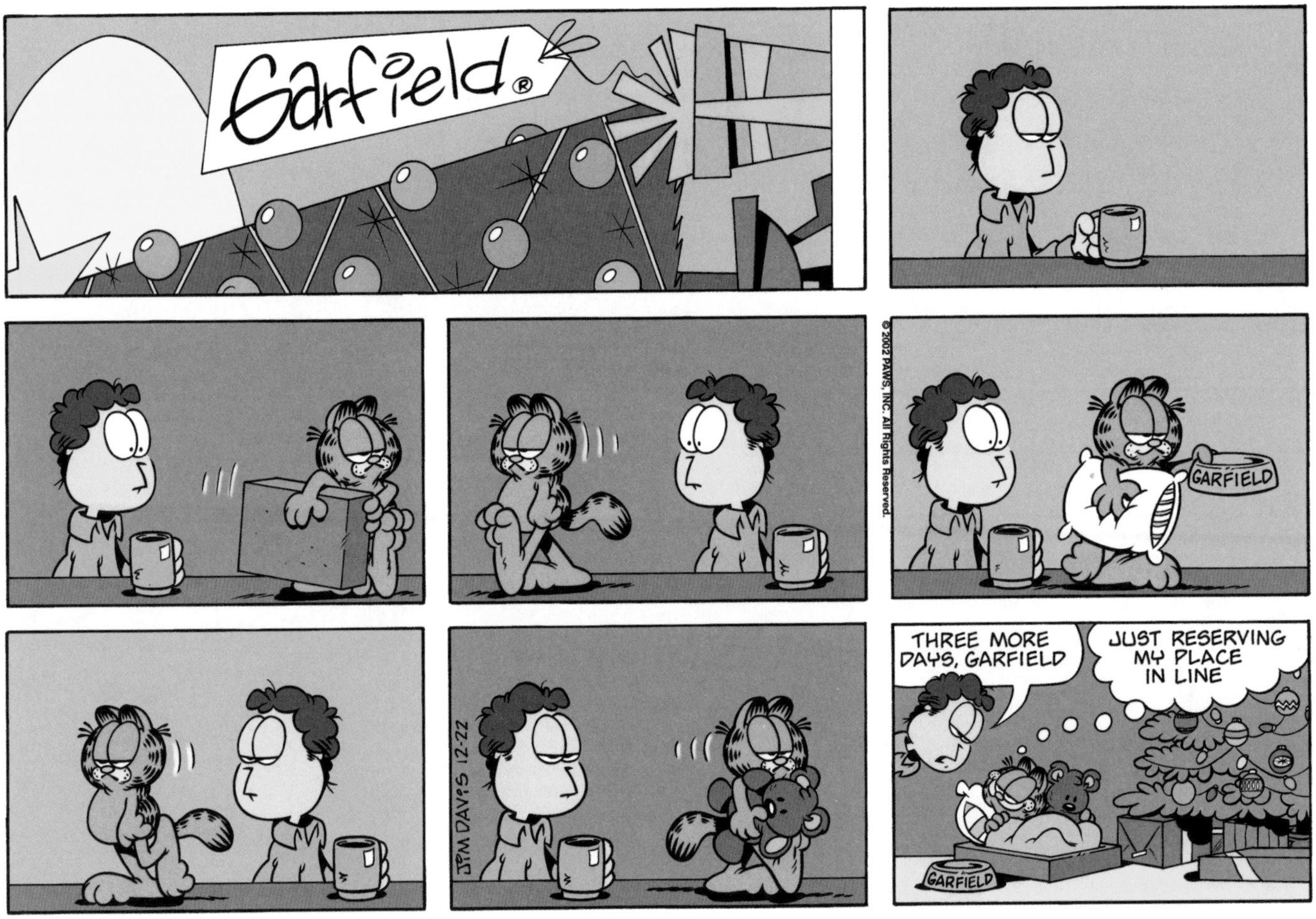
Garfield®
© 2002 PAWS, INC. All Rights Reserved.
GARFIELD
JPM DAVPS 12-22
THREE MORE DAYS, GARFIELD
JUST RESERVING MY PLACE IN LINE
GARFIELD

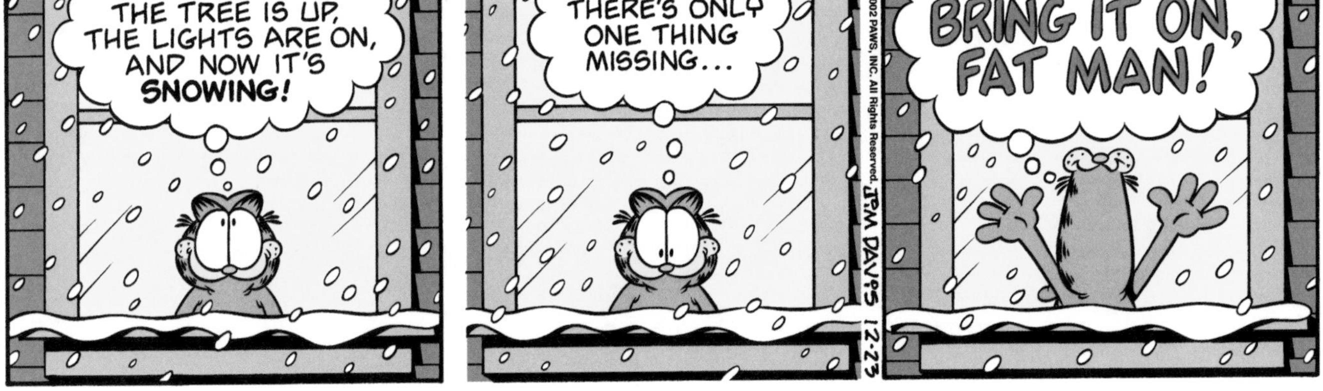
THE TREE IS UP, THE LIGHTS ARE ON, AND NOW IT'S **SNOWING!**
THERE'S ONLY ONE THING MISSING...
© 2002 PAWS, INC. All Rights Reserved.
JPM DAVPS 12-23
BRING IT ON, FAT MAN!

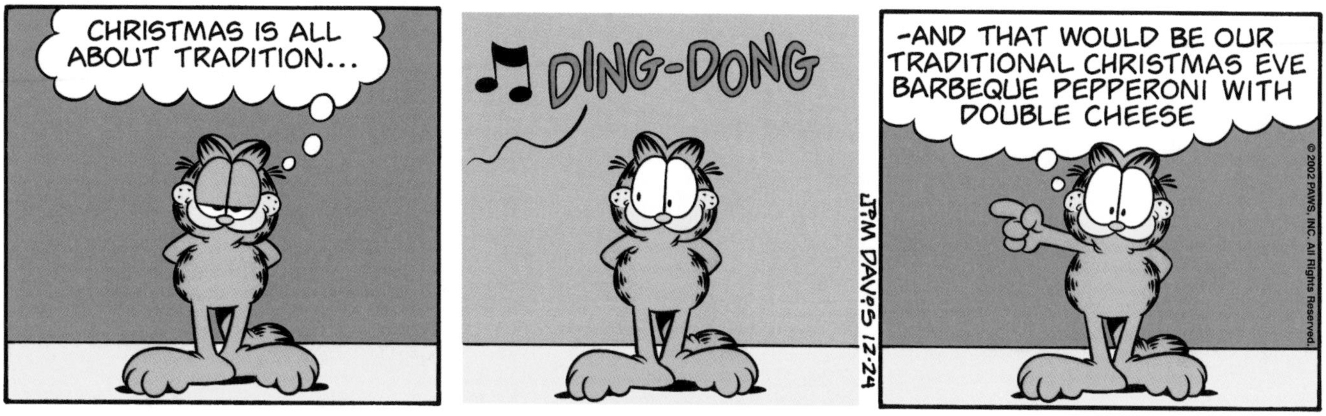
CHRISTMAS IS ALL ABOUT TRADITION...
DING-DONG
-AND THAT WOULD BE OUR TRADITIONAL CHRISTMAS EVE BARBEQUE PEPPERONI WITH DOUBLE CHEESE
JIM DAVIS 12-24
© 2002 PAWS, INC. All Rights Reserved.

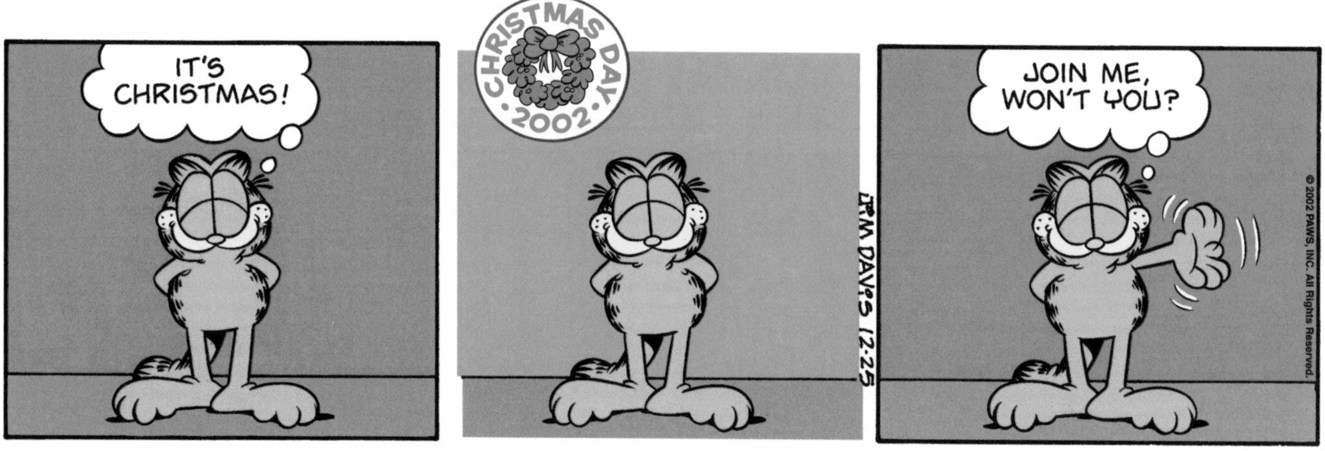
IT'S CHRISTMAS!
CHRISTMAS DAY 2002
JOIN ME, WON'T YOU?
JIM DAVIS 12-25
© 2002 PAWS, INC. All Rights Reserved.

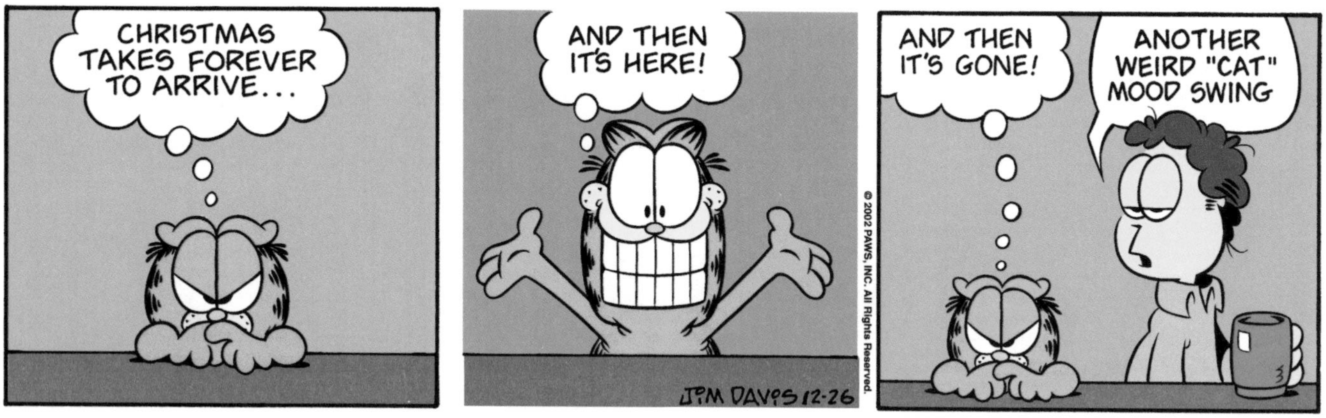
CHRISTMAS TAKES FOREVER TO ARRIVE...
AND THEN IT'S HERE!
AND THEN IT'S GONE!
ANOTHER WEIRD "CAT" MOOD SWING
JIM DAVIS 12-26
© 2002 PAWS, INC. All Rights Reserved.

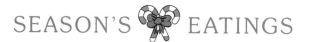

GARFIELD, DID YOU SAVE ALL THE BOWS LIKE I ASKED YOU TO?
© 2002 PAWS, INC. All Rights Reserved.
JPM DAVPS 12-27

OKAY, SO MAYBE MOM IS GETTING A LITTLE FORGETFUL
JPM DAVPS 12-28
IT'S THE THOUGHT THAT COUNTS, RIGHT?...
...RIGHT?
COME CLOSER AND ASK THAT AGAIN
© 2002 PAWS, INC. All Rights Reserved.

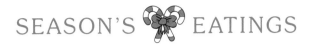

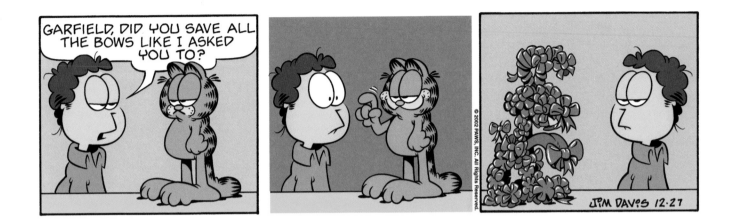

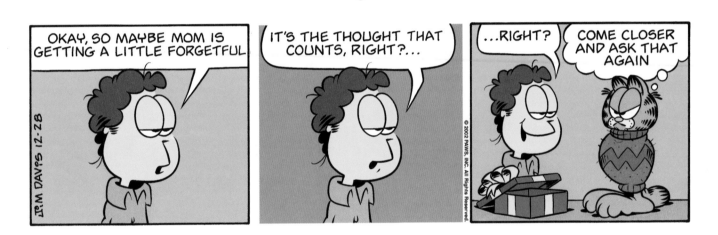

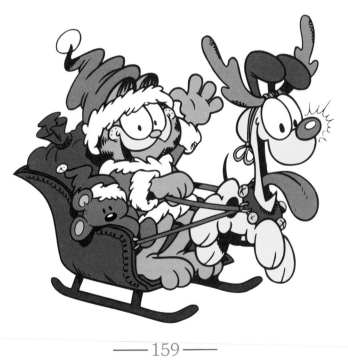